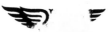

1.50

CAUSES
AND
CONSEQUENCES
OF
WORLD WAR I

CAUSES
AND
CONSEQUENCES
OF
WORLD WAR I

EDITED WITH AN INTRODUCTION BY

JOHN MILTON COOPER, JR.

QUADRANGLE BOOKS

NYT A New York Times Company

Library of Congress Catalog Card Number: 74-190134
International Standard Book Number: cloth 0-8129-0252-1
                                    paper 0-8129-6194-3

Grateful acknowledgment is made to publishers and individuals as noted herein for permission to reprint copy-
righted materials.

PREFACE

The guiding principle in selecting essays for this book has been to suggest how World War I affected the United States and how historians have interpreted its impact. The literature on American involvement in World War I is vast, but the great bulk of it has debated a few well-worn topics. I have tried to furnish a sense of these debates both in my own introduction and in some essays which either are historiographical in nature or summarize previous arguments in the process of advancing fresh interpretations. This book does not, however, take its shape from the main contributions to earlier debates, which have been widely reprinted elsewhere. It strikes me as far more important to consider the limits and directions of scholarly speculation about the meaning of World War I for the United States. At the same time I have tried in the main to select essays with more recent perspectives on the events and with novel methods in research.

My sincere thanks go to the authors who have permitted me to reprint their work and to the scholars with whom I discussed this book as it took shape. My colleagues at the University of Wisconsin, Thomas J. McCormick and John Salapatas, offered valuable suggestions, and the secretarial staff of the history department cheerfully and efficiently typed the manuscript.

CONTENTS

I
Introduction

World War I in American Historical Writing

In the United States, as elsewhere, the passage of time has dimmed little of the interest or controversy surrounding World War I. The continued fascination and argument spring from two different sources. One is the remarkable longevity of some of the quarrels that arose during the war itself over American intervention and participation in peacemaking. To this date there is scant agreement and little critical coolness over such hoary contentions as whether the United States should have entered the war earlier, later, or at all, and for what reasons it did enter; whether the postwar peace treaties were too harsh, too lenient, or reasonably equitable, and what considerations shaped the treaties; whether the country should have entered the League of Nations and why it did not. That such narrowly focused arguments have endured owes something, no doubt, to the delay in opening archival source materials.[1] The effect of belated disclosures has been a periodic refueling of old arguments. The very narrowness of the controversies has also prolonged them. Debates about World War I have, after all, revolved primarily around the actions of one man—Woodrow Wilson—and have probably retained much of their heat because of the intimate connection between basic issues and his distinctive personality.

The other and more important source of interest and controversy is a growing recognition that World War I marked the most significant turning point in recent world history. The years surrounding the war

1. Although most of the relevant American documents were opened to investigators during the twenty years after the war, comparable material from other countries began to be released only after 1945. The circumstances of German and Japanese defeat in World War II led to the opening of those nations' archives. A fifty-year cloture rule prevented access to even the earliest British materials on World War I until 1964. France, according to a recent announcement, opened its diplomatic archives for the war, but not the peace conferences, in 1971. The Russian archives have never been opened.

witnessed the end of a world order dominated politically, culturally, and economically by Western Europe. The destructiveness of the conflict and its unstable resolution undermined the European state system, while former colonial areas began erupting in nationalist revolt. Ideologically, the established complexion of beliefs writhed from injections of revolutionary radicalism, first from Bolshevik Russia in 1917, and soon afterward from fascism in Italy and Nazism in Germany. Intellectually, most of the prevailing assumptions of Western liberalism, such as peaceful, voluntary change and rational progress in human affairs, came under corrosive attack from a great many critics. This view of the era of World War I raises a major new question: What role did the war play in bringing about these changes? Did it in some sense *cause* these momentous overturnings? Or did it merely accelerate developments long afoot and likely to move onward in any event?[2]

The matter of the war as historical turning point has many specific meanings for the United States. America emerged from the conflict as the only Western power not gravely weakened but in fact substantially augmented in physical, economic, and political power. Involvement in the war opened a deep, continuing debate over the nation's proper place in world politics. Harrowing, often tragic domestic confrontations over dissent and civil liberties called into question the meaning of freedom under the American system. Simultaneously, enormous population shifts and technological advances altered the most evident aspects of life. For the first time most people lived in urban areas. Black Americans poured out of the rural South into freshly formed ghettos of Northern cities. The automobile, movies, and radio came within reach of a mass of citizens. Meanwhile, political and intellectual life was convulsed with bitter conflicts. Broad-based reform impulses withered in a new atmosphere apparently polarized between radicals and reactionaries, while openly avowed prejudices wracked all major political groups. Youth in rebellion and intellectuals in varying states of alienation and expatriation became commonplace, along with defensiveness and hostility among the stalwarts of established middle-class culture.

For the United States, too, the major question raised by this perspective is what role the war played in these changes. The fresh approaches to the impact of the war on American life have come

2. It can also be argued, even while accepting the fact of great changes, that the war actually retarded them or prevented or diminished greater transformations.

differently in diplomatic and domestic history. In foreign affairs there is little question that if World War I had not broken out and if the United States had not entered, many aspects of the nation's changing role in world affairs would have been different.[3] New interpretations of the war's impact on American foreign policy have tried to determine the magnitude of this influence. By contrast, new interpretations in domestic history have occasioned something of a debate over identifying the war's direct consequences.

I

The men who took the country into World War I and made peace afterward staked out the basic positions in the historical controversies that followed. The act of entering the conflict spawned three main arguments about the nation's course. First, President Wilson, in his eloquently tortured speech of April 2, 1917, explained that he had chosen to fight both because Germany had attacked the United States via submarine warfare and because the German action threatened those larger political values that America affirmed throughout the world. Second, a few advocates of intervention argued that American national interests required maintaining the balance of power in Europe against German aggression. Finally, though some opponents of the war questioned whether entering it served the nation's interest, most of them charged Wilson with betraying American ideals, both by being partial to the Allies and by pandering to Wall Street investments in the Allied war effort.[4]

3. It can be argued, however, that the United States would have become the leading Western power even if the war had not occurred, since much of the basis of American primacy was already laid. Too, the nation would have remained far stronger than the European nations if it had not entered the war. On the opposite tack, how much change the war caused in American willingness to play an active, aware role in international politics has been questioned by Richard Leopold in his stimulating essay "The Emergence of America as a World Power: Some Second Thoughts," in John Braeman, *et al.*, eds., *Change and Continuity in Twentieth Century America* (Columbus, Ohio, 1964), esp. pp. 22–24, 33–34.

4. For Wilson's speech see Ray Stannard Baker and William E. Dodd, eds., *The Public Papers of Woodrow Wilson* (New York, 1927), Vol. V, 6–16. The strains of argument against intervention were expressed in the speeches of Senators William J. Stone, Robert M. LaFollette, and George W. Norris, *Congressional Record,* 65th Cong., 1st sess., pp. 209–210, 212–214, 228 (April 4, 1917). The balance-of-power argument for intervention was raised in "The Defense of the Atlantic World," *New Republic,*

The principal arguments over the peace settlement originated in the acrid debates of 1919 and 1920 over American membership in the League of Nations. Wilson fashioned a lasting set of contentions when he defended his work at the peace conference as the most equitable possible arrangement and urged full participation in the League as essential to future world peace. The opposition refuted both claims, condemning the peace treaties as selfish and imperialistic and denouncing the League as a disguised war machine designed to maintain the unjust settlement. A separate set of arguments again revolved around concern for national self-interest. Some who favored the League saw it as a way of entering into a defensive military alliance, while a much larger group of critics raised searching questions about how the League might abridge America's sovereignty and thus affect its power and security. Once the United States failed to enter the League because of the stalemate between Wilson and his adversaries in the Senate, these contenders regrouped to argue whether nonparticipation was good or bad, and who deserved the greatest blame for the sorry manner in which the controversy had ended.[5]

These polemical origins of the interpretations of the American role in World War I prefigured two enduring characteristics of the historical controversy. One was that virtually all scholarship for the next generation and beyond would also be "relevant" to the time at which it was being written. Accounts of entry into the war and participation in the postwar settlement almost invariably included analogies to con-

X (February 17, 1917), 59–61, while questions about the utility of intervention to American interests were raised by LaFollette and by Randolph Bourne in "The Collapse of American Strategy," *Seven Arts,* II (August 1917), 409–424.

5. For a sample of Wilson's contentions see his speeches of July 10, 1919, and September 25, 1919, in Baker and Dodd, eds., *Public Papers of Wilson,* V, 537–552; VI, 399–416. Condemnations of the treaties and the League were expressed in the speeches of Senators William E. Borah and Joseph Irwin France, *Congressional Record,* 66th Cong., 1st sess., pp. 6597–6616 (October 19, 1919); pp. 8781–8784 (November 19, 1919), and in Oswald Garrison Villard, "The Truth About the Peace Treaty," *Nation,* CVIII (Apr. 26, 1919), 646–647. The defensive alliance argument for League membership can be found in Henry L. Stimson and McGeorge Bundy, *On Active Service in Peace and War* (New York, 1947), pp. 101–104. Questions about its effect on American sovereignty were raised in the speeches of Senators Philander C. Knox and Henry Cabot Lodge, *Congressional Record,* 65th Cong., 3rd sess., pp. 603–606 (December 18, 1918); 66th Cong., 1st sess., pp. 3778–3784 (August 12, 1919).

temporary situations. In the case of intervention, the best-known examples of this kind of argument came in the 1930's in the writings of such self-styled "revisionists" as C. Hartley Grattan, Walter Millis, and Charles Callan Tansill, who adopted the arguments of the earlier opponents of war and warned against repeating the same mistakes in the face of the rise of Nazi Germany.[6] The history of the peace settlement was applied with similar concern during World War II.[7]

The other continuing characteristic of World War I scholarship has been the fundamentally unaltered shape of the arguments. Clearly, the insistence upon rehashing the same questions about intervention, the work of the peacemakers, and joining the League of Nations grew out of the original debates. Another persistent feature has been the relationship between analyses of American entry and estimates of German intentions. Following Wilson's lead, those who have approved intervention or thought it unavoidable have usually depicted the Kaiser's regime as a gang of militarists and would-be conquerors. Skeptics about intervention have stressed German reasonableness and insecurity, American provocations, and the Allies' tainted record. Also, as in the original debate, arguments about political ideals and national interest have remained separate. For twenty years after World War I, historical controversy rarely strayed from questioning the moralities of intervention and the peace settlement. With the beginning of World War II, however, argument shifted largely to the matter of American self-interest. The sole connection drawn between the two sets of arguments has been the condemnation of Wilsonian idealism by proponents of self-interested policies, regardless of their positions on the specific issues of World War I.

The earliest historical interpretations justifying intervention began to appear during the war and just after its end. Some were produced by scholars who were in government service writing propaganda;

6. For an excellent account of interpretations of intervention up to the end of World War II, see Richard W. Leopold, "The Problem of American Intervention, 1917: An Historical Retrospect," *World Politics,* II (April 1950), 405–425. The revisionists receive detailed treatment in Warren I. Cohen, *The American Revisionists: The Lessons of Intervention in World War I* (Chicago, 1967). It was hardly accidental that Barnes and Tansill joined others, such as Charles A. Beard, in practicing a similar "revisionism" toward American entry into World War II.

7. The outpouring of concern during World War II is treated in Robert A. Divine, *Second Chance: The Triumph of Internationalism in America During World War II* (New York, 1967).

others were the work of unofficial observers who enthusiastically supported the war.[8] Anti-interventionist accounts had their roots in Wilson's opposition. Books which pointed to unneutral biases and profit motives were written soon after the declaration of war by the former anti-interventionist Congressman Charles Lindbergh and the veteran socialist scholar Scott Nearing. The first revisionist account to appear after the war also came from a socialist writer, John Kenneth Turner, in *Shall It Be Again?*, published in 1922.[9] The first interpretations of the peace conference and the fight over League membership came from such participants as Henry Cabot Lodge, with *The Senate and the League of Nations* (1925), and from historians writing campaign documents, for example William E. Dodd with *Woodrow Wilson and His Work* (1920).

Such ties between scholarship and the political debate remained strong in the 1920's, in no small part because leading actors chose particular historians to tell authorized versions of their roles in the events. The practice started when Burton J. Hendrick, a journalist who had helped Admiral William S. Sims write his war memoirs, was commissioned to write a life of Walter Hines Page, the American ambassador to Great Britain who had died in 1918. At the same time, before he left the White House Wilson opened his files to Ray Stannard Baker, who had been his press secretary at the peace conference, to write an account of the negotiations; it appeared in three volumes in 1922 as *Woodrow Wilson and the World Settlement*. Later the President's widow named Baker his authorized biographer with exclusive access to the Wilson papers until the eighth and final volume of *Woodrow Wilson: Life and Letters* was published in 1939. Colonel Edward M. House, Wilson's principal diplomatic adviser, outdid his former chief by turning over his diaries and letters to Charles Seymour, a Yale professor and former member of the peace conference staff, who skillfully edited *The Intimate Papers of Colonel House;* it ap-

8. An example of a book by a scholar who served in the government would be John Spencer Bassett, *Our War with Germany* (New York, 1919); the work of a private pro-war enthusiast is exemplified by John Bach McMaster, *The United States in the World War,* 2 vols. (New York, 1918–1920).

9. See Charles A. Lindbergh, *Why Your Country Is at War and What Happens to Your Country after a War . . .* , (Washington, D.C., 1917); Scott Nearing, *The Great Madness: A Victory for American Plutocracy* (New York, 1917). On Turner, see Leopold, "American Intervention, 1917," p. 408, and Cohen, *American Revisionists,* pp. 45–54.

peared in four volumes in 1926 and 1928. The flow of memoirs also surged in the 1920's, so that almost every surviving member of the Wilson Cabinet eventually left an interpretation of American involvement in the war.[10]

In the 1930's the debate over the war took on a new cast. Public opinion swung sharply to favor the kinds of arguments that had been advanced earlier by anti-interventionists and opponents of League membership. Between 1935 and 1937, new techniques of public opinion polling, pioneered by George Gallup and Elmo Roper, found that an overwhelming majority of Americans surveyed thought that intervention in World War I had been a mistake and that every effort should be made to avoid involvement in future overseas conflicts. These years were, properly speaking, the heyday of American isolationism. Congress passed a series of neutrality acts drawing directly upon the proposals of pre-1917 anti-interventionists. The laws were designed, in the words of one newspaper, "to preserve the United States from intervention in the War of 1914–'18."[11] The most important new source material to be revealed during the decade also grew out of public debate. It came out of the investigation of the special Senate committee headed by Senator Gerald P. Nye of North Dakota into the activities of munitions manufacturers during the war. The Nye Committee had its origins in the ideas of long-time pacifists and marked the ascendancy of the views of such Midwestern and Western progressives as Nye, William E. Borah, George W. Norris, and Hiram Johnson, all of whom were either veterans or political descendants of anti-war and anti-League forces of an earlier generation.[12]

In this climate the revisionists flourished, clearly dominating the

10. Baker has recounted his involvement with telling Wilson's story in his autobiography, *American Chronicle* (New York, 1945), pp. 485–498, 506–516. A single publishing firm, Doubleday Page & Company, which had been co-founded by Ambassador Page and was still managed in part by his sons, made a minor industry out of these books, bringing out the Hendrick biography in three volumes, all eleven of Baker's volumes on Wilson, and most of the Cabinet officers' memoirs.

11. The statement is from the *New York Herald Tribune*, May 1, 1937, as quoted in William E. Leuchtenburg, *Franklin D. Roosevelt and the New Deal, 1932–1940* (New York, 1963), p. 225. On the neutrality laws see Robert A. Divine, *The Illusion of Neutrality* (Chicago, 1962).

12. On the Nye Committee see Wayne S. Cole, *Senator Gerald P. Nye and American Foreign Relations* (Minneapolis, 1962), and John F. Wiltz, *In Search of Peace: The Senate Munitions Inquiry, 1934–36* (Baton Rouge, La., 1963).

scholarly scene and occasionally, as with Millis's *The Road to War* (1935), breaking through to the best-seller lists. Yet it would be wrong to think of the revisionists as simply catering to changing public moods or underpinning contemporary political arguments. Such leading revisionists as Harry Elmer Barnes, Sydney B. Fay, and Charles A. Beard had begun formulating their views in the 1920's and had often been ignored or greeted with hostility. Moreover, Fay was sharply critical of facile parallels drawn between the World War and the 1930's, while Beard warned against indulgence in "the devil theory of war."[13] Despite continuing polemical overtones, the historical controversies of the 1930's marked a gain in maturity and sophistication on both sides. Charles Seymour, who emerged as the leading critic of revisionism, furnished a well-argued defense of Wilson's policies in *American Diplomacy During the World War* (1934). The most impressive revisionist treatment was Tansill's massively documented, deftly wrought *America Goes to War* (1938). At the same time, new studies of propaganda, peace, and military preparedness organizations, and of ethnic groups began to suggest the breadth of the war's impact on the United States.[14] 1936 and 1939 witnessed the publication of the first two volumes of Frederic L. Paxson's *American Democracy and the World War,* a work which offered what was then a remarkably dispassionate view. In its mixture of diplomatic and domestic history it still stands as the most comprehensive treatment of American participation in the war.[15]

For all their heat, the historical arguments of the 1930's did not involve a basic clash of views. They only resurrected the quarrel between Wilson and the main group of anti-interventionists of 1917. Both sides had initially agreed—and still did—that entry into the war was something to be avoided as long as possible, and judged on the ground of how well it served American ideals. Absent entirely in the 1930's were two other positions taken during the original debates of World War I. One was the conviction voiced earlier, by such

13. See Cohen, *American Revisionists,* and Beard, *The Devil Theory of War* (New York, 1936).
14. See, for example, H. C. Peterson, *Propaganda for War* (Norman, Okla., 1939); Clifton Child, *The German-Americans in Politics* (Madison, Wisc., 1939); and Merle Curti, *Peace or War: The American Struggle 1636–1936* (New York, 1936), pp. 228–261.
15. The concluding third volume of Paxson's work was published in 1948.

men as Theodore Roosevelt and Elihu Root, that intervention was a good thing and should have occurred long before April 1917. The other neglected position was the contention that the correct standard for judging participation in the war and the peace settlement was American self-interest. Both of those positions gained favor again toward the end of the 1930's, particularly after the outbreak of World War II in 1939.

Except for Hermann Hagedorn's *The Bugle That Woke America: The Story of Theodore Roosevelt's Last Fight for His Country* (1940), the pre-Pearl Harbor interventionists attempted little rehabilitation of the earlier war hawks. Supporters of aid to the Allies in 1940 and 1941 included such revisionists as Millis, who maintained that "1939 is not 1941," and earlier opponents of World War I, such as Senator Norris, who argued that "there was no similarity in the challenge which confronted the American people."[16] Renewed concern for American self-interest began well before the threat of war in Europe, principally in the work of Charles A. Beard, who for some years had been conducting a thoroughgoing analysis of American foreign policy. It culminated in his two books published in 1934, *The Idea of National Interest* and *The Open Door at Home*. Beard reintroduced the principle of self-interest into the historical argument over participation in World War I when he condemned most of Wilson's decisions for ignoring "the limited nature of American powers to relieve, restore and maintain life beyond its own sphere of interest and control. . . ." Beard's assertion, made in 1940, was part of his increasingly bitter opposition to the pro-Allied policies of President Franklin D. Roosevelt.[17]

16. Millis, "1939 Is Not 1914," *Life,* VII (November 6, 1939), 69–75, 94–98; *Fighting Liberal: The Autobiography of George W. Norris* (New York, 1945), p. 392. Mark Chadwin, *The Hawks of World War II: American Interventionists Before Pearl Harbor* (Chapel Hill, 1968), includes few references to TR and the World War I experience, even though former associates and followers of his, such as Hagedorn, Henry Stimson, and Frank Knox, became leading interventionists. Others, for example Roosevelt's daughter Alice Roosevelt Longworth and such World War I interventionists as Representatives Hamilton Fish and George Holden Tinkham, were leading opponents of pro-Allied policies in World War II.

17. Beard, *A Foreign Policy for America* (New York, 1940), p. 152. Like Tansill and Barnes, Beard became a "revisionist" on World War II as well. For a perceptive analysis of his thought see Richard Hofstadter, *The Progressive Historians: Turner, Beard, Parrington* (New York [Vintage ed.], 1970), pp. 318–346.

Those who used self-interest to justify intervention were more successful. In 1941, Walter Lippmann and Forrest Davis, two spokesmen for a pro-Allied policy, independently argued that the United States had intervened in 1917 in order to protect American security, specifically the community of interest between Britain and the United States over control of the Atlantic and hegemony in the Western Hemisphere.[18] Lippmann elaborated the thesis two years later in his widely read book *U.S. Foreign Policy*. He condemned Wilson for failing to take a tough stand against Germany before 1917. Lippmann also recalled that he had himself urged intervention in 1917 to protect the Atlantic community, and he claimed that similar thinking in administration circles had furnished the true motive for entering the war. Viewing the peace settlement, Lippmann once again found Wilson wanting, because he "identified collective security with antipathy to alliances rather than with constructive development of alliances."[19]

Interpretations of peacemaking, both Wilson's performance at Paris and the fight over League membership, emerged during World War II as a major item of controversy. The first new study of the postwar settlement, Paul Birdsall's *Versailles Twenty Years After,* heralded this revival of concern with its frankly stated purpose of discovering lessons for the 1940's.[20] At the same time, the public was treated to a sentimental apotheosis of Wilson, in which popular writers and even Hollywood moviemakers collaborated in depicting the President as a noble prophet of peace who had been foiled by the jealousy and petty selfishness of his opponents, especially the wily Henry Cabot Lodge. More thoughtful reviews of the events of 1919 often aimed at finding a way to establish international order after World War II. Old-line internationalists called for a neo-Wilsonian approach; other commentators, some of them self-styled "realists," urged reliance upon self-interested military alliances. Lippmann himself continued his attack in *U.S. War Aims* (1944), in which he praised the views of

18. Lippmann, "The Atlantic and America," *Life*, X (April 7, 1941), 84–92; Davis, *The Atlantic System: The Story of Anglo-American Control of the Seas* (New York, 1941), pp. 219–246.

19. Lippmann, *U.S. Foreign Policy: Shield of the Republic* (Boston, 1943), pp. 32–36, 74.

20. During the 1930's, arguments over intervention had largely eclipsed interest in peacemaking. Two earlier studies, Denna Frank Fleming, *The United States and the League of Nations* (New York, 1932), and W. Stull Holt, *Treaties Defeated by the Senate* (Baltimore, 1933), both warmly pro-Wilson and anti-Lodge, just preceded the revisionist debate.

Lodge and Theodore Roosevelt and castigated the "Wilsonian misconception" that international organization "can *replace* the ordinary instruments of international life."[21]

Three historical works treated post–World War I peacemaking directly in the context of what to do after World War II. Ruhl J. Bartlett broadened the perspective somewhat in *The League to Enforce Peace* (1944), a study of the group formed in 1915 to promote the League of Nations idea. But Bartlett's analysis focused largely on how the League to Enforce Peace had either aided or failed Wilson's effort "to direct the American people into a policy of enlightened world leadership" which might have prevented another war.[22] In 1944 and 1945 Thomas A. Bailey published the two volumes which still stand as the major treatment of American participation in the peace settlement—*Woodrow Wilson and the Lost Peace,* on the conference, and *Woodrow Wilson and the Great Betrayal,* on the domestic controversy that followed. Bailey, too, considered broader aspects of peacemaking while remaining squarely within a present-minded concern for eliciting lessons. He paid careful attention to political conditions and the flux of public opinion in the United States, and to personalities and differences of views. Bailey maintained greater detachment than most previous interpreters, and though he expressed sympathy for Wilson's program, he leveled his strongest criticisms at the President's conduct in negotiating the treaty and presenting it to the Senate and the public. Bailey's books each concluded with a list of mistakes made in 1919 to be avoided in 1945; interestingly, the number of items on both lists was fourteen.[23]

After World War II, historical controversy shifted to focus more on intervention. But this time the argument was almost exclusively over the matter of national self-interest and mainly within the confines of a basic approval of intervention in 1917. In 1951 two of the most influential commentators on American foreign policy contended that the United States had gone to war for strategic purposes which Wilson had either failed to appreciate or tried to disguise. George

21. Lippman, *U.S. War Aims* (Boston, 1944), p. 176 and *passim*. Other "realists" included Reinhold Niebuhr and Nicholas Spykman. On the Wilson revival and the debate over postwar peace machinery, see Divine, *Second Chance,* pp. 156–183.

22. Bartlett, *The League to Enforce Peace* (Chapel Hill, 1944), p. 214.

23. Bailey, *Woodrow Wilson and the Lost Peace* (New York, 1944), esp. pp. 322–325; *Woodrow Wilson and the Great Betrayal* (New York, 1945), esp. pp. 362–367.

F. Kennan, in *American Diplomacy, 1900–1950,* condemned Wilson for not openly stating that the United States was seeking to uphold the balance of power; had he done so he might have avoided the moralistic overcommitments that had further unbalanced the international system. Hans J. Morgenthau agreed in *In Defense of the National Interest* that by intervening against Germany, "Wilson pursued the right policy, but pursued it for the wrong reasons." Morgenthau also charged that Wilson's unwillingness to acknowledge American interests had trapped him in a utopian outlook which further confused and deranged American foreign policy.[24]

The debate over the role of self-interest in intervention reached its apex shortly afterward in Robert E. Osgood's magisterial work, *Ideals and Self-Interest in America's Foreign Relations* (1953). Although the book covered diplomatic history from 1898 to 1941, more than half was devoted to World War I and especially to the pre-1917 period. Like Lippmann, Kennan, and Morgenthau, Osgood believed that the United States had no choice but to enter World War I because of its strategic stake in maintaining the European balance of power and Anglo-American supremacy on the Atlantic. Yet he departed somewhat from them by stressing a necessary interdependency of idealism and national interest, and by considering the place of ideals and self-interest not only in Wilson's thinking but also in the views of interventionists and anti-interventionists outside the administration. His conclusions were arresting. He found Theodore Roosevelt and other pro-Allied militants no less idealistic, though in a belligerently romantic way, than Wilson, and no more attuned to considerations of American security. Instead, according to Osgood, the coolest assessments of national self-interest had most often come from the critics of military preparedness and assertive diplomacy. Osgood's scrutiny of how concern for national self-interest and the balance of power had affected the decision to intervene led him to conclude that fear of Allied defeat and its possible effects on American security had played no role in Wilson's final choice to enter the war.[25]

24. Kennan, *American Diplomacy, 1900–1950* (New York [Mentor ed.], 1952), pp. 50–65; Morgenthau, *In Defense of the National Interest: A Critical Examination of American Foreign Policy* (New York, 1951), pp. 25–28.

25. Osgood, *Ideals and Self-Interest in America's Foreign Relations: The Great Transformation of the Twentieth Century* (Chicago, 1953), esp. pp. 143–144, 148–153, 173–174, 181–182, 214–219, 252–254, 261–263.

The controversy over Wilson's perceptions of national self-interest continued after the publication of Osgood's book. Edward Buehrig, in *Woodrow Wilson and the Balance of Power* (1955), contended that security considerations had formed an essential though often sublimated aspect of Wilson's foreign policy. By contrast, a harsh portrait of a moralist unable to depart from abstractions formed the basis of John M. Blum's *Woodrow Wilson and the Politics of Morality* (1956). Simultaneously, the critical attack on the President as a figure somehow removed from reality took a new twist in the psychoanalytic treatment by Alexander and Juliette George, *Woodrow Wilson and Colonel House* (1956). The Georges held that Wilson's peculiar outlook on foreign policy, particularly as expressed in his conduct toward intervention and peacemaking, sprang from "the crushing feelings of inadequacy which had been branded into his spirit as a child."[26] Observance of the centennial of Wilson's birth in 1956 witnessed an outpouring of articles restating previous positions.[27] The final contributions to this debate came with Daniel M. Smith's reappraisal of Secretary of State Lansing, whom he described as keenly aware of the country's strategic stake in World War I and exercising important, but usually indirect, influence on the President.[28]

After 1956 the emphasis shifted from the national-interest debate toward broader reconsideration of the impact of World War I on American foreign policy. The first major contribution came with

26. George and George, *Woodrow Wilson and Colonel House: A Personality Study* (New York, 1956). Psychological views of Wilson had been presented earlier, the first treatment being William Bayard Hale's always hostile, sometimes scurrilous, occasionally incisive *Woodrow Wilson: The Story of a Style* (New York, 1920). Baker sometimes resorted to psychological comments in his biography. It was Wilson's second major biographer, Arthur S. Link, who originated the idea that the Graduate College controversy at Princeton had offered a prefiguration of Wilson's behavior in the League fight. See Link, *Wilson: The Road to the White House* (Princeton, 1947), pp. 90–91. For subsequent examples of this genre, see below.

27. See, e.g., Buehrig, "Idealism and Statecraft," *Confluence,* V (October 1956), 252–263; Osgood, "Woodrow Wilson, Collective Security, and the Lessons of History," *ibid.* (Winter 1957), pp. 341–354; Charles Seymour, "Woodrow Wilson in Perspective," *Foreign Affairs,* XXXIV (January 1956), 175–186; and D. F. Fleming, "Woodrow Wilson and Collective Security Today," *Review of Politics,* XVIII (November 1956), 611–624.

28. See Smith, "Robert M. Lansing and the Formation of American Neutrality Policies, 1914–1915," *Mississippi Valley Historical Review,* XLIII (June 1956), 611–624, and *Robert M. Lansing and American Neutrality, 1914–1917* (Berkeley, 1958).

Arthur S. Link's *Wilson the Diplomatist* (1957), a preview of his multi-volume biography of Wilson. Link considered intervention and peacemaking against several backgrounds, and portrayed the President as a deeply complex statesman who blended idealism, emotion, reflection, and calculating opportunism in his policies. In Wilsonian neutrality Link detected a strategic wisdom of seeking a functional balance between German land superiority and British maritime supremacy. He stressed Wilson's undiminished preference for a compromise settlement as the key to his post-1917 diplomacy. Although Link conceded Wilson's failure to fulfill hopes for a liberal peace, he found much of the cause in Germany's near total collapse after the Armistice, which removed the most effective counterweight to a punitive settlement. The fundamental American division over League membership, in Link's opinion, lay between Wilson's demand for collective security with at least some supranational overtones, and Lodge's insistence upon a more traditional military pact. Finally, Link discounted most of the arguments over the President's physical and psychological condition in 1919. He held that the refusal to compromise was a decision that Wilson could have made in perfect health, since it sprang from an entirely rational, if possibly misguided, recognition of irreconcilable differences of principle.[29]

A different aspect of America's role in World War I was taken up in the late 1950's: its international dimension. Not since the revisionists of the 1930's had relied upon a reasonable, compromising picture of Germany had much attention been paid to the European countries. Four studies which appeared in 1958 and 1959 touched upon Wilson's policies toward Europe from different directions. In *Peace Moves and U-Boat Warfare* (1958), Karl Birnbaum, a Swedish historian, concluded that German views of Wilson as essentially pro-Allied played an important part in the decision to unleash the U-boats

29. Link, *Wilson the Diplomatist: A Look at His Major Foreign Policies* (Baltimore, 1957), esp. pp. 42–43, 51, 99–100, 107–108, 123, 153–155. Link had given an even earlier foretaste of some of his views in his textbook, *American Epoch: The United States in the Twentieth Century* (New York, 1954), and in his general history, *Woodrow Wilson and the Progressive Era* (New York, 1954). The first coverage of the World War in the Wilson biography came with its third volume, published in 1960; the fourth and fifth volumes, appearing in 1964 and 1965, carried the account up to intervention. Link modified some of his interpretations slightly and offered additional interpretations in those volumes, but the overall view remained the same as in *Wilson the Diplomatist*.

in 1917. In *Peace Without Victory* (1958), Laurence W. Martin examined the two-way flow of ideas and influence between Wilsonians and British liberals and moderate socialists, aimed at reconstructing international life along more peaceful and democratic lines. In *Wilson Versus Lenin: Political Origins of the New Diplomacy* (1959), Arno J. Mayer illuminated the ideological conflict that arose after the October Revolution between the middle-class democratic blueprint for world order, espoused by the American President and the moderate left in Western Europe, and the Bolsheviks' revolutionary doctrines.

The most thorough treatment of the international character of the events leading to intervention came in Ernest May's *The World War and American Isolation* (1959), which examined the neutrality of the period from the standpoint of policy-makers in Washington, Berlin, and London. May explained Wilson's policies in light of the classic neutral dilemma of submission or belligerency, and he praised the President's skill and resourcefulness in wending his way between those extremes for as long as he did. British policy also received high marks, at least under Sir Edward Grey's direction at the beginning of the conflict, because it aimed to assure American trade and amity. Grey's actions during the crucial period of the Allied blockade put Anglo-American relations on a favorable footing which later British insensitivity and heavyhandedness could not dislodge. May depicted the Germans as divided in their councils. Among the top rank of leaders he found that only the Chancellor, Theobald von Bethmann Hollweg, genuinely understood the dangers inherent in submarine warfare. When sufficient numbers of the craft became available in 1917 for a serious attack on British shipping, Bethmann Hollweg had to submit to their use, despite the virtual certainty of bringing the United States into the war.[30]

Perhaps the greatest single contribution to understanding the European setting for American participation in the war has come indirectly from Fritz Fischer's monumental study of German war aims, published in Germany in 1961 and in an abridged English translation in 1967. Combining exhaustive research with deft reasoning, Fischer demonstrated that both military chiefs and civilian spokesmen of nearly all political persuasions favored territorial, political, and economic aggrandizement in order to assure German

30. Ernest R. May, *The World War and American Isolation, 1914–1917* (Cambridge, Mass., 1959), esp. pp. 12–32, 314–317, 433–437.

hegemony in Europe and overweening world power. He described German policies toward the United States as fundamentally ignorant and insincere. Bethmann Hollweg's resistance to submarine warfare, in Fischer's view, sprang mainly from a well-founded but irresolute skepticism about its effectiveness against British shipping. Likewise, the Chancellor's encouragement of Wilson's peace initiatives in 1916 and early 1917 amounted to little more than a series of tactical ploys designed to soften American reaction to eventual unleashing of the U-boats. Fischer saw German mistrust of Wilson as not so much a suspicion of Allied favoritism but an accurate presumption that the President opposed their own expansionist war aims. When the final decision was made to resume submarine attacks in January 1917, according to Fischer, the German leaders airily disdained the likelihood of American entry into the war.[31] The implications of Fischer's work for viewing the role of the United States in World War I have only begun to be explored. They point to an important future direction of argument and interpretation.

Thus far, most of the study of the European aspects of American diplomacy has been of relations with Britain. One of the first historians to examine British sources and thus to document both sides of the diplomacy was Seth P. Tillman. In *Anglo-American Relations at the Paris Peace Conference of 1919* (1961), he stressed a basic congruence of interest and, despite Wilson's and Lloyd George's personality differences, a growing concert between the two powers against French efforts to impose a harsher peace. More recently, two books published in 1969 made extensive use of recently opened British archives to explore critical aspects of wartime diplomacy. In *Ambassador to the Court of St. James's,* Ross Gregory told the long overdue story of how Walter Hines Page plummeted from his pre-war pinnacle of intimacy with Wilson to the status of a lonely and ignored advocate of strongly pro-Allied and anti-German policies. In *British-American Relations, 1917–1918,* W. B. Fowler described how Sir William Wiseman, a junior British intelligence officer who became Colonel House's confidant, filled the breach left by the Wilson administration's loss of confidence in Page and the British Ambassador in Washington, Sir Cecil Spring Rice. Both Gregory's and Fowler's books stressed Wilson's mistrust and coolness toward the Allies, especially the British,

31. Fritz Fischer, *Germany's Aims in the First World War* (New York, 1967), esp. pp. 280–309.

attitudes which, as the authors showed, by no means disappeared with American entry into the war.

Some of the most provocative recent work on American diplomacy during and after World War I has been concerned not with relations with the European belligerents but with policies toward Bolshevik Russia and revolutionary nationalism in non-Western areas. Although this concern undoubtedly derived strength from reflections on the Cold War and the rise of the Third World after 1945, it was not simply another reflex response to contemporary events. The idea of the war as a time of combined breakdown of the international order probably originated in the writings of the British historian and political analyst E. H. Carr, especially his *The Twenty Years' Crisis* (1939) and *Conditions of Peace* (1942). From this perspective the European war became a civil war of Western capitalism, owing its larger significance to the occasion it provided for the rise of revolutionary socialism, anti-democratic totalitarianism, and non-Western nationalism.

American diplomacy toward the new Soviet regime attracted considerable interest in the 1950's, in Betty M. Unterberger's *America's Siberian Expedition, 1918–1920* (1956), and George F. Kennan's two-volume *Soviet-American Relations, 1917–1920* (1956–1958), as well as in Arno Mayer's study. Christopher Lasch expanded the discussion in *American Liberals and the Russian Revolution* (1962), in which he demonstrated how the Bolshevik experiment served as a mirror which reflected and sometimes distorted domestic political attitudes inside and outside the Wilson administration. The most important new interpretation came in the writings of William Appleman Williams, who built on the views of Carr and Beard, stressing domestic influences on foreign policy, especially economic interests. Williams argued, notably in *The Tragedy of American Diplomacy* (1962), that Wilson's basic aim was to build a liberal capitalist world order, dominated by the United States and with free access assured everywhere for American economic penetration.

Two important works later elaborated this thesis that response revolution was the most important facet of American participation in the war. Mayer contributed an international perspective in his massive study of the immediate postwar settlement, *Politics and Diplomacy of Peacemaking* (1967), which was based on research in archives and newspapers of several countries. Its ideological analysis drew upon acquaintance with internal conditions in Europe and the United States. Mayer's subtitle, *Containment and Counterrevolution at Versailles, 1918–1919,* suggested his basic interpretation, that the peacemakers acted like a team of firemen putting out blazes and seeking to prevent a conflagration. Wilson, Lloyd George, and Clemenceau functioned as conservators of a capitalist, Western-centered order against the ideological challenge of Bolshevism and the immediate dangers of revolution—as evidenced in uprisings in Hungary and Germany, general strikes on both sides of the Atlantic, and numerous acts of political violence. Mayer believed that the most important discussions at the peace conference were those over the Russian Civil War. He regarded the controversy over terms for Germany as no more than a quarrel over means to reach the common goal of a stable *status quo.*[32]

A comparable analysis was offered by N. Gordon Levin, Jr., in *Woodrow Wilson and World Politics* (1968), which treated the policies of the President and his advisers roughly from 1916 to 1919. Levin characterized Wilson's diplomatic approach as "an effort to construct a stable world order of liberal-capitalist internationalism, at the Center of the global ideological spectrum, safe from both the threat of imperialism on the Right and the danger of revolution on the Left." In short, reformism was the key to the President's foreign policies as much as to his domestic politics. Wilson's international program became, in Levin's estimation, notwithstanding its original action against autocracy, more important for its defensive thrust after it was outflanked by the Bolshevik Revolution and the Leninist critique of world politics. In this light, decisions regarding Russia, China, and Japan, particularly Siberian intervention, assumed greater importance. The efforts at Paris to moderate the terms of the settlement stemmed less from liberal predilections than from a "reintegrationist" desire to include Germany in a centrist, anti-revolutionary system. Finally, Levin maintained that the long-term significance of Wilsonian views lay in their inculcation of an outlook of liberal, capitalist globalism which, after a temporary decline in the 1920's and 1930's, came to dominate American foreign policy during World War II and the Cold War.[33]

Besides viewing the international context and the response to revolu-

32. Mayer, *Politics and Diplomacy of Peacemaking: Containment and Counter-revolution at Versailles, 1918–1919* (New York, 1967), esp. pp. 1–30, 753–812.

33. Levin, *Woodrow Wilson and World Politics: America's Response to War and Revolution* (New York, 1968), esp. pp. 1–10, 125–150, 263–270.

tion, historical assessments of the impact of World War I on American foreign policy have followed one other principal direction. This has been to explore domestic influences and backgrounds to diplomacy. Both Williams and Levin followed Beard's lead in stressing capitalist influences. Other interpreters, however, have studied a variety of men and groups and have discerned a number of different factors influencing American attitudes toward the war and the peace settlement. For example, possible connections between domestic political views and reactions to World War I had long interested nondiplomatic historians. In the early 1950's Eric Goldman and Richard Hofstadter, in their widely read studies of modern American reform, each saw clear links between the crusading spirit of progressives at home and both the zeal to "make the world safe for democracy" and disillusionment with the peace settlement.[34] When Link's biography of Wilson reached the war, beginning in 1960, its focus on the President brought simultaneous examination of domestic and foreign policies. Link carefully appraised such matters as the impact of propaganda and ethnic loyalties on attitudes toward the belligerents, the interplay of party politics with diplomatic attitudes, and the role of domestic reform sentiment in disposing various figures for and against preparedness and intervention.[35]

Since then several works have concentrated on specific aspects of domestic influences. Charles Forcey's *The Crossroads of Liberalism* (1961) examined the thought of *New Republic* editors Lippmann, Herbert Croly, and Walter Weyl, as they struggled to relate their philosophies of democratic nationalism to the diplomatic problems of World War I. Forcey contended that their basic nationalism, especially their fascination with power and their elitist attitude toward political leadership, predisposed them to a tough foreign policy which bordered on interventionism. He depicted their subsequent disillusionment with the nationalistic approach—the result of wartime repression and the peace treaties—as emblematic of the shift of Western liberal

34. Goldman, *Rendezvous with Destiny: A History of Modern American Reform* (New York [Vintage ed.], 1956), pp. 180–219; Hofstadter, *The Age of Reform: From Bryan to F.D.R.* (New York [Vintage ed.], 1960), pp. 272–282.

35. Link's volumes that cover the war from its outbreak to American intervention are *Wilson: The Struggle for Neutrality, 1914–1915* (Princeton, 1960); *Wilson: Confusions and Crises, 1915–1916* (Princeton, 1964); and *Wilson: Campaigns for Progressivism and Peace, 1916–1917* (Princeton, 1965).

sympathies away from middle-class reform to more or less violent social revolution. Christopher Lasch discerned similar shifts of thought in his book on American liberals' reactions to Bolshevism and in a later essay in which he also examined the *New Republic* editors' attitudes toward the war.[36] Roland N. Stromberg treated the arguments over peacemaking as a problem in intellectual history in *Collective Security and American Foreign Policy* (1963), and he paid special attention to the views of experienced diplomatists outside government, such as Elihu Root, who detected deep ambiguities and serious drawbacks in the Wilsonian approach to peace.[37]

Three more recent studies have probed relationships between domestic politics and foreign policy. Seward W. Livermore used a phrase of Wilson's ironically to entitle his book *Politics Is Adjourned* (1966). In it he recorded the partisan strife over diplomatic and military issues from 1916 down to the Armistice and maintained that these contentions laid the foundation for subsequent conflict over the peace treaty. In my own book, *The Vanity of Power* (1969), I traced the development of isolationist attitudes and political support from the outbreak of the war to intervention. I found that the combined influences of political circumstance and intellectual outlook brought together in an isolationist coalition self-interested nationalists and idealists, almost all of whom were affected by partisan, ethnic, sectional, or reformist affiliations. Ralph J. Stone discerned a similarly diverse set of viewpoints and backgrounds in his account of the opponents of League membership in 1919 and 1920, *The Irreconcilables* (1970). Stone's scrutiny of their public and private statements disclosed a variety of arguments which could also be roughly divided between nationalistic concerns for sovereignty and security and idealistic solicitude over peace and freedom. Because previous interpretations had stressed ignorance and prejudice, both my own and Stone's analyses countered with observations on the intellectual respectability of the ideas and criticisms offered by isolationists and irreconcilables.[38]

36. Forcey, *The Crossroads of Liberalism: Croly, Weyl, Lippmann, and the Progressive Era, 1900–1925* (New York, 1961), esp. pp. 220–241, 286–291; Lasch, "The New Republic and the War: 'An Unanalyzable Feeling,'" in *The New Radicalism in America: The Intellectual as a Social Type, 1889–1963* (New York, 1965), pp. 181–224.

37. Stromberg, *Collective Security and American Foreign Policy, From the League of Nations to NATO* (New York, 1963).

38. The impact of the war on American pacifism has also been examined recently in Charles Chatfield, *For Peace and Justice: Pacifism in America,*

Although these studies of the war's influence on American foreign policy have formed the major thrust of recent historical scholarship, earlier arguments over intervention and peacemaking have remained remarkably alive. For example, the national-interest debate continues to attract attention from some historians and political scientists, as do questions about responsibility for failure to join the League.[39] Perhaps the most amazing survival has been the emotion still sure to be aroused over assessments of Wilson's personality. This unabated contentiousness was spectacularly displayed when a psychoanalytic biography done in the early 1930's by William C. Bullitt, purportedly in collaboration with Sigmund Freud, was published, like the disinterment of a long-buried skeleton, in 1967. Most scholars condemned the book as a callow misuse of psychoanalytic concepts for destructive purposes, and called into doubt the degree and quality of Freud's contribution. Yet the book not only gained wide publicity, but its general view of Wilson as a vindictive, inhuman psychic cripple elicited surprisingly hot praise and condemnation.[40] Perhaps the best thing that can be said about these residues of time-worn arguments is that they are no longer in the main line of historical inquiry. Historians have clearly moved toward a broader, more sophisticated

---

1914–1941 (Knoxville, Tenn., 1971). See also Chatfield's earlier article, "World War I and the Liberal Pacifist in the United States," *American Historical Review,* LXXV (December 1970), 1920–1937.

39. On the national-interest debate see Daniel M. Smith, "National Interest and American Intervention, 1917: An Historiographical Appraisal," *Journal of American History,* LII (June 1965), 5–24; and *The Great Departure: The United States and World War I, 1914–1920* (New York, 1965). For continued interest in the League controversy see Kurt Wimer, "Woodrow Wilson Tries Conciliation: An Effort that Failed," *Historian,* XXV (August 1963), 419–438.

40. The Bullitt-Freud study is entitled *Thomas Woodrow Wilson: Twenty-Eighth President of the United States—A Psychological Study* (Boston, 1967). For astute criticisms see Erik H. Erikson and Richard Hofstadter, "The Strange Case of Freud, Bullitt and Woodrow Wilson," *New York Review of Books* (February 9, 1967), pp. 3–8. For condemnation of the book see Link, "The Case for Woodrow Wilson," *Harper's,* CCXXXIV (April 1967), 85–93; and for praise, Barbara W. Tuchman, "Can History Use Freud? The Case of Woodrow Wilson," *Atlantic,* CCXIX (February 1967), 39–44. The best answer in many ways to the psychological arguments comes from the distinguished neurologist Dr. Edwin Weinstein in his article "Woodrow Wilson's Neurological Illness," *Journal of American History,* LVII (September 1970), 324–351.

understanding of the impact of World War I on the foreign policy of the United States.

II

Arguments over what the war meant to the domestic life of the United States originated, too, with those who participated in the events. Opponents of intervention, especially progressive anti-interventionists, predicted that the previous decade's reform accomplishments would be swiftly reversed as the forces of wealth and reaction regained control of the nation. Wilson himself evidently felt a similar dread of the effects of intervention as he grappled with conflicting perceptions and desires in the final crisis of 1917.[41] After the war, the downfall of progressivism and the massive conservative resurgence of 1920 seemed to confirm those earlier forecasts. Others besides liberals and reformers, who engaged in extensive recriminations and often blamed their troubles on the war, believed that intervention had fundamentally altered American life. The victorious Republican right wing of 1920, which upheld Warren Harding's banner of a return to "normalcy," was equally convinced that the country had departed fundamentally from its pre-war condition.[42]

This general agreement that World War I caused enormous changes marked the main difference between assessments of its domestic and diplomatic consequences. There never was any serious debate about the domestic impact; historians simply accepted the basic assumption that the conflict brought fundamental shifts at home. The war quickly came to be viewed as the most vivid turning point in twentieth-century American history. Beginning with Frederick Lewis Allen's enormously influential treatment of the 1920's, *Only Yesterday* (1931), interpreters argued that the war separated the "progressive era" from the 1920's and was responsible for all the transformations implied in the different images of those two periods. The trauma, frenzy, and repression generated by the war supposedly replaced political reform with reaction, social tolerance with prejudice, intellectual

41. On the anti-interventionist arguments and Wilson's qualms about the end of reform, see John Milton Cooper, Jr., *The Vanity of Power: American Isolationism and the First World 1914–1917* (Westport, Conn., 1969), esp. pp. 100–109, 174–191, 197–200, 205–206.

42. The most famous example of liberal castigation is Harold Stearns, *Liberalism in America* (New York, 1919). On the 1920 campaign the best account remains Wesley M. Bagby, *The Road to Normalcy: The Election of 1920* (Baltimore, 1962).

optimism with disillusionment, and overall public concern and engage-
ment with retreat into privacy and apathy. Until the mid-1950's, nearly
all of the writing on the period between 1914 and 1920 accepted or
elaborated this view of the domestic consequences of World War I.[43]

When questions finally began to be raised about the war's impact,
doubts about the traditional view surfaced in piecemeal fashion, the
result of investigations in separate areas of domestic history. One
study to chip away part of the established picture was John Higham's
history of anti-foreign attitudes, *Strangers in the Land* (1954), which
offered a perspective on wartime nativist reactions. Far from souring
a harmoniously tolerant situation, Higham thought American entry
into the war relieved some of the hostility against the most maligned
immigrant groups. This was either because, like the Italians, they
came from Allied nations, or because, like the various Slavic peoples,
they belonged to subject nationalities of the Austro-Hungarian Empire
who opposed the Central Powers. Although Higham did not discount
post-intervention drives for "One Hundred Per Cent Americanism,"
he saw the war as providing both opportunities and complications
for nativist sentiments.[44] Earlier, Charles Fenton, a literary historian,
had partially challenged the view that disillusionment born of combat
experience had spawned the famous "lost generation" of young American writers of the 1920's. Fenton concluded from a careful examination of the volunteer ambulance drivers, who included Ernest Hemingway, E. E. Cummings, and John Dos Passos, that the most sensitive
among them had grown disgusted with prevailing middle-class culture
before they enlisted, and were more or less deliberately seeking the
disillusioning experiences that they found at the battlefront.[45]

The broadest attack on the belief in World War I as the *cause*
of sweeping changes opened in 1956 with an article by Henry F.

43. Two examples of acceptance and elaboration of this view can be
found in Goldman, *Rendezvous with Destiny,* esp. pp. 220–225, and in
Hofstadter, *Age of Reform,* esp. pp. 272–279.

44. See Higham, *Strangers in the Land: Patterns of American Nativism,
1860–1925* (New Brunswick, N.J., 1955), ch. 7–9.

45. Charles Fenton, "Ambulance Drivers in France and Italy,
1914–1918," *American Quarterly,* III (Winter 1951), 326–343. Interestingly,
another member of the ambulance service volunteers and one of the most
influential formulators of the "lost generation" interpretation had himself
suggested much of this counter-interpretation at the same time. See Malcolm
Cowley, *Exile's Return: A Literary Odyssey of the 1920's* (New York
[Compass ed.], 1956), esp. pp. 18–19, 36–47.

May, "The Rebellion of the Intellectuals, 1912–1917." May asserted that most of the ferment of the 1920's had erupted well before the outbreak of the European conflict. May developed his thesis further in *The End of American Innocence* (1959), a more extended account of advanced thinking and broader cultural currents in the five years before intervention. His basic contentions were, first, that youthful and intellectual rebellion against middle-class culture had broken out in the heyday of highminded idealists like Wilson and Roosevelt rather than in reaction to the crass materialism of Harding and Coolidge; and, second, that the erosion of the central faith of liberalism in rational human progress had started before the onset of the World War, which served mainly to confirm pre-existing doubts. Although he was not primarily concerned with political history, May also suggested that internal criticisms and social strains had cracked and shrunk the broad areas of agreement underlying progressivism well in advance of intervention, and that the major disagreements had occurred over issues other than foreign policy.[46]

Closer investigation of political change during the war came in William E. Leuchtenburg's *The Perils of Prosperity* (1958). Leuchtenburg did not challenge the view that wartime disillusionment had deeply affected liberals and radicals, but he did question whether the shift from progressivism to the business-oriented regime of the 1920's really signified a great change. Specifically, Leuchtenburg suggested that many reformers of 1912 and conservatives of 1920 held important views in common, especially commercial and organizational values, and he noted how a number of leading figures made a smooth transition from one outlook to the other.[47] Arthur Link similarly questioned the extent of political change in his article "What Happened to the Progressive Movement in the 1920's?" (1959), though he argued that reform forces retained much greater strength after World War I than had commonly been appreciated. Link did not deny that progressivism declined, nor did he discount the war's influence in its loss of support. But he stressed a variety of other factors, too,

46. May, "The Rebellion of the Intellectuals, 1912–1917," *American Quarterly,* XIII (Summer 1956), 114–126; *The End of American Innocence: A Study of the First Years of Our Own Time, 1912–1917* (New York, 1959), esp. pp. vii–xii, 193–216, 279–329, 333–354.

47. Leuchtenburg, *The Perils of Prosperity, 1914–1932* (Chicago, 1958), pp. 126–127. Overlaps and areas of agreement are also suggested in Paul W. Glad, "Progressives and the Business Culture of the 1920's," *Journal of American History,* LIII (June 1966), 75–89.

including disagreements among reformers over social issues and government action, together with severe political setbacks on domestic grounds before intervention.[48] The upshot of Link's and Leuchtenburg's interpretations was clearly to make the war only one of several factors behind political change between 1916 and 1920.

Meanwhile, other historians were discovering fresh aspects of the war's significance. Probably the most important new area to be discussed in the late 1950's and early 1960's was civil liberties. In *Red Scare* (1955) Robert K. Murray recounted the anti-radical hysteria of 1919 and 1920, which he interpreted as a reaction to the unsettlement of the war and an expression of the patriotic frenzy left unsatisfied by the early end of the conflict. Later, Stanley Coben filled out this interpretation, first with a biography of the major instigator of the Red Scare, Attorney General A. Mitchell Palmer, and then with an article in which he used psychological and anthropological concepts to link the expressions of mass hysteria to social and economic tensions heightened mainly by the war.[49] Two books published in 1963 dealt with wartime suppression of free speech and civil rights. Donald O. Johnson's *The Challenge to American Freedoms* described the formation of the American Civil Liberties Union as a response to the more systematic repressions caused by the war. William Preston, Jr.'s *Aliens and Dissenters* similarly viewed participation in the World War as opening the way for unprecedented government interference with individuals' lives.

Essentially, historical interpretation of the war's domestic impact has followed these two lines of approach since the early 1960's: an elaboration and at the same time a questioning of its influence. Only occasionally have historians of these different persuasions argued with one another, and neither of these viewpoints can be said to constitute a school of interpretation.[50]

To date there has been little attempt at synthesis about the effects

48. Link, "What Happened to the Progressive Movement in the 1920's?" *American Historical Review*, LXIV (July 1959), 833–851.

49. Coben's biography is *A. Mitchell Palmer: Politician* (New York, 1963), and the article is "A Study in Nativism: The American Red Scare of 1919–20," *Political Science Quarterly*, LXXIX (March 1964), 52–75.

50. Curiously, one of the few cases of direct confrontation has come in literary history, where Fenton has challenged May's relative de-emphasis of the effects of the conflict on "the lost generation." See Fenton, "A Literary Fracture of World War I," *American Quarterly*, XII (Summer 1960), 119–132.

of World War I on American domestic history. In some ways such an attempt at synthesis might be premature. For one thing, much of the American experience during the war remains to be studied; important questions about its domestic impact have thus far received little attention. For example, despite frequent remarks on economic and social change wrought by the war, there has been little detailed investigation or intelligent speculation about such obvious questions as what jobs were created and who filled them; how many people moved where and how often; and what shifts in personal values may have come out of experiences with the draft, war work, and military service. Furthermore, much of the recent work on domestic aspects of the war has generated contradictory interpretations. One area which has lately received attention is government intervention in the wartime economy. Historians have known for a long time that experiments in 1917–1918 with centralized control of transportation, industry, and agriculture marked a highly significant departure in public policy. Not only did the activities of the War Industries Board in those years offer the chief precedent for planning and regulation in fighting the depression of the 1930's, but such figures as George N. Peek and Hugh M. Johnson, who served in Washington during the war, returned to head the major New Deal economic agencies in 1933.[51] Only recently, however, have the War Industries Board and other wartime instruments of economic management been carefully studied.

Several historians have investigated this major turning point in governmental relations with industry and in economic thinking. Robert F. Himmelberg concentrated on the proposals, developed by businessmen serving in government agencies, that prices be stabilized by suspending the anti-trust laws. These proposals, Himmelberg argued, influenced ideas of government-business cooperation in a managed economy, both in the trade association movement and Herbert Hoover's policies in the 1920's, and in the National Recovery Administration in the 1930's. Similarly, Paul A. C. Koistinen contended that cooperation between military and civilian officials and business leaders in running the American war machine after 1917 laid the foundation for the "military-industrial complex."[52]

51. World War I precedents for the New Deal are discussed in Leuchtenburg's essay "The New Deal and the Analogue of War," in Braeman, et al., eds., *Change and Continuity in Twentieth-Century America*, pp. 81–143.
52. See Robert F. Himmelberg, "The War Industries Board and the

In contrast, some interpreters have doubted the influence and originality of wartime ideas and practices. Daniel R. Beaver and Robert D. Cuff independently emphasized the relative weakness of the War Industries Board's direction of the economy and the lack of cooperation among various government agencies and business interests. Also working separately, Harry N. Scheiber, in a study of the financier Willard Straight, and James Weinstein, in *The Corporate Ideal in the Liberal State* (1968), concluded that plans for partnership between government and business in managing the economy were highly developed before World War I and that proponents of such programs simply used the war effort as a testing ground for their ideas.[53]

A comparable set of conflicting interpretations has emerged from recent investigations of the war's influence on American politics. Studies of the behavior of ethnic groups in the 1916 election produced evidence that German- and Irish-Americans differed little from "native" elements in their alignments. The only likely influence of the war on these groups was that they may have responded (like other voters) to Wilson's appeal as a peace candidate, rather than believing the anti-administration strictures of leading German and Irish organizations.[54] Analyzing political changes after 1916, David

---

Anti-Trust Question in November 1918," *Journal of American History,* LII (June 1965), 59–74; "Business, Antitrust Policy, and the Industrial Board of the Department of Commerce, 1919," *Business History Review,* XLII (Spring 1968), 1–23; and Paul A. C. Koistinen, "The 'Industrial-Military Complex' in Historical Perspective: World War I," *ibid.,* XLI (Winter 1967), 378–403.

53. Daniel R. Beaver, "Newton D. Baker and the Genesis of the War Industries Board, 1917–1918," *Journal of American History,* LII (June 1965), 43–58; Robert D. Cuff, "Bernard Baruch: Symbol and Myth in Industrial Mobilization," *Business History Review,* XLIII (Summer 1969), 115–133; Harry N. Scheiber, "World War I as Entrepreneurial Opportunity: Willard Straight and the American International Corporation," *Political Science Quarterly,* LXXXIV (December 1969), 486–511; James Weinstein, *The Corporate Ideal in the Liberal State, 1900–1918* (Boston, 1968), esp. pp. 214–254. On mobilization see also Beaver, *Newton D. Baker and the American War Effort, 1917–1919* (Lincoln, Nebr., 1966); and on pre-war ideas of government-business cooperation see Gabriel Kolko, *The Triumph of Conservatism: A Reinterpretation of American History, 1900–1916* (New York, 1963).

54. See esp. Link, *Wilson: Campaigns for Progressivism and Peace,* pp. 161–163; William M. Leary, Jr., "Woodrow Wilson, Irish Americans, and the Election of 1916," *Journal of American History,* LIV (June 1967), 57–62; and Edward Cuddy, "Pro-Germanism and American Catholicism,

Burner produced a mixed set of findings in *The Politics of Provincialism* (1968). On the one hand, Burner seconded Link's earlier observation that Wilson's winning coalition in 1916 had been fortuitous and unstable and offered no real indication of having broken the electorate's normal Republican majority. On the other hand, Burner argued that the massive repudiation of the Democratic party in 1920 sprang mainly from wartime discontents and frustrations. He also blamed Wilson's policies for dissipating the slender bases of cohesion that had held the Democrats together, thereby initiating the fratricidal warfare that helped keep them a minority.[55]

The faltering of socialism and political radicalism was another subject that provoked reassessments of the impact of the war. In the *Decline of Socialism in America* (1967), James Weinstein attacked prevailing views that a combination of progressive reforms before 1917 and patriotism afterward obliterated the appeal of the Socialist party. Instead, Weinstein argued, the Socialists showed impressive and in some areas growing strength. Far from losing favor as a result of their anti-interventionist stands and official repression in 1917 and 1918, they actually gained further support by appealing to widespread public hostility to the conflict. What doomed socialism as a major political movement, in Weinstein's view, was the divisiveness and shortsightedness of the party leaders in responding to the Russian Revolution. Weinstein, himself a committed radical, contended that longings to imitate European, especially Bolshevik, ideas and practices fragmented American Socialists into three inimical sects which were more interested in fighting one another than in establishing ties with discontented and dispossessed blacks, ethnics, and workers.[56]

The role of the war in introducing social change has also been reappraised in recent studies of women and blacks. In different ways, James R. McGovern and William L. O'Neill revised the view that World War I won the vote for American women and transformed them from demure Gibson Girls to frenetic, liberated Flappers. McGovern maintained that most of the relaxed restraints and new opportunities associated with the 1920's took hold before the outbreak

1914–1917," *Catholic Historical Review,* LIV (October 1968), 427–454; and "Irish-Americans and the 1916 Election: An Episode in Immigrant Adjustment," *American Quarterly,* XXI (Summer 1969), 228–243.

55. Burner, *The Politics of Provincialism: The Democratic Party in Transition, 1918–1932* (New York, 1968), pp. 28–73.

56. Weinstein, *The Decline of Socialism in America, 1912–1925* (New York, 1967), esp. pp. 119–176, 324–339.

of the war, while O'Neill questioned whether women's participation in the war really opened new jobs for them and advanced the triumph of woman suffrage.[57] In tracing the history of the nation's two largest black ghettos, New York's Harlem and Chicago's South Side, Gilbert Osofsky and Allen Spear acknowledged that demands for labor drew hundreds of thousands of Negroes out of the South to swell the size of those neighborhoods during the war. But they also pointed out that substantial black migration to New York and Chicago began in the 1890's, and that the location and basic institutions of both ghetto communities were firmly established before 1914.[58] Other historians have drawn mixed conclusions about the effects of the war on race relations, citing a sharp increase in interracial violence yet also noting new efforts to promote greater justice and harmony.[59]

So while a synthesis on the domestic impact of World War I has not yet emerged, clearly the basic positions have been staked out. Questions can now be asked in ways that will contribute to a broader view of the war's significance. Perhaps the most pressing demand at the moment is for a greater interchange between diplomatic and domestic historians, in order to get at the full range of the war's consequences for the United States. Interestingly, only Arthur Link, among recent scholars, has made important contributions to studying the effects of the war at home and abroad. His perspective as Wilson's biographer has allowed him to see that participants in the events hardly viewed diplomacy and domestic affairs as separate categories. The lesson for future historians ought to be clear. If they will recapture something of the contemporary view of World War I, they may begin to grasp its full significance for American history.

57. McGovern, "The American Woman's Pre-World War I Freedom in Manners and Morals," *Journal of American History,* LV (September 1968), 315–333; O'Neill, *Everyone Was Brave: The Rise and Fall of Feminism in America* (Chicago, 1969), pp. 169–224. See also O'Neill, *Divorce in the Progressive Era* (New Haven, 1967), pp. 257–259.

58. Osofsky, *Harlem: The Making of a Ghetto: Negro New York, 1890–1930* (New York, 1965), pp. 17–34, 107–123; Spear, *Black Chicago: The Making of a Negro Ghetto, 1890–1920* (Chicago, 1967), esp. pp. ix, 11, 129–130.

59. See George B. Tindall, *The Emergence of the New South, 1913–1945* (Baton Rouge, 1967), pp. 143–183, and William M. Tuttle, Jr., *Race Riot: Chicago in the Red Summer of 1919* (New York, 1970). For a broader treatment of the war's impact on drives to promote social justice, see also Allen F. Davis, "Welfare Reform and World War I," *American Quarterly,* XIX (Fall 1967), 516–533.

A Selected Bibliography on the United States and World War I

I. General Works

A. GENERAL HISTORIES

William E. Leuchtenburg, *The Perils of Prosperity, 1914–1932* (Chicago, 1958).

Arthur S. Link, *Wilson: The Struggle for Neutrality, 1914–1915* (Princeton, 1960).

———, *Wilson: Confusions and Crises, 1915–1916* (Princeton, 1964).

———, *Wilson: Campaigns for Progressivism and Peace, 1916–1917* (Princeton, 1965).

———, *Woodrow Wilson and the Progressive Era, 1910–1917* (New York, 1954).

Frederic L. Paxson, *American Democracy and the World War, 1914–1920* (3 vols., Boston and Berkeley, 1936–1948).

B. HISTORIOGRAPHY AND GENERAL INTERPRETATIONS

BOOKS

E. H. Carr, *The Twenty Years' Crisis: An Introduction to the Study of International Relations* (London, 1939).

———, *Conditions of Peace* (London, 1942).

Warren I. Cohen, *The American Revisionists: The Lessons of Intervention in World War I* (Chicago, 1967).

George F. Kennan, *American Diplomacy, 1900–1950* (Chicago, 1951).

N. Gordon Levin, Jr., *Woodrow Wilson and World Politics: America's Response to War and Revolution* (New York, 1968).

Robert Endicott Osgood, *Ideals and Self-Interest in America's Foreign Relations: The Great Transformation of the Twentieth Century* (Chicago, 1953).

Daniel M. Smith, *The Great Departure: The United States and World War I, 1914–1920* (New York, 1965).

Roland N. Stromberg, *Collective Security and American Foreign Policy, From the League of Nations to NATO* (New York, 1963).

William Appleman Williams, *The Tragedy of American Diplomacy* (New York, 1962).

ARTICLES

Denna Frank Fleming, "Our Entry into the World War in 1917: The Revised Version," *Journal of Politics,* II (February 1940), 75–86.

George F. Kennan, "The Price We Paid for War," *Atlantic,* CCXIV (October 1964), 50–54.

Richard W. Leopold, "The Emergence of America as a World Power: Some Second Thoughts," in John Braeman, *et al.,* eds., *Change and Continuity in Twentieth Century America* (Columbus, Ohio, 1964), pp. 3–34.

————, "The Problem of American Intervention, 1917: An Historical Retrospect," *World Politics,* II (April 1950), 405–425.

Daniel M. Smith, "National Interest and American Intervention, 1917: An Historiographical Appraisal," *Journal of American History,* LII (June 1965), 5–24.

Richard L. Watson, Jr., "Woodrow Wilson and His Interpreters," 1947–1957," *Mississippi Valley Historical Review,* XLIV (September 1957), 207–236.

C. STUDIES OF WOODROW WILSON

BOOKS

Ray Stannard Baker, *Woodrow Wilson: Life and Letters* (8 vols., Garden City, N.Y., 1927–1939).

John Morton Blum, *Woodrow Wilson and the Politics of Morality* (Boston, 1956).

Edward H. Buehrig, *Woodrow Wilson and the Balance of Power* (Bloomington, Ind., 1955).

William Diamond, *The Economic Thought of Woodrow Wilson* (Baltimore, 1943).

Sigmund Freud and William C. Bullitt, *Thomas Woodrow Wilson: Twenty-Eighth President of the United States—A Psychological Study* (Boston, 1967).

John A. Garraty, *Woodrow Wilson: A Great Life in Brief* (New York, 1956).

Alexander L. George and Juliette L. George, *Woodrow Wilson and Colonel House: A Personality Study* (New York, 1956).

Arthur S. Link, *Wilson the Diplomatist: A Look at His Major Foreign Policies* (Baltimore, 1957).

Arthur Walworth, *Woodrow Wilson* (2 vols., New York, 1958).

ARTICLES

Edward H. Buehrig, "Idealism and Statecraft," *Confluence*, V (Autumn 1956), 252–263.

John Morton Blum, "Woodrow Wilson: A Study in Intellect," *Confluence*, V (Winter 1957), 367–375.

Erik H. Erikson and Richard Hofstadter, "The Strange Case of Freud, Bullitt and Woodrow Wilson," *New York Review of Books* (February 9, 1967), pp. 3–8.

Denna F. Fleming, "Woodrow Wilson and Collective Security Today," *Review of Politics*, XVIII (November 1956), 611–624.

John A. Garraty, "Woodrow Wilson: A Study in Personality," *South Atlantic Quarterly*, LVI (April 1957), 176–185.

Richard Hofstadter, "Woodrow Wilson: The Conservative as a Liberal," in *The American Political Tradition and the Men Who Made It* (New York, 1948), pp. 236–282.

Perry Laukhuff, "The Price of Woodrow Wilson's Illness," *Virginia Quarterly Review*, XXXII (Autumn 1956), 598–610.

Arthur S. Link, "The Case for Woodrow Wilson," *Harper's*, CCXXXIV (April 1967), 85–93.

Robert E. Osgood, "Woodrow Wilson, Collective Security and the Lessons of History," *Confluence*, V (Winter 1957), 341–354.

Charles Seymour, "Woodrow Wilson in Perspective," *Foreign Affairs*, XXXIV (January 1956), 175–186.

Barbara W. Tuchman, "Can History Use Freud? The Case of Woodrow Wilson," *Atlantic*, CCXIX (February 1967), 39–44.

Edwin A. Weinstein, "Woodrow Wilson's Neurological Illness," *Journal of American History*, LVII (September 1970), 324–351.

II. Neutrality and Intervention

A. THE "SUBMARINE SCHOOL" AND THE "REVISIONISTS"

BOOKS

Alex M. Arnett, *Claude Kitchin and the Wilson War Policies* (Boston, 1937).

Newton D. Baker, *Why We Went to War* (New York, 1936).

Harry Elmer Barnes, *Genesis of the World War* (New York, 1926).

Charles A. Beard, *The Devil Theory of War* (New York, 1936).

Edwin M. Borchard and William P. Lage, *Neutrality for the United States* (New Haven, 1937).

C. Hartley Grattan, *Why We Fought* (New York, 1929).

Walter Millis, *The Road to War: America, 1914–1917* (Boston, 1935).

Alice M. Morrissey, *The American Defense of Neutral Rights, 1914–1917* (Cambridge, Mass., 1939).

Dexter Perkins, *America and Two Wars* (Boston, 1944).

H. C. Peterson, *Propaganda for War: The Campaign Against American Neutrality, 1914–1917* (Norman, Okla., 1939).

Charles Seymour, *American Diplomacy During the World War* (Baltimore, 1934).

————, *American Neutrality, 1914–1917* (New Haven, 1935).

Charles Callan Tansill, *America Goes to War* (Boston, 1938).

ARTICLES

Thomas A. Bailey, "The Sinking of the *Lusitania*," *American Historical Review,* XLI (March 1934), 14–35.

Harry Elmer Barnes, "The World War of 1914–1918," in W. Waller, ed., *War in the Twentieth Century* (New York, 1940), pp. 71–82.

Paul Birdsall, "Neutrality and Economic Pressures, 1914–1917," *Science and Society,* III (Spring 1939), 217–228.

H. Schuyler Foster, Jr., "How America Became a Belligerent: A Quantitative Study of War News, 1914–1917," *American Journal of Sociology,* XL (January 1935), 464–475.

Joseph V. Fuller, "The Genesis of the Munitions Traffic," *Journal of Modern History,* VI (September 1934), 280–293.

Walter Millis, "Propaganda for War," *Southern Review,* V (Autumn 1939), 201–210.

Richard W. van Alstyne, "Private American Loans to the Allies, 1914–1916," *Pacific Historical Review,* II (June 1933), 180–193.

B. NATIONAL INTEREST AND INTERNATIONAL PERSPECTIVE

BOOKS

Karl Birnbaum, *Peace Moves and U-Boat Warfare* (Stockholm, 1958).

Forrest Davis, *The Atlantic System: The Story of Anglo-American Control of the Seas* (New York, 1941).

Fritz Fischer, *Germany's Aims in the First World War* (New York, 1967).

Ross Gregory, *Ambassador to the Court of St. James's: Walter Hines Page* (Lexington, Ky., 1969).

————, *The Origins of American Intervention in the First World War* (New York, 1971).

Ernest R. May, *The World War and American Isolation, 1914–1917* (Cambridge, Mass., 1959).

Armin Rapaport, *British Press and American Neutrality, 1914–1917* (Stanford, Calif., 1951).

Marion Siney, *The Allied Bockade of Germany, 1914–1916* (Ann Arbor, 1957).

36 INTRODUCTION

Daniel M. Smith, *Robert M. Lansing and American Neutrality, 1914–1917* (Berkeley, 1958).

ARTICLES

Edward Mead Earle, "A Half-Century of American Foreign Policy: Our Stake in Europe, 1898–1948," *Political Science Quarterly,* LXIV (June 1949), 168–188.

Fritz T. Epstein, "Germany and the United States: Basic Patterns of Conflict and Understanding," in G. L. Anderson, ed., *Issues and Conflict* (Lawrence, Kans., 1959), pp. 284–314.

Walter Lippmann, "The Atlantic and America," *Life,* X (April 7, 1941), 84–92.

Daniel M. Smith, "Robert M. Lansing and the Formation of American Neutrality Policies, 1914–1915," *Mississippi Valley Historical Review,* XLIII (June 1956), 611–624.

Alfred Vagts, "Hopes and Fears of an American-German War, 1870–1915," *Political Science Quarterly,* LV (March 1940), 53–76.

C. DOMESTIC BACKGROUNDS TO FOREIGN POLICY

BOOKS

Ray M. Abrams, *Preachers Present Arms* (Philadelphia, 1933).

Ruhl J. Bartlett, *The League to Enforce Peace* (Chapel Hill, 1944).

Charles Chatfield, *For Peace and Justice: Pacifism in America, 1914–1941* (Knoxville, Tenn., 1971).

Clifton J. Child, *The German-Americans in Politics, 1914–1917* (Madison, Wisc., 1939).

John Milton Cooper, Jr., *The Vanity of Power: American Isolationism and the First World War, 1914–1917* (Westport, Conn., 1969).

Edwin M. Costrell, *How Maine Viewed the World War, 1914–1917* (Orono, Maine, 1940).

John C. Crighton, *Missouri and the World War, 1914–1917* (Columbia, Mo., 1947).

Cedric Cummins, *Indiana Public Opinion and the World War, 1914–1917* (Indianapolis, 1945).

Merle Curti, *Bryan and World Peace* (Northampton, Mass., 1931).

———, *Peace or War: The American Struggle, 1636–1936* (New York, 1936).

Marie L. Degen, *A History of the Women's Peace Party* (Baltimore, 1939).

Charles Forcey, *The Crossroads of Liberalism: Croly, Weyl, Lippmann and the Progressive Era, 1900–1925* (New York, 1961).

Sondra Herman, *Eleven Against War: Studies in American Internationalist Thought, 1898–1921* (Stanford, Calif., 1969).

Lawrence W. Levine, *Defender of the Faith: Bryan, The Last Decade, 1915–1925* (New York, 1965).

Armin Rapaport, *The Navy League of the United States* (Detroit, 1962).

Carl Wittke, *German-Americans and the World War* (Columbus, Ohio, 1935).

ARTICLES

Howard W. Allen, "Republican Reformers and Foreign Policy, 1913–1917," *Mid-America,* XLIV (October 1962), 222–229.

Barton J. Bernstein and Franklin A. Leib, "Progressive Republican Senators and American Imperialism, 1898–1916: A Reappraisal," *Mid-America,* L (July 1968), 163–205.

Felice A. Bonadio, "The Failure of German Propaganda in the United States, 1914–1917," *Mid-America,* XLI (January 1959), 40–57.

Charles Chatfield, "World War I and the Liberal Pacifist in the United States," *American Historical Review,* LXXV (December 1970), 1920–1937.

John Milton Cooper, Jr., "Progressivism and American Foreign Policy: A Reconsideration," *Mid-America,* LI (October 1969), 260–277.

Edward Cuddy, "Irish-Americans and the 1916 Election: An Episode in Immigrant Adjustment," *American Quarterly,* XXI (Summer 1969) 228–243.

———, "Pro-Germanism and American Catholicism, 1914–1917," *Catholic Historical Review,* LIV (October 1968), 427–454.

Dean R. Esslinger, "American German and Irish Attitudes Toward Neutrality, 1914–1917: A Study of Catholic Minorities," *Catholic Historical Review,* LII (July 1967), 194–216.

George C. Herring, Jr., "James Hay and the Preparedness Controversy, 1915–1916," *Journal of Southern History,* XXX (November 1964), 383–404.

Charles Hirschfeld, "Nationalist Progressivism and World War I," *Mid-America,* XLV (July 1963), 139–156.

Thomas J. Kerr, IV, "German-Americans and Neutrality in the 1916 Election," *Mid-America,* XLIII (April 1961), 95–105.

William M. Leary, Jr., "Woodrow Wilson, Irish Americans, and the Election of 1916," *Journal of American History,* LIV (June 1967), 57–72.

William E. Leuchtenburg, "Progressivism and Imperialism: The Progressive Movement and American Foreign Policy," *Mississippi Valley Historical Review,* XXXIX (December 1952), 483–504.

Walter A. Sutton, "Progressive Republican Senators and the Submarine Crisis, 1915–1916," *Mid-America,* XLVII (April 1956), 75–88.

———, "Republican Progressive Senators and Preparedness, 1915–1916," *Mid-America,* LII (July 1970), 155–176.

Harold C. Syrett, "The Business Press and American Neutrality,

1914–1917," *Mississippi Valley Historical Review,* XXXII (September 1945), 215–230.

J. A. Thompson, "American Progressive Publicists and the First World War, 1914–1917," *Journal of American History,* LVIII (September 1971), 364–383.

Walter I. Trattner, "Progressivism and World War I: A Re-appriasal," *Mid-America,* XLIV (July 1962), 131–145.

Robert D. Ward, "The Origin and Activities of the National Security League, 1914–1919," *Mississippi Valley Historical Review,* XLVII (June 1960), 51–65.

III. America at War, 1917–1918

A. MILITARY AND DIPLOMATIC POLICIES

BOOKS

Thomas A. Bailey, *The Policy of the United States Toward Neutrals, 1917–1918* (Baltimore, 1942).

Daniel R. Beaver, *Newton D. Baker and the American War Effort, 1917–1919* (Lincoln, Nebr., 1966).

Edward M. Coffman, *The War to End All Wars: The American Military Experience in World War I* (New York, 1968).

Harvey A. DeWeerd, *President Wilson Fights His War: World War I and the American Intervention* (New York, 1968).

John Dos Passos, *Mr. Wilson's War* (New York, 1962).

W. B. Fowler, *British-American Relations, 1917–1918: The Role of Sir William Wiseman* (Princeton, 1970).

Lawrence E. Gelfand, *The Inquiry: American Preparations for Peace, 1917–1919* (New Haven, 1963).

Louis L. Gerson, *Woodrow Wilson and the Rebirth of Poland, 1914–1920* (New Haven, 1953).

Victor S. Mamatey, *The United States and East Central Europe, 1914–1918* (Princeton, 1957).

Laurence W. Martin, *Peace Without Victory: Woodrow Wilson and the British Liberals* (New Haven, 1958).

David F. Trask, *The United States in the Supreme War Council: American War Aims and Inter-Allied Strategy, 1917–1918* (Middletown, Conn., 1961).

Sir Arthur Willert, *The Road to Safety: A Study in Anglo-American Relations* (London, 1952).

ARTICLES

Warner R. Schilling, "Civil-Naval Politics in World War I," *World Politics,* VII (July 1955), 572–591.

John L. Snell, "German Socialist Reaction to Wilsonian Diplomacy: From Neutrality to Belligerency," *Journal of Central European Affairs,* IX (April 1949), 61–79.

———, "Wilsonian Rhetoric Goes to War," *Historian,* XIV (Spring 1952), 191–208.

———, "Wilson's Peace Program and German Socialism, January-March, 1918," *Mississippi Valley Historical Review,* XXXVIII (September 1951), 187–214.

B. RESPONSES TO THE RUSSIAN REVOLUTION

BOOKS

George F. Kennan, *Soviet-American Relations, 1917–1920* (2 vols., Princeton, 1956–1958).

Christopher Lasch, *American Liberals and the Russian Revolution* (New York, 1962).

Arno J. Mayer, *Wilson versus Lenin: Political Origins of the New Diplomacy, 1917–1918* (New Haven, 1959).

Betty Miller Unterberger, *America's Siberian Expedition, 1918–1920: A Study of National Policy* (Durham, N.C., 1956).

ARTICLES

Claude E. Fike, "The Influence of the Creel Committee and the Red Cross on Russian-American Relations, 1917–1920," *Journal of Modern History,* XXXI (June 1959), 93–109.

———, "The United States and Russian Territorial Problems, 1917–1920," *Historian,* XXIV (May 1962), 331–346.

Christopher Lasch, "American Intervention in Siberia: A Reinterpretation," *Political Science Quarterly,* LXXVI (June 1962), 205–223.

Betty Miller Unterberger, "President Wilson and the Decision to Send American Troops to Siberia," *Pacific Historical Review,* XXIV (February 1955), 63–74.

———, "The Russian Revolution and Wilson's Far-Eastern Policy," *Russian Review,* XVI (April 1957), 35–46.

William A. Williams, "American Intervention in Russia, 1917–1920," *Studies on the Left,* III (Fall 1963), 24–47; IV (Winter 1964), 39–57.

C. MOBILIZATION AND REPRESSION ON THE HOME FRONT

BOOKS

Stanley Coben, *A. Mitchell Palmer: Politician* (New York, 1962).

Melvyn Dubofsky, *We Shall Be All: A History of the Industrial Workers of the World* (Chicago, 1969).

John Higham, *Strangers in the Land: Patterns of American Nativism, 1860–1925* (New Brunswick, N.J., 1955).

Donald O. Johnson, *The Challenge to American Freedoms: World War I and the Rise of the American Civil Liberties Union* (Lexington, Ky., 1963).

Robert K. Murray, *Red Scare: A Study in National Hysteria* (Minneapolis, 1955).

William Preston, Jr., *Aliens and Dissenters: Federal Suppression of Radicals, 1903–1933* (Cambridge, Mass., 1963).

James Weinstein, *The Corporate Ideal in the Liberal State, 1900–1918* (Boston, 1968).

ARTICLES

Paul P. Abrahams, "American Bankers and the Economic Tactics of Peace: 1919," *Journal of American History,* LVI (December 1969), 572–583.

Daniel R. Beaver, "Newton D. Baker and the Genesis of the War Industries Board, 1917–1918," *Journal of American History,* LII (June 1965), 43–58.

Richard Brazier, "The Mass I.W.W. Trial of 1918: A Retrospect," *Labor History,* VII (Spring 1966), 178–192.

Stanley Coben, "A Study in Nativism: The American Red Scare of 1919–20," *Political Science Quarterly,* LXXIX (March 1964), 52–75.

Robert D. Cuff, "Bernard Baruch: Symbol and Myth in Industrial Mobilization," *Business History Review,* XLIII (Summer 1969), 115–133.

——, "A 'Dollar-a-Year Man' in Government: George N. Peek and the War Industries Board," *Business History Review,* XLI (Winter 1967), 404–420.

Robert D. Cuff and Melvin I. Urofsky, "The Steel Industry and Price-Fixing During World War I," *Business History Review,* XLIV (Autumn 1967), 291–306.

Arnon Gutfeld, "The Murder of Frank Little: Radical Labor Agitation in Butte, Montana, 1917," *Labor History,* X (Spring 1969), 177–192.

Robert F. Himmelberg, "Business, Antitrust Policy, and the Industrial Board of the Department of Commerce, 1919," *Business History Review,* XLII (Spring 1968), 1–23.

——, "The War Industries Board and the Antitrust Question in November, 1918," *Journal of American History,* LII (June 1965), 59–74.

Donald O. Johnson, "Wilson, Burleson and Censorship in the First World War," *Journal of Southern History,* XXVIII (February 1962), 46–58.

K. Austin Kerr, "Decision for Federal Control: Wilson, McAdoo, and the Railroads, 1917," *Journal of American History,* LIV (December 1967), 550–560.

Paul A. C. Koistinen, "The 'Industrial-Military Complex' in Historical

Perspective: World War I," *Business History Review,* XLI (Winter 1967), 378–403.

Gerald Nash, "Franklin D. Roosevelt and Labor: The World War I Origins of Early New Deal Policy," *Labor History,* I (Winter 1960), 39–52.

Fred D. Ragan, "Justice Oliver Wendell Holmes, Jr., Zechariah Chafee, Jr., and the Clear and Present Danger Test for Free Speech: The First Year, 1919," *Journal of American History,* LVIII (June 1971), 24–45.

Harry N. Scheiber, "World War I as Entrepreneurial Opportunity: Willard Straight and the American International Corporation," *Political Science Quarterly,* LXXXIV (December 1969), 486–511.

Philip Taft, "The Federal Trials of the I.W.W.," *Labor History,* III (Winter 1962), 57–91.

D. SOCIAL AND INTELLECTUAL IMPACT OF THE WAR

BOOKS

Frederick Lewis Allen, *Only Yesterday* (New York, 1931).

Henry F. May, *The End of American Innocence: A Study of the First Years of Our Own Time, 1912–1917* (New York, 1959).

William L. O'Neill, *Divorce in the Progressive Era* (New Haven, 1967).

———, *Everyone Was Brave: The Rise and Fall of Feminism in America* (Chicago, 1969).

William M. Tuttle, Jr., *Race Riot: Chicago in the Red Summer of 1919* (New York, 1970).

ARTICLES

Henry Blumenthal, "Woodrow Wilson and the Race Question," *Journal of Negro History,* XLVIII (January 1963), 1–21.

Heinz Eulau, "Man Against Himself: Walter Lippmann's Years of Doubt," *American Quarterly,* IV (Winter 1952), 291–304.

Charles Fenton, "Ambulance Drivers in France and Italy, 1914–1918," *American Quarterly,* III (Winter 1951), 326–343.

———, "A Literary Fracture of World War I," *American Quarterly,* XII (Summer 1960), 119–132.

Henry F. May, "The Rebellion of the Intellectuals, 1912–1917," *American Quarterly,* VIII (Summer 1956), 114–126.

———, "Shifting Perspectives on the 1920's," *Mississippi Valley Historical Review,* XLIII (December 1956), 405–427.

James R. McGovern, "The American Woman's Pre-World War I Freedom in Manners and Morals," *Journal of American History,* LV (September 1968), 315–333.

Jane Lang Scheiber and Harry N. Scheiber, "The Wilson Administration and the Wartime Mobilization of Black Americans, 1917–1918," *Labor History,* X (Summer 1969), 433–458.

E. POLITICAL CHANGES

BOOKS

Wesley M. Bagby, *The Road to Normalcy: The Presidential Election of 1920* (Baltimore, 1962).

David M. Burner, *The Politics of Provincialism: The Democratic Party in Transition, 1918–1932* (New York, 1968).

Seward W. Livermore, *Politics Is Adjourned: Woodrow Wilson and the War Congress, 1916–1918* (Middletown, Conn., 1966).

James Weinstein, *The Decline of Socialism in America, 1912–1925* (New York, 1967).

ARTICLES

David Burner, "The Breakup of the Wilson Coalition of 1916," *Mid-America*, XLV (January 1963), 18–35.

Milton Cantor, "The Radical Confrontation with Foreign Policy: War and Revolution, 1914–1920," in Alfred Young, ed., *Dissent: Explorations in the History of American Radicalism* (DeKalb, Ill., 1968), pp. 215–249.

Allen F. Davis, "Welfare, Reform, and World War I," *American Quarterly*, XIX (Fall 1967), 516–533.

Paul W. Glad, "Progressives and the Business Culture of the 1920's," *Journal of American History*, LIII (June 1966), 75–89.

Kenneth E. Hendrickson, Jr., "The Pro-War Socialists, the Social Democratic League and the Ill-Fated Drive for Industrial Democracy in America, 1917–1920," *Labor History*, XI (Summer 1970), 304–322.

Arthur S. Link, "What Happened to the Progressive Movement in the 1920's?" *American Historical Review*, LXIV (July 1959), 833–851.

Seward W. Livermore, "The Sectional Issue in the 1918 Election," *Mississippi Valley Historical Review*, XXXV (June 1948), 29–60.

Herbert F. Margulies, "Recent Opinion on the Decline of the Progressive Movement," *Mid-America*, XLV (October 1965), 250–268.

Sally M. Miller, "Socialist Party Decline and World War I: Bibliography and Interpretation," *Science and Society*, XXXIV (Winter 1970), 398–411.

I. A. Newby, "States' Rights and Southern Congressmen During World War I," *Phylon*, XXIV (Spring 1963), 34–50.

Stanley Shapiro, "The Great War and Reform: Liberals and Labor, 1917–19," *Labor History*, XII (Summer 1971), 323–344.

Wilbur S. Shepperson, "Socialist Pacifism in the American West During World War I: A Case Study," *Historian*, XXIX (August 1967), 619–633.

James Weinstein, "Anti-War Sentiment and the Socialist Party, 1917–1918," *Political Science Quarterly*, LXXIV (June 1959), 215–239.

IV. Peacemaking, 1919–1920

A. THE PEACE CONFERENCE

BOOKS

Thomas A. Bailey, *Woodrow Wilson and the Lost Peace* (New York, 1944).

Paul Birdsall, *Versailles Twenty Years After* (New York, 1941).

Russell Fifield, *Woodrow Wilson and the Far East: The Diplomacy of the Shantung Question* (New York, 1952).

John Maynard Keynes, *The Economic Consequences of the Peace* (New York, 1920).

Arno J. Mayer, *Politics and Diplomacy of Peacemaking: Containment and Counterrevolution at Versailles, 1918–1919* (New York, 1967).

Harold Nicolson, *Peacemaking 1919* (Boston, 1933).

Seth P. Tillman, *Anglo-American Relations at the Paris Peace Conference of 1919* (Princeton, 1961).

Lewis A. R. Yates, *The United States and French Security, 1917–1921* (New York, 1957).

ARTICLES

George Curry, "Woodrow Wilson, Jan Smuts, and the Versailles Settlement," *American Historical Review,* LXVI (July 1961), 968–986.

Robert Ferrell, "Woodrow Wilson and Open Diplomacy," in G. L. Anderson, ed., *Issues and Conflicts: Studies in Twentieth Century American Diplomacy* (Lawrence, Kans., 1959), pp. 193–209.

Charles Seymour, "The Paris Education of Woodrow Wilson," *Virginia Quarterly Review,* XXXII (Autumn 1956), 578–593.

B. THE LEAGUE FIGHT

BOOKS

Thomas A. Bailey, *Woodrow Wilson and the Great Betrayal* (New York, 1945).

Denna Frank Fleming, *The United States and the League of Nations* (New York, 1932).

W. Stull Holt, *Treaties Defeated by the Senate* (Baltimore, 1932).

Ralph A. Stone, *The Irreconcilables: The Fight Against the League of Nations* (Lexington, Ky., 1970).

ARTICLES

John H. Flanagan, Jr., "The Disillusionment of a Progressive: U.S. Senator David I. Walsh and the League of Nations Issue, 1918–1920," *New England Quarterly,* XLI (December 1968), 483–504.

Dewey W. Grantham, Jr., "The Southern Senators and the League of Nations, 1918–1920," *North Carolina Historical Review,* XXVI (April 1949), 187–205.

Wolfgang J. Helbich, "American Liberals in the League of Nations Controversy," *Public Opinion Quarterly,* XXXI (Winter 1967–1968), 568–596.

James L. Lancaster, "The Protestant Churches and the Fight for Ratification of the Versailles Treaty," *Public Opinion Quarterly,* XXXI (Winter 1967–1968), 597–619.

Kenneth R. Maxwell, "Irish-Americans and the Fight for Treaty Ratification," *Public Opinion Quarterly,* XXXI (Winter 1967–1968), 620–641.

Dexter Perkins, "Woodrow Wilson's Tour," in Daniel Aaron, ed., *America in Crisis* (New York, 1952), pp. 425–465.

Daniel M. Smith, "Robert Lansing and the Wilson Interregnum, 1919–1920," *Historian,* XXI (February 1959), 135–161.

Ralph A. Stone, "The Irreconcilables' Alternatives to the League of Nations," *Mid-America,* XLIX (July 1967), 155–176.

Kurt Wimer, "Woodrow Wilson and a Third Nomination," *Pennsylvania History,* XXIX (April 1962), 193–211.

————, "Woodrow Wilson's Plan for a Vote of Confidence," *Pennsylvania History,* XXXVIII (July 1961), 279–293.

————, "Woodrow Wilson Tries Conciliation: An Effort That Failed," *Historian,* XXV (August 1963), 419–438.

II
Causes

DIMENSIONS OF INTERVENTION

DANIEL M. SMITH

National Interest and American Intervention, 1917: An Historiographical Appraisal

The problem of intervention has long overshadowed all other concerns in historical writing about the United States and World War I. In the last thirty years questions about the role of security considerations in Wilson's decision to go to war have attracted the greatest interest, especially from writers who continue to want to draw lessons from the events of 1914–1917. Scholarly debate has raged back and forth over differing assessments of the President's perceptions of American national interests, but nearly all of it has taken place within a framework of agreement that self-interested concerns *should have been* paramount and that intervention on the side of the Allies at some point was necessary and wise.

In this essay a leading participant in the debate recounts and analyzes the principal contributions and suggests lines of development away from previously used definitions of security and national interest. For a comparable account of pre–World War II debates between defenders of Wilson and critical revisionists, see Richard W. Leopold, "The Problem of American Intervention, 1917: An Historical Retrospect," *World Politics,* II (April 1950), 405–425. Two recent works in the context of argument over self-interest are Smith, *The Great Departure: The United States and World War I, 1914–1920* (New York, 1965), and Ross Gregory, *The Origins of American Intervention in the First World War* (New York, 1971).

Reprinted by permission from the *Journal of American History,* LII (June 1965), 5–24.

In the two decades since 1945 several significant studies have been published on American involvement in World War I. These works have advanced beyond the revisionist debates of the 1930s to a more balanced consideration of economic, psychological, and political factors. Also they study the causes of hostilities within the context of developments in the principal European belligerent countries. An important aspect has been the investigation of considerations of the national interests in the decision of the United States to enter the great conflict in 1917.[1] The purpose of this essay is to examine these recent studies, with an especial concentration on the theme of the national interest and its influence on American foreign policy makers.

In 1950 Richard W. Leopold published a stimulating article on the historiography of the American involvement in World War I.[2] He pointed out that scholars had not achieved a consensus on the problem and that a general study had not been published since 1938. Until then the historical debate that began almost with President Woodrow Wilson's war message could be categorized into two schools. One was the "submarine" school, best represented by Charles Seymour, which contended that the nation had entered the war primarily because

1. Only a few of the reviews in the major historical journals of the works examined in this paper commented to an appreciable extent on the emergence of the national interest theme, Ernest R. May, *Mississippi Valley Historical Review*, XLIII (June 1956), 147–48, pointed out that Edward H. Buehrig's study was important as a contribution to a more realistic appraisal of Wilsonian diplomacy; Julius W. Pratt, *American Historical Review*, LXIV (July 1959), 1023–24, called the Smith study of Lansing a "partial answer" to the role of balance-of-power concepts in the 1917 intervention; and Richard L. Watson, Jr., *ibid.*, 973–75, gave the best review from that point of view to the May volume.

2. Richard W. Leopold, "The Problem of American Intervention, 1917: An Historical Retrospect," *World Politics*, II (1950), 405–25. Richard L. Watson, Jr., in "Woodrow Wilson and His Interpreters, 1947–1957," *Mississippi Valley Historical Review*, XLIV (Sept. 1957), 207–36, examines recent literature, and especially the Wilson centennial outpouring, on the domestic and foreign policies of the Wilson administration. Ernest R. May, in two short articles, makes perceptive comments on the major currents of interpretation on American involvement in 1898, 1917, and 1941. He describes himself, Arthur S. Link, and others as moving away from earlier "What went wrong" approaches to a Rankean "What happened" emphasis. See May, "Emergence to World Power," John Higham, ed., *The Reconstruction of American History* (New York, 1962), 180–96; and *American Intervention: 1917 and 1941* (Service Center for Teachers of History, Pamphlet 30, 1960).

of violations of neutral rights and international law and morality by the ruthless German submarine campaigns. Another school comprised the unneutrality group, with Charles C. Tansill as the latest spokesman, that emphasized the patent American unneutrality in favor of the Allied Powers.[3]

During World War II, Leopold noted, a new interpretation emerged that the basic motive for intervention in 1917 had been to protect the nation's security against the menace of possible German victory and a disturbance to the balance of power, and to preserve Anglo-American domination of the North Atlantic. In 1943 Walter Lippmann maintained that the submarine issue had been merely the formal occasion for war, while "the substantial and compelling reason . . . was that the cutting of the Atlantic communications meant the starvation of Britain and, therefore, the conquest of Western Europe by imperial Germany."[4] While acknowledging that Wilson officially had justified hostilities on the basis of submarine violations of American neutral rights, Lippmann contended that this would not have sufficed as a rationalization if most Americans had not realized, intuitively or consciously, that a German victory would imperil American security. In another wartime book the newspaperman Forest Davis advanced a similar explanation.[5] As Leopold observed, however, scholars remained skeptical of these interpretations that seemed to project

3. Charles Callan Tansill, *America Goes to War* (Boston, 1938); Charles Seymour, *American Diplomacy During the World War* (Baltimore, 1934) and *American Neutrality, 1914–1917* (New Haven, 1935). Tansill ignored the issue of American security and global aspects of the war. He disclaimed having a particular thesis to offer. Seymour dismissed political and economic factors as peripheral and attributed the war entry primarily to outraged sentiment at submarine warfare and a determination to protect American lives and property on the high seas. Harley Notter, *The Origins of the Foreign Policy of Woodrow Wilson* (Baltimore, 1937), 642–43, 647, 650, concluded that by 1917 Wilson viewed Germany as a danger to the peace and security of America and the world, but that the United States entered the war only because of intolerable violations of its neutral rights. A slim volume by Samuel R. Spencer, Jr., *The Decision for War, 1917* (Rindge, N.H., 1953), adhered to the submarine thesis while stressing the *Laconia* sinking and release of the Zimmermann telegram in Feb. 1917 as events in the transition to full hostilities. Also see Barbara W. Tuchman, *The Zimmermann Telegram* (New York, 1958).

4. Walter Lippmann, *U.S. Foreign Policy: Shield of the Republic* (Boston, 1943), 33–37.

5. Forest Davis, *The Atlantic System: The Story of Anglo-American Control of the Seas* (New York, 1941), 240–46.

the fears of 1941 into the 1917 era, and at most viewed them as insights requiring extensive research and study. Diplomatic historian Thomas A. Bailey, for example, commented that there had been no rushing into war to redress the power balance and save the Allies in 1917, as seemingly they were winning; only after it was in the war did America realize the dire Allied plight.[6]

The diplomat and historian, George F. Kennan, published in 1950 a volume of essays on recent American diplomacy in which he recognized that there had been high American officials in World War I cognizant of the need to preserve a favorable balance of power against the disturbing possibility of a German triumph. Kennan concluded, however, that such a realistic approach had not been shared by the great majority of citizens; instead, the nation plunged into war on the narrow grounds of defending neutral rights and then turned the struggle into a moralistic-legalistic crusade to remold the world order.[7] The more detailed study, *Ideals and Self-Interest in American Foreign Relations,* published in 1953 by Robert Endicott Osgood, in general substantiated that interpretation.[8]

Osgood acknowledged the plausibility of the Lippmann thesis and in his study, based on printed materials, he recorded similar views held by a number of Americans in 1914–1917.[9] As a *New Republic* editor Lippmann had written several articles[10] contending that American security was involved in the continuation of the existing balance of power, as had the American diplomat Lewis Einstein in 1913 and

6. See Thomas A. Bailey, *Woodrow Wilson and the Lost Peace* (New York, 1944), 12–13, and *A Diplomatic History of the American People* (6th ed., New York, 1958), 594n. Richard W. Van Alstyne, *American Diplomacy in Action* (rev. ed., Stanford, 1947), 255–56, 289, conceded, on the other hand, that while the majority of citizens had not been aware of balance of power arguments, some persons including high officials had been influenced by such considerations.

7. George F. Kennan, *American Diplomacy, 1900–1950* (Chicago, 1951), 64–66, 70–74. Also see Edward Mead Earle, "A Half-Century of American Foreign Policy: Our Stake in Europe, 1898–1914," *Political Science Quarterly,* LXIV (June 1949), 168–88.

8. Robert Endicott Osgood, *Ideals and Self-Interest in American Foreign Relations* (Chicago, 1953). Approximately one third of this study is devoted to the Wilson period.

9. *Ibid.,* 115–34.

10. Walter Lippmann, *Annals of the American Academy of Political and Social Science,* LXVI (1916), 60–70; *Stakes of Diplomacy* (New York, 1915), preface; and *New Republic,* X (Feb. 17, 1917), 59–61.

1914.[11] Other prominent Americans publicly advanced arguments that vital national interests would be threatened by a German victory. Theodore Roosevelt mixed with such views a type of belligerent moralism that advocated hostilities in 1916 in order to uphold national honor and save civilization from the new barbarians.[12]

Several of Wilson's advisers, Osgood wrote, analyzed the meaning of the war to America from a balance-of-power view. The list included Colonel Edward M. House; Robert Lansing, Counselor and then Secretary of State in mid-1915; the ambassador to Britain, Walter Hines Page; and James W. Gerard, ambassador to Germany. These men envisioned a German conquest in Europe as a threat to American security in the western hemisphere and analyzed the war in terms of the national interest in Anglo-American naval predominance in the Atlantic. Yet such considerations, though increasing their willingness to support neutrality policies favorable to the Allies, did little more than quicken events which led the United States into the war. That was because the advisers did not really expect Germany to win and therefore their recommendations to the President did not advocate intervention on the grounds of an endangered security. Events did not seem to pose the clear alternative of fighting Germany or confronting a nearly certain later attack by that power, so it was easier to follow the line of submarine violations of honor and morality and to enter the war on that popular basis.[13] In any case, Osgood concluded, it would be difficult to prove that these advisers had any appreciable influence on the idealistic Wilson, for the President was in nearly complete control of foreign affairs and was unusually independent of counselors.[14]

Osgood thus seemed reluctant to accept the implications of his own findings, that presidential assistants had taken a realistic approach toward the European war. Furthermore, Osgood tended to concentrate on the question of immediate security. These advisers saw the national interest in a broader sense as embracing not only security but economic interests and a favorable postwar position. Osgood's own reasoning

11. Lewis Einstein, "The United States and Anglo-German Rivalry," and "The War and American Policy," *National Review,* LX (Jan. 1913), 736–50 and LXIV (Nov. 1914), 357–76.

12. Osgood, *Ideals and Self-Interest, 135–53.* Also see Howard K. Beale, *Theodore Roosevelt and the Rise of America to World Power* (Baltimore, 1956).

13. Osgood, *Ideals and Self-Interest,* 154–71.

14. *Ibid.,* 172–75.

strongly suggests that House, Lansing, and others might not have recommended to Wilson considerations of honor, morality, and ideology as justifications for belligerency if they had not viewed Germany as a menace to broadly defined national interests. Later studies also have revealed that Wilson was capable of a more realistic approach to the war and that he was far more receptive to advice and dependent on counselors than previously assumed.

Osgood and Kennan undoubtedly have been correct that there was little evidence of popular apprehensions of a direct German threat in 1914–1917. Much evidence exists, however, that an influential minority viewed imperial Germany askance. Since 1898 American military and naval leaders increasingly envisioned Germany as offering a threat to American security in the western hemisphere. The Navy General Board in 1901 recommended purchase of the Danish West Indies because "In view of the isthmian canal and the German settlements in South America, every additional acquisition by the United States in the West Indies is of value."[15] In testimony before the House Naval Affairs Committee in 1914, Admiral Charles Vreeland justified naval expansion as needed to cope with Germany and Japan.[16] A Navy General Board estimate of 1910, recirculated in February 1915, concluded that only Germany, driven by population pressures and rivalries in Latin America and the Far East, could undertake singlehandedly war on the United States and was therefore the most probable potential enemy.[17] The War Department also had defensive war plans drawn

15. General Board No. 187, 31–01, Vol. I, 374, Report of Nov. 12, 1901, Naval War Records Office (Arlington, Virginia). Unclassified. Rumors of German endeavors to acquire the Galapagos Islands caused the Navy and War departments on several occasions to object to the State Department on the grounds of proximity to the Panama Canal; similar objections were made against possible German acquisition of Haiti's Mole St. Nicholas, in 1910 and 1912. See correspondence of April 25, 28, 1911, State Department File Number 822.014G/177, 178; Aug. 25, 1910, June 27, 1912, *ibid.*, 838.802/5, 12 (National Archives).

16. Harold and Margaret Sprout, *The Rise of American Naval Power, 1776–1918* (Princeton, 1942), 311–13. The Navy League centered its none too successful propaganda before 1914 for a more powerful navy on the German menace to the Monroe Doctrine. See Armin Rapaport, *The Navy League of the United States* (Detroit, 1962), 31–66.

17. War Portfolio No. 1, Atlantic Station—approved by the General Board, Oct. 19, 1910 and reissued in Feb. 1915, Naval War Records Office.

with Germany as the theoretical opponent.[18] A lengthy War College paper, 1909–1910, by Captain Paul B. Malone, described Germany as the most serious economic competitor of the United States, in contact and conflict with America both in Latin America and China. Although the author did not flatly predict hostilities he commented that, in the past, war had been the virtually inevitable result of such conflicting interests.[19]

The historian Alfred Vagts has attempted to explain the fact that navalists in Germany and the United States, from the late 1890s to 1914, viewed each other as a probable opponent on the grounds that each needed an excuse to justify large naval expansion programs.[20] He concluded that actual commercial competition between the two states was small and that each power lacked coaling stations and naval cruising range for an attack on the other. Talk of rivalry in both countries primarily reflected the propaganda efforts of big navy advocates. No doubt a degree of validity must be accorded Vagts' interpretation, but the evidence indicates that the apprehensions were genuine and were shared by many leading civilians. On the other hand, apparently there were no official interchanges in the 1910–1917 period between the two defense departments and State in regard to American national interests in the outcome of a general Europe war. Officials in all three departments apparently shared similar appraisals of the situation, and perhaps informally discussed it, but no effort was made to plan and coordinate policy to cope with the danger.[21]

18. No. 9433, War Materials Division (National Archives). Still classified as confidential in 1960.

19. "The Military Geography of the Atlantic Seaboard, Considered with Reference to an Invading Force," War College Division, General Staff, 6916-1, War Materials Division.

20. Alfred Vagts, "Hopes and Fears of an American-German War, 1870–1915," *Political Science Quarterly,* LIV (Dec. 1939), 514–35, and LV (March 1940), 53–76. Fritz T. Epstein, "Germany and the United States: Basic Patterns of Conflict and Understanding," G. L. Anderson, ed., *Issues and Conflict* (Lawrence, Kansas, 1959), 284–314, concludes that German-American friction prior to 1914 reflected psychological differences rather than actual clashes of interest.

21. Based on the author's perusal of State-Navy files in the National Archives, and on a recent article by Fred Greene, "The Military View of American National Policy, 1904–1940," *American Historical Review,* LXVI (1961), 354–77. Greene points out that the army and navy staffs often complained of lack of policy guidance from the State Department

The decade before World War I witnessed a slowly maturing conviction among informed Americans that Germany was a potential enemy and Great Britain a natural ally of the United States. Editorials in the New York *Times* envisioned Germany as hostile, thus requiring an American navy of at least comparable size, and repeatedly expressed confidence in an enduring Anglo-American community of interests.[22] From 1898 the American periodical press also occasionally printed articles expressing distrust of Germany's expansionist tendencies. *Munsey's Magazine* in 1901 featured a comparison of the German and American navies and called for greater naval preparations to cooperate with Great Britain in meeting the German challenge in the western hemisphere.[23] Articles from English journals on the theme of German naval threats to the United States were reprinted in American publications.[24] Comparisons of the American and German navies were drawn and parity was strongly recommended.[25] A 1909 article in *The Independent* by Amos S. Hershey, professor of Political Science and International Law at Indiana University, depicted Germany as menacing both world peace and American interests in the Far East and Latin America. To meet that danger Hershey advocated a defensive Anglo-American alliance. He wrote prophetically: "the people of the United States could hardly remain neutral in a war between Germany and Great Britain which might possibly end in German naval supremacy. . . . A blockade of the British Isles by German

---

before 1940 and were compelled to try to define basic national interests themselves as guidelines for defense plans. J. A. S. Grenville, in "Diplomacy and War Plans in the United States, 1890–1917," *Transactions of the Royal Society,* 5th Series, XI (London, 1961), 1–21, notes that American strategic war plans, revised in 1915 and 1916, were defensive in character and were designed not to cope with the current war but to meet the threat of the victor after the war in Europe was over. Also see Ernest R. May, "The Development of Political-Military Consultation in the United States," *Political Science Quarterly,* LXX (June 1955), 161–80.

22. New York *Times,* July 17, Aug. 20, 26, 1898; Feb. 18, 1899.

23. Walter S. Meriwether, "Our Navy and Germany's," *Munsey's Magazine,* XXIV (March 1901), 856–73.

24. See *American Monthly Review of Reviews, XIX* (Jan. 1899), 86–88; *Living Age,* CCXXIX (June 1, 1901), 583–86; *ibid.,* CCLXXVIII (July 12, 1913), 67–81.

25. *Harper's Weekly,* XLVII (March 14, 1903), 428–29; New York *Times,* Feb. 20, 1905; W. G. Fitz-Gerald, "Does Germany Menace the World's Peace?" *North American Review,* CLXXXIV (April 19, 1907), 853–60.

cruisers and submarine mines, or the loss involved in the danger to contraband trade would be severely felt in this country."[26]

Understandably, the general conflagration which began in 1914 increased the conviction of a number of Americans that Germany was in fact a menace and that American interests could best be secured through an Allied triumph.[27] In the 1916 annual volume of the American Academy of Political and Social Science well-known scholars and pundits presented several papers that emphasized that United States security was involved in the preservation of British sea power.[28] To help focus the widespread interest in 1916 in the preparedness question, the editors of *The Independent* printed an outline of pro and con arguments, prepared by Preston William Slosson, entitled: "Resolved: That the United States should enter the Great War on the side of the Entente Allies." The affirmative side asserted among other arguments that a Teutonic victory would endanger the future security of the American people.[29]

These references to public opinion do not indicate that a majority of citizens in 1917 supported intervention on the grounds of vital national concerns. However, the evidence does reveal that for over a decade a number of educated and informed persons were exposed repeatedly to warnings that Germany challenged the security and the economic welfare of the nation. The existence of these attitudes probably made it inestimably easier to condemn Germany on moral and ideological grounds after 1914 and facilitated eventual war entry on the basis of a defense of neutral rights.

Edward H. Buehrig, as Osgood a political scientist, made an important contribution to the "national interest" school in a subtle study entitled *Woodrow Wilson and the Balance of Power*.[30] Based largely

26. Amos S. Hershey, "Germany—The Main Obstacle to the World's Peace," *Independent*, LXVI (May 20, 1909), 1071–76. For a similar analysis by a well-known English journalist, writing for *Fortnightly ·Review*, see Sydney Brooks, "Great Britain, Germany and the United States," reprinted in *Living Age*, CCLXII (July 31, 1909), 259–66.

27. For example, see New York *Times* editorials of Oct. 14, 19, 1914, Nov. 29, 1916, and letters Oct. 16, 18, Nov. 10, 1914.

28. See articles by S. N. Patten, George Louis Beer, and Walter Lippmann, in *Annals of the American Academy of Political and Social Science*, LXVI (1916), 1–11, 60–70, 71–91. Dissenting views were also voiced.

29. *Independent*, LXXXVI (May 8, 1916), 228.

30. *Woodrow Wilson and the Balance of Power* (Bloomington, 1955).

on printed sources and a few manuscript collections, the volume explained the American intervention in the war in 1917 as resulting from the German challenge to Britain's position as the dominant sea power. If Americans had been accustomed to viewing foreign relations in terms of practical power issues the ultimate war entry possibly might have been based squarely on considerations of security and economic connections. As it was, Germany and the United States were soon entrapped in complicated questions of neutral rights and drifted into war because of different attitudes toward British control of the seas. The United States accepted the British role as beneficial to its interests; Germany felt compelled to challenge it with every available weapon. Consequently, even though a bilateral German-American war was highly improbable, an Anglo-German struggle which threatened to alter drastically Britain's position posed serious questions to America's trans-Atlantic connections and created tensions culminating in war.[31]

The submarine issue was a point of departure for an evolving American policy toward the war. Without it, of course, German-American relations would have been smoother. American neutrality was in practice favorable to the Allies, but Germany decided to use fully the submarine weapon in 1917 because it alone seemed to promise victory. Probably no other course by the United States, short of cooperation with Germany to challenge the British blockade in order to renew substantial American trade with the Central Powers, could have averted unrestricted U-boat warfare. Germany naturally resented the American munitions trade with the Allies but, except as a moral justification, it played no important role in German decisions. What really was sought was to reverse British control of the seas and markets. To have satisfied the Berlin government by effecting a major change in neutral trade would have harmed important American economic interests and would have meant a disturbing replacement of British power with German.[32]

Wilson in 1915 adopted the policy of holding Germany fully accountable for losses of American lives and ships by submarine attacks around the British Isles in order to defend the traditional American concept of neutral rights and "freedom of the seas." He chose to uphold international law, and thereby to defend a conception of the national interest, for Americans had long believed that the nation's

31. *Ibid.*, viii–ix, 16–17.
32. *Ibid.*, 79–84, 90, 102–05.

security was closely connected with the preservation of the world legal structure. In speeches advocating defensive military preparations in 1916, Wilson clearly developed that theme: the United States had to defend legal principles and support the international community. Germany's lawless methods of warfare affected American security, the President implied, dependent as it was on maintenance of national honor and rights and the preservation of the structure of international law and morality.[33]

When the *Sussex* controversy in 1916 made imminent the prospect of entering the war over the submarine issue, Wilson turned to diplomatic intervention in hopes of avoiding hostilities. The House-Grey Memorandum, negotiated earlier by Colonel House with British Foreign Secretary Sir Edward Grey, provided that at a time propitious for the Allies Wilson was to propose a conference to terminate the war; if Germany declined or rejected a "reasonable" peace, the United States "probably" would enter the struggle on the Allied side. The refusal of Britain and France to invoke the plan, which Wilson had hoped would end the war before America should be forced in, compelled the President to seek other means for mediation.[34]

In May 1916 President Wilson addressed the League to Enforce Peace and advocated a universal association of nations that would accord with America's national interest by preserving world free trade and access to markets ("freedom of the seas") and would protect all nations through territorial guarantees. This global organization, said Wilson, could prevent future wars by substitution of conferences for force, and the United States could facilitate the transition by making it known that its power would be thrown onto the international scales in behalf of peaceful means of adjustment. Buehrig analyzed the address as revealing not only Wilsonian idealism but also his interest in maintaining a stable world balance of power. Clear indications that the British government would not aid in promoting a negotiated peace caused Wilson in late 1916 to turn to other avenues for peace.[35] Wilson moved beyond considerations of a balance of power to a community of power when in December 1916 he requested statements of belligerent war aims and early in 1917 appealed for "peace without victory." The President thereby completed a shift from the initial policy of defense of maritime neutral rights to media-

33. *Ibid.,* 106–08, 117–21, 149.
34. *Ibid.,* 172–73, 228, 230–35.
35. *Ibid.,* 238–46.

tion efforts and a just peace on which to build a new community of nations. When Germany subsequently launched unrestricted submarine warfare and abolished not only all neutral rights but also made clear the determination to dictate a conqueror's peace, Wilson took the nation into war. He had no real choice, Buehrig concluded, either from the standpoint of maritime legal rights or of future world peace and stability.[36]

In Buehrig's view, Wilson in shaping American policy lacked neither astuteness nor an appreciation of balance-of-power concepts. The idealistic element in his policy finally received the major emphasis, over realistic considerations, because the President's temperament so required. The need to adjust policies to the requirements of an American public not trained to appraise world affairs in practical terms was also a probable factor.[37]

The Buehrig study has made at least two important contributions. In contrast to Osgood he defined the American concept of the national interests as comprising not only immediate but long-term security, economic interest in freedom of the seas, and the desire for world order and safety through preservation of an international regime of law. Buehrig also has carefully analyzed the elements of Wilsonian policies and thereby detected, along with idealistic elements, indications of a realistic consciousness of the balance of power and concrete American interests involved in the war.[38]

36. *Ibid.,* 260–66.
37. *Ibid.,* 274–75.
38. Buehrig noted that Robert Lansing held balance-of-power concepts about the war, but he asked to what degree this was submerged by an ideological view of the struggle. *Ibid.,* 135–37. That question was answered, at least partially, by Daniel M. Smith's *Robert Lansing and American Neutrality, 1914–1917* (Berkeley, 1958), and "Robert Lansing and the Formulation of American Neutrality Policies, 1914–1915," *Mississippi Valley Historical Review,* XLIII (June 1956), 59–81. Lansing, on the basis of his private diaries, was depicted by Smith as combining ideological considerations with a concern for the nation's economic and security interests in the war, and to have concluded in July 1915 that on both grounds a German victory should be prevented, by an American intervention if necessary. Smith shows that Lansing helped shape the basic neutrality policies in the early months of the war and thereafter was a strong advocate of a firm approach toward the submarine issue. Lansing rarely spoke directly to Wilson of security interests, apparently because of an appreciation of the President's psychology, but he did to Colonel House. He also recommended measures to Wilson based on concrete economic considerations, and he couched other suggestions in idealistic terminology.

In an early volume in the New American Nation series, *Woodrow Wilson and the Progressive Era,* Arthur S. Link subscribed to the "submarine" school in interpreting the entry of the United States into World War I.[39] He recognized that House and Lansing had viewed realistically the European struggle, but he maintained that the two advisers "had only an incidental influence" on the President. In the ultimate analysis it was Wilson who, influenced by public opinion, had determined the American course. To mid-1916 Wilson had followed a neutrality course benevolent toward the Allies because of his moralistic appraisal of the war, German violations of international law, and the apparent greater readiness of Great Britain to make a reasonable peace. When he became convinced that the Allies in fact did not desire a fair settlement but sought, as Germany, a conclusive victory, he moved toward a genuinely impartial position. If Germany had not violated the *Sussex* pledge by unrestricted submarine warfare early in 1917, there would have been no war between the two countries. Considerations of finance, economic ties, ideology, or security were not involved in the presidential decision. War finally came because the submarine assaults on American lives and shipping left Wilson no feasible alternative.[40]

As he continued his multi-volume study of Wilson, Link seemed to modify his views of the causes of American intervention. In 1957 his Albert Shaw Lectures on Diplomatic History were published as *Wilson the Diplomatist.*[41] The interpretation generally followed that of the earlier volume: a genuinely neutral America adjusted to British measures, but the U-boat campaigns were opposed for legal and moral reasons.[42] By early 1917, however, after failure of efforts to halt the war short of total victory for either side and thereby to preclude American involvement and establish the basis for a stable postwar world, Wilson apparently decided to effect a diplomatic withdrawal. Continuation of the war, he foresaw, would cause further deterioration of neutral rights. The President seemingly was willing to retreat on strict accountability and perhaps would have accepted a new U-boat campaign against armed merchantmen or all belligerent vessels except

39. Arthur S. Link, *Woodrow Wilson and the Progressive Era, 1910–1917* (New York, 1954).

40. *Ibid.,* 279–81.

41. *Wilson the Diplomatist: A Look at His Major Foreign Policies* (Baltimore, 1957).

42. *Ibid.,* 32–35, 40–54.

passenger liners. The German decision to attack all shipping, neutrals included, forced Wilson to break diplomatic relations.[43]

Link thus considered the submarine issue to have been the immediate cause of hostilities, but he concluded that the agonized Wilson reluctantly accepted full hostilities in 1917, as opposed to armed neutrality or a limited naval war, only because of other factors. One of the most important of these, though supported by little direct evidence, was Wilson's "apparent fear that the threat of a German victory imperiled the balance of power and all his hopes for the future reconstruction of the world community."[44] Wilson seems not to have apprehended a serious German danger to the United States nor did he seek to preserve the old balance of power. Yet the Allies appeared to be on the verge of losing the war and that would mean German conquest and the end of Wilsonian hopes for a new world order. He remarked to Colonel House that Germany seemed to be a madman who required restraining—and he apparently thought that only through American armed intervention could a Central Powers victory be avoided and American prestige among the Allies enhanced so that a just peace could be achieved. The President undoubtedly also was affected in the war decision by an aroused American public and by the reiterated counsel of his close advisers.[45]

In the preface of the third volume in the Link biography, *Wilson: The Struggle for Neutrality*,[46] the author expressed the hope that in this study of the first fifteen months of neutrality he had purged his mind of preconceived interpretations and could let the men and events speak for themselves. He would appear to have succeeded admirably in this exhaustively researched volume. Realistic appraisals of the war by House and Lansing had an important effect on Wilson's mind. House, as Lansing, was favorably inclined toward the Allies and feared the militaristic and expansionist tendencies of Germany. As a result, the Colonel advised Wilson to acquiesce in Allied war measures and to oppose those of Germany. Yet House did not want a sweeping Allied victory, only one sufficient to check Teutonic ambi-

43. *Ibid.*, 70, 80–82.
44. *Ibid.*, 88.
45. *Ibid.*, 89–90.
46. Arthur S. Link, *Wilson: The Struggle for Neutrality, 1914–1915* (Princeton, 1960). An excellent first chapter discusses American public opinion and the role of belligerent propaganda. Link finds invalid the assumptions of many writers that most Americans were irrationally pro-Ally and that German propaganda was generally inept and ineffective.

tions and still leave Germany powerful enough to block Russian imperialism.[47] President Wilson, after initial sympathy for the Allies, achieved a large degree of impartiality on the question of war guilt. As the war continued, Wilson was increasingly persuaded that the greatest opportunity for a just and lasting peace would come from an indecisive conclusion of the war. As he told a newspaperman, however, while "I cannot regard this [a sweeping Allied triumph] as the ideal solution, at the same time I cannot see now that it would hurt greatly the interests of the United States if either France or Russia or Great Britain should finally dictate the [peace] settlement."[48] Wilson thus indicated, by the close of 1914, a realistic view that the preferable result of the war would be a deadlock which would preserve the existing power structure and facilitate a just peace, but that American interests would not be adversely affected by a decisive Allied triumph. As far as American policy was concerned, however, both moral and practical considerations required maintenance of neutrality.

The fourth volume in Link's series, *Wilson: Confusions and Crises,* necessarily lacks the unifying themes present in the earlier volumes. Among other topics, domestic and foreign, it narrates America's relations with the belligerents through the *Sussex* crisis. The section on the House-Grey Memorandum, based on heretofore unexploited sources including French materials which the author could not directly quote or cite, is particularly valuable. Link depicts the divergence of motives behind the scheme: House, believing that intervention in the war was almost inevitable, was prepared to go far in assuring the Allies of American backing, whereas the President apparently contemplated only peaceful mediation. He believes Grey did not take his "understanding" with the Colonel very seriously, as he doubted the possibility of American intervention, and was aware that the Allied governments were adverse to a negotiated peace and sought a decisive triumph over the Central Powers.[49]

These interpretations reveal that Link is constantly reevaluating the materials as he continues his biography of Wilson. Wilson is now seen as not only a moralist and idealist, but also as aware of balance-of-power arguments, responsive to the advice of realistically-

47. *Ibid.,* 45–48.
48. *Ibid.,* 49–56.
49. Arthur S. Link, *Wilson: Confusions and Crises, 1915–1916* (Princeton, 1964), 111–13, 130, 138–40.

inclined counselors, and to a considerable degree framing the American course on the basis of practical considerations of the national interest. Completion of the biography and the concluding judgment of Link can only be awaited with great interest.

The centennial of Wilson's birth in 1956 occasioned a number of commemorative essays and books. Osgood and Buehrig restated their evaluations of Wilsonian neutrality;[50] Charles Seymour reiterated the submarine thesis,[51] and William L. Langer concurred.[52] Two short and unfootnoted but well-researched biographies were published by John A. Garraty and John M. Blum. Garraty described American neutrality as decidedly pro-Ally, because of Wilson's biases, but the President's views and emotions precluded him from either accepting a German victory or intervening in the war. Wilson eventually lost much of his faith in the Allies and attempted to mediate in late 1916, but was forced into the conflict by the submarine issue.[53] Blum believed that Wilson lacked a realistic appraisal of the war's meaning for American interests and that the country entered the conflict only because of unrestricted U-boat warfare.[54] A generally persuasive and solidly-based psychological study, *Wilson and Colonel House,* was published by Alexander L. and Juliette L. George, that pointed out that while Wilson undoubtedly was familiar with the balance-of-power concept, his psychological aversion to frank considerations of power and self-interest made it difficult for him to frame policies clearly

50. Edward H. Buehrig, "Idealism and Statecraft," *Confluence,* V (Oct. 1956), 252–63; Robert E. Osgood, "Woodrow Wilson, Collective Security, and the Lessons of History," *ibid.,* (Jan. 1957), 341–54.

51. Charles Seymour, "Woodrow Wilson in Perspective," *Foreign Affairs,* XXXIV (Jan. 1956), 175–86. In an article, "The House-Bernstorff Conversations in Perspective," A. O. Sarkissian, ed., *Studies in Diplomatic History and Historiography in Honour of G. P. Gooch* (London, 1961), 90–106, Seymour acknowledged that House had some fears of a German threat to American security and that his pro-British sentiments affected his interest in mediation schemes. Seymour credited the protracted and confidential House-Bernstorff negotiations in 1915–1916 with helping to postpone war until the final crisis in 1917.

52. William L. Langer, "From Isolation to Mediation," Arthur P. Dudden, ed., *Woodrow Wilson and the World of Today* (Philadelphia, 1957), 22–46.

53. John A. Garraty, *Woodrow Wilson: A Great Life in Brief* (New York, 1956), 96–97, 99, 112, 116–17.

54. John Morton Blum, *Woodrow Wilson and the Politics of Morality* (Boston, 1956), 96, 100, 129.

based on such grounds.[55] Two years after the centennial, Arthur Walworth published a two-volume biography of Wilson that, while well-researched, hewed to the Seymour interpretation and made little new contribution to understanding the causes of involvement.[56]

The first extensive exploration of the formulation of German policy toward the United States appeared in Karl E. Birnbaum's *Peace Moves and U-Boat Warfare*[57] His book, concentrating on the *Sussex* crisis and after, does not focus on American policy making but it does have important implications for American diplomatic historians. He found that not only did German policy oscillate between peace moves and intensification of submarine warfare, but that a third course was also pursued of trying to manage issues with the United States so that even full underseas warfare would not lead to hostilities.

In the *Lusitania* and *Arabic* crises full compliance with Wilson's demands was precluded by official skepticism of the President's impartiality and by German public opinion, which was embittered at the American war trade and hopeful of the power of submarine warfare.[58] As 1915 ended, Chancellor Theobald von Bethmann-Hollweg came under great military and public pressures for full underseas warfare. Bethmann, deeply fearful of the dire consequences of hostilities with America, was hampered in resistance by the weakness of Kaiser Wilhelm II and by his own lack of energy and will.[59] The *Sussex* pledge, therefore, was only a temporary triumph over the U-boat enthusiasts.[60]

The Chancellor initiated a peace move in late 1916 in the hope of either forcing a general peace conference or of creating an atmosphere of reasonableness that would prevent hostilities with the United States when more drastic submarine warfare began. The overture failed and when Wilson asked on December 18 for a statement of belligerent

55. Alexander L. and Juliette L. George, *Woodrow Wilson and Colonel House: A Personality Study* (New York, 1956), 159–60.

56. Arthur Walworth, *Woodrow Wilson* (2 vols., New York, 1958). For an interesting survey of modern American foreign policy by a French scholar, see Jean-Baptiste Duroselle (trans. by Nancy Lyman Roelker), *From Wilson to Roosevelt: Foreign Policy of the United States, 1913–1945* (Cambridge, 1963). Duroselle attributes involvement to Wilson's desire to establish a just peace and a stable and progressive postwar world society.

57. Karl E. Birnbaum, *Peace Moves and U-Boat Warfare* (Stockholm, 1958).

58. *Ibid.*, 28–32, 36–37, 39.

59. *Ibid.*, 51–53, 58–61.

60. *Ibid.*, 78–79, 86.

war goals, the Berlin government gave it an evasive, negative reply because both the military and civilian officials distrusted the President's motives and suspected collusion with the Allies. Unfortunately, in Birnbaum's view, the quick reply to Wilson's overture doomed the policy of trying to create a rapport sufficiently strong to avoid hostilities over a new underseas campaign. This was the final failure of Germany's American policy.[61] At the decisive, conferences at Pless on January 9, 1917, the military and naval leaders unanimously insisted on unrestricted underseas warfare as the best hope for victory, whereas the Chancellor merely recited his past objections before deferring to the military view. Birnbaum believes that even at this date a more vigorous objection by Bethmann, analyzing the probable results of unrestricted warfare and the effects of an American entry, might have swayed the Kaiser and have postponed the decision at least long enough to try to cushion its impact on Wilson.

German vacillation between peace efforts and the submarine panacea finally broke down in a decision for the latter because of doubts over Wilson's neutrality and goals, and the growing primacy of the shortsighted military voice within the German government. Although the author disavowed in the preface any intention of answering the question of whether German-American hostilities were avoidable, in his conclusions he attributed considerable weight to German skepticism of Wilson engendered by the pro-Ally nature of American neutrality and the different attitudes of Washington toward Allied as opposed to German infractions of international law.[62] In that sense Birnbaum suggests a partial answer to the question if a more impartial American neutrality would not have strengthened the hands of German moderates in resisting pressures for unrestricted U-boat warfare.

The latest one-volume study of the neutrality period is Ernest R. May's *World War and American Isolation.*[63] Utilizing multi-archival research in Europe and the United States, May has examined the evolution of policies from the British and German perspectives as well as the American. He pointed out that in both Great Britain and Germany questions of policy toward neutral America were intertwined in domestic politics. In comparison with the Birnbaum study,

61. *Ibid.,* 270.
62. *Ibid.,* 31, 336–38.
63. *The World War and American Isolation, 1914–1917* (Cambridge, 1959).

May developed in greater detail the story of domestic German political pressures on foreign policy.

British Foreign Secretary Grey successfully shaped the English course in the first six months of the war by proceeding cautiously and considerately in applying maritime measures so that Anglo-American friendship would be preserved and strengthened. Even when Grey had lost the ability to control events because of mounting public pressures in England for a more drastic blockade, he had helped establish a moral basis of friendship capable of surviving a more trying period.[64]

In Germany Bethmann "fought long and hard against reckless opponents, only in the end to fail."[65] May thus gave a more favorable appraisal than did Birnbaum and Link, who portrayed the Chancellor in less flattering terms as failing to make a serious effort either to comprehend Wilson's peace objectives in 1916, to develop a reasonable German peace move, or to subject Admiralty claims for the submarine to close scrutiny and refutation.[66] May depicted the harried Chancellor as convinced that the submarine could not defeat England and that war with the United States would be disastrous for Germany. He could not force abandonment of the U-boat weapon, however, because of the fanatical attitude of the navy admirals, the submarine enthusiasm of the German public, and the pressures of the conservative political parties and press. Caught in a dilemma, complicated by reliance on the vacillating Kaiser, the Chancellor temporized and delayed, making enough concessions to the United States to avoid war in the *Lusitania, Arabic,* and *Sussex* crises and yet endeavoring to permit the navalists use of the submarine just short of that point. At best, therefore, Bethmann could only postpone a decision for war with America.[67] By the fall of 1916 the new supreme army command of Field Marshal Paul von Hindenburg and General Erich F. W. Ludendorff had come to dominate Wilhelm, and Bethmann could no longer control

64. *Ibid.,* 18–19, 21–25, 32–33. May has concluded that American economic retaliation in late 1916 would not have been fatal to Britain, which by then had developed alternative sources of munitions supplies. *Ibid.,* 321–22.

65. *Ibid.,* [vii].

66. Link, *Wilson the Diplomatist,* 79–80. In *The Struggle for Neutrality,* 399, 401–03, 553, Link portrayed Bethmann more favorably as compelled by his precarious position to temporize in regard to U-boat warfare.

67. May, *World War and American Isolation,* 197–205.

the Reichstag. Hence when the army leaders joined the admirals in insistence on unrestricted underseas warfare as the one reliable hope for victory, the Chancellor was compelled to acquiesce. Any other course would have meant his immediate political demise.[68]

In concurrence with Buehrig and other writers, May described American neutrality as generally benevolent toward the Allies. Yet permission of belligerent loans and the arms trade were not deliberately unneutral but merely reflected America's view of international law and its trade interests. Legal and moral factors also were involved in the different American policies toward the British blockade and the submarine zone, but "the central difference in the two cases was a matter of national interest and not of either law or morality." Wilson could be satisfied that he had complied with the requirements of international law and morality and had served the national interests.[69]

May agreed with previous writers that House and Lansing viewed a triumphant Germany as a future threat to American security. House repeatedly warned Wilson in late 1914 and after that Germany would never forgive America for its pro-Ally attitude and if it won the war would hold the United States accountable and might challenge the Monroe Doctrine in South America. The Colonel did not desire a smashing Allied victory, however, for that would leave Russia free to expand.[70] As for Wilson, May stated that "He does appear, however, to have shared the view of Lansing and House that Germany was an enemy. He hoped that she might be too exhausted by the European war to turn immediately upon the United States, but he was not sanguine."[71] Wilson in late 1915 admitted to House that a victorious Germany might well take the western hemisphere as its next target,

68. *Ibid.*, 288–89, 413–15.
69. *Ibid.*, 45–53. Although Link, in the earlier volumes, described American neutrality to 1916 as benevolent but legally neutral toward the Allies, in *The Struggle for Neutrality*, 687, 691–92, he emphasizes the essential impartiality of American policies. Wilson acquiesced in Allied maritime measures, as required by trade, sympathy, and neutrality, but he also sought an adjustment to German submarine warfare by narrowing an initial condemnation of the U-boat as a weapon to mere insistence on the safety of American lives aboard belligerent liners. Thus the Oct. 21, 1915 protest to Britain was "fair warning" not to expect a benevolent neutrality. Neither side could reasonably complain that Wilson was against it.
70. May, *World War and American Isolation*, 77–78.
71. *Ibid.*, 169.

and his speeches for military preparedness in 1916 revealed a deep apprehension for the future security of the Americas. The President differed from these advisers primarily in his emotional attachment to peace. Consequently, although Wilson accepted the judgments of House and Lansing for a firm policy toward Germany, caution and pacifist inclinations caused him to follow a course of patience and delay, hoping for a "miraculous deliverance" from his dilemma. Additionally, Wilson's caution reflected his consciousness of the divided state of American public opinion, military weaknesses of the United States, and the hope of playing a role of peacemaker in the European war.[72]

Ruthless use of the submarine was the only kind of German action that could have engendered German-American hostility, as Germany lacked other means to affect directly American interests. Wilson could have accepted German underseas warfare in early 1915, just as he had British actions, but he instead chose to condemn it. Other alternatives were rejected apparently because the U-boat campaign violated international law and morality, and because it endangered important American economic interests in the war trade with the Allies.[73] After the *Lusitania* crisis American national prestige was fully committed to the strict accountability policy and diplomatic flexibility was greatly circumscribed. If only moral principles and economic interests had been involved, some possibility of compromise would have remained; what prevented Wilson and his advisers from considering such, however, was apprehension that prestige would be lost by a retreat or a compromise. House conceived of prestige in reference to the diplomatic influence of the American government. Lansing saw it also as closely connected to domestic public confidence in the administration, while Wilson thought of prestige as affecting national pride and involving moral purposes.[74] To the American leaders the concept of national interests thus included not only security but legal, economic, and prestige factors as well.

The unrestricted submarine campaign in 1917 caused Wilson to respond with a decision for war apparently in large part because of his concern for the nation's prestige and moral influence as a

72. *Ibid.*, 167–78.
73. *Ibid.*, 137–42. Contrary to Link, May viewed the Feb. 10, 1915 strict accountability note as initially intended to cover loss of American lives on belligerent as well as American merchant ships.
74. *Ibid.*, 156–59.

great power. Acceptance of the new U-boat war would have been a surrender in the light of past American declarations and seemed impossible to Wilson, not so much now on the grounds of immediate economic or security considerations, but because of the damaging blow American prestige and influence would have suffered. Each succeeding crisis with Germany had seen American prestige more deeply committed; and the submarine issue had become a symbol of Wilson's dedication to uphold international law and the rights of humanity.[75] Full belligerency, rather than armed neutrality, was chosen because of the President's growing distrust of Germany, his desire to unite the American people, and his belief that the nation's role in the war would be limited militarily. May concluded that Wilson had held balance-of-power ideas but that they were subsidiary to his idealistic desire for a just and lasting world peace. Although Wilson has been criticized by some historians for not taking the nation into war to protect its security, May believes it difficult to find fault with Wilson's statesmanship. Not perceiving an immediate danger to America from a German victory in the war, Wilson realistically coped with the only endangered national interests, economic and prestige, and idealistically sought to promote world peace through a new international order.[76]

The problem of the role of the national interests in the neutrality period receives at least a partial answer in the studies by Buehrig, Link, and May. The evidence that Wilson was more realistic than portrayed in the past, and that he was aware of and held to some

75. *Ibid.,* 426–27.

76. *Ibid.,* 433–37. Richard W. Leopold, *The Growth of American Foreign Policy* (New York, 1962), has usefully synthesized recent scholarship on the neutrality era. He views Wilson's acquiescence in the Allied maritime system as necessitated by America's economic and other national interests, and by the impossibility of maintaining an absolutely impartial neutrality when challenged by conditions of modern warfare (pp. 299, 303). The President, despite some evidence of pro-Ally feelings and balance-of-power concerns, "steered a course which was dictated solely by what he thought . . . to be best for America" (p. 311). The resultant economic ties with the Allies did not make war inevitable; only the German declaration of unrestricted submarine warfare, based on hopes of victory and not on resentment of America's role, left no alternative but entry into the war (pp. 303, 336). See also Leopold's "The Emergence of America as a World Power: Some Second Thoughts," John Braeman and others, eds., *Change and Continuity in Twentieth-Century America* (Columbus, 1964).

degree balance-of-power and national interest concepts, is too extensive to be dismissed as a mere selection of isolated statements from the larger corpus of Wilsonian materials. Contrary to previous interpretations, the works of Buehrig, Link's recent volumes, and May reveal that Wilson often was influenced by his realistic counselors, and that he shared much of their evaluations of the meaning of the European war. Secretary Lansing had the clearest conviction that American security would be menaced by a German victory and might require intervention to avert that possibility. House and Wilson generally believed that the outcome of the war most favorable to American and world interests would be a peace short of total victory for either side. May pointed out that both the Colonel and Wilson foresaw that a victorious Germany would probably threaten the position of the United States in South America. Yet as Buehrig, Link, and May agree, balance-of-power and other considerations caused Wilson and House in 1915 and 1916 to try to mediate the war and thus to avoid American involvement and to preserve the existing equipoise. When the President finally did take the nation into the conflict in 1917, it was not because he feared an immediate German menace to American security.

How, then, were concepts of the national interest involved in the American war entry? Buehrig saw the answer in a Wilsonian balance-of-power concern being transformed into reliance on a community-of-power concept to protect American interests and preserve a just future peace. The unrestricted submarine announcement of 1917 precipitated war because of past policy stands, and because Germany was seen as a menace to the new world order envisioned by Wilson. Link portrayed Wilson as driven into acceptance of full hostilities over the submarine issue because of fear of a German victory endangering the balance of power and precluding realization of his idealistic and moralistic hopes for world reconstruction. May placed the emphasis on the prestige factor, which in a sense combined both national interests (security, economic, and diplomatic influence) and moralistic ideas of national honor and duty.

The more simplistic explanations of American involvement in the European war, current in the 1920s and 1930s, whether on the narrow grounds of a defense of legal neutral rights or of unneutral economic ties with the Allies, no longer suffice. The Buehrig, Link, and May studies make that conclusion abundantly clear. Just as clearly, the hypothesis that the United States went to war in 1917 to protect its security against an immediate German threat lacks persuasiveness. It appears that a complex of factors, including legitimate economic interests, some fear of a German victory and long-term threat to the western hemisphere, moral and legal reactions to the submarine, a very sensitive awareness of the involvement of American prestige, and especially Wilson's determination to promote a just and enduring postwar system, underlay American policies and the war entry in 1917. Defined as meaning more than immediate security needs, the authors reviewed agreed that the concept of involved American national interests had a large place in Wilsonian policies and war entry. At least as important, however, if not more so, were moral and idealistic factors.

N. GORDON LEVIN, JR.

The Ideology of Wilsonian Liberalism

Perhaps the most fruitful development in the study of American foreign relations during World War I has been the shift toward broader consideration of underlying assumptions and long-range consequences of diplomacy. This new approach has arisen primarily, though by no means exclusively, from the application of an economic-class analysis. Such an analysis has emphasized both the needs and attitudes generated by the domestic economy and the global confrontation between Western capitalism and revolutionary nationalism. The pioneering exponent of this approach has been William Appleman Williams, and its most assiduous practitioner has been Arno J. Mayer, with his massive studies of the ideological thrust of Wilson's wartime and peace-making diplomatic behavior. But the most interesting and in many ways the most useful contribution to the study of the United States and the World War has been N. Gordon Levin, Jr.'s *Woodrow Wilson and World Politics: America's Response to War and Revolution* (New York, 1968), which is both within the main line of the economic-class interpretation and yet somewhat apart from it.

The following selection from the first chapter of Levin's book illustrates the manner in which he has brought together diverse strands of economic, political, and intellectual values to re-create a sense of the ideological perspective from which Wilson plunged into international politics. For other examples of the economic-class interpretation of Wilsonian diplomacy, see Williams, *The Tragedy of American Diplomacy* (New York, 1962), and Mayer's two books, *Wilson versus Lenin: Political Origins of the New Diplomacy* (New Haven, 1958) and *The Politics and Diplomacy of Peacemaking: Containment and Counterrevolution at Versailles, 1918–19* (New York, 1967).

Woodrow Wilson's vision of a liberal world order of free trade and international harmony did not oppose but rather complemented his conception of the national interests of American capitalism. By the turn of the century it was clear to Wilson that the growth of the American economy, especially in heavy industry, meant that America would soon be competing for the markets of the world with the other major industrialized powers. The future President also correctly saw that the Spanish-American War and the subsequent annexation of the Philippines marked the realization by the nation that the next frontier to be conquered consisted of the fertile export market of Asia. Indeed, this new frontier had to be conquered lest the United States burst with the goods its new industrial system was capable of creating. On the eve of his first presidential campaign, Wilson told the Virginia General Assembly that "we are making more manufactured goods than we can consume ourselves . . . and now, if we are not going to stifle economically, we have got to find our way out into the great international exchanges of the world."[1]

A constant *leitmotif* in Wilson's speeches both before and during his campaign for the presidency in 1912 was the concern that recession and stagnation might overtake the American economy if exports were not drastically increased. Wilson also insisted that, in order to achieve the commercial expansion necessary for American prosperity, it would be necessary to remove certain structural defects in the American economy. In this connection, he emphasized the inadequate credit facilities provided by American banking institutions for export expansion[2] and also stressed his opinion that the merchant marine was inferior to those of America's competitors in international trade.[3]

1. Ray Stannard Baker and William T. Dodd (eds.), *The Public Papers of Woodrow Wilson* (6 vols., New York, 1925–27), II, p. 375 (hereafter cited at *PPWW*); see also *PPWW*, II, pp. 332, 359, 408; for Wilson's views on the international significance of American economic growth at the turn of the century and on the Spanish American War, see Woodrow Wilson, *A History of the American People* (5 vols., New York and London, 1902), V, pp. 264–7, 296; William Diamond, *The Economic Thought of Woodrow Wilson* (Baltimore, 1943), pp. 131–55, and William A. Williams, *The Tragedy of American Diplomacy* (New York, 1962), pp. 61–83, are both excellent over-all analyses of Wilson's export orientation.

2. John Wells Davidson (ed.), *A Cross Roads of Freedom, The 1912 Campaign Speeches of Woodrow Wilson* (New Haven, 1956), p. 114; *PPWW*, II, p. 408.

3. Davidson, *Cross Roads of Freedom*, pp. 33, 47, 115, 487–8; *PPWW*, II, pp. 332, 358, 374–5.

Wilson also attacked the high protective tariff because, among other reasons, its rates brought retaliation against American goods by other countries. The essence of trade was reciprocity, and one could not sell unless one was also willing to buy.[4] Wilson had no doubt that technological efficiency guaranteed American success in international commercial competition, and that, given a chance, "the skill of American workmen would dominate the markets of all the globe."[5]

Wilson's Secretary of the Treasury, William G. McAdoo, was no less convinced than the President that American economic stability was dependent on the movement of surplus products into the mainstream of foreign commerce.[6] He championed, therefore, all Wilson's efforts to remedy the defects in American capitalism which were inhibiting our export expansion. In the same vein, McAdoo worked tirelessly throughout most of Wilson's first term for the passage of an act to create a government-supported merchant marine to prevent foreign competitors from shutting the United States out of world markets by discriminatory freight rates.[7] McAdoo also understood that reciprocity was basic to any effort to avoid depression by a policy of export expansion and that for this reason, among others, Wilsonian efforts to lower the tariff were wise.[8] Finally, McAdoo was fully aware of the relationship of banking reform to the growth of America's commercial role in the world. Writing in the summer of 1915, McAdoo said of the Federal Reserve Act that "this great piece of financial legislation has put this country in position to become the dominant financial power of the world."[9]

4. Davidson, *Cross Roads of Freedom*, pp. 33, 47, 119, 487; *PPWW*, II, pp. 333, 359.

5. Davidson, *Cross Roads of Freedom*, p. 119, see also p. 209; and *PPWW*, II, pp. 232–3, 363–5; for a consideration of the legislation of Wilson's first term in the context of the export issue, see Martin J. Sklar, "Woodrow Wilson and the Political Economy of Modern United States Liberalism," *Studies on the Left*, I, 3 (1960), pp. 17–47.

6. McAdoo to R. L. Henry, Feb. 16, 1915, McAdoo to George W. Norris, June 29, 1915, William G. McAdoo MSS, Library of Congress.

7. McAdoo to F. M. Murphy, Nov. 8, 1915, McAdoo MSS; William G. McAdoo, "Address Before the Chicago Commercial Club," Jan. 9, 1915, *Congressional Record*, 63d Cong. 2d sess., pp. 1535–6; William G. McAdoo, *Crowded Years, The Reminiscences of William G. McAdoo* (Boston, 1931), pp. 294–302.

8. McAdoo to P. H. W. Ross, June 26, 1916, McAdoo MSS; McAdoo, *Crowded Years*, p. 198.

9. McAdoo to George W. Norris, Aug. 27, 1915, McAdoo MSS; see

In this general area of commercial expansion, it is also significant that, under Wilson, Chairman Joseph E. Davies and Vice Chairman Edward N. Hurley of the Federal Trade Commission conceived of the role of the FTC, in part, as one of coordinating joint government-business efforts to make American capitalism rational, co-operative, and efficient. Davies and Hurley hoped thereby both to enhance the stability of the American economy and to increase its competitive potential in world trade.[10] In late 1915, Davies proudly announced at an exporters' convention that it was the purpose of the Federal Trade Commission to aid "in the development of the power and greatness of this nation as an industrial, commercial and financial nation in the world."[11] In a similar vein, Secretary of State William Jennings Bryan told the first National Foreign Trade Convention, meeting in Washington in the spring of 1914, that the Wilson Administration was "earnestly desirous of increasing American foreign commerce and of widening the field of American enterprise."[12] Bryan also emphasized that the State Department would work to "obtain for Americans equality of opportunity in the development of the resources of foreign countries and in the markets of the world."[13]

It is little wonder that Wilson's speeches and letters in 1916 radiated pride in what his first Administration had done to promote American trade abroad. Time and again Wilson stressed the aid given by the Federal Reserve Act, the Federal Trade Commission, and the Com-

---

also McAdoo to Claude Kitchin, Aug. 24, 1915, McAdoo, Speech at Fargo, N.D., Oct. 29, 1915, p. 11, McAdoo MSS; for McAdoo's view that Wilsonian banking, tariff, and shipping legislation formed an interrelated program to aid exports, see McAdoo to J. W. Ashley, Dec. 12, 1914, McAdoo to Henry Lee Higginson, Dec. 15, 1914, McAdoo MSS.

10. *Congressional Record,* 64th Cong. 1st sess., Appendix, pp. 185–8; Edward N. Hurley, Address before Advertising Association, New York, Dec. 1, 1915, Edward N. Hurley, Address before Boston Commercial Club, Mar. 28, 1916, Woodrow Wilson MSS, Library of Congress, Files 6 and 2, respectively; *PPWW,* III, pp. 267–79; *PPWW,* IV, pp. 167–8; for a discussion of the business-oriented ideology of the FTC under Wilson, see Gabriel Kolko, *The Triumph of Conservatism* (New York, 1963), pp. 255–78.

11. *Congressional Record,* 64th Cong., 1st sess., Appendix, p. 187.

12. Cited in Sklar, *Wilson and the Political Economy,* p. 31; see also Bryan to Wilson, Oct. 6, 1913, Wilson-Bryan Correspondence, National Archives.

13. Sklar, *Wilson and the Political Economy,* p. 31.

merce Department to American exporters, and called on the nation's business leaders to rise to their global opportunities.[14] It should be noted, however, that the Wilsonian program of commercial expansion did not go uncriticized domestically. On the Right, some Republican and Progressive nationalist spokesmen, such as Theodore Roosevelt, Albert Beveridge, George Perkins, and Henry Cabot Lodge, were not willing to see tariffs lowered as a means of increasing exports, and they were not averse to having exports expanded by the alternate method of international economic rivalry backed by naval preparedness. On the Left, socialists questioned the very concept of trade expansion itself, arguing that there was no real surplus to export, but only those goods which the lower classes were not able to consume at existing price and income levels. Beyond the question of underconsumption, socialists and some radical liberals also saw a danger of navalism, imperialism, and war in any vigorous program of export expansion. In the Center, however, the Wilsonian position implicitly held, against both conservative and radical critics, that it was possible to have economic expansion and yet to avoid such traditional imperialistic practices as protection, economic warfare, and navalism. Yet, in order fully to understand how Wilson could ideologically fuse commercial expansionism with a form of anti-imperialism, it is now important to grasp that, for the President, export was the necessary material aspect of a national mission to spread the values of American liberalism abroad in the interests of world peace and international liberal-capitalist order.

In essence, Wilson approached the question of America's export trade from the perspective of the Puritan sense of "a calling." Like the Puritans, who placed earthly vocations, or callings, in a larger context of service to God and man, Wilson saw the enlargement of foreign commerce in terms of a duty in the service of humanity. During the early years of the war, and American neutrality, the President coupled his exhortations to American businessmen of commercial expansion with a messianic conception of the service which America was able to provide to a suffering world whose productive facilities had been upset by the struggle. "The war," he claimed, "has made it necessary that the United States should mobilize its resources in the most effective way possible and make her credit and her usefulness

14. *PPWW*, IV, pp. 167–8, 228–44, 257–9, 276–8, 287–8, 309–22; see also Woodrow Wilson, "Address to the National Chamber of Commerce, Feb. 10, 1916," *Nation's Business*, IV (Feb. 10, 1916), pp. 18–20.

good for the service of the whole world."[15] In this sense, the competitive advantage in world trade which America possessed due to her technological and productive efficiency was, for Wilson, not a threat to other nations, but rather a godsend. The peaceful triumph of America in the markets of the world was, therefore, to be both a service and a lesson for a suffering humanity. In Wilson's terms:

> America has stood in the years past for that sort of political understanding among men which would let every man feel that his rights were the same as those of another and as good as those of another, and the mission of America in the field of the world's commerce is to be the same: that when an American comes into that competition he comes without any arms that would enable him to conquer by force, but only with those peaceful influences of intelligence, a desire to serve, a knowledge of what he is about, before which everything softens and yields, and renders itself subject. That is the mission of America, and my interest, so far as my small part in American affairs is concerned, is to lend every bit of intelligence I have to this interesting, this vital, this all-important matter of releasing the intelligence of America for the service of mankind.[16]

The fusion which Wilson made here of America's economic and political missions reveals the roots of the President's combined vision of moral and material expansion. The commercial health of America was, for Wilson, the visible evidence of underlying political and moral strength. Having ideologically unified liberalism, capitalism, and missionary-nationalism, Wilson never doubted that "all the multitude of men who have developed the peaceful industries of America were planted under this free polity in order that they might look out upon the service of mankind and perform it."[17] For the President, the extension of American trade around the world was inseparable from the export of American liberalism. In his eyes the national purpose was one of seeking "to enrich the commerce of our own states and of the world with the products of our mines, our farms, and our factories,

15. *PPWW*, III, p. 212; see also *PPWW*, III, pp. 216–17, 241–2; *PPWW*, IV, p. 26.

16. *PPWW*, IV, p. 323; see also *PPWW*, IV, pp. 6–7, 117–18.

17. *PPWW*, IV, p. 301; see also *PPWW*, IV, pp. 243–4.

with the creations of our thought and the fruits of our character."[18] Toward the end of his first term, Wilson addressed a Salesmanship Congress in Detroit in words that speak volumes as to the unity of his world view of liberal-capitalist expansionism:

> This, then, my friends, is the simple message that I bring you. Lift your eyes to the horizons of business; do not look too close at the little processes with which you are concerned, but let your thoughts and your imaginations run abroad throughout the whole world, and with the inspiration of the thought that you are Americans and are meant to carry liberty and justice and the principles of humanity wherever you go, go out and sell goods that will make the world more comfortable and more happy, and convert them to the principles of America.[19]

New Freedom foreign policy in regard to China and Latin America, during Wilson's first term, exemplified the relation of the President's ideology of moral and material export to his liberal anti-imperialism. In the Far East, Wilsonian concern for the territorial integrity, stability, and political independence of China was not an abstract anti-imperialist position arrived at in an economic and social vacuum. Actually, Wilson's opposition to the traditional policies of spheres of influence and territorial annexation in China was inextricably bound up with his concept of the type of liberal world order of commercial freedom within which the genius of American capitalism could best win its rightful place in the markets of the world. Since Wilson never questioned his basic assumption that American commercial and moral expansion into China contributed to the welfare of the Chinese people, there was a unity in his mind of both his allegiance to the export of American surplus products and his opposition to traditional imperialism in China.[20] In this connection, the Wilson Administration refused to continue the Taft policy of encouraging an American banking group to participate in a projected financial consortium of six major

18. *PPWW*, III, p. 227.

19. *PPWW*, IV, p. 233.

20. Tien-yi Li, *Woodrow Wilson's China Policy, 1913–1917* (New York, 1952), pp. 12–13; Burton F. Beers, *Vain Endeavor, Robert Lansing's Attempt to End the American-Japanese Rivalry* (Durham, N.C., 1962), pp. 16–18; Sklar, *Wilson and the Political Economy*, pp. 44–6.

powers for China. The President took the position that the terms of the planned Six-Power Consortium threatened the political and economic independence of China, and that large segments of the American banking community had been refused admittance to the program.[21] In opposing United States participation in the Consortium, Wilson was not, however, opposing the principle of the expansion of American capitalism into underdeveloped areas. On the contrary, the Administration felt that, once free of the restraints of the Consortium, the American banking and business community as a whole could do a better job of serving the Chinese with the aid of the Departments of State and Commerce.[22]

In Latin America, Wilsonian policy sought to relate American economic expansion to the creation of an hemispheric system of free trade and liberal-capitalist order to be led by the United States. Wilson, McAdoo, and Commerce Secretary William C. Redfield were all anxious to promote the extension of American financial and commercial activity in South America, and they emphasized government support to this end.[23] Adding his voice, Secretary of the Navy Josephus Daniels argued that since America had to sell her surplus products abroad in order to maintain domestic prosperity, American businessmen had best learn how to conquer the markets to the South.[24]

Yet, if Wilsonians envisioned a commercial hemispheric harmony transcending power politics, it is also true that in the sensitive Caribbean area the Wilsonian urge to export liberalism and protect America's commercial and strategic interests from any European encroach-

21. Roy Watson Curry, *Woodrow Wilson and Far Eastern Policy, 1913–1921* (New Haven, 1957), pp. 19–24; Arthur S. Link, *Wilson: The New Freedom* (Princeton, 1956), pp. 283–8; Tien-yi Li, *Wilson's China Policy*, pp. 33–9.

22. Williams, *Tragedy of American Diplomacy*, pp. 74–7; Tien-yi Li, *Wilson's China Policy*, pp. 46–7, 163–5; Beers, *Vain Endeavor*, pp. 72–92; Diamond, *Economic Thought of Woodrow Wilson*, pp. 147–8; Russell H. Fifield, *Woodrow Wilson and the Far East, The Diplomacy of the Shantung Question* (New York, 1952), pp. 90–93.

23. Wilson to McAdoo, Nov. 3, 1914, Aug. 26, Oct. 5, 1915, McAdoo MSS; McAdoo to Senator W. J. Stone, Jan. 15, 1915, and McAdoo, Speech at Chapel Hill, N.C., May 30, 1916, McAdoo MSS; Redfield to Wilson, Sept. 17, Nov. 21, 1914, Wilson MSS, File 2.

24. Josephus Daniels, Address at Banquet of Federation of Trade Press Associations, n.p., Sept. 8, 1915, Josephus Daniels MSS, Library of Congress.

ments led to armed interventions to maintain stability.[25] In late 1915 House recorded:

> He [Lansing] laid some memoranda before me concerning the Caribbean countries which he thought needed attention. He believes that we should give more intimate direction to their affairs than we would feel warranted in doing to other South American states. He puts them in the same category with Santo Domingo and Haiti and believes we should take the same measures to bring about order, both financial and civil, as we are taking in those countries. I approved this policy and promised to express this opinion to the President.[26]

As regards Mexico, however, Wilson successfully resisted pressure to apply the traditional interventionist and conservative solutions of Republican nationalism to the problems created by the Mexican Revolution. Instead, he slowly developed a policy of aid to the Mexican Constitutionalists to the end that Mexican feudalism would be destroyed and broad-based land ownership established.[27] Wilson hoped that these changes, coupled with education, would create the prerequisites for liberalism, capitalism, and stability in Mexico.[28]

In the light of coming events in Russia and the future confrontation of Wilson and Lenin, it is important to understand at this juncture

25. Link, *The New Freedom*, pp. 327–46; Arthur S. Link, *Wilson: The Struggle for Neutrality, 1914–1915* (Princeton, 1960), pp. 495–550; see also United States Dept. of State, *Papers Relating to the Foreign Relations of the United States, The Lansing Papers, 1914–1920* (2 vols., Washington, D.C., 1939), II, pp. 459–70, for evidence that the expansion of American trade and orderly liberal values into the Caribbean area, by forceful means on occasion, was related in part to the Administration's desire to keep strong European economic and/or political influence out of the strategic Caribbean area.

26. The Private Diary of Colonel House, Nov. 28, 1915, House MSS, Yale University Library (hereafter cited as House MSS Diary).

27. *PPWW*, III, pp. 111–22; *PPWW*, IV, pp. 339–42; Link, *The New Freedom*, pp. 347–415; Link, *The Struggle for Neutrality*, pp. 488–94.

28. *PPWW*, III, pp. 45–6, 339–40, 400–405; *PPWW*, IV, p. 343; Wilson to Walter Hines Page, June 4, 1914, Ray Stannard Baker MSS, Library of Congress; Wilson to Bryan, Mar. 17, 1915, Wilson-Bryan Correspondence, United States National Archives; Link, *The New Freedom*, pp. 382–9, 410–15; Link, *The Struggle for Neutrality*, pp. 458–84.

that the revolution which Wilson came to support in Mexico was
conceived by him to be basically liberal-capitalist rather than socialist
in intent. There is no evidence that the President ever changed his
mind about a statement that he made in 1913 to the British diplomat
Sir William Tyrrell: "the United States Government intends not merely
to force Huerta from power, but also to exert every influence it
can to secure Mexico a better government under which all contracts
and business concessions will be safer than they have ever been."[29]
In short, Wilson held that the avoidance of crude economic exploitation and of traditional imperialist practices in Mexico and Latin America would lead both to increased legitimate American investment to
the South and to a just liberal-capitalist hemispheric order.[30] In this
fashion both the material and moral missions of American liberal-expansionism could be fulfilled.

Wilson and House hoped to cap their vision of an American-inspired
and American-led liberal order in the Western Hemisphere with a
Pan-American Pact providing for mutual guarantees as to arbitration,
disarmament, and territorial integrity.[31] Even though the pact was
not actualized, Colonel House recorded some thoughts concerning
it which serve to illustrate the universal scope of the Wilsonian non-
socialist critique of existing world politics. "It was my idea," wrote
House, "to formulate a plan, to be agreed upon by the republics
of the two continents, which in itself would serve as a model for
the European nations when peace is at last brought about."[32] Indeed,
the hope that somehow America could supply the answer to the problems of war-torn Europe became a major element in Wilsonian foreign
policy from 1914 to 1917. In the President's eyes, it should be remem-

29. Wilson to Sir William Tyrrell, Nov. 22, 1913, cited in Ray Stannard
Baker, *Woodrow Wilson, Life and Letters* (8 vols., Garden City, N.Y.,
1927–1934), IV, p. 292 (hereafter cited as *Life and Letters*); in relation
to the question of foreign property in Mexico, see Robert Lansing, Remarks
at Luncheon for American-Mexican Joint Commission, New York, Sept.
4, 1916, p. 4, Wilson MSS, File 6, Box 56; on the Wilson-Tyrrell negotiations see Link, *The New Freedom*, pp. 374–7.
30. *PPWW*, III, pp. 64–9, 113; see also *PPWW*, IV, pp. 341–2; *PPWW*,
V, pp. 227–8; House MSS Diary, Nov. 25, 1914; George Creel, "The
Next Four Years, An Interview with President Wilson," *Everybody's Magazine*, XXXVI (Feb. 1917), p. 132.
31. Charles Seymour (ed.), *The Intimate Papers of Colonel House*
(4 vols., Boston, 1926–1928), I, pp. 207–34 (hereafter cited as *Intimate
Papers*); Link, *The New Freedom*, pp. 324–7.
32. *Intimate Papers*, I, p. 209.

bered, the vast wartime expansion of America's export trade was a means of American aid to mankind. In defense of his policy of neutrality, Wilson argued that "we can help better by keeping out of the war, by giving our financial resources to the use of the injured world, by giving our cotton and our woolen stuffs to clothe the world."[33] This missionary ideology of foreign aid through export also extended to a vision of the role which America might play as the reconstructor of devastated Europe in the postwar period. In a statement capturing his conception of the redemptive power of business and international trade, Wilson affirmed early in 1916 that:

> Somebody must keep the great stable foundations of the life of nations untouched and undisturbed. Somebody must keep the great economic processes of the world of business alive. Somebody must see to it that we stand ready to repair the enormous damage and the incalculable losses which will ensue from this war.[34]

This Wilsonian vision of a role for the United States in European reconstruction was intimately related to the President's awareness that the export trade of 1914–16 had made America the major financial power in the world. This development had necessarily greatly enlarged the potential influence of American capitalism on the international commercial and political scene. "We have become not the debtors but the creditors of the world," Wilson told an audience at Shadow Lawn on the day before the 1916 election, adding, "We can determine to a large extent who is to be financed and who is not to be financed . . . we are in the great drift of humanity which is to determine the politics of every country in the world."[35] The President's realization that the United States was "becoming by the force of circumstances the mediating nation of the world in respect of its finances" was clearly a major element in his confident assertion that "we shall someday have to assist in reconstructing the processes of peace."[36] The fact that the aggregate resources of the national banks of the United States exceeded by three billion dollars the aggregate resources of the Bank of England, the Bank of France, the Bank

33. *PPWW*, IV, p. 104; see also *PPWW*, III, pp. 250–51, 406.
34. *PPWW*, IV, p. 59; see also *PPWW*, IV, p. 116.
35. *PPWW*, IV, p. 391; see also *PPWW*, IV, pp. 229, 378–9.
36. *PPWW*, III, p. 303; see also *Life and Letters*, VI, pp. 377–8.

of Russia, the Reichsbank of Berlin, the Bank of Netherlands, the Bank of Switzerland, and the Bank of Japan, helped to give Wilson confidence that America was better prepared than ever before to "lead the way along the paths of light."[37] The ultimate Wilsonian hope was to use America's expanding commercial and political influence to establish on a worldwide scale the type of liberal-capitalist order of commercial freedom which had been the goal of his concern for American moral and material expansion in China and Latin America. To this end, the President, in close co-operation with Colonel House, opted for the role of mediator in the World War. Indeed, House's missions to Europe as Wilson's emissary during the 1914–16 period may be seen as efforts to convince the European powers that their best interests would be served by a negotiated peace to be made lasting by their mutual co-operation with the United States in the creation of a new political and economic world system in which the seas would be free, territorial integrity mutually guaranteed, and financial expansion into underdeveloped areas handled in a co-operative atmosphere. In such a world, traditional imperialism would be obsolete and American liberal-expansionism could prosper in an atmosphere of peaceful international-capitalism.

In 1912 Colonel House wrote a utopian novel entitled *Philip Dru: Administrator,* whose protagonist, upon becoming dictator of America, succeeds in bringing Germany into an Anglo-American inspired world order "of peace and commercial freedom," within which "disarmaments were to be made to an appreciable degree, customs barriers were to be torn down, zones of influence clearly defined, and an era of friendly commercial rivalry established."[38] During his actual trips to Europe, between 1914 and 1916, House used all his diplomatic skills in an effort to reintegrate Germany into a harmonious international-capitalist concert of Western powers led by England and the United States. In the spring and early summer of 1914, on the eve of war, House sought unsuccessfully to bring about an Anglo-German *rapprochement* around the principles of concert of power, naval disarmament, and peaceful commercial rivalry.[39] In his Diary, House

37. *PPWW,* IV, p. 141.

38. E. M. House, *Philip Dru: Administrator* (New York, 1912), p. 273.

39. *Intimate Papers,* I, pp. 238–75; *Life and Letters,* V, pp. 20–50; Burton J. Hendrick, *The Life and Letters of Walter H. Page* (3 vols., Garden City, N.Y., 1924–1926), I, pp. 270–300.

recorded his conception of the best way to approach the Kaiser in the interests of a rational world system of economic and political order:

> My purpose is to try to show the Emperor that if he will consent to take the initiative in the matter I have in mind, it will rebound greatly to Germany's commercial and material welfare. It is not in my mind to suggest to him to lessen at all his military organization or to disturb his Continental relations. It is only to try to show him that an understanding with Great Britain and the United States will place him in a position to curtail his naval program and open up a wider field for German commerce, besides insuring the peace of the world.[40]

The Colonel's desire to reintegrate Germany into a stable Western international structure was intensified by the outbreak of war in August 1914. Writing to James W. Gerard, the American Ambassador in Germany, House expressed the hope that the Kaiser would consider a peace based on mutual disarmament and territorial guarantees. "With Europe disarmed and with treaties guaranteeing one another's territorial integrity," the Colonel reasoned, "she [Germany] might go forward with every assurance of industrial expansion and permanent peace."[41] On his second peace mission to Europe, in early 1915, House sought to fuse America's export-oriented concern for freedom of trade and neutral rights with an appeal to Germany's leaders to exchange their traditional reliance on national power for an Anglo-German *détente* based on freedom of the seas and peaceful commercial expansion.[42] In the fall of 1915, House sought to present his position to Count Bernstorff, the German Ambassador to America:

> During the conversation we spoke of peace overtures, and of when and how they might begin. I impressed upon him my belief that no peace parleys could be started until Germany was willing to consent to abolish militarism and Great Britain to abolish navalism. I enlarged upon Germany's splendid oppor-

40. House MSS Diary, Apr. 10, 1914.
41. House to Gerard, Aug. 17, 1914, cited in *Intimate Papers,* I, pp. 319–20.
42. House MSS Diary, Mar. 19, Mar. 24, 1915; House to Wilson, Feb. 28, Mar. 19, Mar. 26, Mar. 29 (cable), Apr. 12, 1915, Wilson MSS, File 2; *Intimate Papers,* I, pp. 369, 400–402, 410–11, 430–31.

tunity for industrial advancement with the freedom of the seas
assured, and I made it clear that the one thought uppermost
in the mind of the Western Allies was a peace free from the
menace of another such war.[43]

At the core of House's vision of Western unity was a program
through which the bitterly competitive process of financial and commercial expansion by the advanced nations into the undeveloped world
could be restructured in a rational and co-operative manner. In the
Colonel's conception, the American desire to maintain the Open Door
in colonial areas for the export of American surplus products was
joined to the liberal impulse to end a major cause of imperialist
conflict by reforming world politics from within. As House explained
it to British leaders in early summer 1914:

> My plan is that if England, the United States, Germany and
> France will come to an understanding concerning investments
> by their citizens in undeveloped countries, much good and profit
> will come to their citizens as well as to the countries needing
> development. Stability would be brought about, investments
> would become safe, and low rates of interest might be
> established.[44]

Co-operative management of the world's backward areas also provided,
in House's mind, further means of bringing Germany into a peaceful
international-capitalist world system. In his *Philip Dru: Administrator,*
House had already sketched out a program in which Germany would
be allowed commercial expansion in Latin America, the Balkans,
and the Near East.[45] On his actual peace missions, the Colonel often
urged upon Allied and German leaders the possibility of sublimating
Germany's expansive energies into less aggressive channels by giving
her financial opportunities in the undeveloped areas.[46]

43. House MSS Diary, Sept. 28, 1915; see also House to Wilson, Nov.
19, 1915, Wilson MSS File 2.
44. House MSS Diary, June 21, 1914; see also House MSS Diary,
July 3, 1914; *Intimate Papers,* I, pp. 264–7, 275; Hendrick, *Life and Letters
of Walter H. Page,* I, pp. 270–75.
45. House, *Philip Dru: Administrator,* pp. 273–4.
46. House to Wilson, Apr. 11, 1915, Jan. 15, Feb. 9, 1916, Wilson
MSS, File 2; House MSS Diary, Mar. 23, 1915, Feb. 7, 1916; *Intimate
Papers,* I, pp. 238–9, 246, 260; *Intimate Papers,* II, p. 291; *Life and
Letters,* VI, p. 150, n. 5.

In the light of House's efforts to place the "backward" peoples into the context of a harmonious liberal world order, a dimension was added to Wilson's own desire to use American mediation and financial power to reconstruct and reunify the Western world. Wilson tended to view American neutrality and peace-making as a duty due to the system of world leadership by the great "white" nations of the West, a position which would be reinforced by the imminent challenge of Bolshevism to that system from the Left. Secretary of State Robert Lansing records a significant comment of Wilson's made just after the German declaration of unlimited submarine warfare in February 1917, in which the President made explicit his vision of world liberal peace based on unified Western commercial and political leadership:

> The President, though deeply incensed at Germany's insolent notice, said that he was not yet sure what course we must pursue and must think it over; that he had been more and more impressed that "white civilization" and its domination over the world rested largely on our ability to keep this country intact as we would have to build up the nations ravaged by the war.[47]

On close analysis, then, Wilsonian liberal anti-imperialism emerges as a limited form of international reformism. That is to say, Wilson opposed traditional exploitive imperialism involving territorial annexations, armed force, protectionism, and war. The President did not, however, question either the structural inequitability of the commercial and financial relationships between the agrarian and the industrialized areas of the world or the correlative economic and political world predominance of the West. Wilson's basic concern, inspired both by the expansive needs of American capitalism and by his own liberal-internationalist ideology, was to make more rational and humane the existing world economic and social relationships. The mandate system, which he was to advocate at Paris, was a classic example of his paternalistic orientation. In essence, Wilson and House were reformers with a faith that there was a potential for peace and justice latent in the international-capitalist system which would develop once

47. Robert Lansing, *War Memoirs of Robert Lansing* (New York, 1935), p. 212; David F. Houston, *Eight Years with Wilson's Cabinet, 1913–1920* (2 vols., Garden City, N.Y., 1926), I, p. 229; *Intimate Papers*, II, p. 412; Tien-yi Li, *Wilson's China Policy*, pp. 11–12.

it was liberated from imperialist irrationality. This Wilsonian position was, of course, to the Left of the views of many Republican and Progressive nationalists *vis-à-vis* America's role in the world, but it did not go far enough in its anti-imperialism for many socialists, who insisted that capitalism per se was the root cause of imperialism and war. In this connection, Wilson's world view was not unlike that of such English non-socialist anti-imperialists as Norman Angell, E. D. Morel, and J. A. Hobson, who also offered a rational and democratic critique of protectionism, navalism, secret diplomacy, and colonialism. Along with Wilson and House, these liberals argued that Britain and Europe would prosper best under a commercial and political concert of power which would guarantee free trade, international-capitalist stability, and peace.[48]

Undoubtedly the most complete expression of the Wilsonian anti-imperialism of liberal order may be found in the conceptions of formal international co-operation which Wilson and House developed in the 1915–16 period. By 1916 Wilson hoped to associate America in a postwar union with other leading powers, including Germany, to achieve disarmament, freedom of the seas, mutual territorial guarantees, and international arbitrations.[49] Writing to House on the eve of the Colonel's departure for his third peace mission to Europe, Wilson succinctly expressed his vision of a co-operative international order of commercial freedom:

> I agree with you that we have nothing to do with local settlements,—territorial questions, indemnities, and the like—but are concerned only in the future peace of the world and the guarantees to be given for that. The only possible guarantees, that is, the only possible guarantees that any rational man could accept, are (a) military and naval disarmament and (b) a league of nations to secure each nation against aggression and maintain the absolute freedom of the seas.[50]

48. Laurence W. Martin, *Peace Without Victory, Woodrow Wilson and the British Liberals* (New Haven, 1958), pp. 7–13, 55–84; Arno J. Mayer, *Political Origins of the New Diplomacy, 1917–1918* (New Haven, 1959), pp. 25–7, 54–7; E. M. Winslow, *The Pattern of Imperialism* (New York, 1948), p. 102; Henry R. Winkler, *The League of Nations Movement in Great Britain* (New Brunswick, N.J., 1952), pp. 28–49, 200–203.

49. Wilson to House, May 16, 1916, House MSS; House to Grey, May 10, 1916, House to Wilson, May 21, 1916, Wilson MSS, File 2; *Life and Letters,* V, pp. 73–4; *Life and Letters,* VI, pp. 204–5, 216–17.

50. Wilson to House, Dec. 24, 1915, House MSS.

The emphasis here on the freedom of the seas recalls again the intimate connection in Wilsonian ideology between the needs of an expanding American capitalism and the goals of international liberalism and anti-imperialism. In accepting his renomination for the presidency in September 1916, Wilson made this connection clear by affirming:

> We have already formulated and agreed upon a policy of law which will explicitly remove the ban now supposed to rest upon co-operation amongst our exporters in seeking and securing their proper place in the markets of the world. The field will be free, the instrumentalities at hand. It will only remain for the masters of enterprise amongst us to act in energetic concert, and for the Government of the United States to insist upon the maintenance throughout the world of those conditions of fairness and of even-handed justice in the commercial dealings of the nations with one another upon which, after all, in the last analysis, the peace and ordered life of the world must ultimately depend.[51]

An exchange of memoranda between Lansing and Wilson in early 1917 also shows that concern for commercial freedom and an international Open Door were basic elements in the President's hopes for a liberal postwar order.[52] By the latter half of 1916, Wilson's speeches, which were full of the mission of American capitalism to reconstruct a war-torn world, also affirmed the closely related duty of America to join a future concert of powers in the maintenance of international peace and justice.[53] Beyond war there hopefully lay a liberal-internationalist community of civilized powers, inspired by the moral and material expansion of America, which would guarantee world peace, international law, and freedom for commercial expansion. As the

51. *PPWW,* IV, p. 289.

52. U.S. Department of State, *Papers Relating to the Foreign Relations of the United States, The Lansing Papers, 1914–1920* (2 vols., Washington, D.C., 1939–1940), I, pp. 19–23 (hereafter all volumes in this *Foreign Relations* series of the State Department will be cited by the abbreviation *FR,* to be followed by the appropriate subtitles); see also Martin, *Peace Without Victory,* p. 127; William A. Williams, "American Intervention in Russia, 1917–1920," *Studies on the Left,* III (Fall 1963), 29.

53. *PPWW,* IV, pp. 75, 186–7, 194–5, 348, 381–2; see also Wilson to House, May 16, 1916, House MSS; House to Wilson, May 21, 1916, Wilson MSS, File 2.

President told an audience in Indianapolis during the campaign of
1916:

> I have said, and shall say again, that when the great present
> war is over it will be the duty of America to join with the
> other nations of the world in some kind of league for the main-
> tenance of peace. Now, America was not a party to this war,
> and the only terms upon which we will be admitted to a league,
> almost all the other powerful members of which were engaged
> in the war and made infinite sacrifices when we apparently
> made none, are the only terms which we desire, namely, that
> America shall not stand for national aggression, but shall stand
> for the just conceptions and bases of peace, for the competition
> of merit alone, and for the generous rivalry of liberty.[54]

*   *   *

Wilson's conception of the origin of the world war was a basic component of his American exceptionalist ideology, and his conception
was closely related as well to his desire to use the moral and economic
strength of America to establish a liberal world order. In Cincinnati,
late in the 1916 campaign, Wilson addressed himself to the causes
of the European holocaust:

> Nothing in particular started it, but everything in general. There
> had been growing up in Europe a mutual suspicion, an inter-
> change of conjecture about what this Government and that
> Government was going to do, an interlacing of alliances and
> understandings, a complex web of intrigue and spying, that
> presently was sure to entangle the whole of the family of man-
> kind on that side of the water in its meshes.[55]

Several things should be noted in relation to this statement. First
of all, by placing the locus of responsibility for the war on "European"
phenomena, such as secret diplomacy and entangling alliances, Wilson
remained consistently within the ideological pattern formed by his
fusion of liberal anti-imperialism and American exceptionalism. While
Lenin saw the war as the inevitable result of competition among
imperialist nations in an era of monopoly capitalism, Wilson blamed

54. *PPWW*, IV, pp. 360–61.
55. *PPWW*, IV, p. 381; see also *PPWW*, IV, p. 185.

atavistic and irrational patterns of European national behavior and retained a faith in the peaceful and orderly potential of international-capitalism in general and of American moral-commercial expansionism in particular. Nonetheless, despite the great differences between the liberal-capitalist and the revolutionary-socialist critiques of the war, the two ideologies had one thing in common. From the particular levels of abstraction which each afforded, it was possible to transcend views of the war held by the partisans of the nations involved and to see the conflict critically and objectively as a historical experience emerging from a particular set of political and economic institutions. This was true even if the definition of those institutions offered by Wilsonians and Leninists differed greatly. Indeed, many American radicals and socialists retained positions of critical objectivity *vis-à-vis* the war during the 1914–18 period, which positions could be placed on an ideological continuum at varying points between the poles of liberal and socialist anti-imperialism. The problem becomes further complicated, however, by the fact that by April 1917 the President had moved from his position of liberal objectivity toward the war to a position advocating liberal war against Germany in association with the Entente. The point was that the very missionary liberal nationalism which gave Wilson his neutral and critical objectivity toward the war was also paradoxically capable of supplying an ideological basis for American participation in a war against German autocratic imperialism. To understand fully the Wilsonian transition from liberal mediation to liberal war, it is necessary to consider both the problem of German submarine warfare and the presence within the Wilsonian anti-imperialist mind of certain latent ideological tendencies which would help to motivate an American liberal war against Germany.

The submarine warfare used by Germany during the war could not help but be threatening to Wilson, whose vision, both of America's expansionist mission and of a liberal world order, was so deeply related to a concern for freedom of the seas and the maintenance of international law. The President sought to make his position on the necessity to defend American rights on the seas clear to an audience in Topeka, Kansas, early in 1916:

> There are perfectly clearly marked rights guaranteed by international law which every American is entitled to enjoy, and America is not going to abide the habitual or continued neglect of those rights. Perhaps not being as near the ports as some other

Americans, you do not travel as much and you do not realize
the infinite number of legitimate errands upon which Americans
travel—errands of commerce, errands of relief, errands of business for the Government, errands of every sort which make
America useful to the world. Americans do not travel to disturb
the world; they travel to quicken the processes of the interchange
of life and of goods in the world, and their travel ought not to be
impeded by a reckless disregard of international obligations.[56]

This conviction, that Americans were justified in traveling to serve
the world commercially, was often affirmed by the President during
his speaking tour of the Mid-West on behalf of his military preparedness program in the early weeks of 1916.[57] In this connection, it
should be kept in mind that by the end of 1915 American exports
to the Allies had grown to such proportions that the recession which
plagued the country early in Wilson's first term had been overcome
by the effects of the immense war trade.[58] Related to the material
issue, however, was the fact that, for Wilson, the very process of
defending the nation's rights on the seas became an important aspect
of America's unique liberal service to mankind. If it was the exceptional destiny of the United States to feed, clothe, and morally instruct
the world, it was also its duty to maintain the rule of law on the
high seas for the benefit of all neutral trading nations. As the chief
representative and trustee of neutral rights, Wilson was convinced
that the mission of the United States was "to assert the principles
of law in a world in which the principles of law have broken down."[59]
In defending America's neutral rights, then, the President was as
certain as always that there was complete unity between the national

56. *PPWW*, IV, pp. 89–90.

57. *PPWW*, IV, pp. 30, 37–8, 109–10.

58. On the economic importance of American-Allied wartime trade to
the American economy, see Alice M. Morrissey, *The American Defense
of Neutral Rights* (Cambridge, Mass., 1939), pp. 4–24, 90–104, 132–53;
Ernest R. May, *The World War and American Isolation* (Cambridge,
Mass., 1959), pp. 156–7, 336–46; Daniel M. Smith, *Robert Lansing and
American Neutrality* (Berkeley, 1958), pp. 92–5; Edward H. Buehrig,
Woodrow Wilson and the Balance of Power (Bloomington, 1955), pp.
85–105; see also the speeches by McAdoo on Sept. 28, 1917, and Oct.
4, 1917, in McAdoo MSS, Box 563, in which McAdoo argued that German
submarine warfare had constituted a threat to America's trade and economic
health.

59. *PPWW*, IV, p. 61; see also *PPWW*, IV, pp. 75, 122–3, 171.

interest of the United States and the values of liberal-internationalism. This was the uniqueness of America, a nation which since its inception had "undertaken to be the champions of humanity and the rights of men. Without that ideal there would be nothing that would distinguish America from her predecessors in the history of nations."[60]

It must be emphasized that Wilson and his leading advisers made a clear moral distinction between British naval encroachments on commerce alone and the German submarine threat to both trade and lives.[61] After the torpedoing of the *Lusitania,* it was clear that Wilson was prepared, if pressed, to go to war with Germany on an issue which he saw as involving basic principles of neutral rights and international law.[62] Convinced that unrestricted submarine warfare posed a total challenge to the liberal world order which it was America's duty to foster, the President told his audiences on the preparedness tour that the armed forces of the United States were ready to defend those American rights which were identical with universal human rights, and that the defense of basic principles by force was preferable to ignoble compromise.[63] Speaking in Washington in late February 1916, Wilson expressed succinctly his willingness to take America to war, if that were necessary to defend her most cherished ideals:

> America ought to keep out of this war. She ought to keep out of this war at the sacrifice of everything except this single thing upon which her character and history are founded, her sense of humanity and justice. If she sacrifices that, she has ceased to be America; she has ceased to entertain and to love the traditions which have made us proud to be Americans, and when we go about seeking safety at the expense of humanity, then I for one will believe that I have always been mistaken in what I have conceived to be the spirit of American his-

60. *PPWW,* IV, p. 44; see also *PPWW,* III, pp. 147–8; *PPWW,* IV, pp. 158, 394.

61. *PPWW,* IV, pp. 282, 430–32; *FR, Lansing Papers,* I, pp. 221–2, 555–8; Lansing to Dr. E. M. Gallaudet, June 2, 1915, Lansing MSS, Library of Congress; House to Wilson, July 17, 1915, Wilson MSS, File 2; May, *American Isolation,* pp. 137–9, 325–35; Arthur S. Link, *Wilson the Diplomatist* (Baltimore, 1957), pp. 40–43.

62. May, *American Isolation,* pp. 110–52; Smith, *Robert Lansing,* pp. 49–61; Buehrig, *Balance of Power,* pp. 18–57; Morrissey, *Neutral Rights,* pp. 50–77.

63. *PPWW,* IV, pp. 4, 8, 26, 55–6, 145.

tory. . . . I would be just as much ashamed to be rash as
I would to be a coward. Valor is self-respecting. Valor is circum-
spect. Valor strikes only when it is right to strike. Valor with-
holds itself from all small implications and entanglements and
waits for the great opportunity when the sword will flash as
if it carried the light of heaven upon its blade.[64]

The President also felt that the armed defense of American and neutral
rights would not be at odds with but would rather complement his
conception of America's responsibility to join a postwar community
of powers in the maintenance of international peace and justice.[65]
In short, Wilson's response to German submarine warfare proved
that a propensity for war in defense of the particular and universal
values of American liberal-nationalism was latent in his thought well
before the actual entry into the war.

Nevertheless, the President hoped to be able both to defend his
principles and to keep the United States at peace. The Wilson-House
vision of a reunified Western world functioning with liberal-capitalist
harmony has already been discussed at length. Indeed, the President's
conception of America's duty to pacify Europe and reconstruct a
liberal world order seemed often to assert itself most strongly in
his thought at those times when the submarine issue seemed about
to force a final break between the United States and Germany.[66]
The climactic Wilsonian peace effort of the winter of 1916–17 reflected
both Wilson's desire to co-opt Germany into a liberal concert of
powers and a fear on the President's part that an imminent resumption
of unrestricted submarine warfare by Germany might force the United
States to enter the war.[67] The evidence also suggests that, until February 1917, Colonel House never fully gave up the hope that a German-
American conflict could be avoided through the voluntary acceptance

64. *PPWW*, IV, pp. 127–8.

65. *PPWW*, IV, pp. 347–8.

66. Wilson to House, July 14, 1915, House MSS; House MSS Diary,
Feb. 1, 1917; Josephus Daniels's Diary, Mar. 19, Mar. 20, 1917,
Daniels MSS; *Intimate Papers*, II, pp. 227–8; *Life and Letters*, VI, p.
358; Joseph Tumulty, *Woodrow Wilson as I Know Him* (Garden City,
N.Y., 1921), pp. 233–5.

67. House MSS Diary, Nov. 14 and 17, 1916; Wilson to House, Jan.
24, 1917, Ray Stannard Baker MSS, LC; *Intimate Papers*, II, p. 390;
Arthur S. Link, *Woodrow Wilson and the Progressive Era* (New York,
1954), pp. 254–6; Buehrig, *Balance of Power*, p. 253.

of the Wilsonian vision of Western commercial and political unity by Germany's leaders.[68]

Wilson and House were both concerned with the consequences of a total Allied victory over the Central Powers. Should German power be crushed, it was possible that Tsarist imperialism would menace the West.[69] Then too, both the President and House were disturbed lest high-handed actions by the British navy and Allied plans for postwar economic competition indicate that British naval- and protectionist-oriented Toryism might overcome British liberalism and constitute a serious postwar threat to freedom of the seas and the international commercial Open Door.[70] Such apprehensions as to the possibilities latent in total Entente victory served to counterbalance the Wilsonian urge toward war with Germany over the use of submarines, and to reinforce the Wilson-House conviction that only a compromise peace without victory could provide the foundation necessary for international liberal stability.[71]

Because Wilson has such a strong urge to re-establish Western liberal-capitalist unity under American guidance, another ideological element was needed to justify fully war with Germany to the President. This element was supplied to the Administration by House and Lansing in the form of the theory that the World War was a conflict between aggressive German autocracy and defensive Allied democracy. This theory was capable of neutralizing Wilson's countertendencies to view the war, from the perspective of liberal American exceptionalism, as having emerged from a welter of universal "European" institutions

68. House to Wilson, Dec. 22, 1915, Dec. 27, 1916, Jan. 15, 1917, Wilson MSS, File 2; House MSS Diary, Dec. 27, 1916, Jan. 15, 1917; House to Wilson, Jan. 18, 1917, House to Lansing, Jan. 26, 1917, House MSS; *Intimate Papers,* I, p. 318.

69. House MSS Diary, Sept. 28, 1914; *Intimate Papers,* I, pp. 328, 388; *Life and Letters,* V, pp. 64–5; Christopher Lasch, *The American Liberals and the Russian Revolution* (New York, 1962), pp. 12–13.

70. Wilson to House, May 16, May 18, July 23, 1916, Wilson MSS; House MSS Diary, Jan. 14, May 13, June 23, Sept. 24, 1916; House to Wilson, Dec. 20, 1916, Wilson MSS, File 2; Martin, *Peace Without Victory,* pp. 111–12.

71. House MSS Diary, Sept. 3, 1916, Jan. 19, 1917; House to Wilson, Dec. 7, 1915, Wilson MSS, File 2; *Life and Letters,* VI, pp. 208–9; *Intimate Papers,* I, pp. 284–5; *PPWW,* IV, p. 410; Martin, *Peace Without Victory,* pp. 90–91, May, *American Isolation,* pp. 77–8; for a statement of Wilson's distrust of the war aims of all the major belligerents, see also Wilson to Bryan, Apr. 27, 1915, Wilson-Bryan Correspondence, National Archives.

such as alliances, secret diplomacy, and militarism. The autocracy vs. democracy concept also gave an ethical finality to the schism in Western unity which Wilson was hesitant to accept irrevocably until March 1917, when the resumption of German unrestricted submarine warfare led the President finally to believe that Imperial Germany could not be peacefully reintegrated into a liberal-capitalist international community. Wilson's eventual full acceptance of the autocracy vs. democracy concept also, as we shall see, widened the gulf between him and Lenin.

In Colonel House's wish-fulfillment fantasy, *Philip Dru: Administrator,* the American dictator Dru appeals to the British people over the head of their anti-American conservative government, thereby achieving its replacement by a liberal regime with whom Dru co-operates in creating an Anglo-American-sponsored program designed to uphold "the peace and commercial freedom of the world."[72] House himself, despite his desire to include Germany in a postwar commercial and political community of the powers, did place his greatest hopes for the future on what he conceived to be the enlightened liberalism of such British leaders as Sir Edward Grey, a man, according to the Colonel, of "unselfish outlook, broad vision and high character."[73] By the end of 1915, House had come to believe that Grey shared with Wilson the vision of the maintenance of postwar stability and international freedom of trade through a league of major Western powers.[74] This faith in the possibility of a future Anglo-American partnership in the maintenance of liberal world order was the basis of the moderately pro-Allied character of House's mediation efforts during 1915 and 1916. Given the commanding position of Germany on the war map in the early stages of the war, his concern for a liberal compromise peace would alone have been enough to bring the Colonel's sympathy to the beleaguered Allied cause in the interests of maintaining a balance of power as the basis for negotiation. When one adds the submarine issue and pronounced liberal Anglophilia to the formula, however, it is even easier to see why the Colonel's mediation efforts operated on the assumption that all peace proposals had to have prior Allied approval and should in no way interfere

72. House, *Philip Dru: Administrator,* pp. 272–4.

73. House MSS Diary, Feb. 14, 1916; see also *Intimate Papers,* I, pp. 364, 428.

74. House to Wilson, Nov. 10, 1915, Wilson MSS, File 2; *Intimate Papers,* I, pp. 363–5; *Intimate Papers,* II, pp. 54–5, 87–92.

with necessary Entente military activity.[75] House felt that, even if the Entente ought not to achieve total victory, it must not lose.

In a larger sense, moreover, the evidence suggests that, although House's over-all aim as a mediator was to bring about the peaceful reintegration of Germany into a liberal-capitalist world order, by early 1915 the Colonel had in reality grave doubts about the willingness of autocratic Germany to enter a Wilsonian international community. These doubts were much stronger than similar fears House had as to the future intentions of reactionary elements in the Entente. Indeed, there ran through the Colonel's correspondence and diary a stream of concern, broken by momentary periods of optimism as to German developments, to the effect that an aggressive Germany, dominated by the military, constituted a future threat to America, and that Germany would try to place a diplomatic wedge between the United States and the Allies in order to win an imperialist peace based on the German-dominated war map.[76] As he came to see the German autocracy as the principal threat to his and Wilson's vision of a liberal world order, House felt increasing solidarity with the Allies as the defenders of democratic values.[77] The Colonel wrote to Wilson early in 1916 that were Germany to win a victory "the war lords will reign supreme and democratic governments will be imperilled throughout the world."[78] Earlier, House had theorized that English power was not objectionably exercised due to the existence of British democracy,[79] and that only a democratic Germany could be a "satisfactory member of the society of nations."[80] By early 1916, through negotiating the House-Grey Memorandum, the Colonel succeeded in making explicit his conception that the United States should co-operate with the Allies, peacefully if possible but with force if necessary, in ending the war and creating a new international order

75. *Intimate Papers,* I, pp. 362–4, 372–5, 380–83; May, *American Isolation,* pp. 82–9.

76. House MSS Diary, Nov. 25, 1914, Nov. 9, 1915, Dec. 15, 1915, Jan. 31, 1917; House to Wilson, Feb. 15, 1915, Apr. 11, 1915, Dec. 22, 1915, Feb. 3, 1916, Mar. 22, 1916, Nov. 6, 1916, Nov. 30, 1916, Jan. 20, 1917, Wilson MSS, File 2; *Intimate Papers,* I, pp. 281–2, 298–300.

77. House MSS Diary, Apr. 22, 1915, Jan. 6, 1916, Feb. 11, 1916, Apr. 30, 1916; House to Walter H. Page, Aug. 4, 1915, House to Wilson, Jan. 11, 1916, Wilson MSS, File 2; *Intimate Papers,* I, pp. 469–70.

78. House to Wilson, Feb. 3, 1916, Wilson MSS, File 2.

79. House to Wilson, Sept. 6, 1914, Wilson MSS, File 2.

80. House MSS Diary, Oct. 15, 1915; see also House MSS Diary, Feb. 20, 1915; House to Wilson, Apr. 18, 1915, Wilson MSS, File 2.

on Wilsonian terms.[81] House's goal remained the same as it had been
on his first trip to Europe in early summer 1914, namely, to foster
a new and rational concert of liberal-capitalist powers. By 1916, however, the Colonel had well advanced the ideological process through
which, with the impetus of German submarine warfare, this goal
would no longer be sought by the diplomacy of mediation and would
become a Wilsonian war aim.

Secretary of State Lansing was far more committed than the somewhat ambivalent House to the theory that Imperial Germany could
not be an acceptable partner in a liberal world community. By the
summer of 1915, Lansing was convinced both that German submarine
warfare was symptomatic of a total threat to democracy posed by
German absolutism throughout the world, and that the United States
should be prepared to take part in the war, if necessary, to prevent
the Central Powers from either winning or breaking even.[82] During
1916 and early 1917, Lansing was worried by Wilson's and House's
efforts in the area of mediation, and was also concerned by the President's periodic efforts to prod the British on the question of neutral
rights. The Secretary felt that such policies might result at best in
a compromise peace with German imperialism, and at worst in an
irrevocable split between the United States and the Allies, leading
to a German victory.[83] Convinced that only democracies were fit partners for a peace league, Lansing opposed any plan to include the
Central Powers in a projected postwar concert of nations.[84] With
the German declaration of resumption of unrestricted submarine warfare in February 1917, Lansing pressed unrelentingly for war. Angered
by Wilson's hesitation to make the final decision to enter the conflict
that as President he had tried so long to end, Lansing repeatedly
emphasized the necessity for a liberal crusade to defeat German abso-

81. House MSS Diary, Feb. 7, 10, 11, 14, 1916; *Intimate Papers,* II,
pp. 85–6, 90–1; *Life and Letters,* VI, pp. 124–34, 147–54; May, *American
Isolation,* pp. 348–59.

82. Lansing, "Confidential Memoranda and Notes, July 11, 1915, Jan.
9, 1916," Lansing MSS; House MSS Diary, Oct. 13, 1915; Smith, *Robert
Lansing,* pp. 60–61; Buehrig, *Balance of Power,* pp. 131–7.

83. Lansing, "Confidential Memoranda and Notes, Sept. n.d., Dec. 3,
1916, Jan. 28, 1917," Lansing MSS; Lansing to Wilson, Dec. 10, 1916,
Wilson MSS, File 2; Smith, *Robert Lansing,* pp. 132–7, 146–7; Buehrig,
Balance of Power, pp. 138–41.

84. Lansing, "Confidential Memoranda and Notes, Dec. 3, 1916," Lansing MSS.

lutism and thereby lay the foundation for permanent peace in universal democracy.[85] Writing to a close friend in late February 1917, Lansing affirmed his view "that modern civilization is threatened by military Absolutism and that the only hope of a permanent peace lies in the triumph of the principle of Democracy."[86] We shall see that Lansing's militant commitment to liberalism proved important not only as a basis for an Administration opposition to German autocracy but because it later became a basis for the hostile Wilsonian response to the Bolshevik challenge to the values of liberal-capitalism.

It is not surprising, then, that neither House nor Lansing opposed the subtle but steady process through which Sir Edward Grey, while appearing to encourage Wilsonian mediation efforts, was in reality working to enlist American influence and power behind the achievement of Allied war aims. Of course, this British policy was in no sense predetermined to succeed. Had Germany's leaders been willing to give up their hopes for a total victory, to abandon submarine warfare and accept their defeat on the seas, and to use their military superiority on the land to sue openly for an honest compromise peace in late 1916, there is no doubt that they could have seriously undermined the Wilson Administration's ties with the Allies. This was true because whatever political, ideological, and economic ties were growing between the Wilson Administration and the embattled Allies in the 1914–16 period, there always remained, especially in the President's mind, an element of suspicion of Allied imperialism and a continued irritation with Britain's wartime naval and blockade policies. Moreover, until the Germans made their final decision to try for total victory through unlimited submarine warfare, Wilson remained more committed than House, and especially more committed than Lansing, to the vision of an American-inspired liberal world order to be built on the foundations of a true compromise peace without victory for either side.

Wilson himself proved far less prepared to accept completely the autocracy vs. democracy theory of the war than either of his two principal foreign policy advisers. It is true, of course, that at times Wilson seemed to reveal a latent moral commitment to the Allied cause; one evening in the fall of 1915 he confided to House that

85. Lansing, "Confidential Memoranda and Notes, Feb. 4, 1917," Lansing MSS; *FR, Lansing Papers,* I, pp. 591–2; Smith, *Robert Lansing,* pp. 157–8; Buehrig, *Balance of Power, pp.* 142–7.

86. Lansing to Edward N. Smith, Feb. 27, 1917, Lansing MSS.

"he had never been sure that we ought not to take part in the conflict and if it seemed evident that Germany and her militaristic ideas were to win, the obligation upon us was greater than ever."[87] Nonetheless, despite his latent tendency to make an identification between the cause of the Entente and the values of American missionary liberalism, the main thrust of Wilson's thought and action in the 1914–17 period was in the direction of critical and objective neutrality toward the war coupled with an effort to end the conflict by mediation and the re-establishment of international commercial and political stability. In this connection, Wilson looked upon the House-Grey negotiations of early 1916, which implied extremely close Anglo-American co-operation, as part of the mediation process and in no sense a commitment to go to war in alliance with the Entente.[88] In fact, Wilson's anger both with Allied reluctance to ask him to move for peace and with British infringements on American neutral rights was instrumental in his decision to act publicly for peace in December 1916 despite Allied objections.[89] In the end, it took not only the resumption of unrestricted German submarine warfare in February 1917 but also the liberal March Revolution in Russia to bring the President to accept the war on the terms of a conflict between autocracy and democracy.

The presence of the Tsarist regime among the Allies, in addition to British recalcitrance on neutral rights, had been of concern to Colonel House as he tended more and more to see in the Entente the nucleus for a liberal postwar world. The Colonel was convinced of the possibility that a separate peace could be arranged between Russian and German reactionaries, for, as he told Wilson, "there is no doubt that the Russian bureaucracy and the German militarists have some understanding and will work together so far as the Russian and German people will permit."[90] This fear of a relationship between

87. House MSS Diary, Sept. 22, 1915; see also *Intimate Papers,* I, p. 293; *Intimate Papers,* II, pp. 239–40, *Life and Letters,* V, pp. 214, n. 3, 375–6.

88. *Intimate Papers,* II, pp. 231–2; Martin, *Peace Without Victory,* pp. 98–102; May, *American Isolation,* pp. 351, 356.

89. *Intimate Papers,* II, pp. 390–402; May, *American Isolation,* pp. 358–70; Arthur S. Link, *Wilson: Campaigns for Progressivism and Peace, 1916–1917* (Princeton, 1965), pp. 165–289.

90. House to Wilson, Jan. 20, 1917, Wilson MSS, File 2; on House's fear of a Russian separate peace, see also House to Wilson, Jan. 11, Feb. 9, 1916, Wilson MSS, File 2; *Intimate Papers,* II, p. 129; Lasch, *American Liberals,* pp. 20–23.

German and Russian reaction was, of course, evidence that House saw the war as a potential liberal crusade even prior to American entry. The news of the March Revolution thrilled House, who had "been fearful lest bureaucratic Russia and autocratic Germany would link fortunes and make trouble for the democracies of the world";[91] and he urged Wilson, as the great liberal of modern times, to recognize the new Russian Government as soon as England and France did so.[92]

The significance of the March Revolution was also grasped by Lansing, who sought to convince Wilson that "the Russian Government founded on its hatred of absolutism and therefore of the German Government would be materially benefitted by feeling that this republic was arrayed against the same enemy of liberalism."[93] Actually, the reactions of House and Lansing were typical of those of many liberals in the United States and the Allied countries, who responded to the March Revolution by claiming that it had purified the Entente cause of the stigma of Tsarist reaction, and thereby removed the last barrier to seeing the war ideologically in terms of a contest between autocracy and democracy.[94] Wilson himself, in the Cabinet meeting of March 20, 1917, "spoke of the glorious act of the Russians, which in a way had changed conditions," but added the doubt that he could "give that as reason for war."[95] By April 2, when he asked Congress for a declaration of war, however, Wilson had clearly resolved the question of Russia in his mind and had adopted the House-Lansing view of the significance of the March Revolution both to the Allied cause and to America's war aims:

> Does not every American feel that assurance has been added to our hope for the future peace of the world by the wonderful and heartening things that have been happening within the last few weeks in Russia? Russia was known by those who knew it best to have been always in fact democratic at heart, in all the vital habits of her thought. . . . The autocracy that crowned the summit of her political structure, long as it had

91. House MSS Diary, Mar. 17, 1917.

92. House to Wilson, Mar. 17, 1917, House MSS.

93. *FR, Lansing Papers,* I, pp. 626–8; see also pp. 628–9; Lansing, "Confidential Memoranda and Notes, Mar. 20, 1917," Lansing MSS; George F. Kennan, *Soviet American Relations, 1917–1920, Russia Leaves the War* (Princeton, 1956), pp. 14–16.

94. Mayer, *Political Origins,* p. 70; Lasch, *American Liberals,* pp. 27–9.

95. Daniels MSS Diary, Mar. 20, 1917.

stood and terrible as was the reality of its power, was not in fact Russian in origin, character, or purpose; and now it has been shaken off and the great, generous Russian people have been added in all their naïve majesty and might to the forces that are fighting for freedom in the world, for justice, and for peace. Here is a fit partner for a League of Honor.[96]

For the next three years Wilson would seek to defend this vision of a liberal Russia against the threats posed both by German imperialism on the Right and by Bolshevism on the Left.

The ideological implications of the President's final conversion to the autocracy vs. democracy theory of the war also extended beyond the Russian question, however. We have seen that Wilson and House sought to end the split in the Western community of nations through mediation, and that the President took his mission as world reconstructor and peace-maker with great conviction. If, however, the Entente alliance could be transformed by the Russian Revolution and Wilsonian participation into the nucleus of a postwar liberal world system, then America could enter the war without doing violence to Wilson's overriding desire to create a liberal-capitalist community of Western powers. The unchanged goal of reintegrating Germany into a reunified West could eventually be accomplished in a postwar climate of universal democracy, despite the momentary unwillingness of Germany's existing rulers to accept a peaceful role in a liberal world order. Assuming that a Germany liberalized by war would be generously treated by a democratic Entente at the eventual peace conference, the President saw no necessary contradiction between his desire on the one hand for a liberal war against German imperialism and his hope on the other for a compromise peace to form the basis of a new commercial and political world harmony. Indeed, Wilson told Congress in his war message that "only free peoples can hold their purpose and their honour steady to a common end and prefer the interests of mankind to any narrower interest of their own."[97] Then too, once it was accepted that the war was caused by German militarism, rather than by general "European" imperialistic practices, as Wilson had originally held, it was possible for Wilsonians to handle their American exceptionalist distrust of possible Entente imperialism by emphasizing a belief in the peaceful proclivities of liberal states. What was basically needed,

96. *PPWW*, V, pp. 12–13.
97. Ibid.

according to Wilson, was the remaking of a peaceful liberal-capitalist Germany which could act with international restraint and responsibility. Until then, German imperialism had to be fought militarily.

In a larger sense, it could be said that the decision to bring the United States into the war solved the problem of finding a method of actualizing the President's world view by firmly wedding American military strength to Wilson's missionary liberal-internationalism. Actually, Colonel House had been urging this seemingly contradictory fusion of national power and international-liberalism on the President since 1914. On the one hand, the Colonel insisted that Wilson's voice could carry prestige abroad only if American dignity were maintained in Mexico and if the United States embarked on an impressive program of military and naval preparedness.[98] House was also convinced that American firmness in regard to German submarine warfare was essential to the retention of the respect of the Allies and their willingness to co-operate with the United States in building a postwar world.[99] On the other hand, the Colonel often declared that it was his and Wilson's purpose to eliminate militarism and navalism,[100] and that the President, in working for peace and a new world order, should seek to "rally the liberals of the world"[101] even possibly in opposition to conservative elements in the Entente.[102] It should be stressed, however, that House did not feel that he was inconsistent in trying to join nationalism with liberal anti-imperialism. As if to reassure Wilson on this point, the Colonel wrote in the spring of 1916 that "your desire to stop the war and your willingness to help maintain the peace of the world afterwards would not be inconsistent with a demand for a navy commensurate with these purposes."[103]

In reality, Wilson seemed as able as House to combine the exercise of national power with an appeal to international-liberalism. The Presi-

98. House MSS Diary, Mar. 17, 1916; House to Wilson, Mar. 15, 1915, Jan. 15, 1916, Jan. 16, 1916, Apr. 7, 1916, June 1, 1916, June 18, 1916, June 25, 1916, Wilson MSS, File 2.

99. House MSS Diary, Apr. 19, 1916; House to Wilson, May 11, 1915, May 14, 1915, Jan. 8, 1916, Apr. 19, 1916, Apr. 22, 1916, Wilson MSS, File 2; *Intimate Papers,* I, pp. 442–3.

100. House MSS Diary, Jan. 14, 1916; House to Wilson, May 1, 1915, Nov. 19, 1915, Jan. 11, 1916, Wilson MSS, File 2.

101. House to Wilson, Aug. 3, 1916, Wilson MSS, File 2.

102. House to Wilson, June 10, July 30, 1916, Wilson MSS, File 2; House MSS Diary, May 3, 1916; House to Frank L. Polk, July 28, 1916, Frank L. Polk MSS, Yale University Library.

103. House to Wilson, May 17, 1916, Wilson MSS, File 2.

dent's willingness to use American military force against Germany in defense of his conception of the freedom of the seas has already been discussed. In late 1916 Wilson responded to House's theory that friction with Great Britain was caused by commercial rivalry by suggesting, "let us build a navy bigger than hers, and do what we please."[104] At the same time, however, there is no doubt that Wilson conceived of himself as "speaking for liberals and friends of humanity in every nation" in a struggle for a new international system of peace, disarmament, and commercial freedom against entrenched reaction.[105]

Only a supreme faith in the universal righteousness of their conception of America's national interests could have enabled House and Wilson to conceive of themselves as operating simultaneously as the wielders of traditional forms of national power and as the leaders of world liberalism. The point was, as has been shown, that Wilson's vision of a liberal world order of free trade and international harmony was not opposed to but rather served to complement his conception of the national interests of American liberal-capitalism.[106] Wilsonian foreign policy in an era of war and revolution, then, can best be understood as a combination of liberal opposition to imperialism and of missionary nationalism, and this is the basic explanation of why, once the President accepted it, the concept of a war to make the world safe for democracy served to hold both the national and international elements of the Wilsonian world view in balance.

104. House MSS Diary, Sept. 24, 1916.

105. *PPWW*, IV, p. 413; see also Wilson to House, June 22, 1916, House MSS; Wilson to Thomas Dixon, Jan. 25, 1917, Wilson MSS, File 7; *Life and Letters*, VI, pp. 372, 388–9, 397.

106. For a recent sophisticated statement of the manner in which the work of Link, Buehrig, and E. May has broadened the concept of Wilson's motivations in the 1914–17 period to include a fusion of both national interest and international idealism, see Daniel M. Smith, "National Interest and American Intervention, 1917: An Historiographical Appraisal," *The Journal of American History*, LII (June 1965), 5–24.

DOMESTIC ROOTS OF FOREIGN POLICY ATTITUDES

CHARLES CHATFIELD

World War I and the Liberal Pacifist in the United States

Only in the last several years have historians begun to assess the impact of World War I on the development of basic American attitudes toward world politics. Earlier books such as Merle Curti's general history of pacifism, *Peace or War: The American Struggle, 1636–1936* (New York, 1936), Ray H. Abrams's study of fire-eating militarist clergymen, *Preachers Present Arms* (Philadelphia, 1933), and Ruhl J. Bartlett's work on the main internationalist organization, *The League to Enforce Peace* (Chapel Hill, 1944) suggested some of the ways in which the war had engaged different groups. Similarly, H. C. Peterson's study, posthumously completed by Gilbert Fite, *Opponents of War, 1917–1918* (Madison, Wisc., 1957), exposed some of the motives that led various segments of society to resist intervention. But not until recently have historians probed the interaction and change of attitudes toward both domestic and foreign affairs under the impress of World War I.

Among the most important contributions in this area of interest have been Charles Chatfield's studies of pacifism. This article, which analyzes the changes wrought in American pacifism by the war, has been followed and amplified by Chatfield's book *For Peace and Justice: Pacifism in America, 1914–1941* (Knoxville, Tenn., 1971). For a new look at the advocates of international conciliation, see Sondra Herman, *Eleven Against War: Studies in American Internationalist Thought, 1898–1921* (Stan-

Reprinted by permission from the *American Historical Review*, LXXV (December, 1970), 1920–1937.

ford, 1969). My book, *The Vanity of Power: American Isolationism and the First World War, 1914–1917* (Westport, Conn., 1969), treats another aspect of developing attitudes toward world affairs.

The meaning of the word pacifist changed under the pressure for patriotic conformity in 1917–18. Having had the benign connotation of one who advocated international cooperation for peace, it narrowed to mean one who would not support even a "war to end war." Pacifists were linked with draft dodgers, socialists, and communists, portrayed in hues from yellow to red; a rude inscription in the lobby of 70 Fifth Avenue in New York, where some pacifist groups were housed, read, "Treason's Twilight Zone."[1] The word was thenceforth plagued with double meaning, and more than one prowar peace advocate hastened to explain that "those who are now called 'pacifists' here do not include all or most of those who were called 'pacifists' before the war."[2] Later, when it was respectable to be against the war, the word sometimes was used in its original, broader sense, but it would be used by pacifists themselves, as it is used here, to designate those who worked for peace and refused to sanction any given war—absolute and religious but also selective and political objectors.[3] The narrowness of this definition masked a new dimension in the American peace movement.

There had been pacifists in the strict sense before World War I, but for the most part they had been sectarians motivated by obedience to religious injunctions against killing and against complying with the military. Their churches supplied most of the conscientious objec-

1. This graffito is mentioned in "Memoir of Frances Witherspoon and Tracy Mygatt," p. 8, Oral History Collection, Columbia University. Both women were active in the peace movement and especially the civil liberties groups in New York during World War I.
2. Julia Grace Wales to Clark F. Hunn, Nov. 28, 1917, Wales Papers, Wisconsin Historical Society, Madison, Wisconsin (italics in the original are omitted). Julia Wales was an instructor in English at the University of Wisconsin and the author of a plan for continuous mediation by an international commission of citizen experts.
3. Pacifism is sometimes defined still more narrowly as the position of only those who are opposed to all war. This is the basis for legal recognition of conscientious objection in the United States, and there is considerable merit in its usage. Philosophically and politically speaking, this is a tidy definition, but it is not historically useful since the impact and significance of pacifism varied with its changing constituency and since pacifists of all persuasions responded to the same historical events.

tors in the Civil War and both world wars, but these were nonresistants obedient to the claims of religious faith and not challenging governmental authority or social policy except in the specific cases of their military service.[4]

If sectarians had eschewed social reform, few progressives had stressed the war question, and even fewer seriously considered conscientious objection to war service. Indeed, the prewar advocates of peace hardly sensed the possibility of divided loyalties. They assumed that war was anachronistic. Reason, embodied in arbitration and law, in treaties and international juridical institutions such as the Hague Court, would obviate recourse to war. In this respect peace advocates were internationalists, and so they liked to think of themselves. But with few exceptions they were solid nationalists as well, for they assumed that America's virtues were unique and her interests paramount. If the nation ever should go to war, they believed, its democratic politics and humanitarian traditions would guarantee its cause to be just and necessary.

These peace advocates either were directors of business and educational institutions or accepted such men as models. They gave their movement a literary, patriarchal, and elitist quality, and relied on education and discussion rather than political action. They operated the Carnegie Endowment for International Peace (founded in 1910), the World Peace Foundation (1910), the Church Peace Union (1914), the American School Peace League (1908), the American Peace Society (1828), and various other groups organized to promote study, friendship, and arbitration. They were established men who valued order and distrusted radical challenge to authority, successful men who assumed that progress was inevitable and who aimed at the further perfection of society.[5]

4. The peace churches are traditionally designated as the Quaker, Mennonite, and Brethren, but others important for pacifism include the Disciples of Christ and Jehovah's Witnesses. The definitive study of religious pacifism is Peter Brock, *Pacifism in the United States: From the Colonial Era to the First World War* (Princeton, 1968). See also Roland Bainton, *Christian Attitudes Toward War and Peace: A Historical Survey and Critical Re-evaluation* (Nashville, 1960), and, regarding the Quakers, Elbert Russell, *The History of Quakerism* (New York, 1942), Rufus M. Jones, *The Later Periods of Quakerism* (London, 1921) and *A Service of Love in War Time: American Friends Relief Work in Europe, 1917–1919* (New York, 1920), and Lester Jones, *Quakers in Action* (New York, 1929).

5. The prewar peace movement is studied thoroughly in David S. Patterson, "The Travail of the American Peace Movement, 1887–1914" (Ph.D.

Sarajevo shattered the doctrine of perfection, at least as it applied to Europe. The established peace movement faltered and fell into disarray; by April 1917 most of its leaders had joined the war effort, determined to establish a universal peace along American lines. Accustomed to look for evil on the surface, not in the heart of man, they identified it with one nation—Germany. Peace was held at bay by Prussianism, they said; victory became the prerequisite of progress.[6]

Those who rejected this view and advanced alternatives to it were the wartime pacifists. They reorganized the American peace movement, giving it much of the structure, leadership, social concern, and rationale that would characterize it for over a generation. Where it had been educational and legalistic, the peace movement became political as well; where it had been polite it also became aggressive; where it had been conservatively Brahmin, it also acquired a socialist base; where it had assumed progress, it would claim only possibility. The movement remained divided—perpetually, it seems—between competing points of view and programs, but the wartime pacifists gave it vital leadership and broad social concern.

They brought to it an unresolved dilemma, too, for their experience imparted both a more radical view of society and an ethic of conflict that proscribed the use of violence for social change. No less committed to liberal values than were the intellectuals who stoutly defended the war, pacifists interpreted it differently. No less fervent in their opinions than the patriots, they were virtually isolated from public opinion. When they were subjected to social pressure to conform,

---

dissertation, University of California, Berkeley, 1968), and interpreted in Charles R. Marchand, "The Ultimate Reform: World Peace in American Thought During the Progressive Era" (Ph.D. dissertation, Stanford University, 1964). Varying strands of the movement's rationale are developed in Sondra R. Herman, *Eleven Against War: Studies in American Internationalist Thought, 1898–1921* (Stanford, 1969). The older and established histories of this movement are, of course, Merle Curti, *Peace or War; the American Struggle 1636–1936* (New York, 1936), and Devere Allen, *The Fight for Peace* (New York, 1930).

6. This argument is oversimplified in comparison with its most restrained and balanced presentation (Harry Emerson Fosdick, *The Challenge of the Present Crisis* [New York, 1917]), but it is underplayed in comparison with many contemporary slogans—even those of religious and peace organizations. See Ray H. Abrams, *Preachers Present Arms* (Philadelphia, 1933), and Horace C. Peterson and Gilbert Fite, *Opponents of War, 1917–1918* (Madison, 1957).

pacifists came to distrust authoritarianism itself and to connect it in their minds with violence. That is one reason why their leftward movement stopped short of revolutionary socialism. Associating injustice with war, they hobbled the drive for social justice with a commitment to peace.

Liberal pacifists were the remnant of a peace coalition composed largely of progressives who viewed the war as a threat to the values for which they had worked. War must not come to America, they agreed; and, moreover, its very existence in Europe challenged that notion of an open-ended world of social possibility in which these problem-solvers believed. This war was no abstraction. It was a compelling problem, they insisted, and its solution required concerted social action. This was the response of Louis Lochner who, with the help of George Nasmyth and the American Peace Society, had organized the Cosmopolitan Club movement in American universities, the man who before 1914 had personified internationalism to thousands of college students. After the outbreak of war he left the American Peace Society, tried to refashion the Chicago Peace Society, and together with Jane Addams and others launched a National Peace Federation.[7] It was one of several new organizations federating liberal and peace forces that emerged from such centers of social reform as the Henry Street settlement house founded in New York by Lillian Wald. There social workers, clergymen, educators, and publicists who were conscious of a bond of social concern they had formed in response to industrialism and urbanism met in response to war.[8]

When the Woman's Peace Party was founded in Washington on January 10, 1915, it was clear that advocacy of peace "provided a common ground upon which could meet American women from

7. Other organizations in which Lochner played a leading role included the Ford Peace Expedition (November-December 1915), the First American Conference for Democracy and the Terms of Peace (May 30-31, 1917), and the People's Council of America (May 30-31, 1917). He was also active in other peace movements of the period.
8. Groups whose primary impetus came from New York included the American Union Against Militarism (April 1916), the American Neutral Conference Committee (July 1916), the Emergency Peace Federation (February 1917), the People's Council, and the National Civil Liberties Bureau (a separate organization as of October 1, 1917). The Woman's Peace Party (established January 10, 1915) and the Fellowship of Reconciliation (November 11, 1915), although New York oriented, did not stem primarily from the Henry Street group but included many of its members.

almost every important section of their organizational life."[9] The
women quickly joined hands with their counterparts in Europe; together they developed a plan for a conference of neutral nations
that would stand ready to clarify the war aims of belligerents and
to negotiate peace. They sent emissaries to the belligerent leaders
and tried to induce President Wilson to adopt their program. He
seemed unresponsive, and so their diplomacy evolved into a commission of private citizens to which Henry Ford gave funds and publicity.
Ridicule of Ford's Peace Expedition obscured the serious purpose
of a significant nongovernmental international organization. Still, the
women who promoted it had forged organizational links with civic
and professional groups, connections that would survive the war. They
brought new leadership into the peace movement and created a modern
pressure group of a kind familiar to progressive reformers.

Meanwhile, some Quakers, social gospel clergymen, and YMCA
leaders responded to the organization of religious pacifists in England
when, on November 11, 1915, they created the Fellowship of Reconciliation (FOR), which became the central body for religious objectors
for the next half century.[10] Moreover, liberal journals such as the
Survey, the Independent, and the Nation opened their pages to proposals for a neutral conference for peace in Europe and to arguments
against preparations for war at home. Indeed, by the time the Ford

9. Marie Louise Degen, The History of the Woman's Peace Party (Balti-
more, 1939), 40. For the history of the successor to the WPP, see Gertrude
Bussey and Margaret Tims, Women's International League for Peace and
Freedom: 1915–1965 (London, 1965). The story is told through biography
in James Weber Linn, Jane Addams, a Biography (New York, 1937),
John C. Farrell, Beloved Lady: A History of Jane Addams' Ideas on
Reform and Peace (Baltimore, 1967), Mercedes M. Randall, Improper
Bostonian: Emily Greene Balch (New York, 1964), Jane Addams, Peace
and Bread in Time of War (New York, 1945) and Second Twenty Years
(New York, 1930), and Louis Lochner, Henry Ford—America's Don
Quixote (New York, 1925). Regarding the role of Julia Wales, see Walter
Trattner, "Julia Grace Wales and the Wisconsin Plan for Peace," Wisconsin
Magazine of History, XLIV (1961), 203–61.

10. Membership in the FOR involved signing a declaration of principles.
Consequently its membership rolls are the best index of pacifist intention
for peace advocates, and its minutes and publications are the best sources
on the rationale of religious pacifism. They are collected in the Swarthmore
College Peace Collection (hereafter SCPC), but since much from the
was period is missing, they must be supplemented with the papers of
Gilbert Beaver, Norman Thomas (New York Public Library, hereafter
NYPL), John Nevin Sayre (personal possession, Nyack, N.Y.), and others.

project became a laughingstock, peace workers from Henry Street were bringing the progressive peace coalition to its culmination in the American Union Against Militarism.[11] Historically important for its large-scale antipreparedness campaign of April and May 1916 and for its role in preventing a full-scale war with Mexico in June, the American Union became a model for postwar peace lobbies, and from its ranks emerged both the Foreign Policy Association and the National Civil Liberties Bureau. Its leaders included many of those active in domestic reform and Progressive politics who feared that militant nationalism would sap social progress and frustrate open diplomacy and world federation. Throughout 1916 they supported Wilson with alternating reluctance and enthusiasm as he seemed to act against or speak for their principles.

In 1917 three events shook the progressive peace coalition and reduced it to pacifism. First, when Wilson severed relations with Germany in February, the American Union lost one of its most ardent members, the influential rabbi of New York's Free Synagog, Stephen Wise. Antiwar leaders who had valued his example included Paul Kellogg, editor of the *Survey,* and Emily Balch, founder of the Denison House settlement in Boston and active in the Woman's Peace Party. They were stunned, but nonetheless participated heartily in a new Emergency Peace Federation to keep America out of war. Throughout the spring pacifists enlisted much popular support, but when in April the United States entered the war, prominent peace leaders, including David Starr Jordan, the chancellor of Stanford University, left their ranks.[12] Even so, they were encouraged by the

11. The Anti-Preparedness Committee, established in November 1915, became the American Union Against Militarism (AUAM) on April 3-4, 1916. Only the name changed in the context of a determined antipreparedness drive from April 6 to May 6; the leadership and rationale of the organization remained the same. The best published account of the AUAM is in Donald Johnson, *The Challenge to American Freedom: World War I and the Rise of the American Civil Liberties Union* (Lexington, 1963), but see also Robert L. Duffus, *Lillian Wald: Neighbor and Crusader* (New York, 1938), John Haynes Holmes, *I Speak for Myself* (New York, 1959), Rabbi Stephen S. Wise, *Challenging Years* (New York, 1949), Michael Wreszin, *Oswald Garrison Villard: Pacifist at War* (Bloomington, 1965), and David Starr Jordan, *Days of a Man* (New York, 1922), II, 690–707, 712–36.

12. *Ibid.,* 734–36. Regarding Wise's change of view see Carl Herman Voss, *Rabbi and Minister: The Friendship of Stephen S. Wise and John Haynes Holmes* (New York, 1964), 141–43.

The Emergency Peace Federation was formed out of the American

fact that six senators and fifty representatives voted against the war resolution and by the opposition voiced by the Socialist party after the resolution passed. There was still some basis for hoping that they might influence public policy, and so pacifists created the People's Council of America for Peace and Democracy in order to advance civil liberties and democratic peace terms during the war. By September 1917, however, the Council had aroused so much public opposition by criticizing conscription and defending the Russian Revolution that it did not seem useful to Lillian Wald, Paul Kellogg, and some others who had initiated the new peace coalition.

The American Union Against Militarism was divided during the summer by the efforts of some of its leaders to commit it to the cause of conscientious objectors. Three pacifists were particularly active: Roger Baldwin, who came to the staff from a position as secretary of the Civic League of St. Louis and who shortly organized the Civil Liberties Bureau; Norman Thomas, who was a socially concerned Presbyterian minister and who later joined the Socialist party because of his pacifist beliefs; and vivacious Crystal Eastman, an expert on the legal aspects of industrial accidents who was active in the women's suffrage campaign and the New York branch of the Woman's Peace Party and who with her brother Max later edited the antiwar *Liberator*. The membership of the American Union was at no time entirely pacifist in the strict sense, and these driving leaders threatened to undercut its constituent base and respectability.

On August 20, in the absence of Miss Wald, the executive board of the American Union voted to send delegates to the People's Constituent Assembly of the People's Council of America. She eventually resigned from the board; others followed, and the Union was shattered. It continued to exist in nominal fashion, but the National Civil Liberties Bureau separated itself on October 1, 1917, and thereafter the American Union Against Militarism operated largely on paper only.[13] During the war liberal pacifists affiliated with several other groups that have lasted over half a century: the Civil Liberties Bureau, the

---

Committee for a Neutral Conference, but its leadership overlapped with the AUAM. Lillian Wald and Paul Kellogg helped to found a "Committee on Nothing at All" in April 1918, which had the nucleus of the original AUAM and which evolved into the Foreign Policy Association. See Lillian Wald, *Windows on Henry Street* (Boston, 1934), 311.

13. Minutes of Aug. 30, Sept. 13, and Oct. 1, 1917, and *passim,* AUAM Papers, SCPC.

Fellowship of Reconciliation, the Woman's Peace Party and its successor, the Women's International League for Peace and Freedom, and the American Friends Service Committee (founded in 1917 to provide humanitarian alternatives to fighting).

In their opposition to the war the remnant of the progressive peace coalition was linked with literary radicals (including most of the staff of *The Masses*) and with those Socialists who supported the antiwar resolution that their party made in St. Louis on April 7, 1917. The party convention had been largely middle class in composition, and although its majority report was cast in the language of anticapitalism, it advocated a platform like those of the peace groups rather than a program of revolution or general strike.

These opponents of war were joined by new recruits who in the long run were most important of all, since they virtually staffed the pacifist movement after peace was re-established. They included, among others: A. J. Muste, a Presbyterian minister who subsequently became a leader in the labor and Trotskyite movements, chairman of the Fellowship of Reconciliation, and the symbol of radical pacifism to a cold-war generation; John Nevin Sayre, an Episcopal minister who was never far from the center of the International Fellowship of Reconciliation or its American branch; Evan Thomas, an outstanding conscientious objector of World War I and chairman of the War Resisters League during the Second World War; Kirby Page, a YMCA worker who became the most influential pacifist speaker and writer of the interwar period; Ray Newton, active in Quaker relief work, who later directed the Peace Section of the American Friends Service Committee; Frederick Libby, Florence Boeckel, and Dorothy Detzer, who operated an influential peace lobby in Washington during the thirties; Devere Allen, a student at Oberlin College who became the chief advocate of war resistance in the Socialist party; and the subsequent leader of that party, Norman Thomas.

Few of those converted to pacifism during the war had been active in peace groups before 1917, and they thought through the war question by themselves. They had not been active in domestic reforms, but they were, indeed, just discovering social problems—some through college experiences, some through church work, and others in the fresh idealism of the YMCA, then promoting international concern through the Student Volunteer Movement. In short, the young pacifists encountered World War I when they were coming of age socially, just as progressives of a previous generation had awakened to contemporary problems when they were choosing personal directions. It is hardly surprising that many of those whose pacifism commenced in the war years made peace work a vocation.

There were liberal pacifists of various hues, then, and their language and experiences differed significantly. The very corollary of conscience is, in the apt phrase of Rufus Jones, "a final farewell to uniformity," so that any analysis of the movement is hazardous.[14] Moreover, pacifists' ideas appear more coherent in retrospect than they did when first published, because ideas that we now analyze in terms of common postulates were first advanced polemically by persons whose lives were strikingly dissimilar. This is not to suggest that pacifists acted altogether rationally. Rather, they were drawn together in action through their similar interpretations of their various experiences. If the history of ideas is the story of men's reflections upon their experiences, then it is the study of what meaning they assigned to life; and meaning, if not life, has logical form. What pacifists had in common that set them apart from war supporters was neither a covert conspiracy nor any discernible personality or set of social characteristics. They shared, instead, a distinctive view of the war and a disposition to elevate that view into a matter of principle.

To begin with, pacifists accepted such liberal values of progressivism as the pragmatic approach to choices, the democratic process, and the ultimate worth of the individual. These were hardly more than loosely defined notions, but they implied at least the following: that decisions should be made in the light of consequences rather than of a priori rules and that the meaning of social institutions is found by experiencing them; that political power should be distributed in a society in which economic power is highly concentrated and that decision making should be broadly based; and that individuals are the ends for whom society is ordered. Sentiments like these can be found in a wide variety of objections to the war, even among the disparate arguments of socialists.

The leaders of the Fellowship of Reconciliation put their notion of human value in religious terms, agreeing with Norman Thomas that war is "absolutely opposed to Christ's way of love and His reverence for personality."[15] Although they did not define personality, they

14. Jones, *A Service of Love,* 105.
15. Thomas, "Some Objections Considered," in *The Conquest of War: Some Studies in a Search for a Christian World Order,* ed. Norman Thomas (New York, 1917).

often referred to it in the sense of a man's total being and latent possibility. They rejected the notion of prowar clergymen that combat or even death could leave men undefiled, could even ennoble them. War immolates personalities, they said. In the oldest tradition of their faith, religious pacifists revolted "not only against the cruelty and barbarity of war, but even more against the reversal of human relationships which war implied."[16] The doctrines of love, fatherhood, and brotherhood and such symbols as the cross expressed the normative value of personality for pacifists. Their rhetoric would sound formal to a later generation, but to them it expressed a long-neglected doctrine of Christian faith, the fundamental worth of each individual in the sight of God.

If human personality was sacred to religious pacifists, it had nearly absolute value for some who stood on secular grounds as well. Roger Baldwin, the director of the National Civil Liberties Bureau, spoke for them. On trial for refusing to take the physical examination required in the draft, he said, "The compelling motive for refusing to comply with the Draft Act is my uncompromising opposition to the principle of conscription of life by the state for any purpose whatever, in time of war or peace."[17] At the same time, he felt an intense social concern. As Norman Thomas explained shortly after the war, the individual is a "product of the group, but the group is only valuable as it permits personalities, not automatons to emerge."[18] Liberal pacifists, unlike Spencerian individualists, supported social reform, but, unlike those whose individualism derived from concepts of natural law, they believed that every man is of intrinsic value. Some of them reconciled individualism and socialism, for example, by assuming that man is essentially a social animal and that an individual's personality is most fully realized in altruistic impulses.

16. Jane Addams, *Peace and Bread*, 4. See also W. Fearon Halliday, *Personality and War* (New York, 1916).

17. "Statement in Court," Oct. 30, 1918, enclosed in a letter from Norman Thomas to Henry W. L. Dana, Oct. 31, 1918, Dana Papers, SCPC. It was subsequently printed as *The Individual and the State: the Problem as Presented by the Sentencing of Roger N. Baldwin* (New York, 1918). For other examples of this position see Ernest L. Meyer, *"HEY! YELLOWBACK!": The War Diary of a Conscientious Objector* (New York, 1930), and the discussion of nonreligious objection in Clarence M. Case, *Non-Violent Coercion: A Study in Methods of Social Pressure* (New York, 1923), 251–64.

18. Thomas, *The Conscientious Objector in America* (New York, 1923), 29.

The sense of the individual was muted for most socialists by awareness of class, but even so they argued that the organized proletariat itself was "proclaiming the glad tidings of the coming emancipation," freedom from the tyranny of class over men.[19] Socialists were most strongly united against military conscription. A few supported it, to be sure. William English Walling accused his opponents of accepting conscription by foreign governments that they favored while "leaving America helpless."[20] On the contrary, most socialists who opposed conscription believed that "it robs the individual of freedom" and is "the readiest tool of the military class."[21] As Emily Balch wrote, "It means conscription of mind, hierarchical stratification of society, industrial discipline on [a] military model, obedience as the prime virtue."[22] Even those socialists who could support a war to save the country from militarism could not conceive of "militarism to save us from war."[23] The commitment to individual worth and freedom permeated the publications of pacifists of all political views. For many this commitment was in itself sufficient reason to refuse military service; for all it guaranteed the right of conscientious objection.

Objection to military service was interpreted as the right to dissent by many pacifists who regarded that right as a corollary to the democratic process of majority decision. Like abolitionists before them, the pacifists won support on civil liberties that they could not get on the war issue.

19. *Voices of Revolt: Speeches of Eugene V. Debs,* introd. Alexander Trachtenberg (New York, 1928), 74.

20. "Socialists and the Problems of War: A Symposium," *Intercollegiate Socialist,* V (1917), 26. Socialist views on the war are interpreted in their diversity in James Weinstein, *The Decline of Socialism in America, 1912–1925* (New York, 1967), but see also Peterson and Fite, *Opponents of War,* and Morris Hillquit, *Loose Leaves from a Busy Life* (New York, 1934). The best sources for the period are pamphlet literature, notably *The American Socialists and the War,* ed. Alexander Trachtenberg (New York, 1917), and periodicals such as *The Masses, New Review,* and *Intercollegiate Socialist.* The latter is particularly useful as it printed reasoned arguments representative of both sides as a matter of editorial policy (see statement of May 7, 1917, Intercollegiate Socialist Society Papers, Tamiment Institute, New York). The Socialist Party Collection of manuscript sources at Duke University is not strong for this period.

21. William E. Bohn and Randolph Bourne in "Socialists and the Problems of War," *Intercollegiate Socialist,* V (1917), 10.

22. *Ibid.,* 9.

23. Joseph D. Cannon, *ibid.,* 12. Cannon wrote that he could conceive of a legitimate war of national defense.

The American Union Against Militarism had come into being largely in the vague apprehension that preparedness, conscription, and war would undermine the gains of the Progressive era.[24] Its programs and techniques expressed the progressive faith in the power of public opinion and in government responsible to the people. Woodrow Wilson expressed the same political faith even as he pressed for policies that distressed the pacifists. Even in February 1917 most members of the American Union's executive board preferred to leave foreign policy in Wilson's hands. Increasing numbers of pacifists became apprehensive as the administration geared up for war, although Crystal Eastman wrote in June of the president's wartime appointments:

> It [is] as though he said to his old friends, the liberals, "I know you are disappointed in me—you don't understand my conversion to the draft—my demand for censorship. I have reasons, plans, intentions, that I can't tell you. But as guarantee of good faith I give you Baker and Keppel and Lippman and Creel, to carry out these laws. No matter how they look on paper, they cannot be Prussian in effect with such men to administer them."[25]

The guarantee was not sufficient. The National Civil Liberties Bureau and related organizations expanded their work rapidly, insisting that the civil rights of conscientious objectors to the war were linked to the democratic process itself; majority decision that rested on the suppression of minorities would be a thinly veiled tyranny. This was exactly the premise of those who wanted to keep the Bureau within

24. The theme of war as a threat to progressive gains pervades anti-preparedness literature. Typical are the following: "Around the Circle Against Militarism," *Survey*, XXXVI (1916), 95; John Haynes Holmes, "War and the Social Movement," *ibid.*, XXXII (1914), 629–30; and Oswald G. Villard, "Shall We Arm for Peace?" *ibid.*, XXXV (1915), 299.

25. Crystal Eastman to members of the executive committee, June 14, 1917, AUAM Papers, SCPC. Newton D. Baker, mayor of Cleveland (1912–16), was appointed secretary of war on March 7, 1916; Frederick Keppel, dean of the College of Columbia University, became third assistant secretary of war; Walter Lippmann, liberal commentator for the *New Republic*, was assistant to the secretary of war, June to October 1917; and progressive newspaper editor George Creel became chairman of the Committee on Public Information on April 14, 1917.

the American Union in the fall of 1917. As Norman Thomas said, no other national group was prepared to fight for the "tolerance of minority ideas" that "is absolutely necessary for reasonable social progress."[26] Blatant persecution of dissenters aroused in Eugene Debs the fighting qualities that had been depressed by his sensitivity to the tragedy and anguish of war. His devotion to the workers' cause had never lagged, but his anger was rekindled by the flagrant denial of "the constitutional right of free speech in a country fighting to make democracy safe in the world."[27] He had never ceased to condemn the war, but he stepped onto the platform again on behalf of socialists' freedom. So persistent was the value of democracy in his mind that in 1920 he denied that the Bolsheviks had really intended a dictatorship, even of the proletariat. For Debs "freedom and equal rights" were inseparable.[28]

Similarly, pacifists in the People's Council of America who supported the Russian Revolution during the war regarded it as a vindication of the democratic process and not of the Bolshevik party or even, on the whole, of Marxist economics. As Max Eastman wrote, "what makes us rub our eyes at Russia . . . is the way *our own theories* are proving true."[29] These pacifists supported the revolution, too, because its peace planks accorded with their own demand for a "new diplomacy" embodying democratic principles such as freedom of press, petition, and speech, a progressive tax on war profits, and a "referendum on questions of war and peace."[30]

However impractical a referendum on war might appear to be (it proved no more plausible in 1917 than it would twenty years later as the Ludlow Amendment), most liberal pacifists were responsive to the pervasive currents of pragmatism. Norman Thomas heeded them at Union Seminary, Randolph Bourne at Columbia, Kirby Page at Drake and Chicago; but, in fact, pragmatism was construed to support opposing positions on the war. John Dewey and liberals

26. Edward Evans to Crystal Eastman, Sept. 28, 1917, and Norman Thomas to Crystal Eastman, Sept. 27, 1917, AUAM Papers, SCPC.

27. Quoted in Ray Ginger, *The Bending Cross: A Biography of Eugene Victor Debs* (New Brunswick, 1949), 356.

28. *Speeches of Eugene V. Debs*, 55–56.

29. Eastman, *Love and Revolution: My Journey Through an Epoch* (New York, 1964), 45.

30. "Resolutions of the First American Conference for Democracy and Terms of Peace," May 30-31, New York City, Organizing Committee, People's Council of America Papers, SCPC.

aligned with the *New Republic* (like some prowar socialists) argued that since war prevailed, the intelligent thing to do was to participate so as to be present at that "plastic juncture" when history is being made—the peace settlement.[31]

Randolph Bourne called this a rationalization of intellectual default. By the time of his death in 1918 Bourne's ideas were as familiar to liberal pacifists as was the sight of his hunched back and tortured features. He distrusted religious moralism less only than complacent liberalism, but he came to conclusions similar to those of Christian pacifists, breaking with many of the assumptions and friendships of his past in order to do so. He tried to reach back beyond Dewey's instrumentalism—now a lever for preserving the old order, he thought—to the spirit of William James.

In a world "where irony is dead" he scored prowar intellectuals for their credulity. He was offended as much by the quality of their thought as by their conclusions. "The ex-humanitarian, turned realist, sneers at the snobbish neutrality, colossal conceit, crooked thinking, dazed sensibilities, of those who are still unable to find any balm of consolation for this war," he observed bitterly. The so-called pragmatists had idealized the instruments of policy, he wrote; they had forgotten that "the real enemy is War rather than imperial Germany."[32] Did the realists think that they could control events by joining forces already in motion? Perhaps. But a more consistent pragmatism would be less sanguine: ". . . if it is a question of controlling war, it is difficult to see how the child on the back of a mad elephant is to be any more effective in stopping the beast than is the child who tries to stop him from the ground."[33] The tendency to judge things in terms of results typified all liberals. Bourne was atypical only because he was pessimistic about the consequences of national war.

A number of those who would become professional pacifists between the wars had been impressed in college by the developing field of sociology and the prospect of "discovering concrete ways of getting

31. Regarding the *New Republic* group see Charles Forcey, *Crossroads of Liberalism* (New York, 1961), chaps. 7 and 8, and Christopher Lasch, *The New Radicalism in America, 1889–1963: The Intellectual as a Social Type* (New York, 1965), chap. 6.

32. Randolph S. Bourne, "War and the Intellectuals," in *War and the Intellectuals: Essays by Randolph S. Bourne, 1915–1919*, ed. Carl Resek (New York, 1964), 10. A fuller range of Bourne's thought is suggested in Lillian Schlissel, *The World of Randolph Bourne* (New York, 1965).

33. Bourne, *War and the Intellectuals*, 12.

ideals incarnated in actual institutions."[34] Their disposition to value pragmatic criteria in decision making set them apart from sectarian nonresistants of the past. Kirby Page, working out his position while helping German prisoners of war through the English YMCA, argued that war had to be judged by what it does:

> War is not an ideal, it has an ideal; war is not a spirit, it is waged in a certain spirit; war is not a result, it produces results. War is always and everywhere a *method,* and it is as a method that it must be discussed.[35]

He concluded that it was unchristian, and so his judgment was perhaps not political, but his approach laid the foundation for empirical analysis of international affairs in the postwar years, if not for selective objection to military service. His friend Evan Thomas—Norman's brother—wrote that "on purely sociological grounds I would oppose the war."[36]

These values—pragmatism, democracy, and the sanctity of individual life—were shared in some degree by all liberals and many socialists. Pacifists universalized them. They applied them even to national policy, even in wartime. They made them "axioms of emotional nature" that lent special force to their distinctive view of the politics of the war.

Liberal pacifists concluded that World War I was a product of the European state system and that American national interests were best served by staying out. They identified the causes of the war in European rivalries, in long-standing "misunderstanding, suspicion, fear, diplomatic and commercial struggle to which all nations contributed."[37] All elements of later revisionist writing on the war question

34. *Ibid.,* 10.
35. Kirby Page to Howard E. Sweet, Feb. 3, 1918, and especially the manuscript, "The Sword or the Cross," Page Papers, Southern California School of Theology, Claremont.
36. Evan to Norman Thomas, Nov. 5, 1916, Norman Thomas Papers, NYPL. This sentiment was an integral part of Evan Thomas' agonizing re-evaluation of religion.
37. John Haynes Holmes, *The International Mind* (New York, 1916), 7, but see his full argument in *New Wars for Old* (New York, 1916) and wartime pamphlets, as well as in other pacifist literature, including especially the FOR journal, *The World Tomorrow,* edited by Norman Thomas.

can be found in the antiwar literature of 1917–18. Pacifists and antiwar socialists alike stressed the role of commercial competition, imperialism, secret treaties, and war profits in producing international conflict.

Socialists found in the economic origins of the war clues to its class basis. The workers were as expendable in wartime as they had been in peace, and for the same selfish ends, it was said: "Wars bring wealth and power to the ruling classes, and suffering, death, and demoralization to the workers."[38] At the very least, fighting abroad would "neutralize the class struggle," as some socialists explained.[39] Everything they believed about the war's origins confirmed their view that it was an imperialistic conflict and "not the concern of the workers." Moreover, such leaders as Morris Hillquit and Eugene Debs sensed the power of nationalism with its psychological extensions of fear and pride even in the arguments of those socialists who supported the crusade. Hillquit later ascribed the "stifling terrorism" of a "morbid war psychology" to the circumstance in which the major political parties were rivals in promoting the war effort.[40] Several socialists distrusted the idea of holding a referendum on war precisely because they feared that popular agitation would increase jingoism. Their sensitivity to the power of militant nationalism drew these socialists close to less class-conscious pacifists.

Whereas socialists had a handbook in George Ross Kirkpatrick's unbridled Marxist indictment, *War, What For?*, liberal pacifists found their thinking reflected in Norman Angell's analysis of the fallacy of viewing national defense as security, *The Great Illusion*.[41] Conflict of economic interest was the underlying cause of the war, they agreed, but its catalyst was nationalism itself. In this sense, at least, all the

38. The majority report of the Socialist party, adopted in St. Louis on April 11, 1917, is printed in full in Nathan Fine, *Labor and Farmer Parties in the United States, 1828–1928* (New York, 1928), 310–14. The report was written by Morris Hillquit and Charles Rutherberg, among others. A minority report by Louis Boudin is also printed in full in *ibid.*, 315–17.

39. Alexander Trachtenberg, "Socialists and the Problems of War," *Intercollegiate Socialist*, V (1917), 25.

40. Hillquit, *Loose Leaves from a Busy Life*, 169.

41. About 150,000 copies of *War, What For?* were sold between its publication by the author in 1910 (West Lafayette, Ohio) and its suppression in 1917, and perhaps another 100,000 copies of Kirkpatrick's *Think or Surrender* (New York, 1916) were distributed. Angell's *Great Illusion* (London, 1913) had a great following among internationalists, including those who reluctantly supported the war.

belligerents shared the blame for spreading the war and for the injustice and deceit that characterized it. Indeed, Jane Addams, Kirby Page, and others found that their reports of Allied atrocities were resented by the public simply because it accepted that notion of exclusive national virtues that had led to war in the first place. Pacifists distinguished between the mean motives of all belligerent governments and the high idealism of all the peoples who fought, as did Woodrow Wilson, but they could not support Wilson's idealistic war on behalf of the Allies. Everything they knew of the war's origin pointed to a strictly nationalistic European conflict with which the United States had no business. Private business (war trade and finance) was involved, to be sure, but neither national security nor American ideals were entrenched on one side or the other of no-man's land.

American pacifists were not intentionally isolationist in this regard. They consciously identified with men from all belligerent nations who shared what John Haynes Holmes called an "international mind." Holmes had matched a brilliant record at Harvard University with vigorous leadership in the Unitarian church, where he helped to organize the Fellowship for Social Justice. In 1912 he had written of the revolutionary function of the modern church in America, and four years later he broadened his horizon to include the international scene. There, in the midst of war, he found kindred spirits in Karl Liebknecht, Romain Rolland, and Bertrand Russell, among others. With them he recognized that there were in the world intense struggles for human dignity and decency, for peace itself, but he found these issues active within each nation at war.

Some such transnational humanism characterized pacifists of every hue, from class-conscious socialists to social gospel clergymen—Walter Rauschenbusch, for example, or Paul Jones, an Episcopal bishop who was removed from his diocese because of his views. It was the organizing principle of the Fellowship of Reconciliation and of the American Friends Service Committee. The St. Louis Resolution of the Socialist party implied that American intervention was "a crime against the people of the United States and against the nations of the world."[42] The war seemed irrelevant to the pacifists because, in short, it seemed artificial. Neither side epitomized the values in which pacifists believed, whether phrased socialistically or religiously. No victory promised political justice or the quality of life for which they had labored as progressives. For this reason the famous and radical reporter John

42. Quoted in Fine, *Labor and Farmer Parties,* 313.

Reed wanted to tell the soldiers of both sides, "This is not your war."[43] For this reason Max Eastman found the war "un-interesting for all its gore" and Bertrand Russell called it "trivial, for all its vastness."[44]

This interpretation of the war gained the force of moral commitment from the values that pacifists held. It set them apart from prowar internationalists (just as it would set them apart from isolationists after the war). One after another they described the anguish of being isolated in the midst of idealism about the war. They were able to endure only through the fellowship of other pacifists and their activity for war relief and civil rights.

But, in fact, many did more than endure. The generation of leaders whose pacifism matured between 1914 and 1919 were "as a man . . . awakened out of sleep," suddenly alive to the "moral confusion and disorder that lie concealed in a civilization heavily weighted with materialistic aims."[45] Heightened social responsibility and a more radical view of society led some men to participate in the labor movement after the war. A. J. Muste, for example, joined the strikers, was general secretary of the Amalgamated Textile Workers until 1921, and then became director of Brookwood Labor College and started his sojourn with radicalism. Other pacifists, including Norman Thomas, Devere Allen, and Kirby Page, were led toward active socialism. The sources of this leftward shift were varied; one was the pacifists' association with antiwar socialists, and another was their confrontation with the wartime state.

The radical peace and justice movement of the post-1914 era was international from its inception. A similar devotion to pacifism and social work by religious men and women from London, Berlin, Paris, and Prague led to Quaker relief projects and the creation of the International Fellowship of Reconciliation. A similar concept of the

43. Granville Hicks, *John Reed: The Making of a Revolutionary* (New York, 1937), 169.
44. Eastman, "The Uninteresting War," *The Masses,* VI (1915), 5–8; Russell, *Justice in War Time,* quoted in Holmes, *International Mind,* 13.
45. Typed ms., unsigned, ca. 1917, a draft of a statement on behalf of the Fellowship, probably by Norman Thomas or Paul Jones, FOR Papers, SCPC. This sense of recognition appears not only in the literature of the Fellowship, but also among Quakers such as those in the Friends Service Committee and the Philadelphia Yearly Meeting Committee on the Social Order.

war's origin and of peace terms linked American pacifists with British
left-wing labor, antiwar German socialists, and the Russian Petrograd
Council. In the United States the chief agencies of this first united
front were various civil liberties bureaus and the People's Council
of America.

Launched at a huge Madison Square Garden rally May 30, 1917,
the People's Council was organized by moderate socialists and the
remnant of the progressive antiwar coalition. Its original program
was familiar enough: from May to September it campaigned for
a quick peace on liberal terms, for civil liberties and repeal of conscription, and for economic demands no more radical than fair labor
standards, curbs on the high cost of living, and taxes on war profits.
Hoping to supplant its socialist-pacifist base with a farm-labor coalition, its organizers formed local branches and affiliated labor groups.
By August it claimed just under two million constituents, a measure
of its aspirations more than of its power. Five large meetings were
held across the country as the Council prepared for a grand constituent
assembly on September 1.

Clearly, the Council was associated with international socialism
on war issues. Just as clearly, it was billed as radical and subversive
by fervent patriots and conservative labor leaders, who thwarted its
plan to meet in Minneapolis. Amid great confusion, delegates aboard
a special train from New York pulled into the one Midwest city
willing to be their host—Chicago. Even there the meetings were hasty
and almost covert. Throughout the fall the Council increasingly represented socialist and radical labor; it was the chief defender of Soviet
Russia in 1918–19, but it never quite lost the marks of liberal progressivism. Its program remained virtually unchanged. Scott Nearing, a
socialist economist who was dismissed from the Wharton School
of Finance because of his reform activities, became chairman on
the understanding that the Council would work for "industrial democracy," but when he was asked if that meant socialism, he replied,
"No."[46] Nonetheless, pacifists who associated with socialists, in the
Council or elsewhere, were tarnished with the radical image.

46. Minutes of the executive committee of the People's Council, Sept.
21, 1917, People's Council of America Papers, SCPC. See also the minutes
of the organizing committee, June 21, July 19 and 26, and Aug. 16,
1917, and the *Bulletin* of the People's Council, Aug. 7, 1917, p. 1, *ibid.*
The assembly of September 1, 1917, is fully documented in the People's
Council Papers. The best published versions are in Frank L. Grubbs,
Jr., *The Struggle for Labor Loyalty: Gompers, the A. F. of L., and the*

The nature of that so-called radicalism is important: it derived from the reflection of pacifists upon wartime society in terms of their own experience. Isolation was painful enough, but pacifists were, in fact, the target of persecution because of their opposition to conscription and their association with political radicals. They promised not to obstruct the war effort, but their skeptical neutralism was itself a crime. Pacifists found that their meetings were broken up; their friends were harassed, run out of town, and imprisoned; their literature was withheld from the mails; their headquarters raided; and the president they trusted kept his own peace. Early in the war, before nationalism was virulent, the People's Council printed in facsimile a Russian peace appeal, together with an English translation and this note: "The original copy of the Bulletin from which this reproduction is made was smuggled over to this country—though not, as in the old days—smuggled *out of Russia,* but, as in these strange, new days—smuggled *into America!*"[47] Pacifists now looked upon their earlier warnings as prophetic. The American Union had said in 1916 that "militarism is the real danger" of the war, and Randolph Borne was not alone two years later in describing the "inextricable union of militarism and the State," or in fearing that "War is the health of the State."[48]

Bourne assumed that the ruling classes use the instruments of the state and its military authority to exploit those whose allegiance it commands. There was nothing new in his description of economic injustice or even its connection with war, but he went on to identify violence as the essence of war and authoritarianism as the essence of the state. In a state that identifies itself with democracy, the authority of conformity takes the place of violent, physical force. Wartime patriotism is, therefore, the obverse, the domestic counterpart, of military force. Violence and authoritarianism are essentially and equally objectionable.

Bourne made the most significant statement of this theme, but it was echoed in the diverse literature of liberal pacifism, introducing a political and ethical note into the antiwar socialism of Max Eastman,

---

Pacifists, 1917–1920 (Durham, 1968), and Peterson and Fite, *Opponents of War,* although these authors interpret the Council and also the American Union Against Militarism as being somewhat more radical than the manuscripts seem to warrant.

47. *Bulletin,* Aug. 7, 1917, pp. 2–3.
48. Bourne, "The State," in *War and the Intellectuals,* 89, 84.

Scott Nearing, and Norman Thomas. Only three weeks before he applied for membership in the Socialist party, Thomas had written that he feared its tendency to bind the individual to the class.[49] He did join because he feared more deeply "the undue exaltation of the State" and believed that "radicals ought to stand up and be counted."[50] He was a radical pacifist before he was a socialist, and his distrust of violence and authoritarianism would leave its mark upon the party in the future. Scott Nearing was becoming politically more radical in these years, but he declared that, in the name of liberty and humanity, he was against violence in any cause. Max Eastman was no absolutist—like most socialists he was against World War I specifically—but his fervor against that war modified his radicalism. Later he recalled, "A similar thing happened . . . to a good many American socialists. The reality of armed conflict in Europe dampened the proletarian-revolutionary part of their credo, and stepped up to a high pitch the antimilitary part."[51] They emerged all the more skeptical and alienated from society.

Bourne's understanding was reflected, too, in Kirby Page's influential analysis of war as the method of violence and in the declarations of pacifists in the Fellowship of Reconciliation. Their enemy was war itself, and they concluded that war was the result of the entire competitive economic system. War could be linked to the whole "causal circle," wrote Vida D. Scudder, a socialist professor at Wellesley who had ferreted out the social ideals of English literature, and the pacifist who saw this connection would be forced into a "constructive social radicalism."[52] Under the circumstances it was radical enough to express skepticism of the war or the social system of which it was a part. When conformity is an instrument of war, as in 1917–18 it was, then skepticism is a crime. The liberal pacifists stood accused

49. Thomas to Mrs. Anne C. Brush, Sept. 24, 1918, Thomas Papers, NYPL.
50. Thomas to Alexander Trachtenberg, Oct. 18, 1918, and Thomas to Morris Hillquit, Oct. 2, 1917, Thomas Papers, NYPL.
51. Eastman, *Love and Revolution,* 26; Henry May, *The End of American Innocence: A Study of the First Years of Our Time, 1912–1917* (New York, 1959), 368.
52. Scudder, *On Journey* (New York, 1937), 285. Miss Scudder joined the FOR after she realized that its members were integrating their pacifism with a demand for drastic social reorganization. Similarly, Jane Addams' autobiographical works can be read profitably as records of recognition of injustice on expanding levels of the social order, culminating in a view of the relationship of international injustice and war.

as a group. In their alienation they discovered that what made their pacifism radical was their equal objection to violence and authoritarianism.

This discovery pointed toward a new ethic of conflict, one that looked for the implications of war as a method and related the instrument to its objectives. As Kirby Page wrote, war must be judged by what it does because that is inseparable from what it is for. John Haynes Holmes argued at length that although the logic of force is that it can defend and liberate men, the fallacy of force is that it actually brings new forms of conflict and is the *sine qua non* of tyranny. Jane Addams spoke repeatedly of the futility of using violence in order to deal with the causes of fighting. "Militarism can never be abolished by militarism," as the majority of socialists had agreed in St. Louis when the American government determined to "make the world safe." "Democracy can never be imposed upon any country by a foreign power by force of arms."[53] Their declaration was directed specifically to the international war and was based on a Marxist analysis, but it reflected the very liberal values that absolute pacifists took to imply a universal principle.

The religious pacifists of the FOR abjured fighting on the grounds that it is sinful in its consequences, and agnostic Max Eastman found himself mindful of the "mangled bodies and manic hatreds implied by that lyric word *violence* so dear to humdrum petty-bourgeois dreamers like George Sorel. . . ."[54] For a generation and more pacifists would evaluate choices in terms of the relationship of "ends and means" and, in fact, the phrase would acquire a sanctity independent of tough-minded analysis. The new pacifist ethic was not fully articulated in its inception, in part because the war was brief; the fetters of conformity were shortly removed, and professional peace advocates felt free again to fight militarism without, it seemed, challenging the state.

The memory of World War I was an important consideration in the responses of Americans to foreign affairs for two decades. It was a formative influence upon the pacifist. He tended to universalize the war and apply its example to other events; he used it to popularize his view that wars are always futile and irrelevant to fundamental

53. Majority report of the Socialist party, St. Louis, quoted in Fine, *Labor and Farmer Parties,* 312.
54. Eastman, *Love and Revolution,* 26.

social issues and that the United States could stand aside from a European state system based on force of arms. Revisionist histories of the First World War provided a vehicle for including that view, but they could not convey the internationalism that was a corollary of the pacifist's humanism. To the extent that his memory of the war was accepted by the public, it encouraged isolationism.

There was a deeper dilemma. Pacifism was historically oriented to liberal values. The progressive background of the liberal pacifist reinforced these values even as it socialized them and added a disposition toward political action. In 1917–18 the pacifist began to view war as an integral part of an unjust social order. The instruments of political control involved at least the latent threat of violence, he discovered, and these were in the hands of classes opposed to change. Behind even the system of democratic majority decision he found the tacit sanctions of violent force. To his political right and left were activists for whom violence appeared to be the ultimate authority.

But if the pacifist remembered anything from World War I, it was that violence and authoritarianism were precisely what threatened his every liberal value. Against them he began to define an ethic of conflict, dealing with force as an instrument for social control and rejecting violent means.

Only a few pacifists perceived that their impulse to far-reaching reform might come into conflict with their refusal to sanction violence in any cause: Evan Thomas and his friends on a hunger strike at Ft. Leavenworth, perhaps; John Haynes Holmes trying to find ways to rationalize the passivity out of pacifism, looking for the example of a Gandhi; Kirby Page seeking nonviolent methods of social change; moderate socialists warding off a Bolshevik-communist line. Even these men forgot the dilemma once the war was over, and they returned to normality or took up again the traditional instruments of social change. Liberal pacifists would face it again, however, in the agony of defining the road to power that split the Socialist party in 1934 and in the fight against war and fascism; and their successors would meet it in the sixties in the civil rights movement and the opposition to the war in Vietnam. The terms of the dilemma were exposed in World War I. A willingness to grapple with them would characterize liberal pacifism in the twentieth century.

III
Consequences

"MOBILIZATION" AND ITS EFFECTS

ALLEN F. DAVIS

Welfare, Reform, and World War I

The relationship between war and reform has long fascinated not only historians but also contemporary political participants and observers. The repression and reaction of World War I left many American liberals deeply shaken. For many years William Allen White's aphorism "War is the nemesis of reform" was accepted as sufficient explanation for what happened. The horrors of the European carnage, it was believed, had undermined faith in human progress, while military matters had distracted both attention and funds from social reform. Only recently have historians questioned the correctness of this view.

Political changes after 1914 are discussed in a later section. This essay by Allen Davis shows how advanced progressives, especially professional social workers, saw the war as an opportunity to promote reform, and how their hopes were at least partially fulfilled. Another study which introduces similar findings is Walter I. Trattner, "Progressivism and World War I: A Re-Appraisal," *Mid-America*, XLIV (July 1962), 131–145. Two fine treatments of the *New Republic* editors, Charles Forcey, *The Crossroads of Liberalism: Croly, Weyl, Lippmann and the Progressive Era, 1900–1925* (New York, 1961), and Christopher Lasch, "The *New Republic* and the War: An Unanalyzable Feeling," in his book, *The New Radicalism in America, 1889–1963: The Intellectual as a Social Type* (New York, 1965), also examine the relationship between domestic political ideas and expectations from the war. Interestingly, although these essays depart from the older interpretation of the impact of the war, all of them actually support the idea that, by stricter definition, "nemesis" did help to shape the behavior of many reformers.

Only a decade ago historians were satisfied with the simple generalization that World War I killed the progressive movement, or that the crusade to make the world safe for democracy absorbed the reforming zeal of the progressive era and compounded the disillusionment that followed. "Participation in the war put an end to the Progressive movement," Richard Hofstadter announced. "Reform stopped dead," Eric Goldman decided.[1] It is now obvious that the relationship between social reform and World War I is more complex. Henry May has demonstrated that some of the progressive idealism had cracked and begun to crumble even before 1917,[2] while Arthur Link and Clarke Chambers have discovered that a great deal of progressivism survived into the 1920s.[3] At the same time several historians have shown that for the intellectuals associated with the *New Republic* the war seemed something of a climax to the New Nationalism.[4] And William Leuchtenburg has argued that the economic and social planning of World

1. Richard Hofstadter, *The Age of Reform: From Bryan to F.D.R.* (New York, 1955), p. 273; Eric Goldman, *Rendezvous with Destiny* (New York, 1952), p. 254. See also William E. Leuchtenburg, "Progressivism and Imperialism: The Progressive Movement and American Foreign Policy, 1898–1916," *Mississippi Valley Historical Review*, XXXIX (Dec. 1952), 483–504; Leuchtenburg, *The Perils of Prosperity, 1914–1932* in *The Chicago History of American Civilization,* Daniel Boorstin, ed. (Chicago, 1958), pp. 120–39; George E. Mowry, "The First World War and American Democracy," in Jesse D. Clarkson and Thomas Cochran, eds., *War As a Social Institution* (New York, 1941), p. 182.

2. Henry F. May, *The End of American Innocence: A Study of the First Years of Our Time, 1912–1917* (New York, 1959).

3. Arthur S. Link, "What Happened to the Progressive Movement in the 1920's?" *American Historical Review,* LXIV (July 1959), 933–51; Clarke A. Chambers, *Seedtime of Reform: American Social Service and Social Action, 1918–1933* (Minneapolis, 1963).

4. Charles Forcey, *The Crossroads of Liberalism: Croly, Weyl, Lippmann and the Progressive Era, 1900–1925* (New York, 1961), pp. 221 ff.; Christopher Lasch, *The New Radicalism in America, 1889–1963: The Intellectual as Social Type* (New York, 1965), pp. 181–224; Charles Hirschfeld, "Nationalist Progressivism and World War I," *Mid-America,* XLV (July 1963), 139–56. See also Walter I. Trattner, "Progressivism and World War I: A Re-Appraisal," *Mid-America,* XLIV (July 1962), 131–45.

War I was a much more important model for the New Deal than anything that happened during the progressive era.[5]

It is an overworked truism that there were many progressive movements, but one of the most important and interesting was the social justice movement.[6] Led by social workers, ministers and intellectuals, the social justice movement, in broadest terms, sought to conserve human resources and to humanize the industrial city. The social justice reformers tried to improve housing, abolish child labor, limit the hours of work for both men and women, build parks and playgrounds and better schools. Like all progressives they believed that by altering the environment it was possible to reconstruct society. They combined optimism and a large amount of moral idealism with an exaggerated faith in statistics, efficiency and organization.[7] Of course the social justice reformers did not always agree among themselves; prohibition, immigration restriction and the war itself caused divisions within the group.

The optimism and the idealism of the social justice reformers had been tempered before 1917. In a real sense the formation of the Progressive Party with its platform of industrial minimums had seemed the climax to their crusade.[8] The collapse of the Progressive Party coming almost simultaneously with the outbreak of war in Europe led to shock and disillusionment and to many pronouncements that

5. William E. Leuchtenburg, "The New Deal and the Analogue of War," in John Braeman, Robert H. Bremner, Everett Walters, eds., *Change and Continuity in Twentieth Century America* (Columbus, Ohio, 1964), pp. 81–143.

6. See Arthur Link, *American Epoch: A History of the United States Since the 1890's* (New York, 1955), pp. 68–91, for what seems to me a sensible attempt to define the various progressive movements. The social justice movement was perhaps best represented by organizations like The Consumers' League, The Women's Trade Union League, The American Association for Labor Legislation, the social settlements, and by *The Survey* magazine. A recent book, Irwin Yellowitz, *Labor and the Progressive Movement in New York State, 1897–1916* (Ithaca, 1965), defines a similar group as "social progressives."

7. For one aspect of the efficiency side of progressivism see Samuel Haber, *Efficiency and Uplift: Scientific Management in the Progressive Era, 1890–1920* (Chicago, 1964).

8. See Allen F. Davis, "The Social Workers and the Progressive Party, 1912–1916," *American Historical Review*, LXIX (Apr. 1964), 671–88.

the war had ended social reform.[9] The shock wore off quickly, though some of the disillusionment remained. Many reformers continued to promote social welfare legislation. They lobbied for the La Follette Seaman's bill, and early in 1916 helped to force a reluctant Wilson into supporting a national child labor law. Most of the social justice reformers voted for Wilson in 1916 but without a great deal of enthusiasm.[10] The specter of war hung over them as it hung over all Americans, but for many of them the acceptance or rejection of war was an especially difficult, and in some cases, a shattering experience. A few, like Jane Addams, Lillian Wald and Alice Hamilton, were consistent pacifists. Most of them opposed the preparedness movement and America's entry into the war, and they played important roles in organizations like the American Union Against Militarism. But when the United States declared war most of them went along with the decision, with fear and trembling but with loyalty.[11] They feared that the crisis of war would cancel the victories they had won, that civil liberties would be abridged, that education and recreation and health standards would be neglected, that child labor and long hours for men and women would be resumed in the name of national

9. John Haynes Holmes, "War and the Social Movement," *Survey,* XXXII. (Sept. 26, 1914), 629–30. Lillian Wald, for example, remarked, "War is the doom of all that has taken years of peace to build up," quoted in Robert L. Duffus, *Lillian Wald: Neighbor and Crusader* (New York, 1938), p. 148.

10. Arthur Link, *Wilson: The New Freedom* (Princeton, 1956), pp. 255–59; *Wilson: Campaigns for Progressivism and Peace* (Princeton, 1965), pp. 39–40, 56–60, 124–25; Gregory Weinstein, *The Ardent Eighties: Reminiscences of an Interesting Decade* (New York, 1928), p. 112; "Why Wilson: A Statement by Social Workers," Jane Addams to Paul Kellogg, Oct. 25, 1916; Kellogg to Addams, Oct. 28, 1916, Survey Associates Papers, Box 17, Social Welfare History Archives, University of Minnesota.

11. Donald Johnson, *The Challenge to American Freedoms: World War I and the Rise of the American Civil Liberties Union* (Lexington, Ky., 1963), pp. 1–25; Crystal Eastman to Paul Kellogg, n.d. (received June 15, 1917); Minutes of Henry Street Meeting Sept. 27, 1915, Paul Kellogg MSS, Social Welfare History Archives; Paul Kellogg, "The Fighting Issue," *Survey,* XXXVII (Feb. 17, 1917), 272–277; "War Resolutions Adopted by the Settlements," *Survey,* XXXVIII (June 16, 1917), 265; Ray H. Abrams, *Preachers Present Arms: A Study of the War-Time Attitudes and Activities of the Churches and the Clergy in the United States, 1914–1918* (Philadelphia, 1933). Of course a sizable minority of social justice reformers continued to oppose war after April 1917.

need.[12] Yet gradually, to their own surprise, many of them came to view the war, despite its horror and its dangers, as a climax and culmination of their movement for social justice in America.

Few of the reformers saw the war as a great crusade to make the world safe for democracy, at least in the beginning, but they were soon caught up in the feverish activity and enthusiasm for action that marked the first months of the war. Part of the excitement came from the thrill of being listened to after years of frustration, of plotting and planning and lobbying. "Enthusiasm for social service is epidemic . . . ," Edward T. Devine, the General Secretary of the New York Charity Organization Society, wrote in the summer of 1917, "a luxuriant crop of new agencies is springing up. We scurry back and forth to the national capital; we stock offices with typewriters and new letterheads; we telephone feverishly, regardless of expense, and resort to all the devices of efficient 'publicity work'. . . . It is all very exhilarating, stimulating, intoxicating."[13] The reformers went to Washington; they also joined the Red Cross or the YMCA and went to France. For a time during the war the capital of American social work and philanthropy seemed to have been transferred from New York to Paris. Devine, who in 1918 was in Paris working for the Red Cross, wrote:

> We have moved our offices to 12 Boissy d'Anglas, the Children's Bureau is on the ground floor; the Tuberculosis Bureau with the Rockefeller Foundation was already on the third . . . , the rest of the Department of Civil Affairs is on the first floor, Bureau Chiefs and Associate Chiefs being marshalled along the street side in an imposing array, with Mr. [Homer] Folks and Mr. [John] Kingsbury at one end and Miss Curtis and myself at the other.[14]

12. Arthur P. Kellogg, "The National Conference of Social Work," *Survey,* XXXVIII (June 16, 1917), 253–55; Alice Henry to William Allen White, William Allen White MSS, Box 47, Library of Congress; Edward T. Devine, "Social Problems of the War," *Proceedings of the National Conference of Social Work,* 1917, pp. 44–52.

13. Devine, "Social Forces in Wartime," *Survey,* XXXVIII (July 7, 1917), 316.

14. Devine to Paul Kellogg, Apr. 7, 1918, Survey Associates Papers, Box 22. See also John Kingsbury to Eria Rodakiewics, Dec. 22, 1917, Kingsbury MSS, Box 25, Library of Congress; Kellogg to Newton Baker, Aug. 1, 1917, Survey Associates Papers, Box 18.

John Andrews, Secretary of the American Association for Labor Legislation, surveyed the new kind of administrator being employed by the government, many of them social workers and college professors, and decided that "Perhaps aggressive competition with Germany is having a beneficial effect on bureaucratic Washington." Andrews had gone to Washington in October 1917 to try to get the House to pass a bill, already approved by the Senate, providing workmen's compensation for longshoremen. With Congress ready to adjourn everyone assured him there was no chance for passage. But he went to see President Wilson, and the next day the bill passed the House under the unanimous consent rule. Andrews was amazed and found himself with a great stack of unused facts and statistics. "Usually before our bills are passed, we wear our facts threadbare," he remarked. "Perhaps this is not the most democratic way to secure urgently needed labor laws, but it is effective."[15]

Not everyone of course shared the enthusiasm for war, nor the confidence that war would lead to great social gain. There was some truth in Randolph Bourne's charge that the intellectuals who saw so much good coming out of war were deceiving themselves and falling victim to the worst kind of chauvinism and rationalization. "It is almost demonical," Helena Dudley, a Boston settlement worker, wrote to Jane Addams, "the sweep toward conscription and these enormous war loans which Wall Street is eager to heap on: and labor so passive and the socialists broken up, and the social workers lining up with the bankers." Another woman reported from Seattle that there "the men who feel 'the call to arms' and the women who feel 'the call to knit' for the Red Cross are the men and women generally opposed to labor legislation and all progressive movements to increase the rights and well being of the many."[16] But these were minority views.

Most of the social justice reformers joined John Dewey, Thorstein Veblen and the *New Republic* progressives and applauded the positive action of the Wilson administration in taking over the railroads, mobi-

15. John Andrews to Paul Kellogg, Oct. 6, 1917, Survey Associates Papers, Box 17.

16. Randolph S. Bourne, "The War and the Intellectuals," *Seven Arts,* II (June 1917), 133–46; Helena Dudley to Jane Addams, Apr. 10, 1917, Addams MS, The Peace Collection, Swarthmore College, Swarthmore, Pa.; Theresa McMahon to Stuart Rice, May 17, 1917, enclosed in Rice to John Kingsbury, May 22, 1917, Kingsbury MSS, Box 34.

lizing industry and agriculture. They looked forward to sweeping economic reforms and contemplated the "social possibilities of war."[17] "Laissez-faire is dead," one of them wrote, "Long live social control: social control, not only to enable us to meet the rigorous demands of the war, but also as a foundation for the peace and brotherhood that is to come."[18] Some of them, inspired by the promise of the Russian Revolution and wartime socialism in England, looked forward to a kind of "democratic collectivism."[19]

But the social justice reformers were concerned with more than an extension of the New Nationalism, and their primary interest was not in economic planning. They wanted to continue their crusade for social justice.[20] Nothing was more important to them than the

17. Arthur P. Kellogg, "The National Conference of Social Work," *Survey,* XXXVIII (June 16, 1917), 253–58; Winthrop D. Lane, "The National Conference of Social Work," *Survey,* XL (June·1, 1918), 251–57; John B. Andrews, "Labor Laws in the Crucible," *Survey,* XXIX (Feb. 16, 1918), 542–44. On wartime mobilization and its effect on progressives see esp.: Charles Hirschfeld, "Nationalist Progressivism and World War I," *Mid-America,* XLV (July 1963), 139–56; Leuchtenburg, "The New Deal and the Analogue of War," *Change and Continuity,* pp. 81–91. "The social possibilities of war" is Dewey's phrase; see Dewey, "What Are We Fighting For?" *Independent,* XCIV (June 22, 1918), 480. See also Rexford G. Tugwell, "America's War-Time Socialism," *Nation,* CXXIV (Apr. 6, 1927), 364–67; "The War as a Sociological Laboratory," *Nation,* CVI (Mar. 7, 1918), 258–59.

18. Neva R. Deardorff, "The Demise of a Highly Respected Doctrine," *Survey,* XXXIX (Jan. 12, 1918), 416.

19. "The Russian Instinct for Democracy," *Survey,* XL (Apr. 27, 1918), 85–87; Arthur Gleason, "British Labor and the Issues of Reconstruction," *Survey,* XL (Aug. 3, 1918), 496–504; Paul Kellogg to Charles Elliot, Apr. 13, 1918; Kellogg to John Fitch, June 17, 1918, Survey Associates Papers, Box 24. On reaction to the Russian Revolution see Christopher Lasch, *American Liberals and the Russian Revolution* (New York, 1962), although he finds no place in his rather artificial categories for the social justice reformers or the pacifists; also Lewis Feuer, "American Travelers to the Soviet Union, 1917–32: The Formation of a Component of New Deal Ideology," *American Quarterly,* XIV (Summer 1962), 119–49. The story of the impact of the British Labor Movement on American reform is one that needs to be told.

20. The differences between the social justice reformers and the *New Republic* progressives are ones of emphasis and degree; on many issues they could agree. Men like Paul Kellogg, Edward Devine and John Andrews, women like Lillian Wald and Florence Kelley tended to be more concerned with the ends rather than the means and they spent very little time arguing about a theory of government. They also were

rights of the workingman, and the working woman and child. More
than most progressives they had supported the cause of organized
labor,[21] and they were cheered by the rights won 'by labor during
the war. The National War Labor Policies Board, the United States
Employment Service and other wartime agencies recognized collective
bargaining, the minimum wage and the eight-hour day, improved
conditions of work and reduced the exploitation of women and children in industry.[22] "One of the paradoxes of the war is the stimulus
it is giving to human conservation," a writer in *The Survey* noted.[23]
The social justice reformers spent a large amount of time making
sure labor standards were not weakened, and that women and children
were not exploited during the war. Yet even the invalidation of the
National Child Labor Law by the Supreme Court failed to dim their
enthusiasm. The National Child Labor Committee set to work to
design another and better law, and Congress responded by passing
a bill that levied a 10 per cent tax on products produced by children
under fourteen.[24] A Supreme Court decision did not seem very important when Secretary of War Newton Baker and other members of
the Wilson administration were saying publicly: "We cannot afford,
when we are losing boys in France to lose children in the United
States at the same time . . . , we cannot afford when this nation
is having a drain upon the life of its young manhood . . . , to have
the life of women workers of the United States depressed."[25]

---

usually more interested in child labor and urban housing than they were
in regulating trusts and controlling railroads.

21. See Allen F. Davis, "The Women's Trade Union League: Origins
and Organization," *Labor History*, V (Winter 1964), 3–17.

22. John Commons and Associates, *History of Labor in the United
States* (4 vols.; New York, 1918–35), III, 200–5, 321–25, 341–45; "How
Workingmen Fare at Washington," *Survey*, XXXIX (Feb. 23, 1918), 575.

23. John A. Fitch, "Stretching the Pay Envelope: Some New Methods
of Fixing Wages," *Survey*, XXXIX (Jan. 12, 1918), 411.

24. John B. Andrews, "Federal Government to Uphold Labor Standards,"
Apr. 21, 1917, Survey Associates Papers, Box 17; Winthrop D. Lane,
"Making the War Safe for Childhood," *Survey*, XXXVIII (Aug. 4, 1917),
381–91; Mary McDowell, "Mothers and Night Work," *Survey*, XLI (Dec.
22, 1918), 335–36; "Federal Child Labor Law Invalid," *Survey*, XL (June
8, 1918), 283; "Planning a New Child Labor Law," *Survey*, XL (June
15, 1918), 323; "A New Anti-Child Labor Bill," *Survey*, XL (Sept. 7,
1918), 642.

25. Quoted in Florence Kelley, "The War and Women Workers," *Survey*,
XXXIX (Mar. 9, 1918), 628–31. For complete address, see Survey Associ-

The crisis of war also stimulated the movement to improve urban housing. The housing movement was central to the social justice movement and intertwined with all other reforms from child labor legislation to progressive education. Much of the prewar movement, led by men like Lawrence Veiller, was devoted to passing restrictive legislation, but the war brought the first experiment with public housing.[26] Borrowing something from the English example and spurred to action by the crucial need for housing war workers, the Federal Government, operating through the United States Shipping Board and the Department of Labor, built or controlled dozens of housing projects during the war. For many who had been working to improve urban housing for decades the government experiments seemed like the climax to the movement. Lawrence Veiller himself drew up the "Standards for Permanent Industrial Housing Developments" that were followed by the government agencies. The result was that the projects were much better designed and safer than those built by commercial builders. In addition the architects of the developments, influenced by the English Garden City Movement and by the settlement ideal of neighborhood unity, experimented with row houses, curved streets, recreation and shopping areas. Thus the public housing experiment of World War I was clearly the product of the city planning as well as of the housing movement of the progressive era.[27]

The war also provided a climax to the social insurance movement, which had won very little support in the United States before 1910. Many states had passed workmen's compensation laws by 1917, but

---

ates Papers, Box 18. It is significant that Baker was president of the National Consumers League in 1917. Josephus Daniels and Wilson himself made similar statements; see John B. Andrews, "Federal Government to Uphold Labor Standards," Apr. 21, 1917, Survey Associates Papers, Box 17.

26. For the relation between housing and other movements in the progressive era see Roy Lubove, *The Progressives and the Slums: Tenement House Reform in New York City, 1890–1917* (Pittsburgh, 1962).

27. Bruno Lasker, "The Housing of War Workers: Lessons from British Experience for Fulfillment of an Urgent Task," *Survey*, XLI (Jan. 1919), 390–97; "Toward a Federal Housing Policy," *Survey*, XXXIX (Feb. 16, 1918), 552; Eva W. White, "War Activities as They Have Affected Housing, Health and Recreation," *Proceedings of the National Conference of Social Work, 1919*, pp. 498–500; Lubove, "Homes and a Few Well Placed Fruit Trees: An Object Lesson in Federal Housing," *Social Research*, XXVII (Winter 1960), 469–86.

they were inadequate and filled with loopholes, and the philosophy of the movement was only gradually being accepted by many reformers, let alone the general public, when the United States became involved in World War I.[28] Consequently the Military and Naval Insurance Act, which became law October 6, 1917, was hailed as a great victory by the leaders of the movement.[29] The act, which was drawn up by Judge Julian Mack with the aid of experts like Lee Frankel and Julia Lathrop, required each enlisted man to make an allotment to his family, which the government supplemented. It also provided compensation in case of death or disability, and re-education in case of crippling injury.[30] The architects of the plan hoped that it would prevent the demands for pensions and bonuses that had followed every American war, but more important to those who had fought for social insurance was the fact that the government had assumed the extra hazard involved in military service and guaranteed a minimum standard of subsistence to the soldier's family. The act was slow to get into operation, indeed some families did not receive their allotments until after the Armistice. It also put a heavy burden on the Red Cross, which tried to advance the money to needy families, but at the time the act seemed to mark a victory for an important progressive measure.[31]

Health insurance had made even less progress in the United States before 1917 than had workmen's compensation, but a group of social workers in 1915 picked it as the next great reform. "Health Insurance — the next step in social progress," became their slogan. A few states had amended their workmen's compensation laws to include industrial diseases, and New York, New Jersey, Massachusetts and

28. Robert H. Bremner, *From the Depths: The Discovery of Poverty in the United States* (New York, 1956), pp. 249–59; Yellowitz, *Labor and the Progressive Movement,* pp. 8–9.

29. Arthur Kellogg to John Andrews, Sept. 4, 1917, Box 17; Paul Kellogg to Newton Baker, June 21, 1917, Survey Associates Papers, Box 18; "Compensation for Invalids of the War," *Survey,* XXXVIII (Sept. 22, 1917), 541–44; "Soldiers and Sailors Insurance Law," *Survey,* XXXIX (Oct. 13, 1917), 39–40.

30. Julia C. Lathrop, "The Military and Naval Insurance Act," *Nation,* CVI (Feb. 7, 1918), 157–58.

31. Frank Bruno, *Trends in Social Work* (New York, 1957), pp. 230–32; "The Red Cross Civilian Relief Plan," *Survey,* XXXVIII (May 19, 1917), 162.

a few other states were investigating the possibility of compulsory, contributory workmen's health insurance when the war came.[32] The war seemed to increase the need. The New Jersey commission on old age insurance, in urging the government to enact a health insurance law, declared that "health protection . . . has been raised by the war from a position deserving of humanitarian consideration to one demanding action if we are to survive as a nation."[33] But compulsory health insurance quickly aroused the opposition of the insurance companies and the medical profession, as well as of other groups who denounced it as "Prussianism." Not even the reminder that most of the British troops were protected by government health insurance could stop the opposition.[34]

While health insurance fell victim to the war, or perhaps more accurately to a combination of circumstances, the movement to improve the nation's health was stimulated by the conflict. "War makes sanitation a common cause," Alice Hamilton announced. "We suddenly discovered that health is not a personal matter, but a social obligation," Owen Lovejoy remarked.[35] Early fears that the war, by drawing doctors and nurses into the Army, would lead to a rise in infant mortality, tuberculosis and other diseases proved groundless as a variety of agencies, volunteers and the Federal Government rallied to the cause. Lillian Wald, who opposed American participation in the war, served on the Red Cross Advisory Committee, traveled frequently to Washington as a consultant on health matters, and labored long and hard to keep the district nurses in New York functioning at top efficiency even during the influenza epidemic at the

32. Bremner, *From the Depths,* pp. 258–59; Gurdon Ransom Miller, *Social Insurance in the United States* (Chicago, 1918), pp. 31–51; John B. Andrews, "Progress Toward Health Insurance," *Proceedings NCSW, 1917,* pp. 535–42. In 1917 the American Association for Labor Legislation had reprinted on its letterhead the statement of a Surgeon General in the U.S. Public Health Service: "Health Insurance is the Next Great Step in Social Legislation," Andrews to Paul Kellogg, Jan. 19, 1917, Survey Associates Papers, Box 17.

33. "The Draft and Health Insurance," *Survey,* XXXIX (Mar. 2, 1918), 605.

34. "Health Insurance Argued at Albany," *Survey* (Apr. 6, 1918), 18–19; Isaac M. Rubinow, *The Quest for Security* (New York, 1934), pp. 207–17.

35. Alice Hamilton and Gertrude Seymour, "The New Public Health," *Survey,* XXXVIII (Apr. 21, 1917), 59–62; Owen R. Lovejoy, "A War Program for Peace," *Proceedings NCSW, 1919,* pp. 664–65.

end of the war.[36] Part of the stimulus to the health movement during the war came from the massive attempt to control venereal disease, part came from shock, especially over the rejection of 29 per cent of those drafted as physically unfit for service.[37] But it was more than shock. As one social worker expressed it: "far from arresting public health progress, the war has suddenly defined America's public health problem. And the aroused public conscience has promptly enacted measures which a few months ago would have been tabled by leisurely officials and classed as visionary schemes. Into a year has been packed the progress of a decade."[38]

Other reform movements seemed to make great strides during the war. The use of industrial education in rehabilitation work pleased the supporters of progressive education,[39] while the mental hygiene movement approved the use of psychiatrists and psychiatric tests by the Army.[40] The use of schools as community centers by the Council of National Defense led to the climax of the school social center movement, and the development of community councils and war chests stimulated community organization and led to acceptance of the federated fund drive.[41]

36. Lillian Wald to Joseph Girdansky, July 7, 1917; Wald to Elizabeth Farrell, June 19, 1918, Lillian Wald MSS, New York Public Library.

37. Eva W. White, "War Activities as They Have Affected Housing, Health and Recreation," *Proceedings NCSW, 1919*, pp. 496–502; Lovejoy, "A War Program for Peace," *Proceedings NCSW, 1919*, p. 664.

38. Gertrude Seymour, "The Health of Soldier and Civilian: Some Aspects of the American Health Movement in Wartime," *Survey*, XL (Apr. 27, 1918), 89–94.

39. P. P. Claxton, "Effect of the War on Schools," *National Municipal Review*, VI (Sept. 1917), 571–72; "Government Policies Involving Schools in Wartime," *Survey*, XXXIX (Mar. 9, 1918), 626–28; "Vocational Training Will Be Necessary After the War," *Philadelphia Bulletin*, Feb. 22, 1918, clipping Eva W. White MSS, The Arthur and Elizabeth Schlesinger Library, Radcliffe College.

40. Newton Baker to Paul Kellogg, July 26, 1917, Survey Associates Papers, Box 18; "National Conference of Social Work," *Survey*, XL (May 4, 1918), 130–31; Mark Haller, *Eugenics: Hereditarian Attitudes in American Thought* (New Brunswick, N.J., 1963), pp. 115, 128. The war helped hasten the acceptance and increased the prestige of psychiatry.

41. "School Centers and War Work," *Christian Science Monitor*, Apr. 11, 1918, clipping Eva White MSS; Sidney Dillick, *Community Organization for Neighborhood Development: Past and Present* (New York, 1953), pp. 71–76; Roy Lubove, *The Professional Altruist: The Emergence of Social Work as a Career*, pp. 178, 189–92. The war also increased the

Women also profited from the war. Out of necessity they achieved a measure of equal rights. They entered hundreds of occupations formerly barred to them, and their presence led to the establishment of the Women in Industry Service and ultimately to the Women's Bureau of the Department of Labor. "Wonderful as this hour is for democracy and labor—it is the first hour in history for the women of the world," Mrs. Raymond Robins, the President of the National Women's Trade Union League, announced in 1917. "This is the woman's age! At last after centuries of disabilities and discriminations, women are coming into the labor and festival of life on equal terms with men."[42] The war also seemed to accelerate the movement for woman suffrage. Eight additional states gave women the vote, at least on some issues, during 1917. Wilson, after years of opposition, came out in favor of women voting, and the House of Representatives passed a woman suffrage amendment in January 1918.[43]

The Negro and the immigrant often fell victim to racist hysteria during the war and did not gain as much as other groups. But the war seemed to hold hope even for the disadvantaged. Negroes were drafted and enlisted in the Army in great numbers and often served with distinction. All the training camps, recreation facilities and even the YMCA buildings were segregated, and there were many incidents of racial bitterness and a few of violence. Yet many of the social justice progressives, who had always been more sympathetic to the Negro's plight than had most reformers, hoped that the Negro's willingness to serve and what he learned in the Army would help lead to better conditions after the war. They were cheered by the appointment of Emmett J. Scott, Secretary of Tuskegee Institute, as Special Assistant to the Secretary of War, and by the emergence of a number of young leaders within the Negro community. "We may expect to see the walls of prejudice gradually crumble before the onslaught

---

acceptance of social work as a profession, and led to the further development of psychiatric social work.

42. Eleanor Flexner, *Century of Struggle: The Woman's Rights Movement in the United States* (Cambridge, 1959), pp. 288–89; Pauline Goldmark, "Women Conductors," *Survey*, XL (June 29, 1918), 360; Chambers, *Seedtime of Reform*, pp. 9–10; Mrs. Raymond Robins, "President's Report," *Proceedings, NWTUL, 1917*, pp. v–x.

43. Flexner, *Century of Struggle*, pp. 290–93; "The War and Votes for Women," *New Republic*, XVI (Oct. 10, 1918), 33–35; "War-Time Gains of the Suffragists," *Survey*, XXXVIII (Apr. 28, 1917), 97.

of common sense and racial progress," a writer in *The Crisis* predicted.[44]

It was hard to forget the bloody battle of East St. Louis and the race riot in Houston for which thirteen Negro soldiers were executed. It was easy to dwell on a thousand incidents of prejudice and on the lynchings that continued during the war, but many agreed with William E. B. Du Bois when he called in July 1918 for the Negro to close ranks, support the war effort and put aside special grievances. "Since the war began we have won: Recognition of our citizenship in the draft; One thousand Negro officers; Special representation in the War and Labor Departments; Abolition of the color line in railway wages; Recognition as Red Cross Nurses; Overthrow of segregation ordinances; A strong word from the President against lynching. . . . Come fellow black men," DuBois urged his critics, "fight for your rights, but for god's sake have sense enough to know when you are getting what you fight for."[45]

The war did not end the grievances, but it seemed to improve the Negro's lot. It also stimulated a massive migration. A large number of Negroes had moved north even before 1914 but the war and the lure of jobs increased the flow. Many Negroes did find employment, but they also encountered prejudice and hate. Social workers and a few other reformers continued to struggle against increasing odds to aid the Negro. Yet during the war the problems and the prejudice seemed less important than the promise for the future. The migration north and the large numbers who joined the Army also seemed to create improved wages and better treatment for Negroes in the South. The story of the migration might be told in terms of crime and corruption, of drift and hate, a writer in *Survey* noted, but "Against it, there is a story of careful adjustment to new circumstances, of stimulation to self-help, of education . . . , of job findings and vocational guidance. . . ."[46]

44. Quotation is from "The Turning of the Tide," *Crisis,* XV (Dec. 1917), 77–80. See also Emmett J. Scott, *The American Negro in the World War* (1919); "War-Camp Community Service," *Playground,* XI (1917), 509–10. For the role of the social justice progressives in aiding the Negro, see Gilbert Osofsky, *Harlem: The Making of a Ghetto, Negro New York, 1890–1930* (New York, 1966), pp. 53–67.

45. Du Bois, "Editorial," *Crisis,* XVI (July-Sept. 1918), 3, 217.

46. Quotation from "Negro Migration," *Survey,* XXXIX (Dec. 22, 1917), 342–43; George Edmund Haynes, "Negroes Move North," *Survey,* XL (May 4, 1918), 115–22; John Hope Franklin, *From Slavery to Freedom: A History of American Negroes* (2nd ed.; New York, 1961), pp. 444–68.

The story of the treatment of the immigrant and alien during the war was also not entirely bleak. German-Americans were attacked as radicals, pacifists and traitors, and wartime hysteria led to the development of super-patriotism and the decline of civil liberties. Yet at the time the patriotic enthusiasm seemed in some cases to accelerate the process of Americanization. The sight of many different ethnic groups joining enthusiastically to support Liberty Bond drives and other war activities led one observer to predict that the war would "weld the twenty-five or thirty races which compose our population into a strong, virile and intelligent people . . . ," into "a splendid race of new Americans."[47] The war also strengthened the movement to restrict immigration. In February 1917, a bill requiring a literacy test for the first time passed Congress and became law. There had always been disagreement among social justice progressives on the matter of restriction; some had argued that to help those already here it was necessary to reduce the flow, but the war seemed to end the debate. Not all reformers greeted the new law as a victory for progressivism, but no one, not even the Immigrant Protective League, launched an effective protest against the bill. The National Committee for Constructive Immigration Legislation, formed in 1918, and supported by a great variety of reformers, tried only to soften and define the restrictive legislation.[48]

Despite occasional setbacks reform seemed to triumph in many areas during the war, but perhaps the most impressive victory came with the progressive take-over of the training camps. The Commission on Training Camp Activities was a product of the minds of Newton Baker and Raymond Fosdick. Baker, of course, had been a municipal reformer, and progressive mayor of Cleveland before becoming Secretary of War. Fosdick had been a settlement worker and Commissioner of Accounts in New York and an expert on American and European police systems.[49] As Chairman of the Commission Fosdick picked

47. Alexander Whiteside, "Our New Americans and War Activities," *Survey,* XL (June 15, 1918), 309–12.

48. John Higham, *Strangers in the Land: Patterns of American Nativism, 1860–1925,* pp. 202–3, 302–3; "For a Constructive Law on Immigration," *Survey,* XXXIX (Feb. 23, 1918), 575; Sidney L. Gulick to E. A. Ross, May 8, 1918, E. A. Ross MSS, Wisconsin State Historical Society. Paul Kellogg to Grace Abbott, Feb. 15, 1917; Grace Abbott to Arthur Kellogg, Feb. 19, 1917, Survey Associates Papers, Box 17.

49. C. H. Cramer, *Newton D. Baker: A Biography* (Cleveland, 1961); Raymond D. Fosdick, *Chronicle of a Generation: An Autobiography* (New York, 1958).

men like Joseph Lee of the Playground Association, Lee Hanner of the Russell Sage Foundation and John Mott of the YMCA to serve with him. With the aid of several other private agencies the Commission on Training Camps set out to apply the techniques of social work, recreation and community organization to the problem of mobilizing, entertaining and protecting the American serviceman at home and abroad. They organized community singing and baseball, post exchanges and theaters, and even provided university extension courses for the troops. They moved out into the communities near the military bases and in effect tried to create a massive settlement house around each army camp. No army had seen anything like it before, but it provided something of a climax to the recreation and community organization movement and a victory for those who had been arguing for creative use of leisure time, even as it angered most of the career army men.[50]

The Commission on Training Camp Activities also continued the progressive crusades against alcohol and prostitution. Clearly a part of the progressive movement, both crusades sought to preserve the nation's human resources, and were stimulated by a mixture of moral indignation and the latest medical knowledge. The prohibition movement had a long history, of course, but in its most recent upsurge it had been winning converts and legislative victories since the 1890s. The fight was led by the Anti-Saloon League and the Woman's Christian Temperance Union, but was supported by many social workers and social justice reformers who saw prohibition as a method of improving social conditions in the cities. But many of them had refused to go all the way with the crusade against alcohol. In New York a group of settlement workers had agitated against the Sunday closing of saloons; they appreciated that the saloon served as a social center. The most successful municipal reformers, including Newton Baker in Cleveland, carefully avoided enforcing some of the liquor laws, realizing how easy it was to antagonize the urban masses.[51] The war

50. Fosdick, *Chronicle of a Generation*, pp. 142–86; "The Recreation Movement in War Times," *Playground*, XII (1918), 137–51; Eva White, *Proceedings NCSW, 1919*, pp. 496–502; Mark Sullivan, *Our Times: The United States, 1900–25*, V, *Over Here, 1914–18* (New York, 1933), pp. 330–47.

51. James H. Timberlake, *Prohibition and the Progressive Movement, 1900–1920* (Cambridge, 1963), pp. 153–54; George C. Sikes, "The Liquor Question and Municipal Reform," *National Municipal Review*, V (July 1916), 411–18; Gaylord White, "Legislation Opposed by New York Social Workers," *Commons*, IX (Apr. 1904), 144–46.

stimulated the movement and brought it to a climax; it also ended the lingering doubts among many reformers. It became patriotic to support prohibition in order to save the grain for food, and for the first time in 1917 the National Conference of Social Work came out in favor of prohibition.[52] But it was more than patriotism, for temperance was one key to social advance. Edward T. Devine announced after returning from Russia in 1917 that "the social revolution which followed the prohibition of vodka was more profoundly important and more likely to be permanent than the political revolution which abolished autocracy." Robert Woods, who had long supported prohibition, predicted in 1919 that the 18th amendment would reduce poverty, nearly wipe out prostitution and crime, improve labor organization and "substantially increase our national resources by setting free vast, suppressed human potentialities."[53]

The progressive era also saw a major attack on prostitution, organized vice and the white slave trade, which seemed closely allied with the liquor traffic. Although the progressive vice reformer concentrated his attack on the madams and pimps and business interests which exploited the natural sex instincts of others, he also denied the time-honored defense of the prostitute, that it was necessary for the unmarried male to "sow his wild oats." Using the latest medical statistics, he argued that continence was the best defense against the spread of venereal disease.[54]

Progressive attitudes toward alcohol and prostitution were written into sections twelve and thirteen of the Military Draft Act. They prohibited the sale of liquor to men in uniform and gave the President power to establish zones around all military camps where prostitution and alcohol would be outlawed. There was opposition from a few military commanders, a number of city officials and from at least one irate citizen who protested that red-light districts were "God-pro-

52. Social Workers Stand for Prohibition," *Survey*, XLI (Mar. 23, 1918), 687–88; Irving Fisher to E. A. Ross, Apr. 23, 1917, Ross MSS.; Elizabeth Tilton, "Prohibition for Preparedness," *Survey*, XXXVIII (Apr. 14, 1917), 38.

53. Devine quoted by Arthur P. Kellogg, "The National Conference of Social Work," *Survey*, XXXVIII (June 16, 1917), 255; Robert A. Woods, "Prohibition and Its Social Consequences," *Proceedings NCSW, 1919*, pp. 763–64.

54. Roy Lubove, "The Progressive and the Prostitute," *Historian*, XXIV (May 1962), 308–30; Jane Addams, *A New Conscience and an Ancient Evil* (New York, 1913); Robert Woods, "Prohibition and Social Hygiene," *Social Hygiene*, V (Apr. 1919), 137–45.

vided means for prevention of the violation of innocent girls, by men who are exercising their 'God-given passions.' "[55] But Raymond Fosdick, with the full cooperation of the government, launched a major crusade to wipe out sin in the service; "Fit to Fight" became the motto. It was a typical progressive effort—a large amount of moral indignation combined with the use of the most scientific prophylaxis. Josephus Daniels, the Secretary of the Navy, disapproved of Fosdick's methods. He believed that urging the men to avoid sexual contact was the best and only way to reduce disease; "Men must live straight if they would shoot straight," he told the sailors on one occasion. But when the disease rate in the Navy became the highest in the service he gave in to Fosdick's demand that science as well as moralism be used. The crusade was successful, for by the end of 1918 every major red-light district in the country had been closed, and the venereal disease rate had been lowered to produce what one man called, "the cleanest Army since Cromwell's day."[56]

To protect the health of the soldiers was not enough, however; "We must make these men stronger in every sense, more fit, morally, mentally and physically than they have ever been in their lives . . . ," one recreation worker announced. "These camps are national universities—training schools to which the flower of American youth is being sent." When the boys go to France, "I want them to have invisible armour to take with them," Newton Baker told a conference on War Camp Community Service. "I want them to have armour made up of a set of social habits replacing those of their homes and communities."[57]

France provided a real test for the "invisible armour" of the American soldier. He was forbidden to buy or to accept as gifts any alcoholic beverage except light wine and beer. Despite hundreds of letters of

55. Fosdick, *Chronicle of a Generation,* pp. 144–48; Newton Baker to Fosdick, Sept. 20, 1917, quoted in Frederick Palmer, *Newton D. Baker: America at War* (2 vols.; New York, 1931), I, 311.

56. Fosdick, *Chronicle of a Generation,* p. 147; Fosdick, "The Program of the Commission on Training Camp Activities with Relation to the Problem of Venereal Disease," *Social Hygiene,* IV (Jan. 1918), 71–76; Arthur Kellogg to Charles W. Eliot, Aug. 30, 1917, Survey Associates Papers, Box 24. Josephus Daniels, *The Navy and the Nation: War-Time Addresses* (New York, 1919), pp. 56–69; Fosdick, *Chronicle,* pp. 162–63.

57. "Community and War Recreation Service," *Playground,* XI (1918), 349–54; Newton Baker, "Invisible Armour," *Playground,* XI (1918), 473–81. See also Fred Baldwin, "Invisible Armor," *American Quarterly,* XVI (Fall 1964), 432–44.

protest from American mothers, Fosdick and Baker decided it would be impossible to prevent the soldiers from drinking wine in France. But sex posed a more serious threat, for both the British and French armies had tried to solve the problem of venereal disease by licensing and inspecting prostitutes. Clemenceau could not understand the American attempt to outlaw prostitution and even accused the American Army of spreading disease among the French civilian population. He graciously offered to provide the Americans with licensed prostitutes. General Pershing considered the offer "too hot to handle" and gave it to Fosdick. When Fosdick showed it to Baker, the Secretary of War remarked, "For God's sake, Raymond, don't show this to the President or he'll stop the war." The Americans never accepted Clemenceau's invitation and he continued to be baffled by the American progressive mind.[58]

One of the overriding assumptions of those who sought to protect the American soldier at home and abroad was that he would learn from his experience and return to help make a better America after the war.[59] Indeed one of the major reasons for the optimism of the social justice reformers was their confidence that the experiments and social action of the war years would lead to even greater accomplishments in the reconstruction decade ahead. Robert Woods surveyed the positive actions of the federal government during wartime in the spring of 1918 and asked, "Why should it not always be so? Why not continue in the years of peace this close, vast, wholesome organism of service, of fellowship, of constructive creative power?"[60] Even Jane Addams, who saw much less that was constructive about war than did many of her colleagues, lectured for Herbert Hoover's Food Administration, and looked ahead with confidence and hope for the future.[61] Paul Kellogg, editor of *The Survey*, also mirrored

58. Palmer, *Newton Baker*, II, 292–303; Fosdick, *Chronicle*, p. 171. Just as important for understanding the progressives at war, however, was the long and elaborate scientific report drawn up by the Americans to demonstrate that the venereal disease rate was lower in the American than in the French Army.

59. See, for example, Thomas D. Elliot, "Possible Effects of War upon the Future of the Social Hygiene Movement," *Social Hygiene*, IV (Apr. 1918), 219–23.

60. Woods quoted by Winthrop Lane, "National Conference of Social Work," *Survey*, XL (June 1918), 256–57.

61. Jane Addams, *The Second Twenty Years at Hull House* (New York, 1930), pp. 144–52; Herbert Hoover to Jane Addams, Mar. 2, 1918, Addams

some of the hope for continuing the reform that the war had acceler-
ated when he wrote to his subscribers in September 1918:

> With hundreds of people for the first time shaken out of their
> narrow round of family and business interests and responding
> to public service as a patriotic call, with American help going
> out to the far ends of the earth as at no time since the early
> stages of the missionary movement; with federal action affecting
> housing, labor relations, community life, as never before; with
> reconstruction plans afoot in England and France . . . we feel
> that *The Survey* has never before faced such a great obligation
> and such a great opportunity.[62]

Of course the enthusiasm for the present and optimism for the
future was sometimes tempered by doubts. There was the occasional
glimpse of the horror of war, especially by those who went overseas.
There was the abridgment of the freedom of speech and the persecution of radicals and aliens and pacifists. There was the fear that
opposition or apathy would arise after the war to strike down the
gains, and that the American labor movement, led by Gompers, was
too conservative to take advantage of the opportunity for labor advance. There was even a lingering worry about the very enthusiasm
for reform that made the war years exciting, concern over the disap-
pearance of the opposition and even the decline of debate over immigration restriction, prohibition and other measures. But the doubts
were few and far between. Most of the social justice reformers surveyed the success of social reform at home and looked confidently
toward the future. For them the war was not so much a war to
make the world safe for democracy as it was a war that brought
to a climax their crusade for reform at home.[63]

Yet the progressives deluded themselves. They were the victims

---

MSS; Addams, "World's Food and World's Politics," *Proceedings NCSW,
1918,* pp. 650–56. Jane Addams more than most of the social justice
reformers looked ahead to international reconstruction.

62. Paul Kellogg to Jane Addams, Sept. 20, 1918, Survey Associates
Papers, Box 2.

63. Paul Kellogg to Homer Folks, Apr. 5, 1918, Box 24; Kellogg to
Edward T. Devine, July 2, Aug. 29, 1918, Box 22; Frederick Almy to
Kellogg, Oct. 21, 1918, Box 17; Arthur Gleason to Kellogg, Apr. 23,
1918, Survey Associates Papers; "Free Speech and Peaceable Assembly,"
Survey, XXXVIII (May 12, 1917), 144–45.

of their own confidence and enthusiasm, for the social reforms of the war years were caused more by the emergency situation than by a reform consensus. Quickly after the war, the Wilson administration abandoned public housing and social insurance, and withdrew the government from positive participation in many areas. The gains for labor and the Negro proved ephemeral, and the dream that the newly enfranchised women, together with a generation of young men educated on the battlefields and in the training camps, would lead a great crusade to reconstruct America turned out to be idealistic in the extreme.

By 1920 there was little left from wartime social reform except prohibition, immigration restriction and racist hysteria. The disillusionment that followed can be explained in part by the false hopes raised by the war. Many social justice progressives had been discouraged by the failure of the Progressive Party, then rescued by the excitement of the wartime social experiments. The collapse of the dreams fostered by the war changed American reformers irrevocably. They would never again be quite as optimistic and enthusiastic. Their faith in statistics and their confidence that the American people really wanted reform were shattered. Yet the despair was not complete—it never reached the depths that marked the group of young intellectuals which Ernest Hemingway came to symbolize. Their disillusionment was tempered by a lingering vision of social justice, a vision of government action to protect the rights of labor, and especially the working woman and child, of public housing and social insurance, of equal opportunity for the Negro and other minorities.

A number of social justice progressives worked quietly and sometimes forlornly during the twenties preparing to battle for the success of some of their plans in the 1930s and after. Very often their point of reference was World War I.[64] It is no longer possible to say simply that the war ended the progressive movement. It was not the war itself which killed reform, but rather the rejection afterward of the wartime measures which seemed at the time to constitute the climax to the crusade for social justice. Yet scholars interested in the collapse and survival of progressivism should examine the war years, for here were raised some of the hopes that were later dashed and some of the dreams that were later fulfilled.

64. For the story of the struggle for reform in the twenties see esp. Chambers, *Seedtime of Reform.*

PAUL A. C. KOISTINEN

The "Industrial-Military Complex" in Historical Perspective: World War I

An indisputable consequence of American entry into World War I was an unprecedented measure of government intervention in the economy. Where historians have disagreed has been over the originality, purposes, benefits, and aftereffects of wartime experiences with economic mobilization. Some historians have argued that ideas and programs for government-business cooperation in a managed economy were already well formulated before 1917; others have questioned the extent of government direction and control after the United States went to war. Also, strong evidence has been produced to show that World War I thinking and practices offered precedents for both the pro-business policies of the Republicans in the 1920's and New Deal planning in the 1930's.

A different aspect of economic mobilization which has recently attracted attention is the growth of ties between business and the military. This essay, by a leading student of the "military-industrial complex," detects the beginnings of this phenomenon in the work of various government agencies in 1917–1918. A somewhat different view, which lays greater emphasis on suspicion and hostility among military chiefs, businessmen, and civilians in government, can be found in Daniel R. Beaver's article, "Newton D. Baker and the Genesis of the War Industries Board, 1917–1918," *Journal of American History*, LII (June 1965), 43–58, and in his book, *Newton D. Baker and the American War Effort, 1917–1919* (Lincoln, Nebr., 1966).

The rubric "military-industrial complex" has gained widespread currency in the United States since being coined by President Dwight

Reprinted by permission from *Business History Review*, XLI (Winter 1967), 378–403. Copyright © 1967 by the President and Fellows of Harvard College.

D. Eisenhower in 1961. Though imprecise, the term usually refers to the partial integration of economic and military institutions for the purpose of national security. The nature and consequences of the "complex" remain matters of dispute, but few contest that modern, industrialized warfare has had far-reaching effects upon American life at all levels. Scientific and technological advances have dictated a revolution in weaponry—a revolution which has broken down the distinction between both the civilian and military worlds and the private and public economic functions. Massive spending for war and defense has spread the influence of the "managers of violence" far and wide.

Numerous studies treating the "industrial-military complex" directly and indirectly already exist. Almost without exception, all have concentrated upon the World War II and Cold War years. To focus on those years is quite natural, for it is then that the most blatant manifestations of the "complex" are evident. Nevertheless, to neglect the years before 1940 greatly limits our understanding of the subject for several reasons. In the first place, the so-called "complex" is more difficult to penetrate after 1940 than before. So comprehensive are the effects of twentieth-century warfare that it is often difficult to distinguish the central from the peripheral. Moreover, in many instances essential documents are still denied the scholar. In the second place, and more importantly, the years after 1940 mark not a start but rather a culmination in the process of partially integrating economic and military institutions.

World War I is the watershed. In 1917, the United States had to mobilize its economy totally for the first time. Since a large share of the nation's industrial productivity went to the armed services, their supply and procurement systems had to be integrated into civilian mobilization agencies. The means for doing so were determined by a very chaotic interaction of the federal government as a whole, the industrial community, and the military services. From the wartime experience, the foundations for the so-called "complex" were laid. But the armistice ended the experiment in industrialized warfare before it was complete. What began with the war, however, did not end with it. Directly and indirectly, the 1920's and 1930's were years of consolidation for the government, for industry, and for the armed services in terms of fighting a war under modern conditions. The present article deals with these processes during World War I; the inter-war years will be the subject of a future essay.

According to Professor Ellis W. Hawley, three schools have dominated American thinking about what should be the government's policy toward the concentration of economic power: maintaining competition through the antitrust laws; economic regulation and planning by the federal government; and industrial self-regulation through cooperation within business and between it and the government.[1] Of course, the three schools have never been mutually exclusive; numerous shadings within and among them exist. Industrial self-regulation as the middle way probably best characterizes the political economy of twentieth-century America. The antitrust impulse has had widespread appeal but inadequate political support. Economic planning and regulation has lacked both popularity and sustained backing. For a nation torn between its competitive, *laissez faire* ideology and the massive problems of consolidated economic power, the drift toward industrial self-regulation was quite natural. To varying degrees it found favor in the business community. For the nation at large, cooperation, or a "new competition" as it was often called, had the attraction of meeting the dictates of ideology while still solving some practical economic problems.

In theory and practice, industrial self-rule, policed by the federal government, made impressive gains during the Progressive Era.[2] But its hold was far from absolute. Antitrust sentiments were still strong; numerous divisions still existed within business and the government over matters of political economy. Despite various attempts, industry was not granted immunity from the antitrust laws by having the federal government determine in advance the legality of business practices.

What was not possible during peace became imperative during war. Even if it was politically possible, the federal government lacked the personnel, the information, or the experience necessary for the massive economic regulation World War I demanded. Under the auspices of the government, businessmen had to do it themselves. War

1. *The New Deal and the Problem of Monopoly: A Study in Economic Ambivalence* (Princeton, 1966).

2. Robert Wiebe, *Businessmen and Reform: A Study of the Progressive Movement* (Cambridge, 1962); Gabriel Kolko, *The Triumph of Conservatism: A Reinterpretation of American History, 1900–1916* (New York, 1963); Arthur M. Johnson, "Anti-trust Policy in Transition, 1908: Ideal and Reality," *Mississippi Valley Historical Review,* XLVIII (Dec., 1961), 415–34.

created the ideal conditions for industrial self-regulation. The demand for maximum munitions production and the lavish prosperity federal spending brought about quieted temporarily antitrust and anti-business dissent. Wartime opportunities for rationalizing the economy, however, were matched by grave risks. Converting the huge American economic machine to war production could end disastrously unless exactly the right means were employed.

Neither the Wilson administration, Congress, nor prominent American industrialists, financiers, and the firms they represented appeared excessively concerned about the economics of warfare between 1914 and 1917. Less prominent members of the business community led in the drive for economic preparedness. The Chamber of Commerce of the United States was in the vanguard. Since its organization in 1912, the Chamber was an outstanding advocate for government-policed industrial self-regulation. Backed by the nearly unanimous vote of its membership, the Chamber was consistently far ahead of the administration, the Congress, and the general public in policies it supported for industrial mobilization between 1915 and 1918.[3] Legitimately concerned about the economic effects of war, the Chamber also perceived that a state of hostility would further its peacetime goal. A mobilized economy "will make individual manufacturers and business men and the Government share equally in responsibility for the safety of the nation," declared *The Nation's Business* in mid-1916.[4] Chamber spokesmen never tired of reiterating that the national emergency was the perfect opportunity for businessmen to prove their new morality and patriotism to the country. Writing to the DuPonts in December 1916, the chairman of the Chamber's Executive Committee on National Defense stated:[5]

> The Chamber of Commerce of the United States has been keenly interested in the attempt to create an entirely new relationship between the Government of the United States and the industries of the United States. It is hoped that the atmosphere

3. Galen R. Fisher, "The Chamber of Commerce of the United States and the Laissez-Faire Rationale, 1912–1919" (Ph.D. dissertation, University of California, Berkeley, 1960).

4. *The Nation's Business,* June, 1916, 4.

5. Reproduced in U.S. Congress, Senate, Special Committee Investigating the Munitions Industry, *Hearings, Munitions Industry,* 73rd Cong., 1935, Part 15, 3661—hereafter cited as Nye Committee, *Hearings.*

of confidence and cooperation which is beginning in this country, as shown by the Federal Trade Commission, the Federal Reserve Board and other points of contact which are now in existence, may be further developed, and this munitions question would seem to be the greatest opportunity to foster the new spirit.

Though the Chamber of Commerce was the prominent advocate of economic preparedness, other members of the commercial world initiated the specific action in behalf of industrial preparedness. Their first opportunity came in mid-1915 when Secretary of the Navy Josephus Daniels called upon members of leading engineering and industrial societies to serve as unofficial industrial consultants for the expanding Navy. Called the Naval Consulting Board, this group ultimately organized down to the local level.

The most dynamic accomplishments of the Naval Consulting Board were performed by a subdivision called the Industrial Preparedness Committee. Discovering that neither the Army nor the Navy had adequate information about the nation's industrial potential, the committee during 1916 inventoried thousands of industrial facilities for the services. The detailed work was done by voluntary effort and private financing under the direction of the then virtually unknown Walter S. Gifford, chief statistician for the American Telephone and Telegraph Company. But the real moving spirit behind the project was Howard E. Coffin, vice-president of the Hudson Motor Car Company.[6]

For Coffin, efforts in behalf of preparedness were only an extension of his peacetime endeavors. In 1910, as president of the Society of Automotive Engineers, he had, with the help of others, transformed the society and the auto industry by bringing about the standardization of specifications and materials.[7] Rationalizing the productive process and promoting industrial organization were continuing interests of this restless individual. As few others, he foresaw the threats as well as the possibilities of industrial mobilization.

"Twentieth century warfare," Coffin insisted, "demands that the blood of the soldier must be mingled with from three to five parts of the sweat of the man in the factories, mills, mines, and fields

6. Lloyd N. Scott, *Naval Consulting Board of the United States* (Washington, 1920), 7–37, 220–23.

7. George V. Thompson, "Intercompany Technical Standardization in the Early American Automobile Industry," *Journal of Economic History,* XIV (Winter, 1954), 1–12.

of the nation in arms."[8] World War I was "the greatest business proposition since time began."[9] In the Progressive rhetoric, he and other industrialists were moved by "patriotism." Just as important, however, was the "cold-blooded" desire to protect their own interests.[10] Only industrialists and engineers were qualified to run a mobilized economy, Coffin averred. Under such leadership, war could be fought without untoward damage to the economy.

Coffin and his colleagues had plans for gradually expanding the activities of the Industrial Preparedness Committee as an agency for industrial mobilization. But a committee of unofficial industrial consultants was unsuited for such grandiose responsibilities. In August 1916, the Council of National Defense was created; the council ultimately absorbed the Naval Consulting Board.

The Council of National Defense was the brain child of Dr. Hollis Godfrey, president of the Drexel Institute of Philadelphia—an industrial training and management education institution. As early as 1899, Godfrey was nearly obsessed with the idea of management education as the high road to industrial efficiency and progress. Even before 1914, Godfrey reasoned that his ideas concerning management could serve the nation in war as well as in peace.

Early in 1916, unable to sit by while the nation drifted unprepared into war, Godfrey outlined to General Leonard Wood a plan for applying the principles of management to the economy in order to achieve optimum performance. The two sketched out a proposal for a council of national defense. Over a period of weeks, Godfrey then consulted with numerous industrial colleagues, influential friends, and administrative officials.[11] The final legislation was drafted in the War Department under Secretary Newton D. Baker's instructions. It was shepherded through Congress by the respective chairmen and influen-

8. Quoted in Franklin H. Martin, *Digest of the Proceedings of the Council of National Defense during the World War,* U.S. Congress, Senate, 73rd Cong., 2nd Sess., Document No. 193 (Washington, 1934), 512.

9. U.S. Congress, Senate, Committee on Military Affairs, *Hearings, Investigation of the War Department,* 65th Cong., 2nd Sess., 1917–1918, 2281—hereafter cited as Chamberlain Committee, *Hearings.*

10. U.S. Congress, House, Committee on Naval Affairs, *Hearings, Estimates Submitted by the Secretary of the Navy—1916,* 64th Cong., 1st Sess., 1916, 3360.

11. U.S. Congress, House, Subcommittee No. 2 (Camps), Select Committee on Expenditures in the War Department, *Hearings, War Expenditures,* Serial 3, 66th Cong., 1st Sess., 1920, 880–90—hereafter cited as Graham Committee, *Hearings.*

tial members of the two Military Affairs committees. No meaningful congressional debate took place.

Passed in August 1916, as part of the Army Appropriations Act, the legislation provided for a Council of National Defense consisting of six Cabinet officers. Council members would nominate and the President appoint seven experts in various fields to act as a National Defense Advisory Commission (NDAC) to the Council. Together with the NDAC, the Council would serve as the President's advisory body on all aspects of industrial mobilization.

The creation of the NDAC was actually a formalization of the procedures adopted by the Naval Consulting Board: industrial experts voluntarily donated their talents as public officials without surrendering their positions or incomes as private citizens. The precedent was an important one. It provided the wherewithal for industrialists to guide the process of mobilizing the economy. Moreover, the personnel selected for the National Defense Advisory Commission revealed that it was more an expansion of the Naval Consulting Board than a new agency. Walter S. Gifford was selected as director and Grosvenor B. Clarkson, a journalist, advertising executive, and former civil servant who had handled publicity for the Board, was ultimately to become secretary. Both Coffin and Godfrey were chosen as members along with Bernard M. Baruch and others.

The legislation for the Council of National Defense was predicated on the assumption that private industry would be the primary source of munitions supply in the event of war. Nevertheless, opponents of preparedness zeroed in on the munitions makers in an effort to discredit the drive for an enlarged military force. War mongering, profiteering at the nation's expense, it was charged, would be reduced if the government alone produced munitions. Almost to a man, military personnel opposed the proposition as impractical. It would be prohibitively expensive and would not provide the armed forces the quantity of munitions needed once war was fought, they maintained.[12]

12. Arthur A. Ekrich, Jr., *The Civilian and the Military* (New York, 1956), 160; U.S. Congress, House, Committee on Military Affairs, *Hearings, To Increase the Efficiency of the Military Establishment of the United States,* 64th Cong., 1st Sess., 1916, 62–64, 342, 347, 498–513, 518–20, 532–35, 550–51, 738–39—hereafter cited as HMAC, *Hearings,* 1916; U.S. Congress, Senate, Committee on Military Affairs, *Hearings, Preparedness for National Defense,* 64th Cong., 1st Sess., 1916, 84–85, 519–20, 524–30—hereafter cited as SMAC, *Hearings,* 1916; Marvin A. Kreidberg and Merton G. Henry, *History of Military Mobilization in the United*

Industry, of course, took a similar stand, especially since the armaments industry was threatened as Allied orders were cut back.

To settle the issue, the National Defense Act of 1916 authorized a board of three military officers and two civilians to study the matter and make recommendations. They met in November–December 1916, under the direction of Colonel Francis J. Kernan. Benedict Crowell, chairman of Crowell and Little Construction Company of Cleveland and later Assistant Secretary of War, and R. Goodwyn Rhett, former mayor of Charleston, S.C., president of the People's National Bank of Charleston, and president of the Chamber of Commerce of the United States, served as the civilian members. In its study, the Kernan Board relied heavily on the work of the Naval Consulting Board. Coffin, along with others involved in industrial preparedness, lent their advice.

After inspecting government arsenals and consulting with some leading industrialists, the board reported that it was "not desirable for the Government to undertake, unaided by private plants, to provide for its needs in arms, munitions, and equipment." In the event of war the government should depend "largely upon private plants for war material. . . ." But the board did not stop there. Reading like an editorial from *The Nation's Business,* its report praised businessmen for their patriotism in helping to prepare for an emergency and assured the nation that industry would continue to cooperate in the future. Concerning more immediate problems, the board recommended that plants producing munitions for the Allies not be permitted to remain idle when orders were terminated. It concluded by calling for a comprehensive plan for industrial mobilization.[13]

Though only beginning steps in the long trek toward a mobilized economy, the work of the Naval Consulting Board, the organization of the Council of National Defense and its National Defense Advisory Commission, and the conclusions of the Kernan Board were of the greatest significance. They signaled the beginning of a government-industry partnership for the purpose of national security. The initiative came from industry, but, out of necessity, the federal government, and specifically the military services, appeared willing to go along. When announcing the appointment of the NDAC members in October

States Army, 1775–1945, U.S. Dept. of Army Pamphlet No. 20-212 (Washington, 1955), 336–37.

13. U.S. Congress, Senate, *Government Manufacture of Arms, Munitions, and Equipment,* 64th Cong., 2nd Sess., 1917, Document 664, 5–17.

1916, President Wilson observed: "The organization of the Council [of National Defense] . . . opens up a new and direct channel of communication and cooperation between business and scientific men and all departments of the Government. . . ."[14] Howard E. Coffin had ambitious plans for the Council of National Defense. He wrote to the DuPonts in December 1916:[15]

> Private industry in all the varied lines of Governmental supply must be encouraged and not discouraged. It must be educated, organized, and trained for the national emergency service. A closer and more mutually satisfactory business relation [sic] must be established between the industrial lines and every Department of the Government, and the work of the newly created Council of National Defense must be directed to this end.
>
> .   .   .
>
> The first meeting of the Council of National Defense and its Advisory Commission will be held in the office of the Secretary of War, December 6th, and within six months thereafter it is our hope that we may lay the foundation for that closely knit structure, industrial, civil and military, which every thinking American has come to realize is vital for the future life of this country, in peace and in commerce, no less than in possible war.

Organized in December 1916, the Council of National Defense and its National Defense Advisory Commission did not actively function until March. When war was declared, the Council and the NDAC, authorized only to investigate, advise, and recommend policies to the President and his administration, also assumed responsibilities for mobilizing the economy.

Lack of experience explains in part the failure to create a better, more powerful agency. No one was fully able to anticipate what was required. The nation had to go through the pragmatic process of working out solutions as problems arose. More importantly, there was the widespread desire to avoid permanent political and economic change during the war. Hopefully, a makeshift organization like the Council of National Defense, without clearly defined authority and consisting mainly of existing department heads, would be sufficient to meet war needs. When hostilities ceased, it could easily be dis-

14. New York *Times,* Oct. 12, 1916, 10.
15. Reproduced in Nye Committee, *Hearings,* Part 16, 4056-57.

banded.[16] Moreover, vital issues of political economy were central to any scheme for industrial mobilization. With Progressive divisions still great over the government's role in the economy, any attempt to set up new, powerful mobilization machinery could end in paralyzing debate in Congress and in the nation. Consistently, the President and the Congress avoided facing issues of economic mobilization whenever possible. Not until the mobilization program was on the verge of collapse during the winter of 1917–1918 did President Wilson strengthen the nation's industrial mobilization apparatus. Even then, only the minimal changes essential to the continued operation of the economy were made.

Consistent with prewar precedents, business representatives of the NDAC, not the Cabinet members of the Council of National Defense, led in mobilizing the economy. Haltingly, the commissioners groped their way in search of the proper means. At the outset, they chose to create the most efficient organization possible with the least disturbance to the *status quo*. That meant the federal government would accept, use, and adjust itself to the configuration of power in and the basic pattern of the private sector of the economy.[17]

Several months after its creation, the NDAC divided itself into semiautonomous committees corresponding to the natural subdivisions of the economy: the most important were transportation, raw materials, munitions and manufacturing, and general supplies. In order to relate commission activities to those of the economy as a whole, the commissioners selected or had various industries choose members to represent their interests on committees within the commission. Over 100 such committees were ultimately organized. Almost inevita-

16. For the best expression of this sentiment see: U.S. Congress, Subcommittee of the House Committee on Appropriations, *Hearings, Council of National Defense*, 65th Cong., 1st Sess., 1917, 37–38, 42–43—hereafter cited as Appropriations Subcommittee, *Hearings*. See also, Daniel R. Beaver, *Newton D. Baker and the American War Effort, 1917–1919* (Lincoln, 1966), 51–52, 71–76.

17. Preserving the economic *status quo* during wartime was a central idea of Coffin and was a basic assumption of the Kernan Board. See the discussion of Baruch below and also: Nye Committee, *Minutes of the General Munitions Board From April 4 to August 9, 1917*, 74th Cong., 2nd Sess., 1936, Senate Committee Print No. 6, 1, 2, 4; 6, 39; Nye Committee, *Final Report of the Chairman of the United States War Industries Board to the President of the United States, February, 1919*, 74th Cong., 1st Sess., 1935, Senate Committee Print No. 3, 43–44; Fisher, "Chamber of Commerce," 435–36.

bly, major firms were dominant. Where a trade association like the American Iron and Steel Institute was supreme in its field, it provided the representatives. The Cooperative Committee on Canned Goods, for example, consisted of individuals from the California Packing Corporation, Libby, McNeil & Libby, the H. J. Heinz Company, and others; the steel committee included Elbert H. Gray as chairman and other members from Bethlehem Steel Corporation, Jones and Laughlin Steel Company, Republic Iron and Steel Company, and Lackawanna Steel Company.

The "dollar-a-year" man system was devised to provide the government with the services of experts without undue sacrifice on their part. Because appropriations were limited, businessmen often paid for their own expenses, clerical help, and even office space. Though far from a perfect solution, the system worked for a while. It assured industry's cooperation at a time when the nation's mobilization agency was without authority. Industrialists and merchandisers worked hand in hand with the commissioners. Information on the capacity of the essential industries was collected, the means for curtailing production for civilian uses and converting industry to meet governmental needs were considered, and rudimentary price, priority, and other controls were developed.[18]

Quite early in the war, therefore, the NDAC devised the means for organizing and controlling the private sector of the economy. The methods were often crude and piecemeal, but they could be perfected. Rapid progress was possible because the cooperative efforts of industry and the federal government on behalf of economic regulation during the Progressive Era prepared them to a degree for wartime conditions. Nevertheless, the economic mobilization program floundered for almost a year. Organizing supply—the civilian economy—was not enough. Demand—the multiple needs of claimant agencies like the Army and Navy—also had to be controlled. Throughout the war, demand exceeded supply. Consequently, unless war contracts

18. For a complete list of NDAC committees see: U.S. Council of National Defense, *First Annual Report* (Washington, 1917), 97–127. See also, Nye Committee, *Minutes of the Council of National Defense,* 11–14, 18–19, 30, and *Minutes of the Advisory Commission of the Council of National Defense and Minutes of the Munitions Standard Board,* 3, 11, 28, 30–32, 74th Cong., 2nd Sess., 1936, Senate Committee Prints 7 and 8; Appropriations Subcommittee, *Hearings,* 3–157; Grosvenor B. Clarkson, *Industrial America in the World War: The Strategy Behind the Line, 1917–1918* (New York, 1923), 26–29.

were distributed with care and in order of precedence, the equilibrium of the economy could not be maintained. The NDAC, however, had no authority over the procurement agencies. They were free to do as they liked. A crisis was avoidable as long as claimant agencies procured in an orderly manner and cooperated with the NDAC. To a degree, most did. The Navy Department adjusted to hostilities without major difficulty. That was possible because it was always in a state of semi-preparedness and had an efficient supply system dating back to the late nineteenth century. Other private and public civilian agencies like the American Red Cross, the Emergency Fleet Corporation, and the Fuel and Food Administration also proved to be sufficiently flexible. But not the War Department. The flagrant inadequacies of its supply apparatus undermined the efforts of the NDAC.

When war broke out, five, and later eight, bureaus—the Quartermaster Corps, the Ordnance Department, and the like—independently procured for the Army. Each had its own purchasing staff, handled its own funds, stored its own goods, and transported its own supplies. Determined to meet their own needs, the bureaus competed with one another and other claimant agencies. Contracts were let indiscriminately, facilities commandeered without plan, and equipment transported without regard to need. With such a system, it was virtually impossible for the War Department to come up with reliable statistics concerning requirements.

War Department difficulties did not start with the war. The politics of supply had been a constant source of aggravation within the department for decades.[19] The strife became especially intense around the

19. Testimony of military and other witnesses before congressional committees is the best source for military supply operation immediately before and during World War I. See the relevant portions of: HMAC, *Hearings,* 1916; SMAC, *Hearings,* 1916; Graham Committee, *Hearings,* Serial 1 and 3; Chamberlain Committee, *Hearings;* U.S. Congress, Senate Subcommittee of the Committee on Military Affairs, *Hearings, Reorganization of the Army,* 66th Cong., 2nd Sess., 1919; U.S. Congress, House, Committee on Military Affairs, *Hearings, Army Reorganization,* 66th Cong., 1st Sess., 1919–1920—hereafter cited as HMAC, *Hearings,* 1920.

Secondary sources on the Army are legion. None of them treat adequately with supply factors. The better ones include: John Dickinson, *The Building of an Army: A Detailed Account of Legislation, Administration and Opinion in the United States, 1915–1920* (New York, 1922); J. Franklin Crowell, *Government War Contracts* (New York, 1920); Paul Y. Hammond, *Organizing for Defense: The American Military Establishment in the Twentieth Century* (Princeton, 1961); Samuel P. Huntington, *The*

turn of the century when the Chief of Staff-General Staff system was created by the reforms of Elihu Root (Secretary of War, 1899–1904). Supervising the bureaus and bringing them under some centralized control were part of the responsibility of the Chief of Staff. But the tenaciously independent bureaus successfully resisted control. The staff-bureau conflict continued into the war years. Secretary of War Baker would not move forcefully to resolve it. A Progressive dedicated to applying local solutions to modern problems, Baker opposed temporary changes in the federal government during the war out of fear they might become permanent. Moreover, the former mayor of Cleveland consistently avoided controversy. Attempting to compromise nearly irreconcilable differences between the General Staff and the bureaus, Baker allowed the War Department to drift hopelessly toward disaster.[20]

The General Staff-bureau controversy in part was responsible for the Army failing to anticipate the nature of twentieth-century warfare. Industrial production was as important, or more important, to military success as tactics or strategy. Relating its supply and procurement apparatus to a mobilized economy had to be part of the military mission in modern times.[21] Had the staff-bureau conflict ended with the war and an efficient supply system been fashioned, the Army could have adjusted to emergency conditions with relative ease. Since neither took place, the Army came close to losing its control of supply by threatening the entire civilian economy.

Out of war costs approximating $32,000,000,000, the Army spent $14,500,000,000 between April 1916 and June 1919.[22] Pouring such

---

Soldier and the State: The Theory and Politics of Civil-Military Relations (New York, 1964); Otto L. Nelson, Jr., *National Security and the General Staff* (Washington, 1946); Kreidberg and Henry, *Military Mobilization;* Erna Risch, *The Quartermaster Corps: Organization, Supply, and Services* (Washington, 1953); Constance McLaughlin Green, Harry C. Thomson, and Peter C. Roots, *The Ordnance Department: Planning Munitions for War* (Washington, 1955).

20. Beaver, *Baker,* 5–7, 51–52, 71–72, 80–81, 108–109, 152, 178, 210–11, 215–17, 243–46; C. H. Cramer, *Newton D. Baker: A Biography* (New York, 1961), 136–37.

21. Industrial Mobilization Plan, 1933—contained in U.S. War Policies Commission, *Hearings,* 72nd Cong., 1st Sess., House Document No. 163, 401–402.

22. John M. Clark, *The Cost of the World War to the American People* (New Haven, 1931), 30; Crowell, *War Contracts,* 63. For comparative

vast amounts of money into the economy through the department's antiquated supply system unavoidably produced havoc.

To mitigate the effect, the National Defense Advisory Commission, while still organizing supply and attempting to perfect wartime economic controls, was forced to assume responsibility for coordinating supply and demand. No other agency existed for the purpose. Its task was almost impossible. The procurement agencies had the statutory authority; the NDAC had no more than advisory powers. They were not enough to hold the largest of the procurement agencies in line.

The NDAC's difficulties with the War Department stemmed from two sources. In the first place, according to military dictum, those who controlled strategy must also control supply. The Army looked upon civilian mobilization agencies as a threat to its supply prerogatives. The very weakness of the Army supply system served only to strengthen the suspicion. Secondly, the War Department's supply network did not correspond with that of the civilian economy. The bureaus were organized along functional lines—ordnance, quartermaster, and the like; the economy was informally structured according to commodities—raw materials, industrial products, and so forth.[23] With the NDAC patterned after the economy, effectively coordinating supply and demand was out of the question. Logically, the Army had not only to reform its supply system but also restructure it along commodity lines. It stubbornly resisted until early in 1918.

The Army was able to resist not only because of its statutory authority, but also because Baker was selected as chairman of the Council of National Defense and served as President Wilson's chief adviser on industrial mobilization. Unable to bring order out of confusion in the War Department, Baker failed to rise above departmental interests as chairman of the Council. He used his position to maintain the Army's prerogatives undiminished.[24] For almost a year after the outbreak of war, therefore, the War Department insisted that the

---

purposes, the War Department figures would be slightly lower if estimated normal expenses for the war years were subtracted.

23. U.S. War Department, Purchase, Storage, and Traffic Division, General Staff, Supply Bulletin No. 29, Nov. 7, 1918—reproduced in Graham Committee, *Hearings*, Serial 1, 128–32.

24. Cramer, *Baker*, 122–23; Frederick Palmer, *Newton D. Baker: America at War* (2 vols., New York, 1931), I, 372; Beaver, *Baker*, 71–76; Clarkson, *Industrial America*, 41–42.

civilian economy adjust to its decentralized, inefficient, functional supply system rather than *vice versa*. The tail was attempting to wag
the dog.

At first the NDAC accepted the War Department terms. It attempted to make the War Department system work by serving more
or less as a bridge between the industrial and military worlds. With
the Army bureaus unable to keep up, the recently organized Cooperative Committees of the NDAC performed procurement activities. Individuals and committees aided the Army in distributing contracts
within the industries they represented. In the case of the Quartermaster
Corps, the Committee on Supplies literally built a procurement system
around the corps and assumed many of its functions. NDAC aid
unquestionably kept the Army bureaus from being totally swamped.
But as worked out, the system was not an unmixed blessing. Indeed,
commission operations were often illegal. Actually, if not nominally,
industrialists awarded contracts to themselves and their colleagues.
Small groups of businessmen admittedly engaged in collusive activity—activity sanctioned by the government. Army regulations and
the antitrust laws were being violated.

The expediency, not the legality, of the NDAC's operations was
what bothered its members. Out of need, the NDAC was forced
to assume the responsibilities of a general mobilization agency without
that authority. The Army, and the Navy as well, used or ignored
the NDAC to suit its own purposes. Frustrated, the commissioners
began pressing the Council of National Defense to sanction a more
effective organization. The latter yielded to NDAC entreaties only
reluctantly. At first, a Munitions Standards Board, later a General
Munitions Board, was created. Both were intended to facilitate military
procurement; neither had much effect. As creatures of the Council
of National Defense, they lacked authority. Technically independent
of the NDAC, they were really only extensions of it. After months
of turmoil, the hopelessly inadequate NDAC still remained the principal mobilization agency.[25] As spring gave way to summer in 1917,

25. Testimony of various members of the NDAC before Congressional
Committees is one of the best sources on Commission activities: Chamber-
lain Committee, *Hearings,* 1850–1884—Gifford; Graham Committee, *Hear-
ings,* Serial 3, 869–79, 987–1019—Gifford and Frank A. Scott; Graham
Committee, *Hearings,* Serial 1, 333–447, 1793–1857—Clarkson, Charles
Eiseman, and Baruch; Appropriations Subcommittee, *Hearings,* 3–157. The
day to day evolution of the Council of National Defense and its Advisory
Commission are traced out in: *Council of National Defense Minutes;*

confusion was rife and the efforts to harness the economy were bogging down.

By July 1917, change was essential. The NDAC structure could not maintain economic balance. Backed by influential members of the administration like William G. McAdoo, the Secretary of the Treasury and President Wilson's son-in-law, the commissioners made a plea for the creation of a mobilization agency freed from military control and able to centralize and enforce its decisions.[26]

The impetus for change was strengthened by the first extended debate in Congress involving economic mobilization. NDAC operations, where favored businessmen could serve simultaneously as government agents and contractors, took on the proportions of a national scandal when publicized. The agitation was triggered by those business interests who found themselves excluded from a decision-making process which affected their interests. After acrimonious debate, Congress included in the Lever Act a provision restricting individuals from serving or acting in a capacity to influence the awarding of contracts beneficial to themselves or their firms.[27]

The drive for a more effective mobilization agency combined with congressional criticism led to a general reorganization in July 1917. The Council of National Defense replaced the NDAC structure with the War Industries Board (WIB). As its name implied, the board was to regulate the entire industrial might of the nation, not simply to expedite munitions production. The WIB absorbed the various committees and boards that had proliferated over the months under

---

NDAC Minutes; General Munitions Board Minutes; Nye Committee, Minutes of the War Industries Board from August 1, 1917, to December 19, 1918, 74th Cong., 1st Sess., 1935, Senate Committee Print No. 4; Council of National Defense, *First Annual Report*, and *Second Annual Report* (Washington, 1918).

26. *Council of National Defense Minutes*, 140; *NDAC Minutes*, 75–78, 80–81; Martin, *Digest*, 234; Beaver, *Baker*, 71.

27. *Cong. Rec.*, 65th Cong., 1st Sess., Vol. 55, Part 4, 3335–41, Part 5, 4590–4610, 4651–79, 4814–15, 5001–5049 (intermittent), 5169–89 (intermittent), 5214–25; *Cong. Rec.*, 66th Cong., 2nd Sess., Vol. 59, Part 4, 4089–4091; *Council of National Defense Minutes*, 129; *NDAC Minutes*, 80, 82, 85; *General Munitions Board Minutes*, 131, 142–43, 208–209. For an extended investigation of NDAC committees involving alleged conflict of interest in general and the Committee on Supplies in particular, see: Chamberlain Committee, *Hearings*, 593–1604 (intermittent), 1791–98. See also, Seward W. Livermore, *Politics is Adjourned: Woodrow Wilson and the War Congress, 1916–1918* (Middletown, 1966), 52–57.

the Council of National Defense. For the first time, the federal government had one centralized organization for controlling industry.

In order to meet Congressional and business criticism, the WIB between August and December 1918 disbanded the Cooperative Committees of Industries. It then turned to the Chamber of Commerce of the United States to supervise and certify the formation of new industrial committees. Industries with trade associations or similar societies "democratically" elected members to represent them before the WIB. Precautions were exercised to insure that nonmember firms had a voice. For unorganized industries, the Chamber facilitated organization. The elected bodies were called War Service Committees. Unlike the NDAC committees, their members were private, not public, representatives; industry financed their operations. Many of the committees were new, some—e.g. steel—were the old group with a new name and only minor changes. The Chamber of Commerce had been advocating such a system since before the war. In part it was based on the English mobilization experience.[28]

The War Service Committees granted business far more immunity from the antitrust laws than even the most sanguine advocates of industrial cooperation espoused during the Progressive years. A private, commercial body, not the federal government, certified committees to represent the collective interests of business. As a result, the modern trade association movement began to come of age. Associations grew rapidly in number and importance during the war years.[29]

28. For the creation of the WIB and its War Service Committees, see: *Council of National Defense Minutes,* 151–52, 170–71, 196–97, 215–16; *WIB Minutes,* 31, 38, 50, 69, 78, 93, 111–12, 208, 504–505; Chamberlain Committee, *Hearings,* 1850–84—Gifford testimony; Fisher, "Chamber of Commerce," 335–40, 343–461; William F. Willoughby, *Government Organization in War Time and After: A Survey of the Federal Civil Agencies Created for the Prosecution of the War* (New York, 1919), 80–91; Bernard M. Baruch, *American Industry in the War: A Report of the War Industries Board* (March, 1921), ed. by Richard H. Hippelheuser (New York, 1941), 20–23, 109–116; Clarkson, *Industrial America,* 240, 300–314; Benedict Crowell and Robert F. Wilson, *The Giant Hand: Our Mobilization and Control of Industry and Natural Resources, 1917–1918* (New Haven, 1921), 24–27, 99–103; *Final Report of the WIB,* 13–15, 40–41, 50–51.

29. There is no one outstanding comprehensive work on trade associations. Several of the better volumes include: Joseph H. Foth, *Trade Associations: Their Service to Industry* (New York, 1930); National Industrial Conference Board, *Trade Associations: Their Economic Significance and Legal Status* (New York, 1925); U.S. Department of Commerce, *Trade Association Activities* (Washington, 1927).

The change from the informal, legally tenuous NDAC Cooperative Committees, reminiscent of the ambiguous relations between the government and industry during the Progressive years, was essential. Without the full support of all industrial elements, economic mobilization was difficult, if not impossible. Out of need, the federal government dropped its reservations about trade associations. Indeed, industry could treat with the government only on an organized basis. Writing in *The Nation's Business* in August 1918, Chamber of Commerce President Harry A. Wheeler (vice-president, Union Trust Company of Chicago) declared:[30]

> Creation of the War Service Committees promises to furnish the basis for a truly national organization of industry whose proportions and opportunities are unlimited.
>
> . . .
>
> The integration of business, the expressed aim of the National Chamber, is in sight. War is the stern teacher that is driving home the lesson of cooperative effort.

Representing private interests, the War Service Committees were not officially a part of the WIB. Subdivisions of the board, called Commodity Committees, determined policy for and administered the various industries. The committees were usually staffed with industrialists on a "dollar-a-year" basis but allegedly free from conflicts of interest. Claimant agencies such as the Army and Navy also had representatives on the committees. To maintain a clear line of demarcation between the public and private domains, War Service Committees only "advised" the Commodity Committees. Some 57 Commodity Committees and over 300 War Service Committees were ultimately organized. The former were grouped according to the natural patterns of the economy: chemicals, textiles, finished products, and so forth. The latter operated with the Commodity Committee to which they corresponded.

The WIB never really got under way until early in 1918. By then it was clear that the distinction between public and private interests within the board was more apparent than real. The chief of the Agricultural Implements and Wood Products Section had been manager of the John Deere Wagon Company; at the head of Automotive Products was the former treasurer of the Studebaker Corporation; the former president of the Fisk Rubber Company was chief of the

30. *The Nation's Business,* August, 1918, 9–10.

Rubber and Rubber Goods Section.[31] Serving in such capacities, industrialists were supposed to "dissociate" themselves from their firms. But in November, 1918, the acting chairman of the WIB observed that individuals could absent themselves from negotiations if their own firms were involved. Not until mid-1918 did the board begin to institute precautionary policies against compromising appointments.[32]

Even if no conflict of interest existed, the Commodity Committee–War Service Committee system was not the neat separation of private and public interests that its proponents maintained. At best, the decision-making process was organic. Grosvenor B. Clarkson described it as follows:

> Through the commodity sections on the side of Government and the war service committees on the side of business, all industry was merged in the War Industries Board. Subject to the veto of the chairman of the Board, as the supreme interpreter of the national good, industry imposed its own emergency laws and regulations and assumed nine tenths of the burden and responsibility of enforcing them.

Clarkson went on to say that the Commodity Committee–War Service Committee system was the very nerve center and major source of policy for the WIB.[33] The board was a form of industrial self-regulation writ large. Nonetheless, the organization of the WIB was a giant step forward. Effective industrial control was possible. Private industry was organized, an agency capable of coordinating mobilization existed, and trained personnel were available.

Regardless of the progress, the reorganization did not deal with the fundamental flaw. The WIB was without authority. Created by the Council of National Defense, it had only advisory powers. Actually the board's creation was a victory for Secretary Baker and the War Department. They had resisted the concerted drive for an agency independent of and superior to the military services. Wilson upheld

31. Principal WIB officials, their affiliations, and sources of income are given in Nye Committee, *Hearings,* Part 16, 4142–45. Complete lists of WIB personnel and members of the War Service Committees are conveniently available in Clarkson, *Industrial America,* 501–543.

32. Michael D. Reagen, "Serving Two Masters: Problems in the Employment of Dollar-A-Year and Without Compensation Personnel" (Ph.D. dissertation, Princeton University, 1959), 7–8, 17.

33. Clarkson, *Industrial America,* 98, 303–311.

them.[34] The Army still had the authority to force its methods on the economy. The WIB stood by helplessly. An impasse had been reached. Either the Army had to give way or the mobilization program would halt. The latter occurred before the former.

Chaired by Frank A. Scott, president of Warner and Swasey Company, a Cleveland precision equipment manufacturer, the WIB first faltered and then stumbled. Deterioration was rapid after October, 1917, when Scott resigned, his health broken through agonizing months spent in government service. Daniel Willard, president of the Baltimore and Ohio Railroad Company, was practically drafted to replace him. But on January 11, 1918, he also quit in disgust over the board's impotence. A crippled WIB simply could not fulfill its functions. Various sections remained active but without over-all direction. Like a convulsed person, the WIB's limbs twitched without central motor control. For a time, a so-called War Council, made up of representatives from leading war agencies and others, tried without much success to provide leadership. The crisis was at hand. A new chairman for the WIB was not appointed until March. No one who was considered qualified would take the job without sweeping changes.[35]

The paralysis that gripped the board was matched by that of the economy. Uncontrolled procurement overloaded the Northeast with contracts far beyond its capacity to produce. With the unusually severe winter of 1917–1918, fuel was critically short and the railroad and shipping industries virtually halted in some sections of the nation. The mobilization effort, indeed the entire economy, appeared on the brink of collapse. To remedy the crisis, the administration was forced to bring the railroads under national control in December 1917. But overall coordination of procurement and production was essential to resolve the critical economic conditions. On that crucial issue the administration was stalemated.[36]

34. Beaver, *Baker,* 71–75.

35. *Ibid.,* 75–78; *WIB Minutes,* 2, 6, 13–15, 94, 146; *Council of National Defense Minutes,* 200; Chamberlain Committee, *Hearings,* 2282–83—Coffin testimony; War Policies Commission, *Hearings,* 169–70, 177–78—Daniel Willard testimony; Palmer, *Baker,* I, 378–79; Clarkson, *Industrial America,* 36–49, 83–84, 202–203; Crowell and Wilson, *The Giant Hand,* 22–27.

36. See the following secondary sources for the winter crisis and its resolution: Beaver, *Baker,* 79–109; Alexander D. Noyes, *The War Period of American Finance, 1908–1925* (New York, 1926), 244–78; L. C. Marshall, "A Nation of Economic Amateurs," *Readings in the Economics*

In the absence of executive leadership, the Senate Military Affairs
Committee, under the leadership of a Democratic maverick, Senator
George E. Chamberlain, of Oregon, moved on its own. The committee
conducted an investigation of the War Department from December
12, 1917, until the end of March. It established beyond question
the chaos in Army supply and highlighted its effects on the economy.

The Chamberlain Committee was greatly influenced by Waddill
Catchings, formerly of J. P. Morgan and Company, now chairman
of the War Committee of the Chamber of Commerce of the United
States, and president of ironworks in New York and Ohio. For months,
argued Catchings, Chamber members had devoted full-time effort
to perfecting the nation's mobilization machinery only to have conditions deteriorate rather than improve. Businessmen found their economic fortunes threatened not by government regulation but by
government chaos. With a united Chamber behind him, Catchings
recommended that the United States follow the British experience:
separate procurement from the military and place it under a civilian-
controlled ministry of munitions; and create a War Cabinet to direct
the over-all national war effort.[37]

In January 1918, the Chamberlain Committee presented two bills
to Congress incorporating the Chamber of Commerce recommendations.[38] The proposed legislation led to the most extended and knowledgeable debate on economic mobilization heard in the halls of Congress during World War I. Legislation for a ministry of munitions,
but not the war cabinet, was seriously considered. In order to
circumvent it, the Army began to reform its supply system and the
administration came forth with the Overman Act: a sweeping grant
of authority for the President to reshuffle his administration to meet
the demands of warfare. With the full weight of the administration
behind the compromise proposal, the Chamberlain Committee legis-

of War, ed. by J. Maurice Clark, Walton H. Hamilton, and Harold G.
Moulton (Chicago, 1918), 221–24; Clarkson, Industrial America, 42–45,
51–59, 138–39, 199–200, 234–35, 453; Benedict Crowell and Forrest Wilson,
The Armies of Industry, I (New Haven, 1921), 4–6; Livermore, Politics
Is Adjourned, 62–104; Palmer, Baker, II, 66–84; Frederic L. Paxson, Amer-
ica at War: 1917–1918 (Boston, 1939), 210–228, 250–53.

37. Chamberlain Committee, Hearings, 1885–1924.
38. Cong. Rec., 65th Cong., 2nd Sess., Vol. 56, Part I, 557, 1004,
Part 2, 1077–78; U.S. Congress, Senate, Committee on Military Affairs,
Director of Munitions, 65th Cong., 2nd Sess., 1918, Senate Report No.
200 to accompany S. 3311, 1–2.

tion never stood a chance. In May 1918, the Overman bill passed with only slight opposition.[39]

The compromise succeeded only because Wilson ended the War Department's domination of the mobilization program in March. Under his general powers as President and Commander in Chief, Wilson separated the WIB from the Council of National Defense and placed it directly under himself. After the passage of the Overman Act, the President confirmed his action with an Executive Order. To chair the strengthened board, Wilson selected Bernard M. Baruch. According to the latter's instructions, the WIB's specific and general powers were great indeed. They included general coordinating authority over procurement. Without *statutory* authority, much of the board's action remained legally tenuous. Moreover, the President's directive was vaguely qualified at many points. Nevertheless, with Wilson's full backing, the nearly complete support of business, and the critical conditions the nation faced, the WIB was able to enforce its decisions in most instances. The winter crisis, therefore, was resolved with the military services maintaining control of supply but not of the economy.

Probably without anyone being fully aware of its consequences, the Overman Act set a most important precedent for twentieth-century warfare. Unlike most belligerent nations, in the United States the military services continued to procure their own munitions and, therefore, remained in a position to affect the economy most directly and vitally during war as well as peace. To varying degrees Great Britain and France separated procurement from the services and placed it under civilian-controlled munitions ministries. Even in pre-revolutionary Russia the armed services did not maintain unqualified control of their own purchasing. In Germany, quite a different pattern emerged. The economy was largely mobilized under military authorities in league with large industrial elements.[40]

39. *Cong. Rec.*, 65th Cong., 2nd Sess., Vol. 56, Part 1, 977–79, 980–83, Part 2, 1194–1211, 1242–44, 1607–21, 1686–95, 1747, 1819–32, 1842–52, 2095–2105, Part 3, 2136–49, Part 4, 3815, 4504–26, 4572–83, 4945–73, 5013–23, 5551–71, 5739–66, Part 9, 8616.

40. E. M. H. Lloyd, *Experiments in State Control at the War Office and the Ministry of Food* (London, 1924); John A. Fairle, *British War Administration* (New York, 1919); Pierre Renouvin, *The Forms of War Government in France* (New Haven, 1927); S. O. Zagorsky, *State Control of Industry in Russia during the War* (New Haven, 1928); Robert B. Armeson, *Total Warfare and Compulsory Labor: A Study of the Military-Industrial Complex in Germany during World War I* (The Hague, 1964).

Maintaining procurement in the hands of the armed services was dictated more by political economy than military necessity. Businessmen had directed economic mobilization since April 1917, because they were the only ones qualified to do so. Yet, Wilson, members of his administration, and the public at large doubted the ability of business to place the interests of the nation above its own.[41] Such attitudes, combined with the desire to avoid political and economic changes during the war, led to granting industry a great deal of latitude for perfecting the mobilization machinery, while ultimate authority was continued with the traditional procurement agencies. Only when that expedient failed, did the business-dominated WIB gain some authority under the Overman Act.

To many government officials, going further than the Overman legislation, by separating supply from the armed services, was both undesirable and politically hazardous. It would have meant turning over to industry directly billions of dollars of contracts. The ministry of munitions legislation supported by the Chamberlain Committee was no more than a general grant of authority for a Director of Munitions to perform procurement functions. Out of necessity, the director would have to use the WIB or a similar agency controlled by businessmen to fulfill his responsibilities. Of course, under WIB operations, contracts were virtually in industry's hand anyway. Nonetheless, as long as the armed services maintained the legal right of contracting, ceremonial distinctions between government and business operations were preserved.

Since the Commodity Committee–War Service Committee system nominally separated private and public interests, Congress appeared satisfied with the WIB. Nevertheless, the "dollar-a-year" man and War Service Committee practices—the very life blood of the WIB—were vulnerable. During 1917 they came under repeated attack; in January 1918, legislation was introduced to prohibit the use of industrial advisory committees and government officials serving on a nominal salary. Instead, the wartime economy would be run by paid employees free of compromising affiliations.[42] For the most part,

41. Beaver, *Baker*, 52, 96 (and footnote 64), 105–106. Revering, yet suspecting, the business community has been a long-run trend in American life. See: Thomas C. Cochran, *The American Business System: A Historical Perspective, 1900–1955* (New York, 1962), 2–10, 194–205.

42. *Cong. Rec.*, 65th Cong., 2nd Sess., Vol. 56, Part 1, 558; New York *Times*, January 5, 1918, 3. See also citations for the *Cong. Rec.* in footnotes 27 and 39.

critics of the NDAC and WIB were conveniently ignored. Had Congress moved to place procurement in the hands of the WIB or attempted to write detailed legislation as to how civilians would perform procurement functions, WIB methods at least would have been in jeopardy.

The Overman Act allowed the administration and the Congress to dodge the vexatious problems of industrial mobilization. The WIB was strengthened without in any way disturbing its operations or clearly defining its authority. Moreover, the War Department—the major obstacle to successful mobilization—was forced into line. Issues almost too complex for direct resolution were, thereby, avoided.

Business representatives had every reason to support the Overman compromise and did so. Before the Chamberlain Committee, no one from among the business members on the Council of National Defense or on the WIB favored a ministry of munitions.[43] As members of the Wilson administration they could not have done otherwise. But as long as the President was willing to strengthen the WIB they had no reason to press for the ministry idea. Furthermore, businessmen within government were not unconscious of the threat of a ministry of munitions to the existing mobilization machinery. While still chairman of the crippled and helpless WIB during the winter crisis of 1917–1918, Daniel Willard pleaded with business not to support a supply ministry. It was a risky experiment requiring legislation, he argued. Such legislation, Willard implied, was undesirable.[44] Both Grosvenor B. Clarkson and General Hugh S. Johnson, intimately involved with the wartime economic experience, concluded that the flexibility granted the NDAC and the WIB by the lack of specific statutes was a decided advantage, if not imperative.[45] The attitude of businessmen within the Administration apparently influenced the business community. In February 1918, the Chamber of Commerce of the United States, largely responsible for the Senate Military Affairs Committee's legislation, not only switched its support to the Overman Act, but also defended the bill against its critics. "Those in charge of the administrative machinery of the Government" were opposed to more extended legislation, announced a Chamber member. Through

43. See the testimony of Willard, Baruch, Gifford, and Coffin, Chamberlain Committee, *Hearings*, 1799–1847, 1850–84, 2253–89.

44. *The Nation's Business*, Feb., 1918, 7–9.

45. Clarkson, *Industrial America*, 5–9, 20, 215–16; *Final Report of the WIB*, 3–4—for authorship of the *Report* see Nye Committee, *Hearings*, Part 22, 6393–95, 6642.

the Overman Act, the desired ends could be achieved without weathering the cumbersome legislative process.[46]

Baruch's selection as chairman was as important to the WIB as its new grant of authority. From the day the NDAC was organized, Baruch was a prominent figure. His intimate but detached knowledge and understanding of the American economy and the men who ran it was central to his success. Long before war was declared, Baruch reasoned that successful mobilization depended upon winning industry's voluntary cooperation and maintaining the existing power structure. That meant industry would virtually have to be incorporated into the government. While a member of the NDAC, Baruch was instrumental in devising what ultimately became the Commodity Committee–War Service Committee system.[47]

The nature of the WIB demanded that its chairman have the confidence of industry and yet be above charges of conflict of interests or of favoring private over public welfare. Ironically, Baruch, the "Wolf of Wall Street," was tailor-made for the job. Before joining the NDAC, he divested himself of any connections that could compromise his activities. His speculative career raised opposition to his appointment in some circles, but a congressional committee gave Baruch a clean bill of health. Henceforth, his public image improved. For a time industrialists and financiers approached him with reservation because of his unorthodox occupation. However, uncertainty gradually gave way to trust as Baruch proved his abilities. Because he was largely above suspicion in the eyes of the public and the business community, Baruch could guide the risky process of incorporating industry into government while mostly giving industry its way. A more suspect individual would have met impossible obstacles.

When appointed chairman of the WIB, Baruch instituted policies which he had successfully applied in private business. He selected knowledgeable, competent young men to direct the major subdivisions

46. New York *Times,* Feb. 27, 1918, 4; Fisher, "Chamber of Commerce," 378–80.

47. Concerning Baruch, the NDAC, and his qualifications for the WIB chairmanship, see: sources cited in footnote No. 18; Bernard M. Baruch, *My Own Story* (New York, 1957), 308–312; Bernard M. Baruch, *Baruch, The Public Years* (New York, 1960), 20–25, 28–33, 48–49; Clarkson, *Industrial America,* 66–73, 89, 301–302; Crowell and Wilson, *The Giant Hand,* 24–25, 27–31; Palmer, *Baker,* II, 201–202; Hugh S. Johnson, *The Blue Eagle From Egg to Earth* (New York, 1935), 113–14; Margaret L. Coit, *Mr. Baruch* (Boston, 1957), 147–52, 167–76; Beaver, *Baker,* 104–108.

of the WIB and gave them maximum freedom for carrying out their responsibilities. Authority was centralized, administration decentralized. The Commodity Committees were enlarged and strengthened. In effect they became small war industries boards for the various industries of the nation.[48]

By early 1918, then, a mobilization agency with authority had been perfected. Organized supply was integrated into its structure. But the system would not operate unless demand, and particularly the War Department, was fitted into it. The prospect for a successful merger was better in March 1918 than ever before.

Actually, Baker began patchwork reform of the Army supply network in late summer, 1917. When it became clear, during the winter crisis of 1917–1918, that fundamental change was essential to prevent complete severance of supply from the War Department, the General Staff was reorganized to establish more effective supervision of the bureaus and to better coordinate the Army's operations with those of the WIB.[49]

The more radical reforms Baker initiated did not produce the desired results until March 1918, when General Peyton C. March was appointed first Acting, and later Chief of Staff. In record time, the dynamic, aggressive March fashioned a powerful agency out of the withered General Staff he inherited.[50]

General George W. Goethals became March's chief lieutenant for supply and procurement. Basing his authority on the Overman Act, he directed a near-revolution by managing to break down the old bureau structure and replacing it with a centralized supply system. It was a herculean task that met with intense resistance from the bureaus. At the time of the armistice the job was incomplete.

Ultimately Goethals became an assistant chief of staff and directed

48. The *WIB Minutes* are helpful in tracing the board's development, as are Crowell and Wilson's volumes, *The Giant Hand* and *The Armies of Industry*, I. The 52-page introductory essay to the *Final Report of the WIB* is the one best source on the board. Clarkson, *Industrial America* and Baruch, *American Industry* are indispensable despite their very numerous limitations.

49. Graham Comimittee, *Hearings,* Serial 1, 518–20—Goethals testimony; Nelson, *National Security and the General Staff,* 242–43; Beaver, *Baker,* 93–97.

50. The quality of March's leadership is a main theme of Edward M. Coffman, *The Hilt of the Sword: The Career of Peyton C. March* (Madison, 1966)—see especially, 67–68, 76–77, 149, 151, 247–49. See also, Peyton C. Marsh, *The Nation at War* (New York, 1932), 56.

supply through a subdivision of the General Staff called the Division of Purchase, Storage, and Traffic. All of the Quartermaster Corps and the supply functions of the other bureaus, including purchase, storage, transportation, and finance, were incorporated into the division. In the process, Army supply operations were reorganized along commodity, instead of functional, lines. The War Department's system now paralleled that of the WIB. At last, the Army was adjusting to the civilian economy. Reforms also included methods for obtaining reliable requirements information, centralized procurement of common items, and the standardization of contract forms and procedures.[51]

War Department reforms were originally intended to head off a strengthened civilian agency in order to safeguard Army supply independence.[52] Nevertheless, Army and Navy operations were slowly integrated into those of the WIB. For the Army, that was possible because of new vitality and new personnel. When selected to work with the WIB, officers like General Hugh S. Johnson at first approached the board with typical military suspicion. Soon they came to appreciate that the civilian agency helped secure rather than threaten military prerogatives by aiding the Army in fulfilling its responsibilities.[53] Antagonism gradually gave way to harmony. Flexibility within the WIB helped. At the outset, authority in the Commodity Committees rested exclusively with the civilian section chief. Army members on various committees felt that under the circumstances they were unable to protect War Department interests. Upon the plea of General Johnson, the entire committee was made the source of authority.[54] With similar organization, with a spirit of cooperation, the civilian mobilization agency and the War Department had finally reached a *modus operandi*. From March 1918 forward, the crisis of the economy was resolved.

51. The one best secondary source for analyzing and describing the modernization of the Army's supply structure is Dickinson, *Building of an Army*, 284–307. For primary sources and other secondary sources, see citations in footnote 19.

52. Clarkson, *Industrial America*, 42, 54, 84–85, 128–31; Beaver, *Baker*, 95, 97.

53. Johnson, *Blue Eagle*, 90–93; Clarkson, *Industrial America*, 128–32. Not only did Johnson become an enthusiastic supporter of the WIB, but he was also instrumental in drafting the proposals for restructuring the Army supply system to parallel that of the WIB. See Goethals testimony, Graham Committee, *Hearings*, Serial 1, 529.

54. *WIB Minutes*, 427–28; *Final Report of the WIB*, 14–15; Baruch, *American Industry*, 111–12.

That is not to say that the mobilization machinery ran without flaws or that the munitions picture was bright at war's end. Procurement agencies still set their own requirements; the WIB only determined how they were met. The board lacked the authority, and often the information, for working out a production program that was feasible for the economy. When hostilities ceased, the WIB faced the need to limit demand in order to avoid another crisis.[55]

All of the claimant agencies affected WIB operations, but none as greatly as the War Department. Chief of Staff March looked upon the board as no better than the War Department's equal, perhaps its inferior. As shifts in military requirements took place, March refused to inform the WIB. Only a major showdown between Baruch and March resolved the matter in favor of the board. Realizing that the services tenaciously guarded the right to determine their needs, the WIB never even attempted to institute review procedures. Had the war continued with demand multiplying faster than supply, the explosive military requirements riddle would have become a major divisive issue. The thirty-division American Expeditionary Force program for 1918 was to be increased to eighty for 1919; General John J. Pershing was holding out for even more. Throughout 1918, Pershing's forces were critically short of needed supplies, including ordnance, signal equipment, motor vehicles, and medical provisions; by fall conditions were becoming desperate. Only the armistice saved the day.[56]

Nonetheless, when hostilities ceased, there existed a mobilization scheme that worked. The armed services had preserved control of supply; the business community had experienced a return to stability despite the exigencies of war. The basic pattern was sound even if the mechanics needed perfecting and the lines of authority required clarification.

Scholars and other writers have generally interpreted the War Department's encounter with the WIB and predecessor agencies as a struggle between civilian and military elements over domination of economic mobilization.[57] That is a misconception. The conflict arose as civilian and military institutions were going through the throes

55. David Novick, Melvin Anshen, and W. C. Truppner, *Wartime Production Controls* (New York, 1949), 28–30; Beaver, *Baker,* 172–73.

56. *Ibid.,* 156–61, 165–69, 171–79, 186–88; Baruch, *Public Years,* 56–58; Clarkson, *Industrial America,* 100–102, 128, 132–35; Johnson, *Blue Eagle,* 91; Coffman, *Hilt of the Sword,* 73–74, 76, 84–94, 104–110, 136–41.

57. For the most recent example, see: Beaver, *Baker,* 76.

of adjusting to modern warfare where economically the rigid lines of demarcation between them were no longer possible. Civilian administrations adapted with greater ease to the new conditions. The War Department, however, resisted the minimum changes essential for the successful mobilization of the economy.

Throughout a good part of World War I, the War Department was barely able to manage its own affairs, let alone extend its control over the economy. Its resistance to civilian mobilization agencies was more a result of isolation from, suspicion of, and ignorance about the civilian economy than a desire to dominate it. The Army supply bureaus, really more civilian than military with their close congressional ties and detachment from the line, and Baker's fear of bringing them under control, were a central cause of the friction. Even Chief of Staff March's arrogant attitude toward civilian institutions reflected a failure to grasp the fact that it was no longer possible to compartmentalize civilian and military functions with finality.

Civilians were not anxious to take over military roles. The business community and its representatives were largely responsible for industrial mobilization. Their first concern was finding the means for mobilizing the economy without endangering the *status quo*. Some saw the war as an opportunity for strengthening the Progressive ties between government and industry. From the beginning, however, circumstances made the military services central to any mobilization scheme. While perfecting their own institutions, therefore, members of the NDAC, WIB, and private businessmen worked hand in hand with Army personnel to modernize military supply procedures.[58] Ultimately the War Industries Board proved to be the right means for harnessing the economy. Civilians in general, but businessmen in particular, would not permit the War Department to ruin what they had carefully worked

58. Businessmen, in and out of government service, before and after the winter crisis of 1917–1918, devoted many hours to War Department supply problems. Before war was declared, the Chamber of Commerce organized advisory boards to facilitate the operations of local quartermasters. The following were among those who aided the Army in setting up the Purchase, Storage, and Traffic Division of the General Staff: Otto H. Kahn, of Kuhn, Loeb & Company; C. D. Norton, president of the First National Bank of New York; R. J. Thorne, president of Montgomery Ward & Company, Inc.; H. H. Lehman of Lehman Brothers; Gerard Swope, president of Western Electric Company, Inc.; and F. C. Weems, of J. P. Morgan & Company. See: Fisher, "Chamber of Commerce," 331–34; HMAC, *Hearings*, 1920, 447; Graham Committee, *Hearings*, Serial 1, 293; Dickinson, *Building of an Army*, 305–306.

out to protect their own and the nation's interests. Either the Army had to adjust to the WIB or lose its procurement prerogatives. Since separating procurement from the armed services was politically undesirable, the former rather than the latter solution was adopted with the Overman Act. Wartime industrial self-rule was possible because of the emergency, but only when left undefined. Severing supply from the Army and Navy could have threatened the entire enterprise. Out of those conditions, economic and military institutions were integrated for the duration of the war and the foundation for the "industrial-military complex" was laid.

STANLEY COBEN

A Study in Nativism: The American Red Scare of 1919–1920

The war brought widespread patriotic hysteria and repression in the United States. Much of the intolerance was aimed at German-Americans, with frequent incidents of violence and attempts to impose cultural conformity. Yet, from the beginning, nearly as much repression found targets among assorted radical and nonconformist political groups, and the greatest suppression of civil liberties came with the "Red Scare" of 1919–1920. The basic question for historians has been why these acts of repression occurred when they did. Of course, as contemporary observers recognized, waging war in itself required a degree of conformity not always easy to square with the right to dissent. As several historians have pointed out, every American war has witnessed some curtailment of freedom of expression. Yet World War I still stands as the high-water mark of hysteria and wholesale violation of civil liberties in recent American history.

This essay represents the most sophisticated effort to date to explain the virulence of repression during and just after World War I. It is also a fine example of how conceptual insights borrowed from the social sciences can help to illuminate an historical event. For a somewhat different emphasis on the influence of the war see John Higham, *Strangers in the Land: Patterns of American Nativism, 1865–1925* (New Brunswick, N.J., 1955). It is also useful to note the responses of civil libertarians as recounted in Donald O. Johnson, *The Challenge to American Freedoms: World War I and the Rise of the American Civil Liberties Union* (Lexington, Ky., 1963).

At a victory loan pageant in the District of Columbia on May 6, 1919, a man refused to rise for the playing of "The Star-Spangled Banner." As soon as the national anthem was completed an enraged

Reprinted by permission of the Academy of Political Science from *Political Science Quarterly*, LXXIX (March 1964), 52–75.

sailor fired three shots into the unpatriotic spectator's back. When the man fell, the *Washington Post* reported, "the crowd burst into cheering and handclapping." In February of the same year, a jury in Hammond, Indiana, took two minutes to acquit the assassin of an alien who yelled, "To Hell with the United States." Early in 1920, a clothing store salesman in Waterbury, Connecticut, was sentenced to six months in jail for having remarked to a customer that Lenin was "the brainiest," or "one of the brainiest" of the world's political leaders.[1] Dramatic episodes like these, or the better known Centralia Massacre, Palmer Raids, or May Day riots, were not everyday occurrences, even at the height of the Red Scare. But the fanatical one hundred per cent Americanism reflected by the Washington crowd, the Hammond jury, and the Waterbury judge pervaded a large part of our society between early 1919 and mid-1920.

Recently, social scientists have produced illuminating evidence about the causes of eruptions like that of 1919–20. They have attempted to identify experimentally the individuals most responsive to nativistic appeals, to explain their susceptibility, and to propose general theories of nativistic and related movements. These studies suggest a fuller, more coherent picture of nativistic upheavals and their causes than we now possess, and they provide the framework for this attempt to reinterpret the Red Scare.

Psychological experiments indicate that a great many Americans—at least several million—are always ready to participate in a "red scare." These people permanently hold attitudes which characterized the nativists of 1919–20: hostility toward certain minority groups, especially radicals and recent immigrants, fanatical patriotism, and a belief that internal enemies seriously threaten national security.[2]

1. *Washington Post*, May 7, 1919; Mark Sullivan, *Our Times, The United States 1900–1925* (New York, 1935), VI, 169; *The Nation*, CX (April 17, 1920), 510–11. The most complete account of the Red Scare is Robert K. Murray, *Red Scare, A Study in National Hysteria* (Minneapolis, 1955). But see the critical review of Murray's book by John M. Blum in *Mississippi Valley Historical Review*, XLII (1955), 145. Blum comments that Murray failed to explain "the susceptibility of the American people and of their elite to the 'national hysteria.' . . . About hysteria, after all, psychology and social psychology in particular have had considerable to say." John Higham places the postwar movement in historical perspective in his superb *Strangers in the Land, Patterns of American Nativism, 1860–1925* (New Brunswick, 1955), especially Chaps. 8 and 9.

2. On the incidence of prejudice against minorities in the United States, see Gordon W. Allport and Bernard M. Kramer, "Some Roots of Prej-

In one of the most comprehensive of these experiments, psychologists Nancy C. Morse and Floyd H. Allport tested seven hypotheses about the causes of prejudice and found that one, national involvement or patriotism, proved to be "by far the most important factor" associated with prejudice. Other widely held theories about prejudice—status rivalry, frustration-aggression, and scapegoat hypotheses, for example—were found to be of only secondary importance.[3] Summarizing the results of this and a number of other psychological experiments, Gordon W. Allport, a pioneer in the scientific study of prejudice, concluded that in a large proportion of cases the prejudiced person is attempting to defend himself against severe inner turmoil by enforcing order in his external life. Any disturbance in the social *status quo* threatens the precarious psychic equilibrium of this type of individual, who, according to Allport, seeks "an island of institutional safety and security. The nation is the island he selects. . . . It has the definiteness he needs."

Allport pointed out that many apprehensive and frustrated people are not especially prejudiced. What is important, he found,

> is the way fear and frustration are handled. The institutionalistic way—especially the nationalistic—seems to be the nub of the matter. What happens is that the prejudiced person defines "nation" to fit his needs. The nation is first of all a protection (the chief protection) of him as an individual. It is his in-group. He sees no contradiction in ruling out of its beneficent orbit

---

udice," *Journal of Psychology,* XXII (1946), 9–39; Morris Janowitz and Dwaine Marvick, "Authoritarianism and Political Behavior," *Public Opinion Quarterly,* XVII (1953), 185–201; Bruno Bettelheim and Morris Janowitz, *Dynamics of Prejudice, A Psychological and Sociological Study of Veterans* (New York, 1950), 16, 26, and *passim.*

3. Nancy C. Morse and F. H. Allport, "The Causation of Anti-Semitism: An Investigation of Seven Hypotheses," *Journal of Psychology,* XXXIV (1952), 197–233. For further experimental evidence indicating that prejudiced individuals are no more anxious, neurotic, or intolerant of ambiguity than those with more "liberal" attitudes, Anthony Davids, "Some Personality and Intellectual Correlates to Intolerance of Ambiguity," *Journal of Abnormal and Social Psychology,* LI (1955), 415–20; Ross Stagner and Clyde S. Congdon, "Another Failure to Demonstrate Displacement of Aggression," *Journal of Abnormal and Social Psychology,* LI (1955), 695–96; Dean Peabody, "Attitude Content and Agreement Set in Scales of Authoritarianism, Dogmatism, Anti-Semitism and Economic Conservatism," *Journal of Abnormal and Social Psychology,* LXIII (1961), 1–11.

those whom he regards as threatening intruders and enemies (namely, American minorities). What is more, the nation stands for the status quo. It is a conservative agent; within it are all the devices for safe living that he approves. His nationalism is a form of conservatism.[4]

Substantial evidence, then, suggests that millions of Americans are both extraordinarily fearful of social change and prejudiced against those minority groups which they perceive as "threatening intruders." Societal disruption, especially if it can easily be connected with the "intruders," not only will intensify the hostility of highly prejudiced individuals, but also will provoke many others, whose antagonism in more stable times had been mild or incipient, into the extreme group.

A number of anthropologists have come to conclusions about the roots of nativism which complement these psychological studies. Since the late nineteenth century, anthropologists have been studying the religious and nativistic cults of American Indian tribes and of Melanesian and Papuan groups in the South Pacific. Recently, several anthropologists have attempted to synthesize their findings and have shown striking parallels in the cultural conditions out of which these movements arose.[5] In every case, severe societal disruption preceded the

4. Gordon W. Allport, *The Nature of Prejudice* (Cambridge, 1955), 406; see Boyd C. Shafer, *Nationalism, Myth and Reality* (New York, 1955), 181.

5. See, especially, the works of Anthony F. C. Wallace: "Revitalization Movements," *American Anthropologist,* LVIII (1956), 264–81; "Handsome Lake and the Great Revival in the West," *American Quarterly,* IV (1952), 149–65; "Stress and Rapid Personality Change," *International Record of Medicine and General Practice Clinics,* CLXIX (1956), 761–73; "New Religions Among the Delaware Indians, 1600–1900," *Southwest Journal of Anthropology,* XII (1956), 1–21. Also, Michael M. Ames, "Reaction to Stress: A Comparative Study of Nativism," *Davidson Journal of Anthropology,* III (1957), 16–30; C. S. Belshaw, "The Significance of Modern Cults in Melanesian Development," *Australian Outlook,* IV (1950), 116–25; Raymond Firth, "The Theory of 'Cargo' Cults: A Note on Tikopia," *Man,* LV (1955), 130–32; Lawrence Krader, "A Nativistic Movement in Western Siberia," *American Anthropologist,* LVIII (1956), 282–92; Ralph Linton, "Nativistic Movements," *American Anthropologist,* XLV (1943), 220–43; Margaret Mead, *New Lives for Old* (New York, 1956); Peter Worsley, *The Trumpet Shall Sound* (London, 1957). Several sociologists and psychologists have come to conclusions about the causes of these movements that are similar in important respects to Wallace's, although less comprehensive. See Leon Festinger, *A Theory of Cognitive Dissonance*

184   Consequences

outbreak of widespread nativistic cult behavior. According to Anthony
F. C. Wallace, who has gone farthest toward constructing a general
theory of cult formation, when the disruption has proceeded so far
that many members of a society find it difficult or impossible to
fulfill their physical and psychological needs, or to relieve severe
anxiety through the ordinary culturally approved methods, the society
will be susceptible to what Wallace has termed a "revitalization movement." This is a convulsive attempt to change or revivify important
cultural beliefs and values, and frequently to eliminate alien influences.
Such movements promise and often provide participants with better
means of dealing with their changed circumstances, thus reducing
their very high level of internal stress.[6]

American Indian tribes, for example, experienced a series of such
convulsions as the tide of white settlers rolled west. The Indians
were pushed onto reservations and provided with Indian agents, mis-
sionaries, and physicians, who took over many of the functions hitherto assumed by chiefs and medicine men. Indian craftsmen (and
craftswomen) were replaced by dealers in the white man's implements.
Most hunters and warriors also lost their vocations and consequently
their self-respect. What an anthropologist wrote of one tribe was
true of many others: "From cultural maturity as Pawnees they were
reduced to cultural infancy as civilized men."[7]

(New York, 1957); Hadley Cantril, *The Psychology of Social Movements*
(New York, 1941), especially pp. 3–4, Chaps. 5, 8, and 9; Hans H. Toch,
"Crisis Situations and Ideological Revaluation," *Public Opinion Quarterly,*
XVIX (1955), 53–67.

6. Wallace, "Revitalization Movements." For a recent verification of
Wallace's theories see Thomas Rhys Williams, "The Form of a North
Borneo Nativistic Behavior," *American Anthropologist,* LXV (1963),
543–51. On the psychological results of socially caused stress, Wallace,
"Stress and Rapid Personality Change"; William Caudill, *Effects of Social
and Cultural Systems in Reactions to Stress,* Social Science Research Council Pamphlet No. 14 (New York, 1958); Caudill, "Cultural Perspectives
on Stress," Army Medical Service Graduate School, *Symposium on Stress*
(Washington, D.C., 1953); Hans Selye, *The Stress of Life* (New York,
1956); Roland Fischer and Neil Agnew, "A Hierarchy of Stressors," *Journal
of Mental Science,* CI (1955), 383–86; Daniel H. Funkenstein, Stanley
H. King, and Margaret E. Drolette, *Mastery of Stress* (Cambridge, 1957);
M. Basowitz *et al., Anxiety and Stress: An Interdisciplinary Study of
a Life Situation* (New York, 1955).

7. Alexander Lesser, *The Pawnee Ghost Dance Hand Game. A Study
of Cultural Change* (New York, 1933), 44.

One of the last major religious upheavals among the Indians was the Ghost Dance cult which spread from Nevada through Oregon and northern California in the eighteen-seventies, and a similar movement among the Rocky Mountain and western plains Indians about 1890. Although cult beliefs varied somewhat from tribe to tribe, converts generally were persuaded that if they followed certain prescribed rituals, including the dance, they would soon return to their old ways of living. Even their dead relatives would be restored to life. Most Indians were too conscious of their military weakness to challenge their white masters directly. Ghost Dancers among the Dakota Sioux, however, influenced by the militant proselytizer Sitting Bull, became convinced that true believers could not be harmed by the white man's bullets and that Sioux warriors would drive the intruders from Indian lands. Their dreams were rudely smashed at the massacre of Wounded Knee Creek in December 1890.[8]

The Boxer movement in China, 1898 to 1900, resembled in many aspects the Indian Ghost Dance cults; however, the Boxers, more numerous and perhaps less demoralized than the Indians, aimed more directly at removing foreign influences from their land. The movement erupted first in Shantung province where foreigners, especially Japanese, British, and Germans, were most aggressive. A flood of the Yellow River had recently deprived about a million people in the province of food and shelter. Banditry was rampant, organized government ineffective. The Boxer movement, based on the belief that these tragic conditions were due almost entirely to the "foreign devils" and their agents, determined to drive the enemy out of China. Boxers went into action carrying charms and chanting incantations supposed to make them invulnerable to the foreigners' bullets. The first object of the Boxers' nativistic fury were Chinese who had converted to

8. Cora DuBois, *The 1870 Ghost Dance,* Anthropological Records, III (Berkeley, 1946); Leslie Spier, *The Ghost Dance of 1870 Among the Klamath of Oregon,* University of Washington Publications in Anthropology, II (Seattle, 1927); Lesser, *Ghost Dance;* A. L. Kroeber, *Handbook of the Indians of California,* Bureau of American Ethnology Bulletin 78 (Washington, D.C., 1925). Anthropologists recently have argued about the origins of the Ghost Dance cults. Both sides agree, however, that whatever their origins, the cults took the form they did because of intolerable cultural conditions caused largely by white encroachments. David F. Aberle, "The Prophet Dance and Reactions to White Contact," *Southwest Journal of Anthropology,* XV (1959), 74–83; Leslie Spier, Wayne Suttles, and Melvin Herskovits, "Comment on Aberle's Thesis of Deprivation," *Southwest Journal of Anthropology,* XV (1959), 84–88.

Christianity, the intruders' religion. The patriots then attacked railroad and telegraph lines, leading symbols of foreign influence. Finally, the Boxers turned against the foreigners themselves, slaughtering many. Not until after the Boxers carried on a two-month siege of the foreign community in Peking did American, European, and Japanese armies crush the movement.[9]

Other revitalization attempts proved more successful than the Boxers or Ghost Dancers. The Gaiwiio movement, for example, helped the Iroquois Indians of western New York State to retain their identity as a culture while adjusting successfully to an encroaching white civilization during the first decade of the nineteenth century. The movement implanted a new moral code among the Indians, enjoining sobriety and family stability and encouraging acceptance of Western technology, while revivifying cohesive Indian traditions.[10]

Dominant as well as conquered peoples, Ralph Linton has pointed out, undergo nativistic movements. Dominant groups, he observed, are sometimes threatened "not only by foreign invasion or domestic revolt but also by the invidious process of assimilation which might, in the long run, destroy their distinctive powers and privileges." Under such circumstances, Linton concluded, "the frustrations which motivate nativistic movements in inferior or dominated groups" are "replaced by anxieties which produce very much the same [nativistic] result" in dominant groups.[11]

Communist "brainwashers" have consciously attempted to achieve results comparable to those obtained by prophets of movements like the Ghost Dance cult and the Boxers. They create intolerable stress within individuals, not through rapid societal change, but by intentional physical debilitation and continual accusations, cross-examinations, and use of other anxiety-provoking techniques. Then they offer their

9. The best account of the Boxer movement is Chester C. Tan, *The Boxer Catastrophe* (New York, 1955). Also, George N. Steiger, *China and the Occident, the Origin and Development of the Boxer Movement* (New Haven, 1927); Peter Fleming, *The Siege at Peking* (New York, 1959).

10. Wallace, "Handsome Lake." Wallace compared the Gaiwiio with a Chinese attempt to accommodate their society to Western civilization in "Stress and Rapid Personality Change." For a successful movement in the South Pacific see Mead, *New Lives for Old*.

11. Linton, 237. Also, Carroll L. Riley and John Hobgood, "A Recent Nativistic Movement Among the Southern Tepehaun Indians," *Southwest Journal of Anthropology*, XV (1959), 355–60.

prisoners an escape from the induced psychological torment: conversion to the new gospel.[12]

The similarity in the mental processes involved in "brainwashing" and in the formation of nativistic movements becomes even clearer upon examination of the Chinese Communist attempt to establish their doctrine in mainland China. Again, the Communists intentionally have created conditions like those out of which nativistic cults have arisen more spontaneously in other societies. In addition to the stress which ordinarily would accompany rapid industrialization of an economically backward society, the Chinese leaders have provoked additional anxiety through the systematic use of group confessions and denunciations and have intentionally disrupted family life. Hostility toward the American enemy has been purposely aroused and used to unify the masses, as well as to justify the repression of millions of alleged internal enemies. The whole population has been continually urged to repent their sins and to adopt wholeheartedly the Communist gospel, which has a strong nativistic component. As a psychologist has remarked, to a large extent the Chinese Communists provide both the disease and the cure.[13]

The ferocious outbreak of nativism in the United States after World War I was not consciously planned or provoked by any individual or group, although some Americans took advantage of the movement once it started. Rather, the Red Scare, like the Gaiwiio and Boxer movements described above, was brought on largely by a number of severe social and economic dislocations which threatened the national equilibrium. The full extent and the shocking effects of these disturbances of 1919 have not yet been adequately described. Runaway prices, a brief but sharp stock market crash and business depression, revolutions throughout Europe, widespread fear of domestic revolt, bomb explosions, and an outpouring of radical literature were distressing enough. These sudden difficulties, moreover, served to exaggerate the disruptive effects already produced by the social and intellectual

12. Robert J. Lifton, "Thought Reform in Western Civilians in Chinese Communist Prisons," *Psychiatry,* XIX (1966), 173–95; Edgar H. Schein, "The Chinese Indoctrination Program for Prisoners of War, A Study of Attempted Brainwashing," *Psychiatry,* XIX (1956), 149–72.

13. Edgar H. Schein, with Inge Schneier and Curtis H. Bark, *Coercive Persuasion* (New York, 1961); William Sargent, *Battle for the Mind* (New York, 1957), 150–65; Robert J. Lifton, *Thought Reform and the Psychology of Totalism* (New York, 1961); R. L. Walker, *China Under Communism* (London, 1946).

ravages of the World War and the preceding reform era, and by
the arrival, before the war, of millions of new immigrants. This added
stress intensified the hostility of Americans strongly antagonistic to
minority groups, and brought new converts to blatant nativism from
among those who ordinarily were not overtly hostile toward radicals
or recent immigrants.

Citizens who joined the crusade for one hundred per cent Americanism sought, primarily, a unifying force which would halt the apparent
disintegration of their culture. The movement, they felt, would eliminate those foreign influences which the one hundred per centers believed were the major cause of their anxiety.

Many of the postwar sources of stress were also present during
World War I, and the Red Scare, as John Higham has observed,
was partly an exaggeration of wartime passions.[14] In 1917–18 German-
Americans served as the object of almost all our nativistic fervor;
they were the threatening intruders who refused to become good
citizens. "They used America," a patriotic author declared in 1918
of two million German-Americans, "they never loved her. They clung
to their old language, their old customs, and cared nothing for
ours. . . . As a class they were clannish beyond all other races coming
here."[15] Fear of subversion by German agents was almost as extrava-
gant in 1917–18 as anxiety about "reds" in the postwar period. Attorney General Thomas Watt Gregory reported to a friend in May
1918 that "we not infrequently receive as many as fifteen hundred
letters in a single day suggesting disloyalty and the making of
investigations."[16]

Opposition to the war by radical groups helped smooth the transition
among American nativists from hatred of everything German to fear
of radical revolution. The two groups of enemies were associated
also for other reasons. High government officials declared after the
war that German leaders planned and subsidized the Bolshevik Revolution.[17] When bombs blasted homes and public buildings in nine

14. Higham, 222.
15. Emerson Hough, *The Web* (Chicago, 1919), 23. Hough was a rabid
one hundred per center during the Red Scare also.
16. T. W. Gregory to R. E. Vinson, May 13, 1918, Papers of Thomas
Watt Gregory (Library of Congress, Washington, D.C.).
17. Subcommittee of Senate Committee on the Judiciary, *Hearings,
Brewing and Liquor Interests and German and Bolshevik Propaganda,*
66th Congress, 1st Session, 1919, 2669 ff.; *The New York Times,* July
7, August 11 and 29, September 15-21, 1918.

cities in June 1919, the director of the Justice Department's Bureau of Investigation asserted that the bombers were "connected with Russian bolshevism, aided by Hun money."[18] In November 1919, a year after the armistice, a popular magazine warned of "the Russo-German movement that is now trying to dominate America. . . ."[19]

Even the wartime hostility toward German-Americans, however, is more understandable when seen in the light of recent anthropological and psychological studies. World War I disturbed Americans not only because of the real threat posed by enemy armies and a foreign ideology. For many citizens it had the further effect of shattering an already weakened intellectual tradition. When the European governments decided to fight, they provided shocking evidence that man was not, as most educated members of Western society had believed, a rational creature progressing steadily, if slowly, toward control of his environment. When the great powers declared war in 1914, many Americans as well as many Europeans were stunned. The *New York Times* proclaimed a common theme—European civilization had collapsed: The supposedly advanced nations, declared the *Times,* "have reverted to the condition of savage tribes roaming the forests and falling upon each other in a fury of blood and carnage to achieve the ambitious designs of chieftains clad in skins and drunk with mead."[20] Franz Alexander, director for twenty-five years of the Chicago Institute of Psychoanalysis, recently recalled his response to the outbreak of the World War:

18. *Washington Post,* July 3, 1919. Bureau Director William J. Flynn produced no evidence to back this assertion. Later he claimed to have conclusive proof that the bombers were Italian anarchists. Flynn to Attorney General Harry Daugherty, April 4, 1922, Department of Justice Records, File 202600, Sect. 5 (National Archives, Washington, D.C.).

19. *Saturday Evening Post,* CXCII (November 1, 1919), 28. For similar assertions in other publications, Meno Lovenstein, *American Opinion of Soviet Russia* (Washington, D.C., 1941), Chap. 1, *passim.*

20. Quoted in William E. Leuchtenburg, *The Perils of Prosperity, 1914–32* (Chicago, 1958), 13. There is no comprehensive study of the effects of the war on the American mind. For brief treatments, Henry F. May, *The End of American Innocence* (New York, 1959), 361–67; Merle Curti, *The Growth of American Thought* (New York, 1951), 687–705; Ralph Henry Gabriel, *The Course of American Democratic Thought* (New York, 1956), 387, 404; André Siegfried, *America Comes of Age* (New York, 1927), 3; Walter Lord, *The Good Years, From 1900 to the First World War* (New York, 1960), 339–41.

The first impact of this news is [*sic*] unforgettable. It was the
sudden intuitive realization that a chapter of history had
ended. . . . Since then, I have discussed this matter with some
of my contemporaries and heard about it a great deal in my
early postwar psychoanalytic treatments of patients. To my
amazement, the others who went through the same events had
quite a similar reaction. . . . It was an immediate vivid and
prophetic realization that something irrevocable of immense importance had happened in history.[21]

Americans were jolted by new blows to their equilibrium after
entering the war. Four million men were drafted away from familiar
surroundings and some of them experienced the terrible carnage of
trench warfare. Great numbers of women left home to work in war
industries or to replace men in other jobs. Negroes flocked to Northern
industrial areas by the hundreds of thousands, and their first mass
migration from the South created violent racial antagonism in Northern cities.

During the war, also, Americans sanctioned a degree of government
control over the economy which deviated sharply from traditional
economic individualism. Again, fears aroused before the war were
aggravated, for the reform legislation of the Progressive era had tended
to increase government intervention, and many citizens were further
perturbed by demands that the federal government enforce even higher
standards of economic and social morality. By 1919, therefore, some
prewar progressives as well as conservatives feared the gradual disap-
pearance of highly valued individual opportunity and responsibility.
Their fears were fed by strong postwar calls for continued large-scale
government controls—extension of federal operation of railroads and
of the Food Administration, for example.

The prime threat to these long-held individualistic values, however,
and the most powerful immediate stimulus to the revitalistic response,
came from Russia. There the Bolshevik conquerors proclaimed their
intention of exporting Marxist ideology. If millions of Americans
were disturbed in 1919 by the specter of communism, the underlying
reason was not fear of foreign invasion—Russia, after all, was still

21. Franz Alexander, *The Western Mind in Transition* (New York,
1960), 73–74. Also see William Barrett, *Irrational Man* (Garden City,
N.Y., 1961), 32–33.

a backward nation recently badly defeated by German armies. The real threat was the potential spread of communist ideas. These, the one hundred per centers realized with horror, possessed a genuine appeal for reformers and for the economically underprivileged, and if accepted they would complete the transformation of America.

A clear picture of the Bolshevik tyranny was not yet available; therefore, as after the French Revolution, those who feared the newly successful ideology turned to fight the revolutionary ideals. So the *Saturday Evening Post* declared editorially in November 1919 that "History will see our present state of mind as one with that preceding the burning of witches, the children's crusade, the great tulip craze and other examples of softening of the world brain." The *Post* referred not to the Red Scare or the impending Palmer Raids, but to the spread of communist ideology. Its editorial concluded: "The need of the country is not more idealism, but more pragmatism; not communism, but common sense."[22] One of the most powerful patriotic groups, the National Security League, called upon members early in 1919 to "teach 'Americanism.' This means the fighting of Bolshevism . . . by the creation of well defined National Ideals." Members "must preach Americanism and instil the idealism of America's Wars, and that American spirit of service which believes in giving as well as getting."[23] New York attorney, author, and educator Henry Waters Taft warned a Carnegie Hall audience late in 1919 that Americans must battle "a propaganda which is tending to undermine our most cherished social and political institutions and is having the effect of producing widespread unrest among the poor and the ignorant, especially those of foreign birth."[24]

When the war ended Americans also confronted the disturbing possibility, pointed up in 1919 by the struggle over the League of Nations, that Europe's struggles would continue to be their own. These factors combined to make the First World War a traumatic experience for millions of citizens. As Senator James Reed of Missouri observed in August 1919, "This country is still suffering from shell shock. Hardly anyone is in a normal state of mind. . . . A great

22. *Saturday Evening Post,* CXCII (November 1, 1919), 28.
23. National Security League, *Future Work* (New York, 1919), 6.
24. Henry Waters Taft, *Aspects of Bolshevism and Americanism, Address before the League for Political Education at Carnegie Hall, New York, December 6, 1919* (New York, 1919), 21.

storm has swept over the intellectual world and its ravages and disturbances still exist."[25]

The wartime "shell shock" left many Americans extraordinarily
susceptible to psychological stress caused by postwar social and economic turbulence. Most important for the course of the Red Scare,
many of these disturbances had their greatest effect on individuals
already antagonistic toward minorities. First of all, there was some
real evidence of danger to the nation in 1919, and the nation provided
the chief emotional support for many Americans who responded easily
to charges of an alien radical menace. Violence flared throughout
Europe after the war and revolt lifted radicals to power in several
Eastern and Central European nations. Combined with the earlier
Bolshevik triumph in Russia these revolutions made Americans look
more anxiously at radicals here. Domestic radicals encouraged these
fears; they became unduly optimistic about their own chances of
success and boasted openly of their coming triumph. Scores of new
foreign language anarchist and communist journals, most of them
written by and for Southern and Eastern European immigrants, commenced publication, and the established radical press became more
exuberant. These periodicals never tired of assuring leaders in 1919
that "the United States seems to be on the verge of a revolutionary
crisis."[26] American newspapers and magazines reprinted selections from
radical speeches, pamphlets, and periodicals so their readers could
see what dangerous ideas were abroad in the land.[27] Several mysterious
bomb explosions and bombing attempts, reported in bold front page
headlines in newspapers across the country, frightened the public
in 1919. To many citizens these seemed part of an organized campaign

25. U.S., *Congressional Record,* 66th Congress, 1st Session, August 15,
1919, 3892.

26. Robert E. Park, *The Immigrant Press and Its Control* (New York,
1922), 214, 230–38, 241–45; R. E. Park and Herbert A. Miller, *Old World
Traits Transplanted* (New York, 1921), 99–101; Daniel Bell, "The Background and Development of Marxian Socialism in the United States,"
in Donald Drew Egbert and Stow Persons, *Socialism in American Life*
(Princeton, 1952), I, 334; Lovenstein, 7–50; Leuchtenburg, 67–68; Murray,
33–36.

27. The Justice Department distributed pamphlets containing such material to all American newspapers and magazines; *Red Radicalism, as Described by Its Own Leaders* (Washington, D.C., 1920); National Popular
Government League, *To the American People, Report Upon the Illegal
Practices of the Department of Justice* (Washington, D.C., 1920), 64–66.
The staunchly anti-radical *New York Times* published translations from a
large sample of foreign language radical newspapers on June 8, 1919.

of terror carried on by alien radicals intending to bring down the federal government. The great strikes of 1919 and early 1920 aroused similar fears.[28]

Actually American radical organizations in 1919 were disorganized and poverty-stricken. The Communists were inept, almost without contact with American workers and not yet dominated or subsidized by Moscow. The IWW was shorn of its effective leaders, distrusted by labor, and generally declining in influence and power. Violent anarchists were isolated in a handful of tiny, unconnected local organizations.[29] One or two of these anarchist groups probably carried out the "bomb conspiracy" of 1919; but the extent of the "conspiracy" can be judged from the fact that the bombs killed a total of two men during the year, a night watchman and one of the bomb throwers, and seriously wounded one person, a maid in the home of a Georgia senator.[30]

Nevertheless, prophecies of national disaster abounded in 1919, even among high government officials. Secretary of State Robert Lansing confided to his diary that we were in real peril of social revolution. Attorney General A. Mitchell Palmer advised the House Appropriations Committee that "on a certain day, which we have been advised of," radicals would attempt "to rise up and destroy the Government at one fell swoop." Senator Charles Thomas of Colorado warned that "the country is on the verge of a volcanic upheaval." And Senator Miles Poindexter of Washington declared, "There is real danger that the government will fall."[31] A West Virginia wholesaler, with offices

28. Murray, Chaps. 5, 7–10. Asked by a congressional committee a few weeks after the spate of bombings in June 1919 whether there was real evidence of an organized effort to destroy the federal government, Assistant Attorney General Francis P. Garvan replied, "Certainly." Garvan was in charge of federal prosecution of radicals. *Washington Post,* June 27, 1919.

29. Theodore Draper, *The Roots of American Communism* (New York, 1957), 198–200, 302, 312–14; David J. Saposs, *Left Wing Unionism, A Study in Policies and Tactics* (New York, 1926), 49–50, 152–57; Selig Perlman and Philip Taft (eds.), *Labor Movements* in John R. Commons (ed.), *History of Labor in the United States 1896–1932,* IV (New York, 1935), 431–32, 621; Jerome Davis, *The Russian Immigrant* (New York, 1922), 114–18; Kate Holladay Claghorn, *The Immigrant's Day in Court* (New York, 1923), 363–73; John S. Gambs, *The Decline of the I.W.W.* (New York, 1932), 133; Murray, 107–10.

30. *The New York Times,* May 1, June 3, 4, 1919.

31. "The Spread of Bolshevism in the United States," private memorandum, dated July 26, 1919, Papers of Robert Lansing (Library of Congress,

throughout the state, informed the Justice Department in October 1919 that "there is hardly a respectable citizen of my acquaintance who does not believe that we are on the verge of armed conflict in this country." William G. McAdoo was told by a trusted friend that "Chicago, which has always been a very liberal minded place, seems to me to have gone mad on the question of the 'Reds.' " Delegates to the Farmers National Congress in November 1919 pledged that farmers would assist the government in meeting the threat of revolution.[32]

The slight evidence of danger from radical organizations roused such wild fear only because Americans had already encountered other threats to cultural stability. However, the dislocations caused by the war and the menace of communism alone would not have produced such a vehement nativistic response. Other postwar challenges to the social and economic order made the crucial difference.

Of considerable importance was the skyrocketing cost of living. Retail prices more than doubled between 1915 and 1920, and the price rise began gathering momentum in the spring of 1919.[33] During the summer of 1919 the dominant political issue in America was not the League of Nations; not even the "red menace" or the threat of a series of major strikes disturbed the public as much as did the climbing cost of living. The *Washington Post* early in August 1919 called rising prices "the burning domestic issue. . . ." Democratic National Chairman Homer Cummings, after a trip around the country, told President Woodrow Wilson that more Americans were worried about prices than about any other public issue and that they

---

Washington, D.C.); "One Point of View of the Murders at Centralia, Washington," private memorandum, dated November 13, 1919, Lansing Papers; U.S., *Congressional Record,* 66th Congress, 1st Session, October 14, 1919, 6869; *Washington Post,* February 16, 1919; New York *World,* June 19, 1919.

32. Henry Barham to Palmer, October 27, 1919, Justice Department Records, File 202600; unidentified correspondent to McAdoo, February 10, 1920, McAdoo Papers (Library of Congress, Washington, D.C.); A. P. Sanders to Palmer, November 12, 1919, Justice Department Records, File 202600; *The New York Times,* October 31, 1919.

33. U.S. Bureau of the Census, *Historical Statistics of the United States, Colonial Times to 1952, A Statistical Abstract Supplement* (Washington, D.C., 1960), 91, 92, 126; U.S. Department of Labor, Bureau of Labor Statistics, Bulletin Number 300, *Retail Prices 1913 to December, 1920* (Washington, D.C., 1922), 4; Daniel J. Ahearn, Jr., *The Wages of Farm and Factory Laborers 1914–1944* (New York, 1945), 227.

demanded government action. When Wilson decided to address Congress on the question the Philadelphia *Public Ledger* observed that the administration had "come rather tardily to a realization of what is uppermost in the minds of the American people."[34]

Then the wave of postwar strikes—there were 3,600 of them in 1919 involving over 4,000,000 workers[35]—reached a climax in the fall of 1919. A national steel strike began in September and nationwide coal and rail walkouts were scheduled for November 1. Unions gained in membership and power during the war, and in 1919 labor leaders were under strong pressure to help workers catch up to or go ahead of mounting living costs. Nevertheless, influential government officials attributed the walkouts to radical activities. Early in 1919, Secretary of Labor William B. Wilson declared in a public speech that recent major strikes in Seattle, Butte, Montana, and Lawrence, Massachusetts, had been instituted by the Bolsheviks and the IWW for the sole purpose of bringing about a nationwide revolution in the United States.[36] During the steel strike of early fall, 1919, a Senate investigating committee reported that "behind this strike there is massed a considerable element of I.W.W.'s, anarchists, revolutionists, and Russian soviets. . . ."[37] In April 1920 the head of the Justice Department's General Intelligence Division, J. Edgar Hoover, declared in a public hearing that at least fifty per cent of the influence behind the recent series of strikes was traceable directly to communist agents.[38]

Furthermore, the nation suffered a sharp economic depression in late 1918 and early 1919, caused largely by sudden cancellations of war orders. Returning servicemen found it difficult to obtain jobs during this period, which coincided with the beginning of the Red Scare. The former soldiers had been uprooted from their homes and

34. *Washington Post,* August 1, 4, 1919; *The New York Times,* July 30, August 1, 1919; Philadelphia *Public Ledger,* August 5, 1919.

35. Florence Peterson, *Strikes in the United States, 1880–1936,* U.S. Department of Labor Bulletin Number 651 (Washington, D.C., 1938), 21. More employees engaged in strikes in 1919 than the total over the ten-year period 1923–32.

36. *Washington Post,* February 21, 1919. As late as April 1920, Secretary Wilson agreed with Palmer during a Cabinet meeting that the nationwide rail walkout had been caused by Communists and the IWW. Entry in Josephus Daniels' Diary for April 14, 1920, Papers of Josephus Daniels (Library of Congress, Washington, D.C.).

37. U.S. Senate, Committee on Education and Labor, *Report, Investigation on Strike in Steel Industry,* 66th Congress, 1st Session, 1919, 14.

38. *The New York Times,* April 25, 1920, 23.

told that they were engaged in a patriotic crusade. Now they came back to find "reds" criticizing their country and threatening the government with violence, Negroes holding good jobs in the big cities, prices terribly high, and workers who had not served in the armed forces striking for higher wages.[39] A delegate won prolonged applause from the 1919 American Legion Convention when he denounced radical aliens, exclaiming, "Now that the war is over and they are in lucrative positions while our boys haven't a job, we've got to send those scamps to hell." The major part of the mobs which invaded meeting halls of immigrant organizations and broke up radical parades, especially during the first half of 1919, was comprised of men in uniform.[40]

A variety of other circumstances combined to add even more force to the postwar nativistic movement. Long before the new immigrants were seen as potential revolutionists they became the objects of widespread hostility. The peak of immigration from Southern and Eastern Europe occurred in the fifteen years before the war; during that period almost ten million immigrants from those areas entered the country. Before the anxious eyes of members of all classes of Americans, the newcomers crowded the cities and began to disturb the economic and social order.[41] Even without other postwar disturbances a nativistic movement of some strength could have been predicted when the wartime solidarity against the German enemy began to wear off in 1919.

In addition, not only were the European revolutions most successful in Eastern and to a lesser extent in Southern Europe, but aliens from these areas predominated in American radical organizations. At least ninety per cent of the members of the two American Communist parties formed in 1919 were born in Eastern Europe. The anarchist groups whose literature and bombs captured the imagination of the American public in 1919 were composed almost entirely of

39. George Soule, *Prosperity Decade, From War to Depression: 1917–1929* (New York, 1947), 81–84; Murray, 125, 182–83.

40. *Proceedings and Committees, Caucus of the American Legion* (St. Louis, 1919), 117; *The New York Times,* May 2, 1919; *Washington Post,* May 2, 1919. Ex-servicemen also played major roles in the great Negro-white race riots of mid-1919. *Washington Post,* July 20–23, 28–31.

41. *Historical Statistics of the United States,* 56. On the causes of American hostility to recent immigrants see John Higham's probing and provocative essay "Another Look at Nativism," *Catholic Historical Review,* XLIV (1958), 147–58. Higham stresses status conflicts, but does not explain why some competitors on the crowded social ladder were much more antagonistic to the new immigrants than were others.

Italian, Spanish, and Slavic aliens. Justice Department announcements and statements by politicians and the press stressed the predominance of recent immigrants in radical organizations.[42] Smoldering prejudice against new immigrants and identification of these immigrants with European as well as American radical movements, combined with other sources of postwar stress to create one of the most frenzied and one of the most widespread nativistic movements in the nation's history.

The result, akin to the movements incited by the Chinese Boxers or the Indian Ghost Dancers, was called Americanism or one hundred per cent Americanism.[43] Its objective was to end the apparent erosion of American values and the disintegration of American culture. By reaffirming those beliefs, customs, symbols, and traditions felt to be the foundation of our way of life, by enforcing conformity among the population, and by purging the nation of dangerous foreigners, the one hundred per centers expected to heal societal divisions and to tighten defenses against cultural change.

Panegyrics celebrating our history and institutions were delivered regularly in almost every American school, church, and public hall in 1919 and 1920. Many of these fervent addresses went far beyond the usual patriotic declarations. Audiences were usually urged to join a crusade to protect our hallowed institutions. Typical of the more moderate statements was Columbia University President Nicholas Murray Butler's insistence in April 1919 that "America will be saved, not by those who have only contempt and despite for her founders and her history, but by those who look with respect and reverence upon the great series of happenings extending from the voyage of the Mayflower. . . ."[44]

What one historian has called "a riot of biographies of American

42. Draper, 189–90; *Annual Report of the Attorney General for 1920* (Washington, D.C., 1920), 177; Higham, *Strangers in the Land,* 226–27.

43. The word "Americanism" was used by the nativists of the eighteen-forties and eighteen-fifties. During World War I, the stronger phrase "100 per cent Americanism" was invented to suit the belligerent drive for universal conformity.

44. Horace M. Kallen, *Culture and Democracy in the United States* (New York, 1924), Chap. 3, 154–55; Edward G. Hartman, *The Movement to Americanize the Immigrant* (New York, 1948), Chap. 9; Nicholas Murray Butler, *Is America Worth Saving? An Address Delivered Before the Commercial Club of Cincinnati, Ohio, April 19, 1919* (New York, 1919), 20.

heroes—statesmen, cowboys, and pioneers"[45] appeared in this brief
period. Immigrants as well as citizens produced many autobiographical
testimonials to the superiority of American institutions. These patriotic
tendencies in our literature were as short-lived as the Red Scare,
and have been concealed by "debunking" biographies of folk heroes
and skeptical autobiographies so common later in the nineteen-twenties. An unusual number of motion pictures about our early history
were turned out immediately after the war and the reconstruction
of colonial Williamsburg and of Longfellow's Wayside Inn was begun.
With great fanfare, Secretary of State Lansing placed the original
documents of the Constitution and the Declaration of Independence
on display in January 1920, and the State Department distributed
movies of this ceremony to almost every town and city in the United
States.[46] Organizations like the National Security League, the Association for Constitutional Government, the Sons and the Daughters of
the American Revolution, the Colonial Dames of America, with the
cooperation of the American Bar Association and many state Bar
Associations, organized Constitution Day celebrations and distributed
huge numbers of pamphlets on the subject throughout the country.

The American flag became a sacred symbol. Legionnaires demanded
that citizens "Run the Reds out from the land whose flag they sully."[47]
Men suspected of radical leanings were forced to kiss the stars and
stripes. A Brooklyn truck driver decided in June 1919 that it was
unpatriotic to obey a New York City law obliging him to fly a red
cloth on lumber which projected from his vehicle. Instead he used
as a danger signal a small American flag. A policeman, infuriated
at the sight of the stars and stripes flying from a lumber pile, arrested
the driver on a charge of disorderly conduct. Despite the Brooklyn
patriot's insistence that he meant no offense to the flag, he was repri-
manded and fined by the court.[48]

Recent immigrants, especially, were called upon to show evidence
of real conversion. Great pressure was brought to bear upon the
foreign-born to learn English and to forget their native tongues. As
Senator William S. Kenyon of Iowa declared in October 1919, "The

45. Emerson Hunsberger Loucks, *The Ku Klux Klan in Pennsylvania*
(New York, 1936), 163.
46. Kallen, Chap. 3, 154–55; Division of Foreign Intelligence, "Memorandum about Constitution Ceremonies," January 19, 1920, Lansing Papers;
The New York Times, January 18, 1920.
47. *American Legion Weekly,* I (November 14, 1919), 12.
48. Sullivan, VI, 118; New York *World,* June 22, 1919.

time has come to make this a one-language nation."[49] An editorial in the *American Legion Weekly* took a further step and insisted that the one language must be called "American. Why even in Mexico they do not stand for calling the language the Spanish language."[50]

Immigrants were also expected to adopt our customs and to snuff out remnants of Old World cultures. Genteel prewar and wartime movements to speed up assimilation took on a "frightened and feverish aspect."[51] Welcoming members of an Americanization conference called by his department, Secretary of the Interior Franklin K. Lane exclaimed in May 1919, "You have been gathered together as crusaders in a great cause. . . . There is no other question of such importance before the American people as the solidifying and strengthening of true American sentiment." A Harvard University official told the conference that "The Americanization movement . . . gives men a new and holy religion. . . . It challenges each one of us to a renewed consecration and devotion to the welfare of the nation."[52] The National Security League boasted, in 1919, of establishing one thousand study groups to teach teachers how to inculcate "Americanism" in their foreign-born students.[53] A critic of the prevailing mood protested against "one of our best advertised American mottoes, 'One country, one language, one flag,' " which, he complained, had become the basis for a fervent nationwide program.[54]

As the postwar movement for one hundred per cent Americanism gathered momentum, the deportation of alien nonconformists became

49. *The New York Times,* October 14, 1919.

50. *American Legion Weekly,* I (November 14, 1919) 12.

51. Higham, *Strangers in the Land,* 225.

52. United States Department of the Interior, Bureau of Education, *Organization Conference, Proceedings* (Washington, D.C., 1919), 293, 345–50.

53. National Security League, 4.

54. *Addresses and Proceedings of the Knights of Columbus Educational Convention* (New Haven, 1919), 71. Again note the family resemblance between the attempt to protect America through absolute conformity in 1919–20 and the more drastic, centrally-planned Chinese Communist efforts at national indoctrination. A student of Chinese "coercive persuasion" described the "elaborate unanimity rituals like parades, . . . 'spontaneous' mass demonstrations and society-wide campaigns, the extensive proselytizing among the 'heretics' or the 'infidels,' the purges, programs of re-education, and other repressive measures aimed at deviants." In China, also, past national glory is invoked as evidence of present and future greatness. Schein *et al.,* 62; Lifton, *Thought Reform and the Psychology of Totalism;* Walker, *China Under Communism.*

increasingly its most compelling objective. Asked to suggest a remedy
for the nationwide upsurge in radical activity, the Mayor of Gary,
Indiana, replied, "Deportation is the answer, deportation of these
leaders who talk treason in America and deportation of those who
agree with them and work with them." "We must remake America,"
a popular author averred, "We must purify the source of America's
population and keep it pure. . . . We must insist that there shall
be an American loyalty, brooking no amendment or qualification."[55]
As Higham noted, "In 1919, the clamor of 100 per centers for applying deportation as a purgative arose to an hysterical howl. . . .
Through repression and deportation on the one hand and speedy total
assimilation on the other, 100 per centers hoped to eradicate discontent
and purify the nation."[56]

Politicians quickly sensed the possibilities of the popular frenzy
for Americanism. Mayor Ole Hanson of Seattle, Governor Calvin
Coolidge of Massachusetts, and General Leonard Wood became the
early heroes of the movement.[57] The man in the best political position
to take advantage of the popular feeling, however, was Attorney
General A. Mitchell Palmer.[58] In 1919, especially after the President's
physical collapse, only Palmer had the authority, staff, and money
necessary to arrest and deport huge numbers of radical aliens. The
most virulent phase of the movement for one hundred per cent Americanism came early in 1920, when Palmer's agents rounded up for
deportation over six thousand aliens and prepared to arrest thousands
more suspected of membership in radical organizations. Most of these
aliens were taken without warrants, many were detained for unjusti-
fiably long periods of time, and some suffered incredible hardships.
Almost all, however, were eventually released.[59]

After Palmer decided that he could ride the postwar fears into
the presidency, he set out calculatingly to become the symbol of
one hundred per cent Americanism. The Palmer raids, his anti-labor

55. Emerson Hough, "Round Our Town," *Saturday Evening Post,* CXCII
(February 21, 1920), 102; Hough, *The Web,* 456.

56. Higham, *Strangers in the Land,* 227, 255.

57. Murray, 62–65, 147–48, 159–60.

58. For a full discussion of Palmer's role, Stanley Coben, *A. Mitchell
Palmer: Politician* (New York, 1963).

59. Coben, *Palmer,* Chaps. 11, 12; Claghorn, Chap. 10; Constantine
Panunzio, *The Deportation Cases of 1919–1920* (New York, 1920); Zechariah Chafee, Jr., *Free Speech in the United States* (Cambridge, 1941),
204–17; Murray, Chap. 13.

activities, and his frequent pious professions of patriotism during the campaign were all part of this effort. Palmer was introduced by a political associate to the Democratic party's annual Jackson Day dinner in January 1920 as "an American whose Americanism cannot be misunderstood." In a speech delivered in Georgia shortly before the primary election (in which Palmer won control of the state's delegation to the Democratic National Convention), the Attorney General asserted: "I am myself an American and I love to preach my doctrine before undiluted one hundred per cent Americans, because my platform is, in a word, undiluted Americanism and undying loyalty to the republic." The same theme dominated the address made by Palmer's old friend, John H. Bigelow of Hazleton, Pennsylvania, when he placed Palmer's name in nomination at the 1920 National Convention. Proclaimed Bigelow: "No party could survive today that did not write into its platform the magic word 'Americanism.' . . . The Attorney-General of the United States has not merely professed, but he has proved his true Americanism. . . . Behind him I see a solid phalanx of true Americanism that knows no divided allegiance."[60]

Unfortunately for political candidates like Palmer and Wood, most of the social and economic disturbances which had activated the movement they sought to lead gradually disappeared during the first half of 1920. The European revolutions were put down; by 1920 communism seemed to have been isolated in Russia. Bombings ceased abruptly after June 1919, and fear of new outrages gradually abated. Prices of food and clothing began to recede during the spring. Labor strife almost vanished from our major industries after a brief railroad walkout in April. Prosperity returned after mid-1919 and by early 1920 business activity and employment levels exceeded their wartime peaks.[61] At the same time, it became clear that the Senate would not pass Wilson's peace treaty and that America was free to turn its back on the responsibilities of world leadership. The problems associated with the new immigrants remained; so did the disillusionment with

60. Coben, *Palmer,* Chap. 13; *The New York Times,* January 9, 1920; Atlanta *Constitution,* April 7, 1920; *Official Report of the Proceedings of the Democratic National Convention, 1920* (Indianapolis, 1920), 113–14. Palmer also launched a highly publicized campaign to hold down soaring prices in 1919–20, by fixing retail prices and bringing suits against profiteers and hoarders.

61. Bell, 334; Soule, 83–88; *Seventh Annual Report of the Federal Reserve Board for the Year 1920* (Washington, D.C., 1920), 7.

Europe and with many old intellectual ideals. Nativism did not disappear from the American scene; but the frenzied attempt to revitalize the culture did peter out in 1920. The handful of unintimidated men, especially Assistant Secretary of Labor Louis F. Post, who had used the safeguards provided by American law to protect many victims of the Red Scare, found increasing public support. On the other hand, politicians like Palmer, Wood, and Hanson were left high and dry, proclaiming the need for one hundred per cent Americanism to an audience which no longer urgently cared.

It is ironic that in 1920 the Russian leaders of the Comintern finally took charge of the American Communist movement, provided funds and leadership, and ordered the Communist factions to unite and participate actively in labor organizations and strikes. These facts were reported in the American press.[62] Thus a potentially serious foreign threat to national security appeared just as the Red Scare evaporated, providing a final illustration of the fact that the frenzied one hundred per centers of 1919–20 were affected less by the "red menace" than by a series of social and economic dislocations.

Although the Red Scare died out in 1920, its effects lingered. Hostility toward immigrants, mobilized in 1919–20, remained strong enough to force congressional passage of restrictive immigration laws. Some of the die-hard one hundred per centers found a temporary home in the Ku Klux Klan until that organization withered away during the mid-twenties. As its most lasting accomplishments, the movement for one hundred per cent Americanism fostered a spirit of conformity in the country, a satisfaction with the *status quo,* and the equation of reform ideologies with foreign enemies. Revitalization movements have helped many societies adapt successfully to new conditions. The movement associated with the American Red Scare, however, had no such effect. True, it unified the culture against the threats faced in 1919–20; but the basic problems—a damaged value system, an unrestrained business cycle, a hostile Russia, and communism—were left for future generations of Americans to deal with in their own fashion.

62. Draper, 244, 267–68; New York *World,* March 29, 1920.

POLITICAL CHANGES
AT HOME

ARTHUR S. LINK

What Happened to the Progressive Movement in the 1920's?

The claim that World War I promoted reaction in the United States has been most insistent in the area of politics. The notion of war as the "nemesis of reform" grew out of the harrowing experiences of various progressives as they struggled against rampant pro-business conservatism in the 1920's. In turn, the belief that entering the war had killed off progressivism served to buttress liberal support for isolationist foreign policies in the late thirties and early forties. Questioning of this effect of the war has arisen only in recent years. This essay represents the pioneering work in reconsidering the demise of progressivism. Link does not deny that the war had significant political effects, but he sees a variety of other factors also at work in the waning support for political reform after 1916.

Another article on the same subject is Herbert F. Margulies, "Recent Opinion on the Decline of the Progressive Movement," *Mid-America*, XLV (October 1965), 250–268. Two other essays which provide useful perspectives on the postwar fate of reform are Henry F. May, "Shifting Perspectives on the 1920's," *Mississippi Valley Historical Review*, XLIII (December 1956), and Paul W. Glad, "Progressives and the Business Culture of the 1920's," *Journal of American History*, LIII (June 1966), 75–89. The broadest study of political change in the postwar period is David Burner, *The Politics of Provincialism: The Democratic Party in Transition, 1918–1932* (New York, 1968).

Reprinted by permission of the author from the *American Historical Review*, LXIV (July 1959), 833–851.

If the day has not yet arrived when we can make a definite synthesis of political developments between the Armistice and the Great Depression, it is surely high time for historians to begin to clear away the accumulated heap of mistaken and half-mistaken hypotheses about this important transitional period. Writing often without fear or much research (to paraphrase Carl Becker's remark), we recent American historians have gone on indefatigably to perpetuate hypotheses that either reflected the disillusionment and despair of contemporaries, or once served their purpose in exposing the alleged hiatus in the great continuum of twentieth-century reform.

Stated briefly, the following are what might be called the governing hypotheses of the period under discussion: The 1920's were a period made almost unique by an extraordinary reaction against idealism and reform. They were a time when the political representatives of big business and Wall Street executed a relentless and successful campaign in state and nation to subvert the regulatory structure that had been built at the cost of so much toil and sweat since the 1870's, and to restore a Hanna-like reign of special privilege to benefit business, industry, and finance. The surging tides of nationalism and mass hatreds generated by World War I continued to engulf the land and were manifested, among other things, in fear of communism, suppression of civil liberties, revival of nativism and anti-Semitism most crudely exemplified by the Ku Klux Klan, and in the triumph of racism and prejudice in immigration legislation. The 1920's were an era when great traditions and ideals were repudiated or forgotten, when the American people, propelled by a crass materialism in their scramble for wealth, uttered a curse on twenty-five years of reform endeavor. As a result, progressives were stunned and everywhere in retreat along the entire political front, their forces disorganized and leaderless, their movement shattered, their dreams of a new America turned into agonizing nightmares.

To be sure, the total picture that emerges from these generalizations is overdrawn. Yet it seems fair to say that leading historians have advanced each of these generalizations, that the total picture is the one that most of us younger historians saw during the years of our training, and that these hypotheses to a greater or lesser degree still control the way in which we write and teach about the 1920's, as a reading of textbooks and general works will quickly show.

This paper has not been written, however, to quarrel with anyone or to make an indictment. Its purposes are, first, to attempt to determine the degree to which the governing hypotheses, as stated, are adequate or inadequate to explain the political phenomena of the period, and, second, to discover whether any new and sounder hypotheses might be suggested. Such an effort, of course, must be tentative and above all imperfect in view of the absence of sufficient foundations for a synthesis.

Happily, however, we do not have to proceed entirely in the dark. Historians young and old, but mostly young, have already discovered that the period of the 1920's is the exciting new frontier of American historical research and that its opportunities are almost limitless in view of the mass of manuscript materials that are becoming available. Thus we have (the following examples are mentioned only at random) excellent recent studies of agrarian discontent and farm movements by Theodore Saloutos, John D. Hicks, Gilbert C. Fite, Robert L. Moran, and James H. Shideler; of nativism and problems of immigration and assimilation by John Higham, Oscar Handlin, Robert A. Divine, and Edmund D. Cronon; of intellectual currents, the social gospel, and religious controversies by Henry F. May, Paul A. Carter, Robert M. Miller, and Norman F. Furniss; of left-wing politics and labor developments by Theodore Draper, David A. Shannon, Daniel Bell, Paul M. Angle, and Matthew Josephson; of the campaign of 1928 by Edmund A. Moore; and of political and judicial leaders by Alpheus T. Mason, Frank Freidel, Arthur M. Schlesinger, Jr., Merlo J. Pusey, and Joel F. Paschal.[1] Moreover, we can look forward

1. Theodore Saloutos and John D. Hicks, *Agrarian Discontent in the Middle West, 1900–1939* (Madison, Wis., 1951); Gilbert C. Fite, *Peter Norbeck: Prairie Statesman* (Columbia, Mo., 1948), and *George N. Peek and the Fight for Farm Parity* (Norman, Okla., 1954); Robert L. Moran, *Political Prairie Fire: The Nonpartisan League, 1915–1922* (Minneapolis, Minn., 1955); James H. Shideler, *Farm Crisis, 1919–1923* (Berkeley, Calif., 1957); John Higham, *Strangers in the Land: Patterns of American Nativism, 1860–1925* (New Brunswick, N.J., 1955); Oscar Handlin, *The American People in the Twentieth Century* (Cambridge, Mass., 1954); Robert A. Divine, *American Immigration Policy, 1924–1952* (New Haven, Conn., 1957); Edmund D. Cronon, *Black Moses: The Story of Marcus Garvey and the Universal Negro Improvement Association* (Madison, Wis., 1955); Henry F. May, "Shifting Perspectives on the 1920's," *Mississippi Valley Historical Review,* XLIII (Dec., 1956), 405–27; Paul A. Carter, *The Decline and Revival of the Social Gospel* (Ithaca, N.Y., 1956), Robert M. Miller, "An Inquiry into the Social Attitudes of American Protestantism, 1919–1939," doctoral dissertation, Northwestern University, 1955; Norman F. Furniss, *The Fundamentalist Controversy, 1918–1931* (New Haven, Conn., 1954); Theodore Draper, *The Roots of American Communism*

to the early publication of studies that will be equally illuminating for the period, like the biographies of George W. Norris, Thomas J. Walsh, and Albert B. Fall now being prepared by Richard Lowitt, Leonard Bates, and David Stratton, respectively, and the recently completed study of the campaign and election of 1920 by Wesley M. Bagby.[2]

Obviously, we are not only at a point in the progress of our research into the political history of the 1920's when we can begin to generalize, but we have reached the time when we should attempt to find some consensus, however tentative it must now be, concerning the larger political dimensions and meanings of the period.

In answering the question of what happened to the progressive movement in the 1920's, we should begin by looking briefly at some fundamental facts about the movement before 1918, facts that in large measure predetermined its fate in the 1920's, given the political climate and circumstances that prevailed.

The first of these was the elementary fact that the progressive movement never really existed as a recognizable organization with common goals and a political machinery geared to achieve them. Generally speaking (and for the purposes of this paper), progressivism might be defined as the popular effort, which began convulsively

(New York, 1957); David A. Shannon, *The Socialist Party of America: A History* (New York, 1955); Daniel Bell, "The Background and Development of Marxian Socialism in the United States," *Socialism and American Life,* ed. Donald D. Egbert and Stow Persons (2 vols., Princeton, N.J., 1952), I, 215–405; Paul M. Angle, *Bloody Williamson* (New York, 1952); Matthew Josephson, *Sidney Hillman: Statesman of American Labor* (New York, 1952); Edmund A. Moore, *A Catholic Runs for President: The Campaign of 1928* (New York, 1956); Alpheus Thomas Mason, *Brandeis: A Free Man's Life* (New York, 1946), and *Harlan Fiske Stone: Pillar of the Law* (New York, 1956); Frank Freidel, *Franklin D. Roosevelt: The Ordeal* (Boston, 1954); Arthur M. Schlesinger, Jr., *The Age of Roosevelt: The Crisis of the Old Order* (Boston, 1957); Merlo J. Pusey, *Charles Evans Hughes* (2 vols., New York, 1951); Joel Francis Paschal, *Mr. Justice Sutherland: A Man against the State* (Princeton, N.J., 1951).

2. Wesley M. Bagby, "Woodrow Wilson and the Great Debate of 1920," MS in the possession of Professor Bagby; see also his "The 'Smoke-Filled Room' and the Nomination of Warren G. Harding," *Mississippi Valley Historical Review,* XLI (Mar., 1955), 657–74, and "Woodrow Wilson, a Third Term, and the Solemn Referendum," *American Historical Review,* LX (Apr., 1955), 567–75.

in the 1890's and waxed and waned afterward to our own time, to insure the survival of democracy in the United States by the enlargement of governmental power to control and offset the power of private economic groups over the nation's institutions and life. Actually, of course, from the 1890's on there were many "progressive" movements on many levels seeking sometimes contradictory objectives. Not all, but most of these campaigns were the work of special interest groups or classes seeking greater political status and economic security. This was true from the beginning of the progressive movement in the 1890's; by 1913 it was that movement's most important characteristic.

The second fundamental fact—that the progressive movements were often largely middle class in constituency and orientation—is of course well known, but an important corollary has often been ignored. It was that several of the most important reform movements were inspired, staffed, and led by businessmen with very specific or special-interest objectives in view. Because they hated waste, mismanagement, and high taxes, they, together with their friends in the legal profession, often furnished the leadership of good government campaigns. Because they feared industrial monopoly, abuse of power by railroads, and the growth of financial oligarchy, they were the backbone of the movements that culminated in the adoption of the Hepburn and later acts for railroad regulation, the Federal Reserve Act, and the Federal Trade Commission Act. Among the many consequences of their participation in the progressive movement, two should be mentioned because of their significance for developments in the 1920's: First, the strong identification of businessmen with good government and economic reforms for which the general public also had a lively concern helped preserve the good reputation of the middle-class business community (as opposed to its alleged natural enemies, monopolists, malefactors of great wealth, and railroad barons) and helped to direct the energies of the progressive movement toward the strengthening instead of the shackling of the business community. Second, their activities and influence served to intensify the tensions within the broad reform movement, because they often opposed the demands of farm groups, labor unions, and advocates of social justice.

The third remark to be made about the progressive movement before 1918 is that despite its actual diversity and inner tensions it did seem to have unity; that is, it seemed to share common ideals and objectives. This was true in part because much of the motivation even of the special-interest groups was altruistic (at least they succeeded in convincing themselves that they sought the welfare of society rather than their own interests primarily); in part because political leadership generally succeeded in subordinating inner tensions. It was true, above all, because there were in fact important idealistic elements in the progressive ranks—social gospel leaders, social justice elements, and intellectuals and philosophers—who worked hard at the task of defining and elevating common principles and goals.

Fourth and finally, the substantial progressive achievements before 1918 had been gained, at least on the federal level, only because of the temporary dislocations of the national political structure caused by successive popular uprisings, not because progressives had found or created a viable organization for perpetuating their control. Or, to put the matter another way, before 1918 the various progressive elements had failed to destroy the existing party structure by organizing a national party of their own that could survive. They, or at least many of them, tried in 1912; and it seemed for a time in 1916 that Woodrow Wilson had succeeded in drawing the important progressive groups permanently into the Democratic party. But Wilson's accomplishment did not survive even to the end of the war, and by 1920 traditional partisan loyalties were reasserting themselves with extraordinary vigor.

With this introduction, we can now ask what happened to the progressive movement or movements in the 1920's. Surely no one would contend that after 1916 the political scene did not change significantly, both on the state and national levels. There was the seemingly obvious fact that the Wilsonian coalition had been wrecked by the election of 1920, and that the progressive elements were divided and afterward unable to agree upon a program or to control the national government. There was the even more "obvious" fact that conservative Republican presidents and their cabinets controlled the executive branch throughout the period. There was Congress, as Eric F. Goldman has said, allegedly whooping through procorporation legislation, and the Supreme Court interpreting the New Freedom laws in a way that harassed unions and encouraged trusts.[3] There were, to outraged idealists and intellectuals, the more disgusting spectacles of Red hunts, mass arrests and deportations, the survival deep into the 1920's of arrogant nationalism, crusades against the teaching

3. Eric F. Goldman, *Rendezvous with Destiny* (New York, 1953), 284. The "allegedly" in this sentence is mine, not Professor Goldman's.

of evolution, the attempted suppression of the right to drink, and myriad other manifestations of what would now be called a repressive reaction.[4]

Like the hypotheses suggested at the beginning, this picture is overdrawn in some particulars. But it is accurate in part, for progressivism was certainly on the downgrade if not in decay after 1918. This is an obvious fact that needs explanation and understanding rather than elaborate proof. We can go a long way toward answering our question if we can explain, at least partially, the extraordinarily complex developments that converge to produce the "obvious" result.

For this explanation we must begin by looking at the several progressive elements and their relation to each other and to the two major parties after 1916. Since national progressivism was never an organized or independent movement (except imperfectly and then only temporarily in 1912), it could succeed only when its constituent elements formed a coalition strong enough to control one of the major parties. This had happened in 1916, when southern and western farmers, organized labor, the social justice elements, and a large part of the independent radicals who had heretofore voted the Socialist ticket coalesced to continue the control of Wilson and the Democratic party.

The important fact about the progressive coalition of 1916, however, was not its strength but its weakness. It was not a new party but a temporary alliance, welded in the heat of the most extraordinary domestic and external events. To be sure, it functioned for the most part successfully during the war, in providing the necessary support for a program of heavy taxation, relatively stringent controls over business and industry, and extensive new benefits to labor. Surviving in a crippled way even in the months following the Armistice, it put across a program that constituted a sizable triumph for the progressive movement—continued heavy taxation, the Transportation Act of 1920, the culmination of the long fight for railroad regulation, a new child labor act, amendments for prohibition and woman suffrage, immigration restriction, and water power and conservation legislation.

Even so, the progressive coalition of 1916 was inherently unstable. Indeed, it was so wracked by inner tensions that it could not survive,

4. H. C. Peterson and Gilbert C. Fite, *Opponents of War, 1917–1918* (Norman, Okla., 1957); Robert K. Murray, *Red Scare: A Study in National Hysteria, 1919–1920* (Minneapolis, Minn., 1955).

and destruction came inexorably, it seemed systematically, from 1917 to 1920. Why was this true?

First, the independent radicals and antiwar agrarians were alienated by the war declaration and the government's suppression of dissent and civil liberties during the war and the Red scare. Organized labor was disaffected by the administration's coercion of the coal miners in 1919, its lukewarm if not hostile attitude during the great strikes of 1919 and 1920, and its failure to support the Plumb Plan for nationalization of the railroads. Isolationists and idealists were outraged by what they thought was the President's betrayal of American traditions or the liberal peace program at Paris. These tensions were strong enough to disrupt the coalition, but a final one would have been fatal even if the others had never existed. This was the alienation of farmers in the Plains and western states produced by the administration's refusal to impose price controls on cotton while it maintained ceilings on the prices of other agricultural commodities,[5] and especially by the administration's failure to do anything decisive to stem the downward plunge of farm prices that began in the summer of 1920.[6] Under the impact of all these stresses, the Wilsonian coalition gradually disintegrated from 1917 to 1920 and disappeared entirely during the campaign of 1920.

The progressive coalition was thus destroyed, but the components of a potential movement remained. As we will see, these elements were neither inactive nor entirely unsuccessful in the 1920's. But they obviously failed to find common principles and a program, much less to unite effectively for political action on a national scale. I suggest that this was true, in part at least, for the following reasons:

First, the progressive elements could never create or gain control of a political organization capable of carrying them into national office. The Republican party was patently an impossible instrument because control of the GOP was too much in the hands of the eastern and midwestern industrial, oil, and financial interests, as it had been since about 1910. There was always the hope of a third party. Several

5. On this point, see Seward W. Livermore, "The Sectional Issue in the 1918 Congressional Elections," *Mississippi Valley Historical Review*, XXXV (June, 1948), 29–60.
6. Arthur S. Link, "The Federal Reserve Policy and the Agricultural Depression of 1920–1921," *Agricultural History*, XX (July, 1946), 166–75; and Herbert F. Margulies, "The Election of 1920 in Wisconsin: The Return to 'Normalcy' Reappraised," *Wisconsin Magazine of History*, XXXVIII (Autumn, 1954), 15–22.

progressive groups—insurgent midwestern Republicans, the railroad brotherhoods, a segment of the AF of L, and the moderate Socialists under Robert M. La Follette—tried to realize this goal in 1924, only to discover that third party movements in the United States are doomed to failure except in periods of enormous national turmoil, and that the 1920's were not such a time. Thus the Democratic party remained the only vehicle that conceivably could have been used by a new progressive coalition. But that party was simply not capable of such service in the 1920's. It was so torn by conflicts between its eastern, big city wing and its southern and western rural majority that it literally ceased to be a national party. It remained strong in its sectional and metropolitan components, but it was so divided that it barely succeeded in nominating a presidential candidate at all in 1924 and nominated one in 1928 only at the cost of temporary disruption.[7]

Progressivism declined in the 1920's, in the second place, because, as has been suggested, the tensions that had wrecked the coalition of 1916 not only persisted but actually grew in number and intensity. The two most numerous progressive elements, the southern and western farmers, strongly supported the Eighteenth Amendment, were heavily tinged with nativism and therefore supported immigration restriction, were either members of, friendly to, or politically afraid of the Ku Klux Klan, and demanded as the principal plank in their platform legislation to guarantee them a larger share of the national income. On all these points and issues the lower and lower middle classes in the large cities stood in direct and often violent opposition to their potential allies in the rural areas. Moreover, the liaison between the farm groups and organized labor, which had been productive of much significant legislation during the Wilson period, virtually ceased to exist in the 1920's. There were many reasons for this development, and I mention only one—the fact that the preeminent spokesmen of farmers in the 1920's, the new Farm Bureau Federation, represented the larger commercial farmers who (in contrast to the members of the leading farm organization in Wilson's day, the National Farmers' Union) were often employers themselves and felt no identification with the rank and file of labor.

It was little wonder, therefore (and this is a third reason for the

7. For a highly partisan account of the events see Karl Schriftgiesser, *This Was Normalcy* (Boston, 1948). More balanced are the already cited Freidel, *Franklin D. Roosevelt: The Ordeal,* and Schlesinger, *The Age of Roosevelt: The Crisis of the Old Order.*

weakness of progressivism in the 1920's), that the tension-ridden progressive groups were never able to agree upon a program that, like the Democratic platform of 1916, could provide the basis for a revived coalition. So long as progressive groups fought one another more fiercely than they fought their natural opponents, such agreement was impossible; and so long as common goals were impossible to achieve, a national progressive movement could not take effective form. Nothing illustrates this better than the failure of the Democratic conventions of 1924 and 1928 to adopt platforms that could rally and unite the discontented elements. One result, among others, was that southern farmers voted as Democrats and western farmers as Republicans. And, as Professor Frank Freidel once commented to the author, much of the failure of progressivism in the 1920's can be explained by this elementary fact.

A deeper reason for the failure of progressives to unite ideologically in the 1920's was what might be called a substantial paralysis of the progressive mind. This was partly the result of the repudiation of progressive ideals by many intellectuals and the defection from the progressive movement of the urban middle classes and professional groups, as will be demonstrated. It was the result, even more importantly, of the fact that progressivism as an organized body of political thought found itself at a crossroads in the 1920's, like progressivism today, and did not know which way to turn. The major objectives of the progressive movement of the prewar years had in fact been largely achieved by 1920. In what direction should progressivism now move? Should it remain in the channels already deeply cut by its own traditions, and, while giving sincere allegiance to the ideal of democratic capitalism, work for more comprehensive programs of business regulation and assistance to disadvantaged classes like farmers and submerged industrial workers? Should it abandon these traditions and, like most similar European movements, take the road toward a moderate socialism with a predominantly labor orientation? Should it attempt merely to revive the goals of more democracy through changes in the political machinery? Or should it become mainly an agrarian movement with purely agrarian goals?

These were real dilemmas, not academic ones, and one can see numerous examples of how they confused and almost paralyzed progressives in the 1920's. The platform of La Follette's Progressive party of 1924 offers one revealing illustration. It embodied much that was old and meaningless by this time (the direct election of the president and a national referendum before the adoption of a war resolution, for example) and little that had any real significance for the future.[8] And yet it was the best that a vigorous and idealistic movement could offer. A second example was the plight of the agrarians and insurgents in Congress who fought so hard all through the 1920's against Andrew Mellon's proposals to abolish the inheritance tax and to make drastic reductions in the taxes on large incomes. In view of the rapid reduction of the federal debt, the progressives were hard pressed to justify the continuation of nearly confiscatory tax levels, simply because few of them realized the wide social and economic uses to which the income tax could be put. Lacking any programs for the redistribution of the national income (except to farmers), they were plagued and overwhelmed by the surpluses in the federal Treasury until, for want of any good arguments, they finally gave Secretary Andrew Mellon the legislation he had been demanding.[9] A third and final example of this virtual paralysis of the progressive mind was perhaps the most revealing of all. It was the attempt that Woodrow Wilson, Louis D. Brandeis, and other Democratic leaders made from 1921 to 1924 to draft a new charter for progressivism. Except for its inevitable proposals for an idealistic world leadership, the document that emerged from this interchange included little or nothing that would have sounded new to a western progressive in 1912.

A fourth reason for the disintegration and decline of the progressive movement in the 1920's was the lack of an effective leadership. Given the political temper and circumstances of the 1920's, it is possible that such leadership could not have operated successfully in any event. Perhaps the various progressive elements were so mutually hostile and so self-centered in interests and objectives that even a Theodore Roosevelt or a Woodrow Wilson, had they been at the zenith of their powers in the 1920's, could not have drawn them together in a common front. We will never know what a strong national leader might have done because by a trick of fate no such leader emerged before Franklin D. Roosevelt.

8. For a different picture see Belle C. La Follette and Fola La Follette, *Robert M. La Follette* (2 vols., New York, 1963); and Russell B. Nye, *Midwestern Progressive Politics, 1870–1950* (East Lansing, Mich., 1951). Both works contribute to an understanding of progressive politics in the 1920's.

9. Here indebtedness is acknowledged to Sidney Ratner, *American Taxation: Its History as a Social Force in Democracy* (New York, 1942).

Four factors, then, contributed to the failure of the progressive components to unite successfully after 1918 and, as things turned out, before 1932: the lack of a suitable political vehicle, the severity of the tensions that kept progressives apart, the failure of progressives to agree upon a common program, and the absence of a national leadership, without which a united movement could never be created and sustained. These were all weaknesses that stemmed to a large degree from the instability and failures of the progressive movement itself.

There were, besides, a number of what might be called external causes for the movement's decline. In considering them one must begin with what was seemingly the most important—the alleged fact that the 1920's were a very unpropitious time for any new progressive revolt because of the ever-increasing level of economic prosperity, the materialism, and the general contentment of the decade 1919 to 1929. Part of this generalization is valid when applied to specific elements in the population. For example, the rapid rise in the real wages of industrial workers, coupled with generally full employment and the spread of so-called welfare practices among management, certainly did much to weaken and avert the further spread of organized labor, and thus to debilitate one of the important progressive components. But to say that it was prosperity per se that created a climate unfriendly to progressive ideals would be inaccurate. There was little prosperity and much depression during the 1920's for the single largest economic group, the farmers, as well as for numerous other groups. Progressivism, moreover, can flourish as much during periods of prosperity as during periods of discontent, as the history of the development of the progressive movement from 1901 to 1917 and of its triumph from 1945 to 1956 prove.

Vastly more important among the external factors in the decline of progressivism was the widespread, almost wholesale, defection from its ranks of the middle class—the middling businessmen, bankers, and manufacturers, and the professional people closely associated with them in ideals and habits—in American cities large and small. For an understanding of this phenomenon no simple explanations like "prosperity" or the "temper of the times" will suffice, although they give some insight. The important fact was that these groups found a new economic and social status as a consequence of the flowering of American enterprise under the impact of the technological, financial, and other revolutions of the 1920's. If, as Professor

Richard Hofstadter has claimed,[10] the urban middle classes were progressive (that is, they demanded governmental relief from various anxieties) in the early 1900's because they resented their loss of social prestige to the *nouveaux riches* and feared being ground under by monopolists in industry, banking, and labor—if this is true, then the urban middle classes were not progressive in the 1920's for inverse reasons. Their temper was dynamic, expansive, and supremely confident. They knew that they were building a new America, a business civilization based not upon monopoly and restriction but upon a whole new set of business values—mass production and consumption, short hours and high wages, full employment, welfare capitalism. And what was more important, virtually the entire country (at least the journalists, writers in popular magazines, and many preachers and professors) acknowledged that the nation's destiny was in good hands. It was little wonder, therefore, that the whole complex of groups constituting the urban middle classes, whether in New York, Zenith, or Middletown, had little interest in rebellion or even in mild reform proposals that seemed to imperil their leadership and control.

Other important factors, of course, contributed to the contentment of the urban middle classes. The professionalization of business and the full-blown emergence of a large managerial class had a profound impact upon social and political ideals. The acceleration of mass advertising played its role, as did also the beginning disintegration of the great cities with the spread of middle- and upper-middle-class suburbs, a factor that diffused the remaining reform energies among the urban leaders.

A second external factor in the decline of the progressive movement after 1918 was the desertion from its ranks of a good part of the intellectual leadership of the country. Indeed, more than simple desertion was involved here; it was often a matter of a cynical repudiation of the ideals from which progressivism derived its strength. I do not mean to imply too much by this generalization. I know that what has been called intellectual progressivism not only survived in the 1920's but actually flourished in many fields.[11] I know that the intellectual foundations of our present quasi-welfare state were either

10. Richard Hofstadter, *The Age of Reform: From Bryan to F.D.R.* (New York, 1955), 131 ff.

11. *Ibid.,* 5, 131, 135 ff. For a recent excellent survey, previously cited, see Henry F. May, "Shifting Perspectives on the 1920's." Schlesinger's previously cited *Age of Roosevelt* sheds much new light on the economic thought of the 1920's.

being laid or reinforced during the decade. Even so, one cannot evade the conclusion that the intellectual-political climate of the 1920's was vastly different from the one that had prevailed in the preceding two decades.

During the years of the great progressive revolt, intellectuals—novelists, journalists, political thinkers, social scientists, historians, and the like—had made a deeply personal commitment to the cause of democracy, first in domestic and then in foreign affairs. Their leadership in and impact on many phases of the progressive movement had been profound. By contrast, in the 1920's a large body of this intellectual phalanx turned against the very ideals they had once deified. One could cite, for example, the reaction of the idealists against the Versailles settlement; the disenchantment of the intellectuals with the extension of government authority when it could be used to justify the Eighteenth Amendment or the suppression of free speech; or the inevitable loss of faith in the "people" when en masse they hounded so-called radicals, joined Bryan's crusade against evolution, or regaled themselves as Knights of the Ku Klux Klan. Whatever the cause, many alienated intellectuals simply withdrew or repudiated any identification with the groups they had once helped to lead. The result was not fatal to progressivism, but it was serious. The spark plugs had been removed from the engine of reform.

The progressive movement, then, unquestionably declined, but was it defunct in the 1920's? Much, of course, depends upon the definition of terms. If we accept the usual definition for "defunct" as "dead" or "ceasing to have any life or strength," we must recognize that the progressive movement was certainly not defunct in the 1920's; that on the contrary at least important parts of it were very much alive; and that it is just as important to know how and why progressivism survived as it is to know how and why it declined.

To state the matter briefly, progressivism survived in the 1920's because several important elements of the movement remained either in full vigor or in only slightly diminished strength. These were the farmers, after 1918 better organized and more powerful than during the high tide of the progressive revolt; the politically conscious elements among organized labor, particularly the railroad brotherhoods, who wielded a power all out of proportion to their numbers; the Democratic organizations in the large cities, usually vitally concerned with the welfare of the so-called lower classes; a remnant of independent radicals, social workers, and social gospel writers and preachers;

and finally, an emerging new vocal element, the champions of public power and regional developments.

Although they never united effectively enough to capture a major party and the national government before 1932, these progressive elements controlled Congress from 1921 to about 1927 and continued to exercise a near control during the period of their greatest weakness in the legislative branch, from 1927 to about 1930.

Indeed, the single most powerful and consistently successful group in Congress during the entire decade from 1919 to 1929 were the spokesmen of the farmers. Spurred by an unrest in the country areas more intense than at any time since the 1890's,[12] in 1920 and 1921 southern Democrats and mid-western and western insurgents, nominally Republican, joined forces in an alliance called the Farm Bloc. By maintaining a common front from 1921 to 1924 they succeeded in enacting the most advanced agricultural legislation to that date, legislation that completed the program begun under Wilsonian auspices. It included measures for high tariffs on agricultural products, thoroughgoing federal regulation of stockyards, packing houses, and grain exchanges, the exemption of agricultural cooperatives from the application of the antitrust laws, stimulation of the export of agricultural commodities, and the establishment of an entirely new federal system of intermediate rural credit.

When prosperity failed to return to the countryside, rural leaders in Congress espoused a new and bolder plan for relief—the proposal made by George N. Peek and Hugh S. Johnson in 1922 to use the federal power to obtain "fair exchange" or "parity" prices for farm products. Embodied in the McNary-Haugen bill in 1924, this measure was approved by Congress in 1927 and 1928, only to encounter vetoes by President Calvin Coolidge.

In spite of its momentary failure, the McNary-Haugen bill had a momentous significance for the American progressive movement. Its wholesale espousal by the great mass of farm leaders and spokesmen meant that the politically most powerful class in the country had come full scale to the conviction that the taxing power should be used directly and specifically for the purpose of underwriting (some persons called it subsidizing) agriculture. It was a milestone in the development of a comprehensive political doctrine that it was govern-

12. It derived from the fact that farm prices plummeted in 1920 and 1921, and remained so low that farmers, generally speaking, operated at a net capital loss throughout the balance of the decade.

ment's duty to protect the economic security of all classes and particularly depressed ones. McNary-Haugenism can be seen in its proper perspective if it is remembered that it would have been considered almost absurd in the Wilson period, that it was regarded as radical by non-farm elements in the 1920's, and that it, or at any rate its fundamental object, was incorporated almost as a matter of course into basic federal policy in the 1930's.

A second significant manifestation of the survival of progressivism in the 1920's came during the long controversy over public ownership or regulation of the burgeoning electric power industry. In this, as in most of the conflicts that eventually culminated on Capitol Hill, the agrarian element constituted the core of progressive strength. At the same time a sizable and well-organized independent movement developed that emanated from urban centers and was vigorous on the municipal and state levels. Throughout the decade this relatively new progressive group fought with mounting success to expose the propaganda of the private utilities, to strengthen state and federal regulatory agencies, and to win municipal ownership for distributive facilities. Like the advocates of railroad regulation in an earlier period, these proponents of regulation or ownership of a great new natural monopoly failed almost as much as they had succeeded in the 1920's. But their activities and exposures (the Federal Trade Commission's devastating investigation of the electric power industry in the late 1920's and early 1930's was the prime example) laid secure foundations for movements that in the 1930's would reach various culminations.

Even more significant for the future of American progressivism was the emergence in the 1920's of a new objective, that of committing the federal government to plans for large hydroelectric projects in the Tennessee Valley, the Columbia River watershed, the Southwest, and the St. Lawrence Valley for the purpose, some progressives said, of establishing "yardsticks" for rates, or for the further purpose, as other progressives declared, of beginning a movement for the eventual nationalization of the entire electric power industry. The development of this movement in its emerging stages affords a good case study in the natural history of American progressivism. It began when the Harding and Coolidge administrations attempted to dispose of the government's hydroelectric and nitrate facilities at Muscle Shoals, Alabama, to private interests. In the first stage of the controversy, the progressive objective was merely federal operation of these facilities for the production of cheap fertilizer—a reflection of its exclusive special-interest orientation. Then, as new groups joined the fight to save Muscle Shoals, the objective of public production of cheap electric power came to the fore. Finally, by the end of the 1920's, the objective of a multipurpose regional development in the Tennessee Valley and in other areas as well had taken firm shape.

In addition, by 1928 the agrarians in Congress led by Senator George W. Norris had found enough allies in the two houses and enough support in the country at large to adopt a bill for limited federal development of the Tennessee Valley. Thwarted by President Coolidge's pocket veto, the progressives tried again in 1931, only to meet a second rebuff at the hands of President Herbert Hoover.

All this might be regarded as another milestone in the maturing of American progressivism. It signified a deviation from the older traditions of mere regulation, as President Hoover had said in his veto of the second Muscle Shoals bill, and the triumph of new concepts of direct federal leadership in large-scale development of resources. If progressives had not won their goal by the end of the 1920's, they had at least succeeded in writing what would become perhaps the most important plank in their program for the future.

The maturing of an advanced farm program and the formulation of plans for public power and regional developments may be termed the two most significant progressive achievements on the national level in the 1920's. Others merit only brief consideration. One was the final winning of the old progressive goal of immigration restriction through limited and selective admission. The fact that this movement was motivated in part by racism, nativism, and anti-Semitism (with which, incidentally, a great many if not a majority of progressives were imbued in the 1920's) should not blind us to the fact that it was also progressive. It sought to substitute a so-called scientific and a planned policy of laissez faire. Its purpose was admittedly to disturb the free operation of the international labor market. Organized labor and social workers had long supported it against the opposition of large employers. And there was prohibition, the most ambitious and revealing progressive experiment of the twentieth century. Even the contemned antievolution crusade of Bryan and the fundamentalists and the surging drives for conformity of thought and action in other fields should be mentioned. All these movements stemmed from the conviction that organized public power could and should be used purposefully to achieve fundamental social and so-called moral change. The fact that they were potentially or actively repressive does not mean that they were not progressive. On the contrary, they superbly illustrated the repressive tendencies that inhered in progressivism precisely because it was grounded so much upon majoritarian principles.

Three other developments on the national level that have often been cited as evidences of the failure of progressivism in the 1920's appear in a somewhat different light at second glance. The first was the reversal of the tariff-for-revenue-only tendencies of the Underwood Act with the enactment of the Emergency Tariff Act of 1921 and the Fordney-McCumber Act of 1922. Actually, the adoption of these measures signified, on the whole, not a repudiation but a revival of progressive principles in the realm of federal fiscal policy. A revenue tariff had never been an authentic progressive objective. Indeed, at least by 1913, many progressives, except for some southern agrarians, had concluded that it was retrogressive and had agreed that the tariff laws should be used deliberately to achieve certain national objectives—for example, the crippling of noncompetitive big business by the free admission of articles manufactured by so-called trusts, or benefits to farmers by the free entry of farm implements. Wilson himself had been at least partially converted to these principles by 1916, as his insistence upon the creation of the Federal Tariff Commission and his promise of protection to the domestic chemical industry revealed. As for the tariff legislation of the early 1920's, its only important changes were increased protection for aluminum, chemical products, and agricultural commodities. It left the Underwood rates on the great mass of raw materials and manufactured goods largely undisturbed. It may have been economically shortsighted and a bad example for the rest of the world, but for the most part it was progressive in principle and was the handiwork of the progressive coalition in Congress.

Another development that has often been misunderstood in its relation to the progressive movement was the policies of consistent support that the Harding and Coolidge administrations adopted for business enterprise, particularly the policy of the Federal Trade Commission in encouraging the formation of trade associations and the diminution of certain traditional competitive practices. The significance of all this can easily be overrated. Such policies as these two administrations executed had substantial justification in progressive theory and in precedents clearly established by the Wilson administration.

A third challenge to usual interpretations concerns implications to be drawn from the election of Harding and Coolidge in 1920 and 1924. These elections seem to indicate the triumph of reaction among the mass of American voters. Yet one could argue that both Harding and Coolidge were political accidents, the beneficiaries of grave defects in the American political and constitutional systems. The rank and file of Republican voters demonstrated during the pre-convention campaign that they wanted vigorous leadership and a moderately progressive candidate in 1920. They got Harding instead, not because they wanted him, but because unusual circumstances permitted a small clique to thwart the will of the majority.[13] They took Coolidge as their candidate in 1924 simply because Harding died in the middle of his term and there seemed to be no alternative to nominating the man who had succeeded him in the White House. Further, an analysis of the election returns in 1920 and 1924 will show that the really decisive factor in the victories of Harding and Coolidge was the fragmentation of the progressive movement and the fact that an opposition strong enough to rally and unite the progressive majority simply did not exist.

There remains, finally, a vast area of progressive activity about which we yet know very little. One could mention the continuation of old reform movements and the development of new ones in the cities and states during the years following the Armistice. For example, the steady spread of the city manager form of government, the beginning of zoning and planning movements, and the efforts of the great cities to keep abreast of the transportation revolution then in full swing. Throughout the country the educational and welfare activities of the cities and states steadily increased. Factory legislation matured, while social insurance had its experimental beginnings. Whether such reform impulses were generally weak or strong, one cannot say; but what we do know about developments in cities like Cincinnati and states like New York, Wisconsin, and Louisiana[14] justifies a challenge to the assumption that municipal and state reform energies were dead after 1918 and, incidentally, a plea to young scholars to plow this unworked field of recent American history.

13. Much that is new on the Republican preconvention campaign and convention of 1920 may be found in William T. Hutchinson, *Lowden of Illinois: The Life of Frank O. Lowden* (2 vols., Chicago, 1957).

14. See, e.g., Allen P. Sindler, *Huey Long's Lousiana: State Politics, 1920–1952* (Baltimore, Md., 1956).

Let us, then, suggest a tentative synthesis as an explanation of what happened to the progressive movement after 1918:

First, the national progressive movement, which had found its most effective embodiment in the coalition of forces that reelected Woodrow Wilson in 1916, was shattered by certain policies that the administration pursued from 1917 to 1920, and by some developments over which the administration had no or only slight control. The collapse that occurred in 1920 was not inevitable and cannot be explained by merely saying that "the war killed the progressive movement."

Second, large and aggressive components of a potential new progressive coalition remained after 1920. These elements never succeeded in uniting effectively before the end of the decade, not because they did not exist, but because they were divided by conflicts among themselves. National leadership, which in any event did not emerge in the 1920's, perhaps could not have succeeded in subduing these tensions and in creating a new common front.

Third, as a result of the foregoing, progressivism as an organized national force suffered a serious decline in the 1920's. This decline was heightened by the defection of large elements among the urban middle classes and the intellectuals, a desertion induced by technological, economic, and demographic changes, and by the outcropping of certain repressive tendencies in progressivism after 1917.

Fourth, in spite of reversals and failures, important components of the national progressive movement survived in considerable vigor and succeeded to a varying degree, not merely in keeping the movement alive, but even in broadening its horizons. This was true particularly of the farm groups and of the coalition concerned with public regulation or ownership of electric power resources. These two groups laid the groundwork in the 1920's for significant new programs in the 1930's and beyond.

Fifth, various progressive coalitions controlled Congress for the greater part of the 1920's and were always a serious threat to the conservative administrations that controlled the executive branch. Because this was true, most of the legislation adopted by Congress during this period, including many measures that historians have inaccurately called reactionary, was progressive in character.

Sixth, the progressive movement in the cities and states was far from dead in the 1920's, although we do not have sufficient evidence to justify any generalizations about the degree of its vigor.

If this tentative and imperfect synthesis has any value, perhaps it is high time that we discard the sweeping generalizations, false hypotheses, and clichés that we have so often used in explaining and characterizing political developments from 1918 to 1929. Perhaps we should try to see these developments for what they were—the normal and ordinary political behavior of groups and classes caught up in a swirl of social and economic change. When we do this we will no longer ask whether the progressive movement was defunct in the 1920's. We will ask only what happened to it and why.

JAMES WEINSTEIN

Anti-War Sentiment and the Socialist Party, 1917–1918

If World War I stifled reform in the United States, some historians believe it also affected more radical groups, especially the Socialist party, which lost support because of official repression and the unpopularity of their opposition to the war. Repression, through government action as well as private vigilantism, undeniably occurred, and the Socialists, except for the comparatively large vote for Eugene Debs in the 1920 presidential election, never regained their pre-war strength. But the connection between those two facts has recently come under critical scrutiny, and a by-product of this examination has been to raise questions about how popular intervention was with the American public.

James Weinstein's essay introduces fresh evidence about both the appeal of the Socialists after 1917 and the lack of public support for the war. For a more general treatment of the effects of the war on socialism see Weinstein's book, which incorporates this essay, *The Decline of Socialism in America, 1912–1925* (New York, 1967). Other considerations of the same problem are Milton Cantor, "The Radical Confrontation with Foreign Policy: War and Revolution, 1914–1920," in Alfred Young, ed., *Dissent: Explorations in the History of American Radicalism* (DeKalb, Ill., 1968), pp. 215–249, and Stanley Shapiro, "The Great War and Reform: Liberals and Labor, 1917–19," *Labor History*, XII (Summer 1971), 323–344.

The reëlection of Woodrow Wilson in 1916 was the result of a widespread belief that a Democratic administration would not involve the United States in the World War; yet only five months after the election the United States was at war with Germany. This sudden development left large numbers in opposition to their country's partici-

Reprinted by permission from the *Political Science Quarterly*, LXXIV (June 1959), 215–239.

pation in the war; but the extent of this opposition has not been appreciated. The conventional channels of expression were closed to the opponents of the war. The great majority of newspapers supported the war energetically. Despite the fact that six senators and fifty congressmen voted against the declaration of war, major party opposition was slight. Indeed, opponents of war remained disorganized and almost leaderless: organized opposition was restricted virtually to radical groups. Nevertheless, many Americans, of varied backgrounds and interests, remained firm in the belief that American democracy had nothing at stake in the war.

Probably the main reason that historians have underestimated popular opposition to the war is that the Socialist party was the main vehicle of opposition. The wartime (and, until recently, the pre-war) influence of the party has received scant attention from students of this period.[1] Historians have tended to project the changed character of the Left after 1919 into the pre-war period, and to consider the influence of the Socialists during the war to have been negligible.[2] This is probably a result, in part, of the hostile and disparaging attitude of the wartime press and politicians. Opponents, and particularly radical opponents, of the war became such constant targets of both verbal and physical abuse that they are more remembered for the violence directed against them than for their activity in behalf of peace. Yet, throughout 1917 and 1918, Socialists campaigned vigorously for an immediate conference to end the war on what came to be accepted as democratic peace terms. In a series of local elections in these years the party made unprecedented gains on the basis of its opposition to the continuation of the war.

The Socialist party was, of course, unable to mobilize all opponents of the war. The party's potential as a center of opposition was limited by its radical nature, as well as by a deficiency of press and organization. Much anti-war sentiment was left to find expression through spontaneous local organization, or through individual actions. This

1. H. C. Peterson and Gilbert C. Fite, in *Opponents of War* (Madison, 1957), deal with the Socialists during the war, but from the point of view of the attacks on their civil liberties.

2. See David H. Shannon, "The Socialist Party Before the First World War," *Mississippi Valley Historical Review,* September 1951, p. 279. Even Shannon, in writing of the difference between pre-war and post-war Socialists, omits the war years. He writes of the influence of the party before 1917, and its decline after 1919.

was true also with regard to conscription, which was widely opposed by those who considered it undemocratic and by many who simply did not wish to serve, as well as by those who were opposed to war.

If the motives for opposing the draft varied, so did the forms of opposition. They ranged from widespread attempts at evasion to armed rebellion. The initial form of opposition to the draft was simple failure to register, of which there were occasional reports in the press.[3] Then, with the beginning of the induction process, large numbers of registrants failed to appear for their physical examinations. In Donora, Pennsylvania, 40 per cent of the men who registered gave fictitious addresses, such as vacant lots. In Erie, where one in six was a "slacker," the *Dispatch* proudly reported that Erie men were "showing a greater willingness to serve than in most Pennsylvania cities." One district in Chicago reported that of 345 men called 139 did not appear.[4] In the month of August alone 2,500 slackers were reported in Cleveland. In October 4,000 were reported in Akron.[5] In a two-week period, in Minneapolis, thirty delinquents were picked up and inducted and sixteen deserters found as late as June 1918.[6] Even among those who did appear when called for their physical examinations large numbers were reluctant to serve. Seventy per cent of those appearing in New York City, a center of interventionist sentiment, filed exemption claims. In Philadelphia several draft boards exhausted ten times the number of exemption blanks originally provided; the government was unable to keep up with the demand for these forms.[7]

More direct evidence of anti-war sentiment than efforts to avoid

3. The Reading (Pennsylvania) *News-Times* reported, August 2, 1917, that the Department of Justice was receiving from one hundred to two hundred letters a day giving substantially accurate information of men who had not registered. The New Castle (Pennsylvania) *Herald,* September 18, 1917, reported the arrest of three unregistered men. The Youngstown (Ohio) *Vindicator,* October 22, 1917, reported that many men registering to vote were found to be "shy of serial numbers."

4. Allentown *Democrat,* August 8, 1917; Erie *Dispatch,* August 26, 1917. On November 1, 1917, the *Dispatch* reported: "Slackers Multiply. No Men To Go Friday." Minneapolis *Journal,* August 8, 1917.

5. Dayton *News,* August 20, 1917; Akron *Beacon-Journal,* October 3, 1917.

6. Minneapolis *Journal,* June 15, 1918.

7. *New York Times,* August 8, 1917; Philadelphia *Public Ledger,* August 15, 1917.

personal military service was the generalized attacks on the draft and the Administration's war policies. In some cities draft lists were stolen to delay the induction process. The night before the first scheduled draft in Indianapolis the lists for the entire county were stolen.[8] A few days later a similar incident occurred in New York City.[9] On August 7, the Minneapolis *Journal* reported that antidraft sentiment had "infected large areas of Minnesota," and was "fast spreading." Protest meetings were reported in many places. Merchants and bankers who supported the war were boycotted in Hutchinson, Glencoe and New Ulm.[10] Similarly, in Georgia, as Senator Hardwick later told his colleagues, "there was undoubtedly general and widespread opposition [to] . . . the draft law. Numerous and largely attended mass meetings held in every part of the state protested against it."[11] The outstanding leader of this opposition was Tom Watson, whose energetic activity brought him renewed prominence in Georgia politics. In his newspaper, *The Jeffersonian,* Watson attacked the "dictatorial powers demanded by the President." Nor did he hesitate to attack the Administration's motives in leading America to war. Watson twitted "our sweetly sincere President" for saying "The world must be made safe for democracy." "What he meant," Watson explained, was "that the huge investment, which our blood gorged capitalists had made in French, Italian, Russian, and English *paper* must be made safe.

"Where Morgan's money went, your boys' blood must go, ELSE MORGAN WILL LOSE HIS MONEY."[12]

In June, July and August, Watson appealed for funds to challenge the constitutionality of the Conscription Act. Checks in small amounts, totaling about $100,000, poured in from Atlanta, Chattanooga, Danville, Virginia, and numerous towns throughout the South. Every week Watson published a list of contributors several columns long—until, in mid-August, *The Jeffersonian* was banned from the mails.[13]

There were those, too, whose hostility to the war led them to more forceful resistance. In Dallas, Texas, fifty-three members of the Farmers and Laborers Protective Association were indicted for armed resis-

8. Reading *News-Times,* August 3, 1917.

9. *New York Times,* August 6, 1917.

10. Minneapolis *Journal,* August 6, 7, 22, 1917.

11. *Congressional Record,* 65th Cong., 2nd Session, May 2, 1918, p. 5941.

12. C. Vann Woodward, *Tom Watson* (New York, 1938), pp. 453–55.

13. *Ibid.* and Philadelphia *Public Ledger,* August 5, 1917.

tance to the draft. In Tyler, Texas, six men were arrested with arms in their possession.[14] In North Carolina an armed revolt against the draft was reported among the farmers of Chatham County.[15] Outside of Toledo, Ohio, a troop train was fired upon; three soldiers were wounded. In California, a band of twenty-five men, alleged IWWs, cut off the last two cars of a troop train and fought the soldiers.[16]

The most dramatic, and certainly the most pathetic, anti-war action occurred in eastern Oklahoma, where an armed uprising, known as the Green Corn Rebellion, took place early in August. The rebels were some 800 to 1,000 poor tenant farmers, the vast majority of whom were of old American stock. Peace sentiment among them was particularly strong, as was resentment against President Wilson, to whom they referred as "Big Slick."[17] The Rebellion was organized by the Working Class Union, a syndicalist organization which had its greatest strength among the Socialist farmers of eastern Oklahoma. The farmers, believing that there were groups of men under arms in many states, planned to march on Washington, seize the government and end the "Rich Man's War."[18]

In only six counties of eastern Oklahoma did groups of men actually assemble. A few of these set about cutting telegraph wires and attempting to burn railroad bridges, while the encamped "army" waited with growing restlessness for its four million promised allies to materialize. After two days of waiting, and eating barbecued beef and green corn, realization came: they were alone. Demoralized and without leadership the "army" scattered at the approach of a local posse. By August 16 the last of the known conspirators had been rounded up, and some 450 frightened men rested in Oklahoma jails. The "revolution" was stillborn.[19]

14. *New York Times,* August 4, 1917.

15. *Ibid.,* August 4, 5, 1917.

16. Toledo *News-Bee,* September 16, November 4, 1917.

17. Charles C. Bush, "The Green Corn Rebellion" (unpublished Master's Thesis, University of Oklahoma, 1932), pp. 1, 11, 26.

18. *Ibid.,* pp. 6, 9, 17. The Socialist party received a third of the vote in this part of Oklahoma.

19. Bush, *op. cit.,* p. 50. Oscar Ameringer, in *If You Don't Weaken* (New York, 1940), p. 351, writes that although the rebellion was limited to the eastern counties, opposition to the war "was just as strong in the western half of the state. And there the bitterest opponents were . . . the Democrats who had cast their ballots for the man who 'kept us out of war' . . . only being better situated and educated, they saw the futility of opposing the war by force."

At its Emergency Convention in St. Louis, April 7–9, 1917, the Socialist party branded the declaration of war "a crime against the people of the United States," and pledged "continuous, active opposition to the war" and to conscription.[20] In the months that followed, Socialists tried vigorously to rally the varied anti-war elements under their banner. In many states the party's rôle was extremely limited because of a lack of organization; and in Oklahoma, the state in which the Socialists were strongest, the party dissolved after the Green Corn Rebellion.[21] But in other states Socialists were "in evidence almost everywhere,"[22] speaking against continuation of the war and against conscription. The speakers attracted large crowds, and, along with them, sharp attacks on their right to speak. On July 1, 8,000 Socialists and trade unionists paraded in Boston. They carried banners demanding peace with "No Forcible Annexations" and "No Punitive Indemnities." As they marched, organized groups of soldiers and sailors attacked them. Hundreds of fights broke out, and the Socialist headquarters was ransacked. Ten of the paraders were arrested.[23] A more peaceful gathering was held in Chicago, where 3,000 pacifists were addressed by Congressman William E. Mason and six Socialist speakers. The program adopted by this meeting called for an immediate peace conference based on the Socialist slogan of "No Annexations, No Indemnities."[24] In Evansville, Indiana, Frank Lamonte, Socialist candidate for mayor, had a "thrilling escape" from a group of vigilantes after "flaying" the draft before a large crowd.[25] On New York City street corners countless radicals spoke against the war. So many were jailed on Blackwell's Island that the New York *Call* facetiously suggested that the prisoners might request a local charter.[26]

In Minnesota, Socialists were especially active. They spoke at mass meetings throughout the state, and brought upon themselves the wrath of state officials. On July 25, 5,000 to 10,000 farmers gathered at New Ulm for a meeting presided over by the mayor of the town and the local college president. Conscription was denounced by

20. From the St. Louis Manifesto, *International Socialist Review,* May 1917, pp. 670 *et seq.*
21. Ameringer, *op. cit.*, p. 351.
22. Dayton *News,* August 18, 1917.
23. Peterson and Fite, *op. cit.*, pp. 45–46. *New York Times,* July 2, 1917.
24. *New York Times,* July 9, 1917.
25. Dayton *Journal,* August 7, 1917.
26. September 6, 1917.

Thomas Van Lear, Socialist mayor of Minneapolis.[27] Two weeks later he addressed a meeting in Glencoe, "where 6,000 persons gathered for a protest against sending American troops to France." Petitions against sending conscripts overseas were circulated and 4,500 people were reported to have signed. Van Lear "hinted" that the nations fighting Germany were doing so for private gain. He demanded a statement of war aims, declaring that the people had a right to know for what they were fighting. Another speaker declared his opposition to the Kaiser, but added that the war was being fought "for Wall Street interests . . . not for democracy."[28]

The success of these meetings led to the arrest of many Socialist leaders, and inspired "loyalty" meetings throughout Minnesota. Among those arrested was J. O. Bentall, former Socialist candidate for governor. In a letter from jail he described some of the meetings:

> At Hutchinson at least 10,000 came—some 20 or 30 miles—full of enthusiasm and eagerness. I never saw anything like it. In the middle of my speech the postmaster rushed up on the platform and struck me in the face. He was promptly reduced to quiet by some big farmers, and I talked another hour and a half. People are falling over each other to hear about Socialism these days. They are no longer afraid of it, and the farmers are most radical and fearless. . . . Eight thousand attended a meeting at Dale, including two sheriffs, three judges, and several U.S. deputy marshals and a number of plain clothesmen. . . . I never talk against the war, all I do is talk peace.[29]

At the first big "loyalty" meeting in Minneapolis, Governor Burnquist gave his answer to the critics of the war. He warned:

> If anti-American meetings cannot be stopped by local officials, every resource at our command will be used to punish the offenders and prevent such meetings from being held. If, by means of this action on our part, bloodshed and loss of life will result, the responsibility therefor will rest on those who are back of and support, by their presence, these un-American demonstrations.[30]

27. Peterson and Fite, *op. cit.,* p. 37. Minneapolis *Journal,* August 6, 22, 1917.
28. Minneapolis *Journal,* August 8, 1917.
29. *International Socialist Review,* September 1917, p. 188.
30. Minneapolis *Journal,* August 7, 1917.

The Governor's warning did not stop the peace meetings, and so, in early September, he placed a blanket ban on Socialist meetings in most counties of Minnesota.[31]

Governor Burnquist's attitude toward expressions of anti-war sentiment, although extreme, was by no means unique. Most active interventionists, typified by Theodore Roosevelt, saw in every opponent of the war "the Hun within our gates."[32] The press usually took this attitude toward Socialists, as did several of the Socialist leaders who had resigned from the party to support the war effort.[33] But, although pro-German sentiment was not unknown within the party, the great majority of Socialists opposed the war because they viewed it primarily as a struggle among capitalists for control of world markets. Most Socialists were neutral, as their program, adopted in 1915, indicates. Similar in principle to Wilson's Fourteen Points of early 1918, the program called for an immediate conference to end the war on the following terms:

No indemnities.

No transfer of territories except upon the consent and by the vote of their people.

All countries under foreign rule to be given political independence if demanded by their inhabitants.

International commission to consider and settle international disputes without resort to arms—in place of present secret diplomacy.

Political and industrial democracy. Universal suffrage, including woman suffrage.[34]

Whether the party was neutral or pro-German made little difference in the wartime atmosphere; the relevant fact was that the party opposed the war. The more active the party became in opposition, the more intense were the various attacks on its representatives and its organs. Increasingly, Socialist meetings were banned or broken up, speakers arrested and put on trains leaving town, or kidnapped

31. *International Socialist Review*, October 1917, p. 209; New York *Call*, September 14, 1917.

32. Peterson and Fite, *op. cit.*, p. 81.

33. See "Divergent Effects of the War on the Socialist Movement," *Current Opinion*, August 1917, pp. 73–75; "The Socialist as Patriot," *Literary Digest*, June 16, 1917, pp. 1836–37.

34. Adapted from *American Labor Yearbook: 1916* (New York, 1917), p. 126.

and threatened.[35] Of the many blows suffered by the party during this period, perhaps the most serious from a long-range point of view were those struck by the federal government. Almost immediately after the Espionage Act became law in June 1917, Postmaster-General Burleson proceeded to withhold Socialist periodicals from the mails. In June and July he withheld a dozen or more leading Socialist publications with a total circulation of over a million copies.[36] This harassment helped alter the character of the movement during the war. As Eugene Debs wrote, the press was "the very life-breath of [the] party,"[37] especially in the rural states where its strength had always been relatively greatest. Even in the cities, however, many Socialist papers were forced to suspend publication, once denied second-class privileges.[38]

I

In the face of this mounting tempo of attack on their right to speak, the Socialists saw their best opportunity for further discussion of peace in the relative freedom of the coming municipal election campaigns. This was decided, despite the fact that 1917 was an off year, in the hope that the party could gain sufficient votes in these elections to win a more respectful hearing for its program. The Reverend Herbert S. Bigelow, recent convert to socialism, expressed this hope when he asserted that the government would "have to heed the Socialist votes," adding confidently that "if there are as many as we expect, the war will end."[39] In the hope of securing this goal, Socialists conducted active campaigns in Chicago, and in the cities of Indiana, Ohio, Pennsylvania, New Jersey, New York, Connecticut and Maryland.

35. New York *Call*, September 5, 6, 14, 1917; *New York Times*, July 5, August 16, 1917; Youngstown *Vindicator*, August 22, 1917. Peterson and Fite, *op. cit.*, chapter v.

36. See "Divergent Effects of the War on the Socialist Movement," *loc. cit.*, *International Socialist Review*, August 1917, p. 125; *American Labor Yearbook: 1919–20*, p. 401.

37. *Social Revolution*, October 1917, p. 3.

38. For example, *Current Opinion*, November 1917, reported the Hungarian Socialist paper, *E'lore*, and the Russian, *Novy Mir*, both published in New York City, had been "wiped out of existence speedily by federal authorities" (p. 293).

39. Akron *Beacon-Journal*, October 4, 1917. Bigelow had been chairman of the Ohio State Constitutional Convention in 1912.

Ohio was the scene of greatest Socialist activity in the 1917 elections, and it was in the primary election in Dayton that the first victory was won. Dayton, Democratic in state and national elections, was the home of Ohio's Governor, James Cox. The city's commission government was controlled by the Citizens' Committee, a "nonpartisan" reform group, which, on local issues, differed little from the Socialists, normally a minor force in Dayton's politics.[40] During the primary campaign the Socialists were virtually ignored by the press, which was involved in a battle between the Democrats and the Citizens' Committee; but Socialists from many parts of Ohio campaigned actively in Dayton. They presented the party's demand for a statement of war terms and repeal of the draft at street meetings, and in the pages of the one small Socialist weekly.[41] On primary day, August 14, the Socialists amazed everyone by sweeping nine of Dayton's twelve wards. The Citizens' Committee carried the remaining three, while the Democrats, supported by Governor Cox's *News,* carried none. The Socialists received 11,017 votes, the largest primary total any party had received in Dayton's history. They won an absolute majority and defeated the Citizens' Committee by a record plurality. In doing this the Socialists spent only $395, compared to the $28,058 spent by the other parties.[42]

Overjoyed, Joseph Sharts, local Socialist leader, declared:

> The great victory of the Socialists in Dayton, Ohio, at the primary election in August was won squarely on the anti-war issue, and any attempt to minimize the significance of the victory is an effort to hoodwink the rest of the country. . . . The workers registered their protest against the war and voted for peace.[43]

Governor Cox's paper admitted that the vote was due to the disaffection of Democrats, many of whom were "inimical to the war." The *News* further commented that "a combined fight should be made against the Socialists" in the November election in order to defeat the "cowardly" opponents of the war who, although "afraid to pro-

---

40. See Raymond Moley, "Representation in Dayton and Ashtabula," *National Municipal Review,* January 1918, pp. 28–29.

41. New York *Call,* September 2, 1917; *Chicago Tribune,* August 18, 1917.

42. Dayton *News,* August 15, 25, 1917; *Call,* September 2, 1917.

43. *Call,* September 2, 1917.

claim their convictions to their fellows," were still capable of enjoying the "sensation of the silent stab of the ballot."[44]

As Joseph Sharts hoped, the Dayton primary was "an inspiration to the Socialists the country over."[45] With growing enthusiasm they campaigned in a number of nominally nonpartisan primaries. In September, Pennsylvania Socialists nominated four of eight council candidates elected in Reading; the lone Socialist candidates ran first of eight nominees in Allentown, and second in New Castle; and in Erie the Socialists unexpectedly nominated one of their candidates for council.[46] The same month, the Socialist candidate was among three nominees elected to run for mayor of Toledo.[47] In October, Buffalo Socialists increased their vote over the previous election from 13 per cent to 32 per cent, losing second place to the Republicans by 14,341 to 14,695.[48]

After the news of the large primary vote in Buffalo, the New York *Call* could hardly contain itself. "The world is sick of war; it is sick of bloodshed and destruction," the *Call* wrote. "THE WORLD WANTS PEACE! THE WORLD WANTS SOCIALISM." In a burst of premature enthusiasm, it added: "The great victories that we are winning and that we are going to win are the most significant political events of the century . . . it is not a political revolution. It is *the* political revolution."[49]

Support for the Socialists appeared to be developing so rapidly at the time that this seemingly incredible view is not entirely inexplicable. Even conservatives believed that the Socialists might sweep the country in future elections. The strongest statement of this view was made by C. L. Knight's Akron *Beacon-Journal*. On September 7, the *Beacon* wrote:

> There is scarcely a political observer whose opinion is worth much but what will admit that were an election to come now

44. Dayton *News*, August 15, 1917.
45. *Call*, September 2, 1917.
46. Reading *News-Times*, Allentown *Democrat*, New Castle *Herald*, Erie *Dispatch*—all September 20, 1917.
47. Toledo *News-Bee*, September 12, 1917. The Socialist ran a poor third.
48. *Call*, October 18, 1917. Also Paul H. Douglas, "The Socialist Vote in the 1917 Municipal Elections," *National Municipal Review*, March 1918, p. 135.
49. *Call*, October 19, 1917.

a mighty tide of Socialism would inundate the Middle West and perhaps other—maybe all other sections of the country. . . . The United States has never embarked upon a more unpopular war. However wrong it may be the vast majority of the people have never been convinced that war was necessary either to sustain our honor or to protect our interests and being unconvinced . . . they vote the Socialist ticket as a means of protest.

This estimate of Socialist strength was, of course, far from universal. But it was common enough to cause Democrats and Republicans to unite in an effort to prevent Socialist victories in Chicago, in Dayton, Hamilton and Toledo, Ohio, and in Blairsville, New Castle and Reading, Pennsylvania.

By the end of September the election campaigns were in full swing in most cities. Of these campaigns, the one in New York City ranked first, both in national significance and in drama. There a four-cornered race developed, with the incumbent, John Purroy Mitchel, a highly irregular Democrat, running as a Fusion candidate. Mitchel was an outstanding reform mayor, with a national reputation as an energetic, honest man, equally concerned with municipal efficiency and the welfare of his constituents.[50] Against him Tammany, under heavy pressure from William Randolph Hearst, had nominated John F. Hylan, a singularly undistinguished and obscure judge from Brooklyn. The Republican candidate was William M. Bennett. The Socialists nominated Morris Hillquit.

The initiative in the campaign was seized by Mitchel. Disregarding his excellent record on municipal matters, he chose to center his campaign on all-out support of the war, the issue the Socialists most wanted to test, and one which Tammany turned to its advantage by adopting a policy of silence. Nevertheless, "Americanism" *versus* "Kaiserism" was the challenge Mitchel flung at his opponents.

In the early weeks of the campaign Judge Hylan was the main

---

50. See Burton J. Hendrick, "The Mayor of New York," *The World's Work,* September 1916, pp. 513–21; *World's Work,* February 1917, p. 355; "A Mayor and His Constituents," *Outlook,* April 21, 1915, p. 900, and May 10, 1916, p. 52; "Mayor Mitchel's Administration of New York City," *American Review of Reviews,* April 1916, p. 495; William Hard, "John Mitchel," *Everybody's,* October 1917, pp. 465–78; and *Survey,* November 10, 1917, p. 144.

target of Mitchel's attack. Since Hylan was Hearst's candidate, and since Hearst was a well-known Anglophobe who had expressed pro-German sentiments, Hylan became the "Kaiser's candidate." "Hearst, Hylan, and Hohenzollern" was Mitchel's war cry,[51] while campaign posters depicted Mitchel in a doughboy's uniform, rifle in hand, bayoneting the Tammany Tiger. In this posture Mitchel received the support of powerful politicians, of whom Theodore Roosevelt was the loudest and most prominent.[52] There were a few attempts to focus the campaign on local issues, but they were unsuccessful.[53] As the *Nation* observed, Mitchel "not only wrapped himself in the American flag, but declared that a vote for Hylan was a vote for the Kaiser and every vote for Hillquit a vote for treason."[54]

Although press support for Mitchel was almost unanimous, and interest in his campaign nation-wide,[55] it was Hillquit, rather than Mitchel, for whom there were amazing manifestations of popular support. This was much more than "the usual propaganda campaign" which Hillquit had expected.[56] Indeed, the Socialist campaign rapidly assumed the character of a religious revival. For the first major meeting 20,000 people jammed in and around the old Madison Square Garden. At the "magic" words, "We want peace," the crowd rose in their places and "for five minutes the shouting, whistling and stamping of feet beat in waves upon the scarlet-decked platform from which the demand had come."[57]

Morris Hillquit set the tone of the Socialist campaign as he declared:

> We are for peace. We are unalterably opposed to the killing of our manhood and the draining of our resources in a bewildering pursuit of an incomprehensible "democracy" . . . a pursuit which begins by suppressing the freedom of speech and press

51. New York *World*, October 2, 1917, *passim*, September, October and November 1917.

52. Charles E. Hughes, Alton Parker, Henry Morgenthau and Oscar Straus supported Mitchel actively.

53. See *World*, October 15, 1917. Governor Whitman, in announcing his support for Mitchel, tried to make Tammany the main issue.

54. November 8, 1917, p. 500.

55. See "National Aspects of the Mayoralty Contest in New York City," *Current Opinion*, November 1917, pp. 293 *et seq.*

56. Morris Hillquit, *Loose Leaves from a Busy Life* (New York, 1934) p. 182.

57. *Call*, September 24, 1917.

and public assemblage, and by stifling legitimate political criticism.[58]

Hillquit campaigned not for a separate peace, but for the immediate calling of an international conference to end the war on the principle of no annexations, no indemnities. But the Socialists refused to support the continuation of the war until such a conference be called. In keeping with the St. Louis Manifesto, which had declared that in support of the war Socialists would "not give a single dollar," Hillquit announced that he would not buy Liberty Bonds. This caused a storm of indignation. Mayor Mitchel declared that "Any man who will not buy a liberty bond when he can afford them is not fit to be a citizen of the United States."[59] Theodore Roosevelt and Charles E. Hughes also attacked Hillquit on this issue; but Hillquit stood his ground, asserting that he would gladly contribute to a fund to end the war: that was the way to aid the soldiers.[60]

In Washington, President Wilson considered an indictment of Hillquit for his "outrageous utterances about the Liberty Loan," but decided that the government would "only be assisting Mr. Hillquit by apparently making him a martyr if . . . [it] should pay any attention to his remarks."[61]

Despite Hillquit's refusal to buy bonds, enthusiasm for him continued to mount. In October, Socialist meetings on the East Side drew great throngs. One night 15,000 admirers "surged through the streets," following Hillquit from hall to hall in spontaneous demonstrations. Hillquit asked the crowd: "War or peace? How will you decide?"[62] In the *Herald's* straw poll "Scores of ballots were returned with the crossmark before Morris Hillquit's name, and the words written, 'They are all crooks but Hillquit.'" A meeting at which Hillquit had been "followed by thousands who cheered until they were hoarse" was a "typical Socialist reception."[63]

The greatest manifestations of support for the Socialists occurred after Postmaster-General Burleson initiated proceedings to revoke the

58. *Ibid.*

59. *World,* October 26, 1917.

60. Robert W. Iversen, "Morris Hillquit, American Social Democrat" (unpublished Ph.D. Dissertation, University of Iowa, 1951), p. 204.

61. Woodrow Wilson, *Life and Letters,* ed. R. S. Baker, VII (New York, 1939), 333.

62. *New York Times,* October 19, 1917; *World,* October 19, 1917.

63. *Herald,* November 1, 1917.

second-class mailing privilege of the *Call.* Burleson's tactics, which in the long run greatly weakened the party, had the immediate effect of rallying non-Socialist support to Hillquit. Several pro-war liberal leaders supported Hillquit as a protest against "Burlesonism," although most of them also endorsed the Socialist demand for a statement of war terms including no indemnities, no annexations. Among the liberals who supported Hillquit were Amos Pinchot, Dudley Field Malone, J. A. H. Hopkins and Harry Hopkins.[64]

Despite the intense barrage from Mayor Mitchel and the press, Judge Hylan maintained a prudent silence on the war. Tammany saw Mitchel's arrogant superpatriotism alienating him from the voters, and came to view the growing strength of Hillquit as its main concern. The *World* reported, on October 21, that Hillquit had "gained strength at an almost alarming rate," and that Tammany,

> trying to cut the ground from under the Socialistic program [was] giving paramount importance to the municipal ownership pledge and the other vagrant features of the Socialistic doctrine.
>
> Instructions to the leaders [were] . . . to star municipal ownership and the high cost of living and to *evade any agitation of patriotism or other issues resulting from war conditions.* [Italics added]

The commercial press, with the exception of the Hearst papers, followed Mitchel in attacking nonsupport of the war as alien and non-American. The *Tribune,* for example, on October 28, had "Morris Hillquit of Riga" as its subject in the current number of a series on "Who's Who Against America." Hillquit was described as "a Jew, born at Riga, the Milwaukee of Russia, 48 years ago. Now he is rich and lives on Riverside Drive." The *Herald,* on November 2, ran a cartoon on page 1 showing a hook-nosed man named "Hillkowitz or Hillquitter" waving a flag which said "Peace at any price" at a smiling "Kaiser."[65]

64. *New York Times,* October 15, 27, 29, 1917; New York *American,* November 5, 1917, advertisement. On Harry Hopkins see Robert E. Sherwood, *Roosevelt and Hopkins* (New York, 1948), p. 25.

65. This anti-Semitism appeared to confirm fears previously expressed by conservative Jewish leaders. The pro-Mitchel *American Hebrew* protested: "It is regrettable that the shortsighted policy of making the Jew the scapegoat for all radical movements, having been abandoned by the reactionary Russian press since the outbreak of the Revolution, has been adopted now by some of our New York dailies." Quoted in *World,* November 5, 1917.

Colonel Roosevelt's attitude toward dissenters was similar. In a speech in support of Mitchel, Roosevelt bellowed: "I don't like the Hun outside our gates, but I tell you, I like the Hun inside them still less. (Applause) And even worse than the Hun is the man who cringes before them! Traitors! (Applause)"[66]

Even the liberal *World* was carried away. It editorialized on Hillquit, Hylan and Mitchel: "Today's election will determine whether New York is a traitor town, or a quasi-Copperhead town or an American town devoted to American ideals and pledged without reservation to the war policies of the United States government."[67]

On election day, Mayor Mitchel's militantly pro-war campaign ended in disaster. Hylan swept in, receiving the greatest plurality in the history of the city, while Mitchel finished just barely ahead of Hillquit. The vote was 313,956 for Hylan, 155,497 for Mitchel, 145,332 for Hillquit, and 55,438 for Bennett. Two thirds of the vote had gone either to the candidate widely accused of disloyalty, or to the one openly opposed to the war. Hillquit's 21.7 per cent represented nearly a fivefold increase over the normal Socialist vote. For the first time the party put candidates on the Board of Aldermen, electing seven. They also elected a municipal court justice and ten assemblymen, an increase of eight.[68]

Hillquit hailed the result as a repudiation of Administration policies.[69] Hylan, however, "proclaimed his loyalty"[70] the day after the election, and newspapers the country over, which during the campaign had attacked Hylan as the Kaiser's candidate, took this belated declaration as proof that Hylan's victory was no reflection of peace sentiment. "New York is not against the war," the *Tribune* wrote. "It is not ready to accept the programme of surrender which Mr. Hillquit so boldly preached."[71] The Des Moines *Register* echoed: "Whatever satisfaction the Kaiser got out of the New York election will be due to the large minority vote cast for the Socialist candidate."[72] It was

66. *Herald,* November 1, 1917.
67. *World,* November 6, 1917.
68. *Call,* November 7, 8, 1917; *Annual Report of the Board of Elections in the City of New York: 1917.* One other Socialist assembly candidate was tied until the soldier vote was counted; an aldermanic candidate lost by 11 votes.
69. *Literary Digest,* November 17, 1917, p. 12.
70. *Herald,* November 8, 1917.
71. November 7, 1917.
72. Quoted in *Literary Digest,* November 17, 1917, p. 12.

left to the *Survey* to state the obvious: that although "Hillquit polled much of the anti-war vote . . . some non-Socialist pacifists voted for Hylan as more practical."[73]

As in New York, so in most other cities, the war was the main issue projected by the Socialists; and where they failed to stress the issue it was raised against them with vigor.[74] In Reading, Pennsylvania, James Maurer, Socialist President of the Pennsylvania Federation of Labor, told the voters: "On election day you have on one side a party which has plunged you into war . . . on the other hand you have the Socialist party which is opposed to the war and demands an immediate peace. Which are you going to choose?"[75]

In Cleveland, the Socialist candidate for mayor was C. E. Ruthenberg, co-author of the St. Louis Manifesto, who was under indictment for inciting resistance to conscription. Some Socialists believed that "if all the anti-war sentiment in Cleveland were put behind Ruthenberg, he would be the next mayor." But, they conceded, "Unfortunately many . . . will stick by their [traditional] political organizations."[76] Calling Ruthenberg "the Hillquit of Cleveland," the *Plain Dealer* wrote that Cleveland—"200 percent city in patriotism"—would be "shamed before the world," should this "candidate of Prussianism" be given a respectable showing.[77]

In Toledo, where a two-way race developed,[78] Senator LaFollette attacked war profiteers in a speech in support of Haworth, the Socialist candidate for mayor.[79] In turn he was attacked by Charles Edward Russell, one of the pro-war Socialist leaders. Russell called the Senator "a perjurer and a traitor," and, accusing him of sympathizing with

73. November 10, 1917, p. 144.

74. Blairsville, Pennsylvania, was an exception. There the main issue seemed to be that Reuben Einstein, the Socialist candidate, was the richest man in town. He was accused of being a parasite, and was chided for his Socialist ideals. Einstein conceded being a parasite, but explained that "The actual difference between me and the other parasites is this: They want to stay on your backs and continue to live off you, while . . . I am willing to get entirely off your backs just as soon as you have enough sense to keep others off. . . . [Until then] I refuse to join your ranks and starve. . . ." Blairsville *Courier,* October 25, 1917, advertisement.

75. Reading *News-Times,* November 5, 1917.

76. Letter to New York *Call,* September 8, 1917.

77. November 3, 1917.

78. The third nominee died several weeks before the election.

79. Toledo *News-Bee,* September 24, 1917; New York *Tribune,* November 7, 1917.

Germany, urged him to "Go live there."[80] The Toledo *News-Bee,* concerned over the possibility of, Haworth's election, warned "that to elect a Socialist mayor at this time would be to encourage sedition and treason, to stimulate German intrigue, to aid in dividing our own people when we should stand together as one man."[81]

In Dayton the Citizens' Committee campaign had active support from the Democratic governor. In attacking the Socialists, Governor Cox argued that

> In their declaration against this war they insolently assume that our people are not opposed to war in the abstract, while everybody knows that the war is being fought to prevent wars in the future; that when the Kaiser is destroyed the great menace to peace shall have been destroyed.[82]

The Dayton *Journal,* organ of the Citizens' Committee, was also deeply concerned at the prospect of Socialist victory. It quoted New York Socialists as declaring that a Socialist victory "WILL BE A CLEAR MANDATE TO THE GOVERNMENT OF THE UNITED STATES TO OPEN NEGOTIATIONS FOR AN IMMEDIATE PEACE." This prospect was more than the *Journal* could bear. "When the votes are counted," it declared, "we are going to know, for a truth, whether we really have a nation, or as Colonel Roosevelt expresses it, 'only a polyglot boarding house.' "[83]

In Hamilton, Ohio, too, where the Socialist candidate for mayor faced a single opponent, the *Evening Journal* noted that many intended to vote Socialist "as a means of saying they want the war to stop." But, the *Journal* argued: "Such a vote cannot stop the war. If every man in Hamilton voted the Socialist ticket it would and could have no effect on our nation at war. . . . The only thing a vote for the Socialist ticket can do is say you . . . are in sympathy with the Kaiser."[84]

On election day Socialist mayors were elected in only five municipalities: two in Indiana, two in Ohio, and one in Pennsylvania. Yet the party recorded sweeping gains in almost every city in which it

80. *News-Bee,* November 6, 1917.
81. November 3, 1917.
82. Cleveland *Plain Dealer,* November 4, 1917. The Governor also challenged the Socialists to "produce one Socialist leader that had bought a war bond."
83. November 1, 1917.
84. November, 5, 1917.

TABLE 1

THE SOCIALIST VOTE IN 1916 AND 1917 AND PERCENTAGES
OF FOREIGN BORN IN 1920[a]

	1917 Per Cent[b]	1916 Per Cent	Elected Socialist Officials, 1917	Per Cent Foreign Born
Ohio[c]				
Byesville	...	...	Mayor and others	7.0
Hamilton	44.1	15.5	1 Councilman	6.7
Dayton	44.0	6.5	None	8.6
Toledo	34.8	5.9	3 Councilmen	15.7
Piqua	33.0	8.1	Mayor, 2 Councilmen	3.9
Sandusky	48.9	4.7	1 City Commissioner	11.7
Massillon	29.6	10.2	1 Councilman	12.5
Springfield	30.0	3.6	?	4.5
Canton	21.0	3.8	?	16.9
Cleveland	22.4	4.5	2 Councilmen, 1 Member School Board	30.1
Lima	19.9	3.7	None	4.6
Akron	16.3	3.8	8 Assessors, 1 Constable	18.2
Cincinnati	11.9	2.9	None	10.7
Pennsylvania[d]				
Garrett	...	33.0	Burgess (Mayor)	?
McKeesport	55.0	7.0	Controller	25.4
Allentown	4151[b]	4.7 (513)	1 Councilman (of 4)	11.7
Slatington	42.3	5.0	?	8.2
Blairsville	45.0	11.3	None	7.3
Reading	32.6	14.3	None	8.9
Erie	3403[b]	6.4 (702)	None	22.5
New Castle	1488[b]	6.0 (307)	None	19.3
Maryland[e]				
Hagerstown	15.0	1.6	None	1.5
New York[f]				
Buffalo	30.2 (Primary)	2.6	None	
Schenectady	23.7	8.0	None	
New York	21.7	4.5	10 Assemblymen, 7 Aldermen, 1 Municipal Court Justice	
Rochester	19.5	3.4	3 Constables, 2 Aldermen, 2 Supervisors	
Gloversville	18.7	?	None	
Syracuse	11.9	3.0	None	
Olean	597[b]	4.1 (138)	?	
Albany	4.0	.8	None	
New Jersey[g]				
Passaic County	14.0	7.5	None	
Hudson County	13.2	3.7	None	
Camden County	8.3	4.8	None	
Newark	12.0	...	None	

TABLE 1—*Cont.*

	1917 Per Cent[b]	1916 Per Cent	Elected Socialist Officials, 1917	Per Cent Foreign Born
Illinois[h]				
Chicago	34.7	3.6 (1915)	None	
Connecticut[i]				
Bridgeport	7.0	3.0	None	

[a] Foreign-born percentages compiled from *U.S. Census, 14th Census, 1920*, vol. III.

[b] In some instances, absolute figures are given for 1917, as it is not possible to convert these into percentages, for various reasons.

[c] Figures for 1916 from *Annual Report of the Secretary of State* of Ohio for 1917, pp. 299 *et seq.*, vote for Governor. Figures for 1917 from Paul H. Douglas. "The Socialist Vote in the 1917 Municipal Elections," *National Municipal Review*, March 1918, pp. 136-37; Hamilton *Evening Journal;* Dayton *News;* Toledo *News-Bee;* Piqua *Leader-Dispatch;* Sandusky *Register;* Massillon *Evening Independent;* Cleveland *Plain Dealer;* Lima *News;* Akron *Beacon-Journal*—all November 7 or 8, 1917.

[d] Figures for 1916 from *Smull's Legislative Handbook and Manual for the State of Pennsylvania: 1917*, pp. 667 *et seq.*, vote for President. For 1917 from New York *Call;* Allentown *Democrat;* Blairsville *Courier;* Reading *News-Times;* Erie *Dispatch;* New Castle *Herald*—all November 7 or 8, 1917.

[e] For 1916, *Maryland Manual: 1915-1916*, p. 249, vote for Governor. For 1917, Hagerstown *Globe*, November 7, 1917.

[f] For 1916, *Manual for the Use of the Legislature of the State of New York: 1917*, pp. 898 *et seq.*, vote for Governor. For 1917, Douglas, *loc. cit.*, pp. 133-35; New York *Call*, October 18, November 7, 8, 1917; New York *Tribune;* Albany *Times-Union;* Rochester *Democrat and Chronicle;* Gloversville *Herald;* Syracuse *Herald*—all November 7, 1917.

[g] Douglas, *loc. cit.*, p. 134; *Manual of the Legislature of New Jersey: 1916, 1917*, vote for Assembly.

[h] For 1915 see Douglas, *loc. cit.*, p. 135. For 1917, *Chicago Daily News Almanac and Yearbook*, p. 624.

[i] For 1916, *Connecticut Register and Manual, 1917*, p. 484, vote for President. For 1917, New York *Call*, November 7, 1917.

campaigned. (See Table 1.) The most striking gains were in Ohio, where the Socialists received 30 per cent of the vote, or more, in at least seven cities and one town. All told, they received from 20 to 48 per cent of the vote in at least eleven municipalities in Ohio, eight in Pennsylvania, six in Indiana, four in New York, and they received 34 per cent of the vote in Chicago. A number of Socialists were elected to office in Ohio, Indiana, Pennsylvania and New York. (See Tables 1 and 2.)

The Socialist vote in New York City received nation-wide press

244 CONSEQUENCES

TABLE 2
The Socialist Vote and the Percentage of Foreign Born in Indiana Cities in 1917[a]

City or Town	Percentage of Vote	Percentage of Foreign Born
Gas City	40.4 (elected mayor)	4.9
Elwood	38.9 (elected mayor)	4.2
Marion	30.9	2.2
Anderson	29.1	3.2
Elkhart	22.5 (2 councilmen)	6.3
Fort Wayne	19.6 (1 alderman)	7.7
Kokomo	18.3	3.9
Evansville	17 3	3.7
Columbus	13.6	1.5
Bedford	12.1	3.3
Princeton	11.6	1.2
Alexandria	11.3	5.3
Clinton	11.3	21.3
Goshen	10.9	3.1
Logansport	10.3	4.9
Gary	6.2	29.7
South Bend	5.2	18.9
Mishawaka	5.1	15.2
Indianapolis	4.0	8.5
East Chicago	2.8	40.0

[a] Election figures compiled from *Yearbook of the State of Indiana* for the year 1917. Foreign born compiled from *U.S. Bureau of Census, 14th Census, 1920*, vol. III.

[b] Douglas, *loc. cit.*, p. 138.

comment, but in other cities it was minimized. In reporting the results in Chicago, for example, the *New York Times* stated that the " 'anti-war, anti-Wilson, Anti-American' judicial ticket of the Socialists" had been snowed under "in a blizzard of ballots."[85] But the Socialist defeat was decisive only because the Democrats and Republicans had united in a single opposition slate. Actually, the 34 per cent which the Socialists received represented almost a tenfold increase over their normal vote. Indeed, the vote was sufficient to induce Roger Sullivan, Chicago Democratic leader, to suggest that it might be "time to amalgamate the Republican and Democratic parties in the nation in a new lineup of conservatives and radicals."[86]

85. November 8, 1917.
86. Paul H. Douglas, "The Socialist Vote in the 1917 Municipal Elections," *National Municipal Review*, March 1918, p. 139; *Nation*, November 27, 1917, p. 712; Milwaukee *Leader*, November 8, 1917. Election figures, *Chicago Daily News Almanac and Yearbook: 1918*, p. 624.

In further depreciation, the press widely attributed the Socialist vote in these elections to the foreign born. The Philadelphia *Public Ledger* declared that the Hillquit vote was "almost entirely due to . . . alien discontent, intensified by conditions peculiar to foreign populations of New York in wartime."[87] The *National Municipal Review* saw the "immense foreign influence" as responsible for the large Socialist vote in New York City, Buffalo, Cleveland and Chicago.[88] In many cities Socialists were the political beneficiaries of large concentrations of immigrant populations. This was so in New York City, where Hillquit's strength was concentrated in immigrant Jewish working-class communities.[89] Contrary to popular belief, however, this was not typical. The Socialists also received substantial popular support in many cities where foreign born were few. (Tables 1 and 2.) Indeed, in Indiana cities the results show a negative correlation between the percentage of foreign born and the Socialist vote in 1917. In Ohio there is little or no correlation. For example, Hamilton and Dayton, each of which gave the Socialists 44 per cent of the vote, had foreign-born population of 6.7 per cent and 8.6 per cent. In Reading, Pennsylvania, as the *News-Times* wrote, the "election dispelled another fallacy. It proved that the German-American citizens were absolutely loyal, for they voted almost as a unit against the Socialist candidates."[90] What is true, however, was that in most cities the Socialists received their heaviest vote in the working-class districts. In those cities with large numbers of working-class immigrants, therefore, the Socialist vote came predominantly from the foreign born. This was so in Chicago, Cleveland, Buffalo, New York City, Rochester and several other cities.

II

After the election the New York *Evening Post* commented that "The Socialists have won admission, as it were, to the family of political parties,"[91] a sentiment confidently echoed by Socialist party

87. November 9, 1917.

88. January 1918, p. 44.

89. Harry Best, "The Melting Pot in the United States," *Social Forces,* May 1936, pp. 591 *et seq.* Best uses the heavy Socialist vote among the Jewish immigrants in New York City as proof that these foreigners had not become "Americanized."

90. November 7, 1917.

91. Quoted by Douglas, *loc. cit.*

leaders.[92] But just before the election the Dayton *News* had indicated more accurately what was in store for the party:

> Ever since the outbreak of the war we have heard sedition preached and it has been allowed to pass in the name of free speech. . . . Now we see riot and disorder encouraged in political campaigns by Socialist candidates, who hope thereby to collect under their banner all who have grievances. . . . Action must take the place of forbearance.[93]

In the months that followed, mass sedition indictments were returned against almost every major Socialist leader. These indictments, added to the previous attacks on the civil liberties of the Socialists, further hampered the party's attempts at organization.

While the attacks on the Socialists sharpened, President Wilson enunciated the principles he was soon to embody in his Fourteen Points, thereby enabling many wearying opponents of war to change gracefully to supporters of the Administration. The *Appeal to Reason,* which had been banned from the mails for most of the late summer and fall of 1917, announced on December 15 that "President Wilson Has Heard the 'Voices of Humanity That Are in the Air' and Declares in Favor of Democratic Settlement of War." Commenting on Wilson's address to Congress in early December—in response to the plea made by Pope Benedict XV, in August—the *Appeal* added: "Until your President delivered his address to Congress last week the democratic slogan of 'No annexations; no contributions; no punitive indemnities,' was practically sounded by the Socialists and liberals alone while the reactionary elements condemned this slogan as being tainted with pro-Germanism."[94]

Two weeks later the *Appeal to Reason* was the *New Appeal,* and an ardent supporter of Wilson.

The war, however, continued to be an issue in elections which took place in the spring and fall of 1918. In these elections, under conditions much more difficult than those of the previous year, nonsupporters of the war received unexpectedly high votes. In Wisconsin, in April, a special election for senator was held. The candidates were Joseph E. Davies, Irvine Lenroot and Victor Berger. Davies received

92. See *Literary Digest,* November 17, 1917, p. 12; *Social Revolution,* December 1917, p. 5.
93. November 3, 1917.
94. December 15, 1917.

strong support from President Wilson.[95] Lenroot, although one of Wisconsin's two congressmen who voted for the declaration of war (nine voted against it), was attacked for having a record which did not square with the "interests of the nation," and for accepting support from Senator LaFollette. Berger, indicted for sedition in the middle of the campaign, ran on a platform which stated that America had been plunged into war "by the treachery of the ruling class."[96]

The election was won by Lenroot, who polled 163,980 votes, to 148,713 for Davies, and a surprising 110,487 for Berger.[97] The *Milwaukee Journal* commented that, in electing Lenroot, Wisconsin might have "gone as far as she can go. It may be, in other words, that Wisconsin's Americanism is lukewarm. The large vote polled by the anti-war Socialists, and . . . Mr. Lenroot, with his record, may indicate a mild, negative sort of interest in America's cause."[98]

In the Milwaukee mayoralty election, which also took place in April, the Socialist mayor was reëlected with an increased plurality; while in November, for the first time since 1910, the Socialists elected their entire county ticket. They also increased the number of state senators from two to five, and assemblymen from 11 to 18;[99] Victor Berger was elected to Congress from the Fifth District, and in the Fourth District the Socialist candidate polled 42 per cent of the vote.[100]

In Minnesota, in June 1918, Charles A. Lindbergh, Nonpartisan League candidate, ran against Governor Burnquist in the Republican primary. He campaigned jointly with Thomas Van Lear, Socialist mayor of Minneapolis, who was seeking renomination in a nonpartisan primary. A "Loyalty ticket" was put up against them and the Minneapolis *Journal* urged the people of Minnesota to "Let Lindbergh know that he cannot preach sedition and treason, and yet aspire to the chief magistracy of the state." Van Lear was told that "stirring up of class feeling will not avail to return him to the seat he does not deserve, and that his acceptance of the disloyal St. Louis platform was emphatically 'a local issue.' "[101] Repression in the campaign was

95. *Milwaukee Journal*, April 1, 1918.
96. *Ibid.*
97. *Ibid.*, April 10, 1918. The Socialists had polled 27,846 votes for president in Wisconsin in 1916.
98. April 3, 1918.
99. *Milwaukee Journal*, April 4, 1918; *Milwaukee Leader*, November 6, 1918.
100. *Milwaukee Journal*, November 6, 1918.
101. Minneapolis *Journal*, June 15, 1918.

so intense that Lindbergh was forced to conduct at least one meeting in the state of Iowa.[102] Yet he received 43 per cent of the primary vote, while Van Lear was renominated.[103] In November Van Lear was narrowly defeated, but the number of Socialist aldermen increased from three to seven, while two Socialists were elected to the State Assembly and two to the State Senate.[104]

Finally, in Georgia, Tom Watson began his amazing political comeback by almost defeating Carl Vinson in the primary election in the Tenth Congressional District in 1918. Vinson, a "super patriot," made the war the main issue, charging, among other things, that Watson had never bought a Liberty Bond. Watson admitted the charge. He campaigned for "free speech; re-establishment of the press . . . and . . . stronger individual liberty." The election was so close that Watson contested the result. He lost, but two years later was elected to the Senate by a large plurality.[105]

Although the Socialist party of World War I has been remembered primarily for the persistent attacks upon it, the intensity of these attacks has not been satisfactorily explained. Recently H. C. Peterson and Gilbert C. Fite have implied that it was not the activities of the opponents of war that inspired the assaults upon them. On the contrary, "patriotism," they write, was merely a "cloak" which "served as an ideal camouflage for the conservative economic and political interests which sought to crush the radical labor and farmer movements"[106] during the war. There is undoubtedly much truth in this explanation, but it is not complete. The size of the Socialist vote in 1917 suggests that there was genuine reason for viewing the party as a potential menace to the war effort; that the almost universal sanction for the anti-Socialist assaults was based, partially, upon apprehension of increasing Socialist popularity.

The popular response to Socialist and non-Socialist anti-war appeals demonstrates considerable and continuing opposition to America's participation in the World War. The opposition, furthermore, was probably appreciably greater than the Socialist vote, in the states examined here, would indicate. This is so partly because of the severe limitation of the Socialist party as an effective center of opposition to the war.

102. Peterson and Fite, *op. cit.*, pp. 189 *et seq.*

103. Minneapolis *Journal*, June 19, 23, 1918.

104. *Ibid.*, November 7, 8, 9, 13, 1918. Van Lear received 27,652 votes to 28,967 for J. E. Myers, the "loyalty" candidate.

105. Woodward, *op. cit.*, pp. 462, 473.

106. *Op. cit.*, p. 73.

In addition, this study does not indicate the full extent of anti-war sentiment because the states in which the Socialist campaigns were conducted, in 1917, were not those in which opposition was greatest. If congressional votes against the declaration of war are used as a measure, then Wisconsin, Nevada, South Dakota, Colorado, Nebraska, Montana, Minnesota and Washington, in that order, were the main centers of opposition. Of the 42 congressmen from these states who voted on the declaration of war, 24 were opposed; while only 8 of 162 congressmen from Illinois, Indiana, Ohio, Pennsylvania, Maryland, New Jersey, New York and Connecticut voted "no."[107]

It seems clear, also, that opposition to the war was not restricted to any one section of the population or nation. In Minnesota, Oklahoma and Georgia opposition was primarily rural,[108] while in New York, New Jersey, Ohio, Pennsylvania and Indiana it appears to have been primarily urban. The Socialist vote indicates that in some cities where Socialist votes were numerous, foreign born were few; in the rural areas of Oklahoma and Georgia foreign born were curiosities. What emerges is a pattern of opposition which indicates disagreement with Administration policies among diverse groups in the population—an opposition which cannot be explained in terms of Midwest "isolationism" or of urban alienism, but which indicates that many Americans, of varied interests and origins, felt that American democracy had nothing at stake in the European war.

107. *Congressional Record,* 65th Congress, Special Session, April 5, 1917, pp. 412–13.
108. Lindbergh carried many of the rural counties by better than two to one, while running well behind Burnquist in most cities. (Minneapolis *Journal,* June 23, 1918.) In Oklahoma the opposition was among tenant farmers. In Georgia, Watson's strength was among the "red-neck" farmers.

THE INTELLECTUAL
AND SOCIAL IMPACT
OF THE WAR

HENRY F. MAY

The Rebellion of the Intellectuals, 1912–1917

One of the most influential interpretations of the impact of World War I concerns the emergence of those younger American writers who proudly called themselves the "lost generation." For a long time it was thought that in going to war these men and women had re-enacted the classic confrontation between New World innocence and Old World experience, with the result that they grew at once deeper and wiser yet also disillusioned and hedonistic. The most prominent critic of this view—not only of the war's literary legacy but, by extension, of its whole intellectual and cultural effect—has been Henry F. May. Beginning with this essay, May has argued that the confidence and optimism usually associated with pre-war America actually began to break down before the outbreak of the war. The disintegration was simply intensified by the conflict and by American intervention. May later expanded this interpretation in his book *The End of American Innocence: A Study of the First Years of Our Own Time, 1912–1917* (New York, 1959).

The literature by and about the "lost generation" is vast. The classic account of its experience, by one of its members, is Malcolm Cowley, *Exile's Return: A Literary Odyssey of the 1920's* (New York, 1934). The first critic to question whether the war had initiated the writers' disillusionment was Charles

Reprinted by permission from *American Quarterly*, VIII (Summer 1956), 114–126. Copyright © 1956 by the Trustees of the University of Pennsylvania.

Fenton, in "Ambulance Drivers in France and Italy, 1914–1918," *American Quarterly,* III (Winter 1951), 326–343. Interestingly, however, Fenton later reasserted that the war caused a generational division among American writers in "A Literary Fracture of World War I," *ibid.,* XII (Summer 1960), 119–132.

As the nineteen-twenties move from memory into history, a standard picture of the decade emerges from reminiscence and research into the textbooks. This picture is a puzzling one. The decade is still, as it was in the thirties, the last island of normalcy and isolation between wars and crises. Yet it is also, clearly, a period of major cultural revolution. Both the "revolt of the highbrows" and the "rebellion of youth," first sketched by F. L. Allen, are a standard part of our semiofficial self-picture. In response to current historical fashions and perhaps also to their own changing worries about their country, historians are giving more attention to the revolutionary aspect of this conservative decade.

Having dealt with other revolutions, historians should be able to appreciate both the importance and complexity of this one. For instance, they should be able to avoid taking to task the rebellious intellectuals of the twenties in the manner of some critics of the forties. The spokesmen of a revolution are not, after all, its sole cause, and a healthy regime is seldom overthrown. Yet anybody, today, must recognize that revolutions are expensive. They may release, as this one certainly did, a burst of creative vigor; but they inevitably leave behind division, hatred, and shock. In the twenties, for instance, beliefs and customs that still commanded the deepest loyalties of one part of the population became to another group a dead and repressive Genteel Tradition, to be ceremonially flouted whenever possible. Suspicions dating from this cultural cleavage still poison the air. The historian must hope that analysis of the revolution and its causes can eventually help a little to clear away some of the resentment.

Starting backward, as historians must, we arrive immediately at the First World War, and there many have stopped. It is obvious that America's first major venture into world tragedy, with its rapid cycle of national exaltation, exhaustion, and revulsion played a very large part in the emotional life of the postwar rebels. By contrast with 1918 or 1919 or even 1925, hundreds of autobiographies paint the prewar period as a time of unity, moderation, progress, and sheltered childhood.

Yet we all know that postwar reminiscence, whether of the old plantation or the old literary culture, is a dubious guide for history. Those who have looked even briefly at the social and literary criticism of the prewar years know that the period 1912–1917[1] was itself, for some, a time of doubt and fragmentation, of upheaval in ideas, of the disintegration of tradition—in other words it was a pre-revolutionary or early revolutionary period. Nearly every phenomenon of the twenties from Freudianism to expatriation or the abandonment of politics was present before the war, on a smaller scale and with certain differences. If we can recapture any of the meaning or content of this prewar ferment, we may be able to understand better in what sense the revolution of the twenties was and was not postwar. In this way we may even get a few suggestions as to the perenially baffling problem of the relation between ideas and events.

In an essay published in 1913 George Santayana made an attempt to catch and pin down on paper "The Intellectual Temper of the Age." To do this for one's own time is one of the hardest tasks a writer can undertake, yet for anybody who has been for a while immersed in the records of that period it is astonishing how well this brilliant essay seems to order and illuminate the times. To Santayana it seemed that "the civilisation characteristic of Christendom has not disappeared, yet another civilisation has begun to take its place."[2] In the resulting age of confusion and transition, men were giving up the search for lasting values and firm intellectual conclusions. Instead of these, they were placing a premium on sheer vitality, on movement, change, and emotion. According to Santayana, who sometimes enjoyed but did not admire this taste, the result was that in thought and art, his generation was "in full career toward disintegration."[3]

Whether or not one shares Santayana's cool disapproval of the tendencies of his day, the vitalist spirit he describes stares out from the sources. One recognizes on all sides its gaiety, its irresponsibility,

1. Through this essay I treat this period as one instead of dividing it in August, 1914. The outbreak of the war in Europe shocked American intellectuals but did not immediately become their main preoccupation. Until about the winter of 1916, radical and progressive politics, together with the new literary and philosophical tendencies, get more space than the war in the liberal and literary periodicals.

2. George Santayana, *Winds of Doctrine* (London and New York: Charles Scribner's Sons, 1913), p. 1.

3. *Ibid.*, p. 10.

its love of change, and also its contempt for reason. And it does not take much knowledge of American intellectual history to know that this spirit meant trouble. For a century and a half the dominant ideas in the national faith had been a confidence in secure moral values and a belief in progress. These two commitments had often been in conflict and formed at best a somewhat unstable compound. Now both at once were brought under devastating attack.

If one starts, as Santayana does, with philosophy, the tendencies he describes emerge very clearly. The young intellectuals of America were still most widely influenced by pragmatism, by what Morton G. White has called the revolt against formalism. Experience and movement were reality; potentiality more important than actuality. Dewey's program for intelligence remaking both the world and itself probably attracted the largest number of conscious disciples, some of them, like Randolph Bourne, soon to break away in a more emotionally satisfying direction. But it may well be that the influence of James, with his catholic and dangerous acceptance of the irrational, personal, and mysterious, went deeper in a generation nourished on idealism. Emerson, universally read though misunderstood and underrated, and Whitman, the sole American patron of some of the rebels, as well as the German idealists casually studied in college courses, must have prepared them for a philosophy of intuition. Whatever the reason it was the destructive elements in pragmatism that were the most influential. The avant-garde of 1912–17, the aggressive young innovators, were perfectly willing to see all of life as an experiment. But their purpose in experimenting was rather to express themselves and experience emotion than to solve problems in a disciplined manner.

Those who were sensitive to Atlantic breezes felt most keenly the swelling winds of antirationalism, which had been gathering force for a long time. Nietzsche, for long known vaguely by the American public as an Antichrist, was becoming a major prophet. The most vigorous, though not the most accurate, of his American interpreters was H. L. Mencken, who in a widely read and widely praised book published first in 1908 and again in 1913 used the German prophet to belabor religion, women, and, most roughly of all, democracy in his already familiar manner.[4] But the most fashionable of Europeans was the still living and lecturing Henri Bergson, who pushed the

4. Henry L. Mencken, *The Philosophy of Friedrich Nietzsche* (Boston: Luce and Co., 1908).

current tendency to an extreme, contending that reality, being in constant flux and change, is only distorted by efforts to think about it and must be apprehended through intuition. His was not the only, but it was probably the dominant direction in which philosophy was moving in 1913, and there is plenty of evidence that he was extraordinarily attractive to up-to-date American intellectuals. Irving Babbitt, already an alarmed defender of traditional values, saw the rise of Bergsonism as the culmination of a long, deplorable irrationalist trend, and found it in 1912 "allied with all that is violent and extreme in contemporary life from syndicalism to 'futurist' painting."[5]

Psychology, as well as philosphy, was dealing heavy blows to dominant assumptions and beliefs. From the time of Freud's famous trip to Clark University in 1908, the Viennese theories cropped up in popular magazines and political treatises as well as learned journals. Whether or not, as his supporters claim, Freud is to be regarded as himself a brave and determined champion of reason, the first impact of his doctrines in the United States seemed to confirm and deepen the hedonism, emotionalism, and egocentricity that were beginning to spread so widely.[6] On the other hand, Behaviorism, a movement launched in its most dogmatic form by John B. Watson in 1912, had to wait for its vogue until after the war.[7] Its extreme practicalism, its rejection not only of reason but of consciousness, its suspicion of emotion, did not fit the tastes of the prewar rebels.

It does not need demonstrating that restless and vigorous innovation in the graphic arts got its American start before the war. Two major tendencies already dazzled the intellectuals and startled the public. One was apparently native, the harsh and sometimes violent Ash Can realism of Sloan, Bellows and the *Masses* cartoons. The other

5. Irving Babbitt, "Bergson and Rousseau," *Nation,* November 14, 1912, p. 455. One of the more influential of the considerable number of books on Bergson appearing in these years was H. M. Kallen, *William James and Henri Bergson* (Chicago: University of Chicago Press, 1914). There is a very large volume of periodical discussion from 1911.

6. For a helpful review see Frederick J. Hoffman, *Freudianism and the Literary Mind* (Baton Rouge, La: Louisiana State University Press, 1945). The early impact of Freud and many other foreign influences is clearly recorded in the works of Floyd Dell, one of Freud's important American exponents. Dell deals most specifically with these influences in his retrospective *Intellectual Vagabondage* (New York: George H. Doran Co., 1926).

7. See Lucille C. Birnbaum, "Behaviorism in the 1920's," *American Quarterly, VII* (1955), 15–30, esp. p. 20.

was imported from Paris, and consisted of a kaleidoscopic series of schools of experiment in form and technique. Commenting on "Current Impressionism," a term already well out of date but helpful as a catch-all, Louis Weinberg extended his observations from and beyond contemporary art:

> Impressionism as a technique is a means of recording the transitory nature of phenomena and the fluidity of motion. As a principle it is based on a philosophy of change. . . .
>
> But this is not alone a description of the art of our times. It is the very essence of our lives.[8]

Wherever the impressionist or vitalist tendency arose, it was expressed most frequently and characteristically not in painting or philosophy, but in politics and literature. These are the forms in which most American cultural change has been recorded, and it is to them that we must turn for a slightly closer look at prewar tendencies. Santayana's brilliant summary suggests that in politics alone the current drift toward fragmentation and chaos may have reversed itself in the constructive and integrating (though to Santayana most uncongenial) movement towards collectivism.[9] In this one opinion, regarding an area which concerned him little, I think Santayana missed the current drift and underrated the force of his own generalization. It is true that progressivism, optimistic, gradual, and in some forms mildly collectivist, was the officially dominant ideology; and that socialism was a swelling movement on the left that seemed to many sober Americans to possess the future. Yet both these political tendencies were in the early teens already under devastating attack, and from much the same irrationalist quarter.

Progressivism in all its varieties took for granted one or both of the two fundamental assumptions which had so far underlain the whole American political tradition. One of these was that we possess secure criteria by which we can judge our political achievement, the other that human beings are able consciously to remold their environment. Now both of these basic assumptions were being seriously shaken by new doctrines that had penetrated the house of progressivism itself.

Recent studies have shown that moral standards of a highly tradi-

8. Louis Weinberg, "Current Impressionism," *New Republic,* March 6, 1915, pp. 124–25.

9. George Santayana, *Winds of Doctrine,* p. 10.

tional sort motivated a great many of the prewar progressives. Truth and falsehood, good and evil, stand out in nearly all the speeches of Theodore Roosevelt and Wilson and good men threw out bad in most American cities. These venerable distinctions were the first to go; the younger progressive intellectuals, nourished on Dewey and H. G. Wells, were quite willing to throw out moral categories and rely on the shaping intelligence. On a popular level Lincoln Steffens spread the picture of the good boss and the honest crook. James Harvey Robinson, speaking for the main organ of the pragmatic progressives, lumped together as obsolete the ideals of "sound doctrine, consistency, fidelity to conscience, eternal verities, immutable human nature, and the imprescriptable rights of man."[10]

With these went the state and law, the traditional locus and method of American reform. Many of the ablest political theorists of various schools, led by the brilliant Harold Laski, were redefining the state almost out of existence. To some it was a congeries of associations, to others the tool of a class, to still others the expression of the wish of those at present in authority. Its acts were no more final and deserved no greater obedience than those of other human groups, and it was less likely than many to be rationally motivated. Similarly, law, to the followers of the French positivist Leon Duguit or the American Roscoe Pound, was no longer either the embodiment of a principle nor the command of a sovereign, but the complex resultant of social forces, prevailing opinion, and judicial will.

There remained the conscious intelligence, remolding the goals of action together with its methods. This was a moving conception, and a sufficient loyalty for many in this generation. Yet this too was seriously menaced by ideas that were attractive to the youngest generation of progressives. From the new and flourishing disciplines of sociology, anthropology and social psychology came an increasingly fashionable emphasis on custom and group emotion. It was sometimes hard to see what function this newest tendency left for intelligence and purpose.[11]

10. James H. Robinson, "A Journal of Opinion," *New Republic*, May 8, 1915, pp. 9–10.

11. An account of all these tendencies in prewar thought, together with a vast bibliography, can be found in two helpful summaries. These are W. Y. Elliott, *The Pragmatic Revolt in Politics* (New York: The Macmillan Company, 1928) and C. E. Merriam and H. E. Barnes, eds., *A History of Political Theories, Recent Times* (New York: The Macmillan Company, 1924).

Walter Lippmann's two prewar studies, *A Preface to Politics* (1913) and *Drift and Mastery* (1914), bring together the pragmatist attack on tradition and the implicit Freudian attack on pragmatism. Appealing for a radically instrumental state, he denounces the "routineers" who rely on political machinery, law, and conventional morality. His fellow progressives seem to draw most of his fire for their naïve adherence to literal numerical democracy and narrow utilitarian goals. What is needed in politics is passion and creative emotion, still of course somehow constructively channeled and used by the far-seeing for purposes which will transcend woman suffrage or the eight-hour day.

> . . . the goal of action is in its final analysis aesthetic and not moral—a quality of feeling instead of conformity to rule.[12]

This formulation seems to me far closer to the view of postwar literary intellectuals than to that of the progressive standard-bearers. And the sources are explicit. Lippmann's friend Graham Wallas, the British author of *Human Nature in Politics*[13] had opened the eyes of his Harvard seminar to political psychology. Steffens had helped to guide Lippmann and so, in a negative direction, had his brief experience with municipal socialism in Schenectady. But beyond these immediate guides one finds recurring references to James, Nietzsche and Bergson and frequent, specific acknowledgment of the work of Freud.[14]

All these new insights enriched the social sciences, and for many they doubtless furnished in practice new sources of power and freedom. Traditional progressivism, with its facile assumptions and sometimes shallow purposes, needed—and for that matter still needs—rethinking. Yet much had been accomplished under the auspices of ideas that were beginning to seem stale and boring. And the new beliefs that buzzed and swarmed through the immediate postwar years were not easy to introduce into the progressive hive. To combine Lippmann or Laski with Wilson was, and soon proved to be, as difficult as to match Bergson and Nietzsche with Lyman Abbott.

It is tempting to wonder whether the actual practical difficulties of progressivism from about 1914 to 1917 were not related in part to confusion of purposes and motives. It is true at least that the

12. Walter Lippmann, *A Preface to Politics* (New York: M. Kennerley, 1913), p. 200.

13. London: A. Constable and Co., 1908.

14. *E.g.,* Walter Lippmann, *Drift and Mastery* (New York: M. Kennerley, 1914), pp. 249, 274.

Wilsonian impetus began to bog down in these years. Already one finds in the up-to-the-minute *New Republic* troubled editorials that ask the common postwar question: what has happened to the progressives?[15]

On the far left much the same process was taking place, whether one labels it fertilization or disintegration or both. Not the Marxian dialectic, but the Bergsonian and mystical syndicalism of Sorel or the anarchism of Max Stirner or Emma Goldman seemed most exciting to the younger radical intellectuals.[16] Not the earnest socialism of Milwaukee or Schenectady, with its respectability and its reliance on the discredited machinery of the state, but the romantic activism of the I.W.W. captured the emotions of the sympathizers. One of America's waves of labor violence, running through the Northwest, Colorado, West Virginia and other centers of direct action, reflecting the primitive brutality of employers' methods in the same areas, aroused the generous emotions and seemed to some to make political action irrelevant. The climax came in 1912 at Lawrence and in 1913 at Paterson, when the I.W.W. penetrated the East and the writers and artists went to its aid, when Bill Haywood was a Greenwich Village social lion and John Reed staged an immense pageant in Madison Square Garden with the letters I.W.W. flaming from the roof in red electric signs ten feet high. Even Lippmann, viewing radicalism from the outside, approved the I.W.W. rather than the Socialist Party as less formalist and more in possession of the kind of emotional force that needed only to be constructively channeled.[17]

Naturally, when Max Eastman, a young man of impeccable ministerial stock, joined the Socialist Party, he chose the left wing rather than the gradualists. Under Eastman's editorship the *Masses,* focus of so much later radical nostalgia, became perhaps even more clearly than the sober *New Republic* the organ of youth. Publishing the magnificent and not always political cartoons of Sloan and Bellows, an occasional Picasso drawing, stories by Sherwood Anderson, and reporting by Reed, it fought for the new literature and the new sexual morality as well as the social revolution. The *Masses* was rich in

15. *E.g.,* January 16, 1915, pp. 6–8; November 6, 1915, p. 1; June 17, 1916, pp. 159–61; July 1, 1916, pp. 211–13.

16. See Daniel Bell, "Marxian Socialism in the United States," in D. D. Egbert and Stow Persons, eds., *Socialism and American Life* (Princeton, N.J.: Princeton University Press, 1952), I, 289–90.

17. Walter Lippmann, *Preface to Politics,* pp. 277–78.

humor and human emotion—qualities often enough lacking on the far left—and practically negligible in social program. Smashing idols was, in these years as after the war, a flourishing business, while Socialism as a political movement was already losing momentum in 1914–16.[18]

More spectacularly than anywhere else, the new spirit of 1910 or 1912 to 1917 was reflected in a literary renaissance. The story of this sudden creative outburst has often been told, and only two points need making for our present purpose. One of these is that literary departures in the prewar years were closely related to contemporary movements in other fields of thought, the other that prewar writing contains in embryo nearly all of the developments of the twenties.

Here too the stimulus came in large part from abroad. Young Americans, brought up on Matthew Arnold and Thackeray, were following before he gave it the advice of Yeats at the *Poetry* dinner in 1912 to forget London and look to Paris for all that was excellent.[19] In Kroch's bookstore in Chicago, in the translations issued by a series of daring new publishers, in the eager if undiscriminating reviews by the young critics, this generation of rebels was nourished on a whole series of movements extending over the last generation in Europe. All the writers that had for so long been belaboring the European bourgeoisie—French symbolists and decadents and naturalists, Scandinavian pessimists and social critics, Russian apostles of mysticism and emotion; even from England D. H. Lawrence as well as Shaw, suddenly began to penetrate the American barrier. What this series of reagents produced was a series of explosions, and what exploded was more than the genteel tradition in literature, more than conventional moral categories. With the conventions of literary form and language went the underlying assumptions about thought and communication. Randolph Bourne perhaps described this grand explosion better than he realized in June, 1917:

> What becomes more and more apparent to the readers of Dostoevsky, however, is his superb modern healthiness. He is

18. See David L. Shannon, *The Socialist Party of America, A History* (New York: The Macmillan Company, 1955). As Shannon and other historians of socialism have pointed out, the apparent revival of the Socialist Party in the big Debs vote of 1920 is misleading. It belongs in the category of protest rather than party success.

19. Harriet Monroe, *A Poet's Life* (New York: The Macmillan Company, 1938), p. 337.

healthy because he has no sense of any dividing line between the normal and the abnormal, or even between the sane and the insane.[20]

When Harriet Monroe, full of civic feeling as well as poetic zeal, founded *Poetry* in 1912 she seemed to tap immediately a rich underground gusher of poetic impulse. Soon the flood of experiment became too thick and varied even for *Poetry* to contain and overflowed into *Others* and the *Little Review*. As in the visual arts, a rapid series of schools succeeded each other, but perhaps the literary movement most characteristic of the period, and most obviously related to its philosophic tendencies, was that of the Imagists, with its manifestoes in favor of complete freedom, concentration on the fleeting and immediate image for its own sake, and refusal to assign an image any "external" meaning or reference. Already before the war the revolution in the use of language was under way toward its ultimate destinations; Joyce was being published in the London *Egoist* and Gertrude Stein, settled in Paris, had developed her opinions and her characteristic style.

It would be misleading to divide this literary outpouring into precise categories, yet one can find suggestions of two emergent ways of thinking and feeling among writers. One group demanded freedom from European forms, confidence in emotion and spontaneity, and in general preached democratic optimism in the Whitman tradition. The other, more disciplined but also more deeply rebellious against American culture, called for concentration, rejection of irrelevant moral and political purposes, and the development of conscious intellectual aristocracy.

Obviously the former, democratic and optimist group is more distant than the other from postwar directions. This is the tendency one associates particularly with the sudden and brief Chicago Renaissance, with Sandburg and Lindsay and Miss Monroe, though it is found also in other areas, for instance in the organized and vigorous character of what Francis Hackett labeled and dated forever as Miss Amy Lowell's "Votes for Poetry movement."[21] Yet even the most exuberant of the Chicago poets were, like contemporary political radicals, destroying for the sake of redemption, like Sandburg's personified city "Shovelling, wrecking, planning, building, breaking, rebuilding."

20. Randolph Bourne, "The Immanence of Dostoevsky," *The Dial,* LXIII (1917), 25.
21. In the *New Republic,* November 10, 1917, p. 52.

And even in Chicago pessimistic and sceptical tendencies were also, and had long been, at work. Dreiser's not exactly rosy picture of American city life was finally finding its audience; and the small town, from E. A. Robinson's New England Tilbury town to Masters' Middlewestern Spoon River, was preparing the way for Winesburg and Gopher Prairie. In the bosom of *Poetry* magazine, at the official heart of the Chicago movement, Ezra Pound, the magazine's foreign editor, was chafing at its cover slogan, the statement of Whitman that "to have great poets there must be great audiences too." Pound preferred Dante's pronouncement that the wisest in the city is "He whom the fools hate worst" and denied that poets have any need for the rabble.

> It is true that the great artist has always a great audience, even in his lifetime; but it is not the *vulgo* but the spirits of irony and of destiny and of humor, sitting with him.[22]

In that sentence lies the germ of a dozen ponderous manifestoes of the postwar Young Intellectuals. Pound stayed on *Poetry* long enough to persuade Miss Monroe to publish Eliot's "Prufrock" in 1915 and then found a refuge from uplift and Whitmanism in the *Little Review*.

In the Eastern centers of the new literary movement the mixture of optimism and nihilism, of reform and rejection was somewhat different. Harvard, which was incubating an extraordinary number of important writers, seemed to produce a strange and special mixture of ideas.[23] The dominant note in its teaching of literature was aestheticism, worship of Europe, and contempt for the native production. Irving Babbitt's vigorous attack on democratic sentimentality was already a major influence. Yet Walter Lippmann, for one, managed to combine presidency of the Harvard Socialist Club with assisting Professor Santayana. A certain survival of Emersonian and Puritan responsibility seems to have been a part of the prevalent passionate concern for literature. America might be vulgar and materialistic

---

22. Ezra Pound, "The Audience," *Poetry, A Magazine of Verse*, V (1914–15), 30.

23. See the following helpful autobiographies of Harvard graduates: Malcolm Cowley, *Exile's Return* (New York: W. W. Norton & Company, 1934); Harold E. Stearns, *The Street I Know* (New York: L. Furman, 1935); Van Wyck Brooks, *Scenes and Portraits* (New York: E. P. Dutton & Co., 1954).

and nearly hopeless; if so one's duty was to search the harder for seeds of literary springtime, and literary revival would bring social regeneration as well. Like so many writers after the war, Van Wyck Brooks went to Europe to look for these seeds. He found in London in 1913–14 Ezra Pound, T. S. Eliot, John Gould Fletcher, Conrad Aiken, Elinor Wylie, Robert Frost and Walter Lippmann.[24] Across the channel he could already have run into an equally significant group of fellow-countrymen. It was in London that Brooks began to struggle seriously with the typical problem of the expatriate of the next decade: the love of European tradition and the nostalgic turning toward American vitality. He solved this problem by writing, in London in 1914, the book that most influenced the writers of the next decade, an attack on the Genteel Tradition and an appeal for a literary renaissance that seemed then, as its title implies, to mark an arrival and not just a beginning: *America's Coming-of-Age*.

From here we can see, even more clearly than Santayana could in 1913, the unrest, the disintegration of old standards, the search for vitality and movement that already was under way at that time.[25] We know, too, that what was then unrest later became cultural revolution and angry intellectual civil war. This brings us to the compelling question, what started it all? Why did this search for novelty, this gay destruction of traditional standards, occur at just this moment in the midst of an apparently placid and contented period?

This is hardly a question that can be answered with certainty. All that we know for sure is that a movement so general and noticeable in the prewar years was not started by the war. Perhaps the most obvious forces at work in early twentieth-century civilization were technological change and urban growth, but these had been at work reshaping American culture for several generations and do not afford a direct and simple explanation for the sudden restlessness of 1912–17. Moreover, an increase of mechanistic materialism rather than a new vitalism would seem a more easily understandable product of machine civilization. It may be that the prewar rebellion was in part a protest against such a long-run tendency; in 1915 the *Nation* suggested that the rising "Bergsonian school . . . owes not a little of its popularity

24. Brooks, *op. cit.*, pp. 123–48, 210 ff.
25. The same traits that one finds in the ideas of the period characterize much of its social life. Ragtime and the dance craze, the furore over alleged white slave disclosures, in 1913 seem to prefigure the feverishness and the moral divisions of the postwar decade.

to its expression of revolt from the dreary materialistic determinism of the closing years of the last century."[26]

One is tempted to wonder whether the new physics was at work already disintegrating the comparatively simple universe of nineteenth-century science. It seems, however, that although the Einstein revolution was being discussed before the war by American scientists and reported in the serious periodical press, it did not directly affect as yet the literary and political intellectuals to any great extent, and it was not, as it became after the war, a newspaper sensation.[27]

In part the American intellectual rebellion may be considered merely a belated phase of an European antirationalist tendency. Yet it remains puzzling that Nietzsche and Dostoevsky and Baudelaire waited for their most telling American impact until they competed with Freud and Joyce. Part of the violence of the American literary and intellectual battles of the next decade arises from the fact that influences that had gradually permeated European thought presented themselves to many Americans all at once and in their extreme forms.

The time and special character of the prewar rebellion were, I believe, determined in part by the very surface placidity of the Progressive Era. Traditional American beliefs in moral certainty and inevitable progress had for some time been subjected to inner strain and external attack, yet in the prewar decade, for the last time, the official custodians of culture were able to maintain and defend a common front. Yet these almost hereditary leaders—Roosevelt and Royce and Howells in their several spheres—were growing weaker. A new generation, full of confidence and provided with leisure and libraries, was fairly literally looking for trouble. What attracts us about the standard culture of America in the early years of the century is its confident consensus, its lack of passion and violence. Passion and violence were exactly the demand of the young intellectuals of 1913 and 1914, of Lippmann and Brooks and Bourne and Pound. This was what they wanted, and this was what they got.

The war, then, was not the cause of the cultural revolution of the twenties. It played, however, the immense part that the Civil War played in the economic and political revolution of the mid-nine-

26. From a review of Croly's *Progressive Democracy,* which the *Nation* associates with the Bergson influence (April 29, 1915), pp. 469–70.

27. This impression comes from an examination of periodicals and is confirmed by an intensive though brief examination of popular scientific literature by Robert G. Sumpter.

teenth century, speeding, widening and altering in kind a movement already under way.

The experiences of 1917–19 darkened and soured the mood of the rebels. Even at its most iconoclastic and even in those spokesmen who adopted the most pessimistic doctrines, the prewar renaissance was always exuberant. Pound, amid his fierce negations, still found it possible to make his famous and somewhat rash prophecy that the coming American Risorgimento would "make the Italian Renaissance look like a tempest in a teapot!"[28] The rejection of easy rationalism, the spurning of dull politics were to make America better and brighter. In the war and its aftermath however the rebellious generation learned something of the price of destruction and experienced personally both tragedy and (in 1919) failure. Many who had been rebellious optimists became despairing nihilists and those who had already been preaching the futility of conscious effort preached it with different emotional corollaries.

The other effect of the war was that the disintegration of traditional ideas spread far more widely among the population. Most of the prewar rebellion was confined to a small and isolated, though articulate and potentially influential, group of intellectuals. As yet the overwhelming bulk of the people took for granted the truth of the old political and moral slogans. As long as this was so rebels could be ignored or patronized; they did not have to be feared and fought. Without the political events of 1917–19 traditional beliefs might perhaps have been slowly adapted to new realities instead of, for the moment, either smashed or blindly defended. And without the currents of doubt and disintegration already abroad, these political events themselves might have lacked their willing and ready Cassandras.

In 1913 *Sons and Lovers, A Preface to Politics,* and *Winds of Doctrine* were published, but *Pollyanna* and *Laddie* were the best-sellers. In 1925 the best-seller list itself had to find place for *An American Tragedy*.

---

28. Pound to Harriet Monroe, 24 September, 1914, in D. D. Paige, ed., *The Letters of Ezra Pound 1907–1941* (New York: Harcourt, Brace and Co., 1950), p. 10.

JAMES R. McGOVERN

The American Woman's Pre-World War I Freedom in Manners and Morals

More than anyone or anything else, the "new woman" of the 1920's, with her short skirt, bobbed hair, and at least a verbal sexual liberation, has symbolized the evident social metamorphosis brought about by the war. This intepretation, too, has been revised in recent years. In this essay James R. McGovern argues that before 1914 women had already achieved much of the emancipation commonly associated with the Flappers of the twenties.

The classic account of the social impact of World War I was first advanced by Frederick Lewis Allen in *Only Yesterday* (New York, 1931). Allen's version is repeated in the main, with somewhat greater historical grounding, in William E. Leuchtenburg, *The Perils of Prosperity, 1914–1932* (Chicago, 1958). The extent of changes for women brought about by the war is also questioned in William L. O'Neill's *Divorce in the Progressive Era* (New Haven, 1967) and *Everyone Was Brave: The Rise and Fall of Feminism in America* (Chicago, 1969).

The twenties have been alternately praised or blamed for almost everything and its opposite;[1] but most historians hold, whether to praise or to condemn, that this decade launched the revolution in manners and morals through which we are still moving today. This judgment seems to be part of an even more inclusive one in American historiography to exceptionalize the Twenties. No other decade has invited such titles of historical caricature as *The Jazz Age, This Was Normalcy, Fantastic Interim,* or *The Perils of Prosperity.* Richard Hofstad-

Reprinted by permission from the *Journal of American History*, LV (September 1968), 315–333.
1. Henry F. May, "Shifting Perspectives on the 1920's," *Mississippi Valley Historical Review*, XLIII (Dec. 1956), 405–27.

ter's classic, *The Age of Reform,* subtly reinforces this view by seeing the Twenties as "Entr'acte," an interim between two periods of reform, the Progressive era and the New Deal, which themselves display discontinuity.[2]

Revisionism, in the form of a developmental interpretation of the relationship between the Progressive era and the Twenties, has been gaining strong support in recent years. De-emphasizing the disruptive impact of World War I, Henry F. May asked whether the 1920s could be understood fully "without giving more attention to the old regime."[3] He declared that "Immediately prewar America must be newly explored," especially "its inarticulate assumptions—assumptions in such areas as morality, politics, class and race relations, popular art and literature, and family life."[4] May pursued his inquiry in *The End of American Innocence* and showed that for the purposes of intellectual history, at least, the Twenties were not as significant as the preceding decade.[5] Political historians have been reassessing the relationship of the Progressive era to the Twenties as well. Arthur Link has demonstrated that progressivism survived World War I,[6] and J. Joseph Huthmacher has established continuity between progressivism and the New Deal in the immigrant's steadfast devotion to the ameliorative powers of the government.[7] Together with May's

2. Richard Hofstadter, *The Age of Reform: From Bryan to F. D. R.* (New York, 1955), 282–301.

3. May, "Shifting Perspectives on the 1920's," 426. See also Henry F. May, "The Rebellion of the Intellectuals, 1912–1917," *American Quarterly,* VIII (Summer 1956), 115, wherein May describes 1912–1917 as a "pre-revolutionary or early revolutionary period."

4. May, "Shifting Perspectives on the 1920's," 427.

5. Henry F. May, *The End of American Innocence: A Study of the First Years of Our Own Time, 1912–1917* (New York, 1959).

6. Arthur S. Link, "What Happened to the Progressive Movement in the 1920's?" *American Historical Review,* LXIV (July 1959), 833–51.

7. J. Joseph Huthmacher, "Urban Liberalism and the Age of Reform," *Mississippi Valley Historical Review,* XLIX (Sept. 1962), 231–41. Other political and economic historians concur on a developmental interpretation. Gerald D. Nash, *State Government and Economic Development: A History of Administrative Policies in California, 1849–1933* (Berkeley, 1964), 250, 291, 326, views the period 1900–1933 as a unit because it was characterized by notable coordination and centralization of authority by agencies of state government in California. Donald C. Swain, *Federal Conservation Policy, 1921–1933* (Berkeley, 1963), 6, sees the national conservation program making continuous advances through the 1920s based upon beginnings in the Progressive period.

analysis, their writings suggest that the 1920s are much more the result of earlier intrinsic social changes than either the sudden, supposedly traumatic experiences of the war or unique developments in the Twenties. Since this assertion is certain to encounter the formidable claims that the 1920s, at least in manners and morals, amounted to a revolution, its viability can be tested by questioning if the American woman's "emancipation" in manners and morals occurred even earlier than World War I.

Even a casual exploration of the popular literature of the Progressive era reveals that Americans then described and understood themselves to be undergoing significant changes in morals. "Sex o'clock in America" struck in 1913,[8] about the same time as "The Repeal of Reticence."[9] One contemporary writer saw Americans as liberated from the strictures of "Victorianism," now an epithet deserving criticism, and exulted, "Heaven defend us from a return to the prudery of the Victorian regime!"[10] Conditions were such that another commentator asked self-consciously, "Are We Immoral?"[11] And still another feared that the present "vice not often matched since [the time of] the Protestant Reformation" might invite a return to Puritanism.[12] Yet, historians have not carefully investigated the possibility that the true beginnings of America's "New Freedom" in morals occurred prior

8. "Sex O'clock in America," *Current Opinion,* LV (Aug. 1913), 113–14. The anonymous author borrowed the phrase from William M. Reedy, editor of the St. Louis *Mirror.*

9. Agnes Repplier, "The Repeal of Reticence," *Atlantic Monthly,* CXIII (March 1914), 297–304, objected to the "obsession of sex which has set us all a-babbling about matters once excluded from the amenities of conversation" (p. 298). Articles on birth control, prostitution, divorce, and sexual morals between 1910 and 1914 were cumulatively more numerous per thousand among articles indexed in the *Reader's Guide to Periodical Literature* than for either 1919 to 1924 or 1925 to 1928. Hornell Hart, "Changing Social Attitudes and Interests," *Recent Social Trends in the United States: Report of the President's Research Committee on Social Trends* (2 vols., New York, 1933), I, 414.

10. H. W. Boynton, "Ideas, Sex, and the Novel," *Dial,* LX (April 13, 1916), 361. In Robert W. Chambers, *The Restless Sex* (New York, 1910), 143, the heroine remarks, "What was all wrong in our Victorian mothers' days is all right now."

11. Arthur Pollock, "Are We Immoral?" *Forum,* LI (Jan. 1914), 52. Pollock remarks that "in our literature and in our life to-day sex is paramount."

12. "Will Puritanism Return?" *Independent,* 77 (March 23, 1914), 397.

to 1920.[13] The most extensive, analytical writing on the subject of changing manners and morals is found in Frederick L. Allen's *Only Yesterday* (1931), William Leuchtenburg's *The Perils of Prosperity* (1958), May's *The End of American Innocence* (1959), and George Mowry's *The Urban Nation* (1965).

Allen and Leuchtenburg apply almost identical sharp-break interpretations, respectively entitling chapters "The Revolution in Manners and Morals" and "The Revolution in Morals."[14] Both catalogue the same types of criteria for judgment. The flapper, as the "new woman" was called, was a creature of the 1920s. She smoked, drank, worked, and played side by side with men. She became preoccupied with sex—shocking and simultaneously unshockable. She danced close, became freer with her favors, kept her own latchkey, wore scantier attire which emphasized her boyish, athletic form, just as she used makeup and bobbed and dyed her hair. She and her comradely beau tried to abolish time and succeeded, at least to the extent that the elders asked to join the revelry. Although there were occasional "advance signals" of "rebellion" before the war, it was not until the 1920s that the code of woman's innocence and ignorance crumbled.

May, who comes closest to an understanding of the moral permissiveness before the 1920s, describes in general terms such phenomena of the Progressive era as the "Dance Craze," birth control, the impact of the movies, and the "white-slave panic."[15] He focuses on the intellectuals, however, and therefore overlooks the depth of these and similar social movements. This causes him to view them as mere "Cracks

13. Mark Sullivan, *Our Times: The War Begins* (New York, 1932), 165–93, states in colorful and impressionistic terms that significant changes in moral attitudes had taken place in the Progressive era. He attributes much of this to the influence of Freud, Shaw, and Omar Khayyám. Preston William Slosson, *The Great Crusade and After: 1914–1928* (New York, 1930), describes the period 1914–1928 as a unit, but his material dealing with morals centers on the 1920s. For example, there are only five footnotes based on materials written between 1914 and 1919 in his chapter, "The American Woman Wins Equality," 130–61. Samuel Eliot Morison makes brief mention of a "revolution in sexual morals" before 1920 in *The Oxford History of the American People* (New York, 1965), 906–08.

14. Frederick Lewis Allen, *Only Yesterday: An Informal History of the Nineteen-Twenties* (New York, 1931), 88–122; William E. Leuchtenburg, *The Perils of Prosperity: 1914–32* (Chicago, 1958), 158–77.

15. May, *The End of American Innocence,* 334–47, is lightly documented; there are only twelve footnotes to support his discussion of these and similar developments.

in the Surface" of an essentially conservative society. He quotes approvingly of the distinction made by the *Nation* "between the fluttering tastes of the half-baked intellectuals, attracted by all these things, and the surviving soundness of the great majority."[16] His treatment also ignores one of the most significant areas of changing manners and morals as they affected the American woman: the decided shift in her sex role and identification in the direction of more masculine norms. Again, *The End of American Innocence* does not convincingly relate these changes to the growth of the cities. Perhaps these limitations explain Mowry's preference for a "sharp-break" interpretation, although he wrote seven years after May.

Mowry, who acknowledges especial indebtedness to Leuchtenburg,[17] is emphatic about the "startling" changes in manners and morals in the 1920s.[18] He highlights "the new woman of the twenties"[19] whose "modern feminine morality and attitudes toward the institution of marriage date from the twenties."[20] Mowry concedes to the libidos of progressives only the exceptional goings-on in Greenwich Village society.

These hypotheses, excluding May's, hold that the flapper appeared in the postwar period mainly because American women en masse then first enjoyed considerable social and economic freedom. They also emphasize the effect of World War I on morals.[21] By inference, of course, the Progressive era did not provide a suitable matrix. But an investigation of this period establishes that women had become sufficiently active and socially independent to prefigure the "emancipation" of the 1920s.

16. *Ibid.*, 347. May's view of women's changing attitudes is contradicted by Margaret Deland: "Of course there were women a generation ago, as in all generations, who asserted themselves; but they were practically 'sports.' Now, the simple, honest woman . . . the good wife, the good mother—is evolving ideals which are changing her life, and the lives of those people about her." Margaret Deland, "The Change in the Feminine Ideal," *Atlantic Monthly*, CV (March 1910), 291.

17. George E. Mowry, *The Urban Nation: 1920–1960* (New York, 1965), 250.

18. *Ibid.*, 23.

19. *Ibid.*

20. *Ibid.*, 24.

21. "By 1930 more than ten million women held jobs. Nothing did more to emancipate them." Leuchtenburg, *Perils of Prosperity*, 160. See also Allen, *Only Yesterday*, 95–98. For estimates of the effects of World War I on morals, see Leuchtenburg, *Perils of Prosperity*, 172–73; Allen, *Only Yesterday*, 94; Mowry, *Urban Nation*, 24.

A significant deterioration of external controls over morality had occurred before 1920. One of the consequences of working and living conditions in the cities, especially as these affected women, was that Americans of the period 1900–1920 had experienced a vast dissolution of moral authority, which formerly had centered in the family and the small community. The traditional "straight and narrow" could not serve the choices and opportunities of city life.[22] As against primary controls and contacts based on face-to-face association where the norms of family, church, and small community, usually reinforcing each other, could be internalized, the city made for a type of "individualization" through its distant, casual, specialized, and transient clusters of secondary associations.[23] The individual came to determine his own behavioral norms.

The "home is in peril" became a fact of sociological literature as early as 1904.[24] One of the most serious signs of its peril was the increasing inability of parents to influence their children in the delicate areas of propriety and morals.[25] The car, already numerous enough to affect dating and premarital patterns,[26] the phone coming

22. Population in urban territory comprised only about 28 per cent of the total American population in 1880; but by 1920, approximately 52 per cent were living there. Department of Commerce, Bureau of the Census, *Historical Statistics of the United States, Colonial Times to 1957* (Washington, 1960), 14.

23. Scott Nearing and Nellie M. S. Nearing, *Woman and Social Progress* (New York, 1912), 137–41. The Nearings wrote: "The freedom which American Women have gained through recent social changes and the significance of their consequent choice, constitutes one of the profoundest and at the same time one of the most inscrutable problems in American life" (p. 138). William I. Thomas, *The Unadjusted Girl: With Cases and Standpoint for Behavior Analysis* (Boston, 1923), 86. Ernest R. Mowrer, *Family Disorganization* (Chicago, 1927), 6–8. Mowrer attributes "Family Disorganization" to the "conditions of city life" which resulted in a "rebellion against the old ideals of family life. . . ."

24. George Elliott Howard, "Social Control and the Functions of the Family," Howard J. Rogers, ed., *Congress of Arts and Sciences: Universal Exposition, St. Louis, 1904* (8 vols., Boston, 1906), VII, 702.

25. Louise Collier Willcox, "Our Supervised Morals," *North American Review*, CXCVIII (Nov. 1913), 708, observes: "The time is past when parents supervised the morals of their children. . . ."

26. There was a surprisingly large number of cars sold and used in America between 1910 and 1920. Approximately 40 per cent as many cars were produced each year between 1915 and 1917 as were manufactured between 1925 and 1927. *Facts and Figures of the Automobile Industry* (New York, 1929), 6, 22. There were approximately 7,500,000 cars regis-

to be used for purposes of romantic accommodation,[27] and the variety of partners at the office or factory,[28] all together assured unparalleled privacy and permissiveness between the sexes.

Individualization of members served to disrupt confidence between generations of the family, if not to threaten parents with the role of anachronistic irrelevance. Dorothy Dix observed in 1913 that there had been "so many changes in the conditions of life and point of view in the last twenty years that the parent of today is absolutely unfitted to decide the problems of life for the young man and woman of today. This is particularly the case with women because the whole economic and social position of women has been revolutionzed since mother was a girl."[29] Magazine articles lamented "The Passing of the Home Daughter" who preferred the blessed anonymity of the city to "dying of asphyxiation at home!"[30] The same phenomenon helps to explain the popularity in this period of such standardized mothers as Dorothy Dix, Beatrice Fairfax, and Emily Post, each of whom was besieged with queries on the respective rights of mothers and daughters.

Woman's individualization resulted mainly because, whether single or married, gainfully employed or not, she spent more time outside her home. Evidence demonstrates that the so-called job and kitchen revolutions were already in advanced stages by 1910. The great leap forward in women's participation in economic life came between 1900 and 1910; the percentage of women who were employed changed only slightly from 1910 to 1930. A comparison of the percentages of gainfully employed women aged 16 to 44 between 1890 and 1930

---

tered in 1919. "Existing Surfaced Mileage Total" on a scale of 1,000 miles was 204 in 1910, 332 in 1918, 521 in 1925, and 694 in 1930. *Historical Statistics of the United States*, 458. Newspapers reported the impact of the automobile on dating and elopements. For a moralistic reaction to the phenomenon, see Dorothy Dix, Boston *American*, Sept. 5, 1912. For an enthusiast of "mobile privacy" in this period, see F. Scott Fitzgerald, "Echoes of the Jazz Age," *Scribner's Magazine*, XC (Nov. 1931), 460. Fitzgerald wrote: "As far back as 1915 the unchaperoned young people of the smaller cities had discovered the mobile privacy of that automobile given to young Bill at sixteen to make him 'self-reliant.' "

27. Dorothy Dix, "A Modern Diana," Boston *American*, April 7, 1910.

28. Beatrice Fairfax, *ibid.*, May 28, 1908; Dorothy Dix, *ibid.*, Sept. 9, 1912.

29. *Ibid.*, Aug. 21, 1913.

30. Marion Harland, "The Passing of the Home Daughter," *Independent*, LXXI (July 13, 1911), 90.

shows that they comprised 21.7 per cent of Americans employed in 1890, 23.5 per cent in 1900, 28.1 per cent in 1910, 28.3 per cent in 1920, and 29.7 per cent in 1930.[31] While occupational activity for women appears to stagnate from 1910 to 1920, in reality a considerable restructuring occurred with women leaving roles as domestics and assuming positions affording more personal independence as clerks and stenographers.[32]

Married women, especially those in the upper and middle classes, enjoyed commensurate opportunities. Experts in household management advised women to rid themselves of the maid and turn to appliances as the "maid of all service."[33] Statistics on money expended on those industries which reduced home labor for the wife suggest that women in middle-income families gained considerable leisure after 1914.[34] This idea is also corroborated from other sources,[35] espe-

31. Sophonisba P. Breckinridge, *Women in the Twentieth Century: A Study of Their Political, Social and Economic Activities* (New York, 1933), 112. Overall percentages of women gainfully employed rose from 19 per cent of the total work force in 1890 to 20.6 per cent in 1900, 24.3 per cent in 1910, 24 per cent in 1920, and 25.3 per cent in 1930. *Ibid.*, 108.

32. While the number of women who worked as domestics declined after 1910, large numbers of women were employed for the first time as clerks and stenographers. In fact, more women were employed in both these occupations between 1910 and 1920 than between 1920 and 1930. *Ibid.*, 129, 177.

33. Martha Bensley Bruere and Robert W. Bruere, *Increasing Home Efficiency* (New York, 1914), 236–41.

34.

Item	Total Amount Expended in Millions of Dollars				
	1909	1914	1919	1923	1929
(a) canned fruits and vegetables	162	254	575	625	930
(b) cleaning and polishing preparations	6	9	27	35	46
(c) electricity in household operation	83	132	265	389	615.5
(d) mechanical appliances (refrigerators, sewing machines, washers, cooking)	152	175	419	535	804.1
Percentage of expenditures on household equipment to total expenditures	9.9%	9.2%	10.3%	11.6%	13.2%

cially from the tone and content of advertising in popular magazines when they are compared with advertising at the turn of the century. Generally speaking, women depicted in advertising in or about 1900 are well rounded, have gentle, motherly expressions, soft billowy hair, and delicate hands. They are either sitting down or standing motionless; their facial expressions are immobile as are their corseted figures.[36] After 1910, they are depicted as more active figures with more of their activity taking place outside their homes.[37] One woman tells another over the phone: "Yes[,] drive over right away—I'll be ready. My housework! Oh that's all done. How do I do it? I just let electricity do my work nowadays."[38] Vacuum cleaners permitted the housewife to "Push the Button—and Enjoy the Spingtime!"[39] Van Camp's "Pork and Beans" promised to save her "100 hours yearly,"[40] and Campbell's soups encouraged, "Get some fun out of life," since it was unnecessary to let the "three-meals-a-day problem tie you down to constant drudgery."[41] Wizard Polish, Minute Tapioca, and Minute Gelatine also offered the same promise. The advertising image of women became

---

(a-b) is found in William H. Lough, *High-Level Consumption: Its Behavior; Its Consequences* (New York, 1935), 236, 241. These figures are tabulated in millions of dollars for 1935. Items (c-d) and the percentage of expenditure on household equipment to total expenditures were taken from James Dewhurst, *America's Needs and Resources: A New Survey* (New York, 1955), 702, 704, 180.

35. Realistic novelists noted the leisure of the middle-class women. David Graham Phillips, *The Hungry Heart* (New York, 1909) and *Old Wives for New* (New York, 1908); Robert Herrick, *Together* (New York, 1908), especially 515–17.

36. For example, see *Cosmopolitan*, XXXV (May-Oct. 1903); *Ladies Home Journal*, XXI (Dec. 1903–May 1904). A notable exception showing a woman riding a bicycle may be found in *ibid*. (April 1904), 39.

37. *Ladies Home Journal*, XXXIV (May 1917), for example, shows a woman entertaining stylish women friends (34, 89, 92), driving the car or on an automobile trip (36–37, 74), economizing on time spent in housework (42), the object of "outdoor girl" ads (78), beautifying at a social affair or appearing very chic (102, 106). Perhaps the best illustration for woman's activity in advertisements was employed in *Ladies Home Journal* by Williams Talc Powder. It read, "After the game, the ride, the swim, the brisk walk, or a day at the sea-shore, turn for comfort to Williams Talc Powder." *Ibid.*, XXXIV (July 1917), 74.

38. *Collier's*, 56 (Nov. 27, 1915), 4.

39. *Cosmopolitan*, LIX (June 1915), advertising section, 50.

40. *Collier's*, 56 (Sept. 25, 1915), 22.

41. *Ibid.* (Nov. 27, 1915), 25.

more natural, even nonchalant. A lady entertaining a friend remarks: "I don't have to hurry nowadays. I have a Florence Automatic Oil Stove in my kitchen."[42] It had become "so *very* easy" to wax the floors that well-dressed women could manage them.[43] And they enjoyed a round of social activities driving the family car.[44]

It was in this setting that the flapper appeared along with her older married sister who sought to imitate her. No one at the office or in the next block cared much about their morals as long as the one was efficient and the other paid her bills on time. And given the fact that both these women had more leisure and wished "to participate in what men call 'the game of life' " rather than accept "the mere humdrum of household duties,"[45] it is little wonder that contemporaries rightly assessed the danger of the situation for traditional morals by 1910.

The ensuing decade was marked by the development of a revolution in manners and morals; its chief embodiment was the flapper who was urban based and came primarily from the middle and upper classes. Young—whether in fact or fancy—assertive, and independent, she experimented with intimate dancing, permissive favors, and casual courtships or affairs. She joined men as comrades, and the differences in behavior of the sexes were narrowed. She became in fact in some degree desexualized. She might ask herself, "Am I Not a Boy? Yes, I Am—Not."[46] Her speech, her interest in thrills and excitement, her dress and hair, her more aggressive sexuality, even perhaps her elaborate beautification, which was a statement of intentions, all point to this. Women, whether single or married, became at once more attractive and freer in their morals and paradoxically less feminine. Indeed, the term sexual revolution as applied to the Progressive era means reversal in the traditional role of women just as it describes a pronounced familiarity of the sexes.

The unmarried woman after 1910 was living in the "Day of the

42. *Ladies Home Journal,* XXXV (April 1918), 58.

43. *Ibid.,* 57.

44. *Ibid.,* XXXIII (Jan. 1916), 46–47. Women drove their friends and families about in their cars. *Ibid.,* XXXII (July 1915), 34–35; (Aug. 1915), 38–39; (Oct. 1915), 86; XXXIII (Nov. 1916), 71.

45. Susanne Wilcox, "The Unrest of Modern Women," *Independent,* LXVII (July 8, 1909), 63.

46. Nell Brinkley, a nationally syndicated cartoonist and commentator on women's activities, asked this question of one of her young women. Boston *American,* July 14, 1913.

Girl."[47] Dorothy Dix described "the type of girl that the modern young man falls for" in 1915 as a "husky young woman who can play golf all day and dance all night, and drive a motor car, and give first aid to the injured if anybody gets hurt, and who is in no more danger of swooning than he is."[48] Little wonder she was celebrated in song as "A Dangerous Girl"; the lyrics of one of the popular songs for 1916 read, "You dare me, you scare me, and still I like you more each day. But you're the kind that will charm; and then do harm; you've got a dangerous way."[49] The "most popular art print . . . ever issued" by *Puck* depicts a made-up young lady puckering her lips and saying "Take It From Me!"[50] The American girl of 1900 was not described in similar terms. The lovely and gracious Gibson Girl was too idealized to be real.[51] And when young lovers trysted in advertising, they met at Horlick's Malted Milk Bar; he with his guitar, and she with her parasol.[52] Beatrice Fairfax could still reply archaically about the need for "maidenly reserve" to such queries as those on the proprieties of men staring at women on the streets.[53] And the *Wellesley College News* in 1902 reported that students were not permitted to have a Junior Prom because it would be an occasion for meeting "promiscuous men," although the college sanctioned "girl dances."[54]

The girls, however, dispensed with "maidenly reserve." In 1910, Margaret Deland, the novelist, could announce a "Change in the Feminine Ideal."

> This young person . . . with surprisingly bad manners—has gone to college, and when she graduates she is going to earn her own living . . . she won't go to church; she has views upon marriage and the birth-rate, and she utters them calmly,

47. Nell Brinkley coined the phrase. *Ibid.*, Nov. 14, 1916.

48. *Ibid.*, May 4, 1915. See also *Ladies Home Journal,* XXXII (July 1915), which depicts a young woman driving a speedboat while her boyfriend sits next to her.

49. Boston *American,* Oct. 1, 1916.

50. *Collier's,* 56 (March 4, 1916), 38.

51. Emma B. Kaufman, "The Education of a Debutante," *Cosmopolitan,* XXXV (Sept. 1903), 499–508.

52. *Cosmopolitan,* XXXIX (Oct. 1905).

53. "Girls, Don't Allow Men to be Familiar," Boston *American,* June 17, 1904; *ibid.,* July 15, 1905.

54. *Wellesley College News,* Feb. 20, 1902. Wellesley relented on "men dances" in 1913.

while her mother blushes with embarrassment; she occupies herself, passionately, with everything except the things that used to occupy the minds of girls.[55]

Many young women carried their own latchkeys.[56] Meanwhile, as Dorothy Dix noted, it had become "literally true that the average father does not know, by name or sight, the young man who visits his daughter and who takes her out to places of amusement."[57] She was distressed over the widespread use by young people of the car which she called the "devil's wagon."[58] Another writer asked: "Where Is Your Daughter This Afternoon?" "Are you sure that she is not being drawn into the whirling vortex of afternoon 'trots' . . . ?"[59] Polly, Cliff Sterrett's remarkable comic-strip, modern girl from *Polly and Her Pals,* washed dishes under the shower and dried them with an electric fan; and while her mother tried hard to domesticate her, Polly wondered, "Gee Whiz! I wish I knew what made my nose shine!"[60]

Since young women were working side by side with men and recreating more freely and intimately with them, it was inevitable that they behaved like men. Older people sometimes carped that growing familiarity meant that romance was dead[61] or that "nowadays brides hardly blush, much less faint."[62] And Beatrice Fairfax asked, "Has Sweet Sixteen Vanished?"[63] But some observers were encouraged to note that as girls' ways approximated men's, the sexes were, at least, more comradely.[64] The modern unmarried woman had become a "Diana,

55. Deland, "The Change in the Feminine Ideal," 291.
56. *Ibid.,* 289.
57. Boston *American,* May 6, 1910.
58. *Ibid.,* Sept. 5, 1912.
59. Ethel Watts Mumford, "Where Is Your Daughter This Afternoon?" *Harper's Weekly,* LVIII (Jan. 17, 1914), 28.
60. Boston *American,* Sept. 5, 1916; *ibid.,* Jan. 4, 1914.
61. Alice Duer Miller, "The New Dances and the Younger Generation," *Harper's Bazaar,* XLVI (May 1912), 250.
62. Deland, "Change in the Feminine Ideal," 293.
63. Boston *American,* March 24, 1916. In a letter to the editor of the New York *Times,* one critic of the "women of New York" complained that they seemed to be part of a "new race" or even a "super-sex." He waxed poetic: "Sweet seventeen is rouge-pot mad, And hobbles to her tasks blase, . . . Where are the girls of yesterday?" New York *Times,* July 20, 1914.
64. Miller, "New Dances and the Younger Generation," 250. According to Helen Rowland, the woman was "no longer Man's plaything, but his

Hunting in the Open."[65] Dorothy Dix reported that "nice girls, good girls, girls in good positions in society—frankly take the initiative in furthering an acquaintance with any man who happens to strike their fancy." The new ideal in feminine figure, dress, and hair styles was all semi-masculine. The "1914 Girl" with her "slim hips and boy-carriage" was a "slim, boylike creature."[66] The "new figure is Amazonian, rather than Miloan. It is boyish rather than womanly. It is strong rather than soft."[67] Her dress styles, meanwhile, de-emphasized both hips and bust while they permitted the large waist. The boyish coiffure began in 1912 when young women began to tuck-under their hair with a ribbon;[68] and by 1913–1914, Newport ladies, actresses like Pauline Frederick, then said to be the prettiest girl in America, and the willowy, popular dancer Irene Castle were wearing short hair.[69] By 1915, the *Ladies Home Journal* featured women with short hair on its covers, and even the pure type of woman who advertised Ivory Soap appeared to be shorn.[70]

The unmarried flapper was a determined pleasure-seeker whom novelist Owen Johnson described collectively as "determined to liberate their lives and claim the same rights of judgment as their brothers."[71] The product of a "feminine revolution startling in the shock of its abruptness," she was living in the city independently of her family. Johnson noted: "She is sure of one life only and that one she passionately desires. She wants to live that life to its fullest. . . . She wants adventure. She wants excitement and mystery. She wants to see, to know, to experience. . . ." She expressed both a "passionate revolt against the commonplace" and a "scorn of conventions." Johnson's heroine in *The Salamander,* Doré Baxter, embodied his views. Her carefree motto is reminiscent of Fitzgerald's flappers of the Twenties:

playmate. . . ." Helen Rowland, "The Emancipation of 'the Rib,'" *Delineator,* LXXVII (March 1911), 233.

65. Boston *American,* April 7, 1910.
66. *Ibid.,* March 20, 1914.
67. *Ibid.,* June 11, 1916.
68. *Ibid.,* Nov. 27, Dec. 8, 1912.
69. On Newport and Boston society women see *ibid.,* July 6, 27, Aug. 10, 24, 1913. Pauline Frederick's picture may be found in *ibid.,* Aug. 2, 1913. For Irene Castle, see Mr. and Mrs. Vernon Castle, *Modern Dancing* (New York, 1914), 98, 105.
70. *Ladies Home Journal,* XXXII (July and Sept., 1915); *ibid.* (Nov. 1915), 8.
71. Owen Johnson, *The Salamander* (Indianapolis, 1914), Foreword, n.p.

" 'How do I know what I'll do to-morrow?' "[72] Her nightly prayer, the modest " 'O Lord! give me everything I want!' "[73] Love was her "supreme law of conduct,"[74] and she, like the literary flappers of the Twenties, feared "thirty as a sort of sepulcher, an end of all things!"[75] Johnson believed that all young women in all sections of the country had "a little touch of the Salamander," each alike being impelled by "an impetuous frenzy . . . to sample each new excitement," both the "safe and the dangerous."[76] Girls "seemed determined to have their fling like men," the novelist Gertrude Atherton noted in *Current Opinion,* "and some of the stories [about them] made even my sophisticated hair crackle at the roots. . . ."[77] Beatrice Fairfax deplored the trends, especially the fact that "Making love lightly, boldly and promiscuously seems to be part of our social structure."[78] Young men and women kissed though they did not intend to marry.[79] And kissing was shading into spooning (" 'To Spoon' or 'Not to Spoon' Seems to Be the Burning Question with Modern Young America")[80] and even "petting," which was modish among the collegiate set.[81] In fact, excerpts from the diary of a co-ed written before World War I suggest that experimentation was virtually complete within her peer group. She discussed her "adventures" with other college girls. "We were healthy animals and we were demanding our rights to spring's awakening." As for men, she wrote, "I played square with the men. I always told them I was not out to pin them down to marriage, but that this intimacy was pleasant and I wanted it

72. *Ibid.,* 9.

73. *Ibid.,* 129.

74. *Ibid.,* 66.

75. *Ibid.,* 61.

76. *Ibid.,* Foreword, n.p. Chambers' young heroine Stephanie Cleland in *The Restless Sex,* 191, practiced trial marriage in order to learn by experience. See also Phillips, *Hungry Heart,* 166–80; Terry Ramsaye, *A Million and One Nights: A History of the Motion Picture* (2 vols., New York, 1926), II, 702–04.

77. "Mrs. Atherton Tells of Her 'Perch of the Devil,' " *Current Opinion,* LVII (Nov. 1914), 349.

78. Boston *American,* Feb. 8, 1917.

79. The "kiss of friendship" criticized by Fairfax had become a major issue of her mail by 1913. See, for example, *ibid.,* July 5, 1913. Girls shocked her with inquiries as to whether it was permissible to "soul kiss" on a first date. *Ibid.,* Feb. 13, 1914. An engaged girl asked whether it would be all right to kiss men other than her fiance. *Ibid.,* May 2, 1916.

80. *Ibid.,* Feb. 8, 1917.

81. Fitzgerald, "Echoes of the Jazz Age," 460.

as much as they did. We indulged in sex talk, birth control. . . .
We thought too much about it."[82]

One of the most interesting developments in changing sexual behavior which characterized these years was the blurring of age lines
between young and middle-aged women in silhouette, dress, and cosmetics.[83] A fashion commentator warned matrons, "This is the day
of the figure. . . . The face alone, no matter how pretty, counts
for nothing unless the body is as straight and yielding as every young
girl's."[84] With only slight variations, the optimum style for women's
dress between 1908 and 1918 was a modified sheath, straight up
and down and clinging.[85] How different from the styles of the high-
busted, broad-hipped mother of the race of 1904 for whom Ella
Wheeler Wilcox, the journalist and poet, advised the use of veils
because "the slightest approach to masculinity in woman's attire is
always unlovely and disappointing."[86]

The sloughing off of numerous undergarments and loosening of
others underscored women's quickening activity and increasingly self-
reliant morals. Clinging dresses and their "accompanying lack of
undergarments" eliminated, according to the president of the New
York Cotton Exchange, "at least twelve yards of finished goods for
each adult female inhabitant."[87] Corset makers were forced to make
adjustments too and use more supple materials.[88] Nevertheless, their
sales declined.[89]

82. Thomas, *Unadjusted Girl,* 95.

83. "Today in the world of fashion, all women are young, and they
grow more so all the time." Doeuilet, "When All the World Looks Young,"
Delineator, LXXXIII (Aug. 1913), 20. Advertisements used flattery or
played up the value of youth for women and warned that they might
age unless certain products were used. *Cosmopolitan,* LIX (Nov. 1915),
112; *ibid.* (July 1915), 81; *Ladies Home Journal,* XXXII (Nov. 1915),
65; *Cosmopolitan,* LIX (Oct. 1915), 57.

84. Eleanor Chalmers, "Facts and Figures," *Delineator,* LXXXIV (April
1914), 38.

85. Boston *American,* March 20, 1910; *Delineator,* LXXXIX (Oct.
1916), 66.

86. Boston *American,* March 28, 1904.

87. New York *Tribune,* April 4, 1912; Eleanor Chalmers, "You and
Your Sewing," *Delineator,* LXXXIII (Aug. 1913), 33.

88. Eleanor Chalmers, *Delineator,* LXXXIV (April 1914), 38. The sense
of relief these changes brought is amusingly described in Dorothy A.
Plum, comp., *The Magnificent Enterprise: A Chronicle of Vassar College*
(Poughkeepsie, 1961), 43–44.

89. Percival White, "Figuring Us Out," *North American Review,*
CCXXVII (Jan. 1929), 69.

The American woman of 1910, in contrast with her sister of 1900, avidly cultivated beauty of face and form. In fact, the first American woman whose photographs and advertising image we can clearly recognize as belonging to our times lived between 1910 and 1920. "Nowadays," the speaker for a woman's club declared in 1916, "only the very poor or the extremely careless are old or ugly. You can go to a beauty shop and choose the kind of beauty you will have."[90] Beautification included the use of powder, rouge, lipstick, eyelash and eyebrow stain. Advertising was now manipulating such images for face powder as "Mother tried it and decided to keep it for herself."[91] or "You can have beautiful Eyebrows and Eyelashes. . . . Society women and actresses get them by using Lash-Brow-Ine."[92] Nearly every one of the numerous advertisements for cosmetics promised some variation of "How to Become Beautiful, Fascinating, Attractive."[93]

In her dress as well as her use of cosmetics, the American woman gave evidence that she had abandoned passivity. An unprecedented public display of the female figure characterized the period.[94] Limbs now became legs and more of them showed after 1910, although they were less revealing than the promising hosiery advertisements. Rolled down hose first appeared in 1917.[95] Dresses for opera and restaurant were deeply cut in front and back, and not even the rumor that Mrs. John Jacob Astor had suffered a chest cold as a result of wearing deep decolleté[96] deterred their wearers. As for gowns, "Fashion says—Evening gowns must be sleeveless. . . . afternoon gowns are made with semi-transparent yokes and sleeves."[97] Undoubtedly,

90. Boston *American*, Dec. 10, 1916.

91. *Delineator*, LXXXV (July 1914), 55.

92. Boston *American*, Sept. 3, 1916.

93. *Cosmopolitan*, LIX (July 1915).

94. An editorial declared that women's dresses in 1913 had approached "the danger line of indecency about as closely as they could." New York *Times*, July 6, 1914.

95. *Ladies Home Journal*, XXXIV (Oct. 1917), 98.

96. Boston *American*, June 8, 1907. "The conventions of evening dress have changed radically in the last four or five years. Not so very long ago a high-necked gown was considered *au fait* for all evening functions except formal dinners and the opera. Nowadays, well-dressed women wear decolleté dresses even for home dinners, and semi-decolleté gowns for restaurants and theaters." *Delineator*, LXXV (Jan. 1910), 60.

97. *Cosmopolitan*, LIX (July 1915).

this vogue for transparent blouses and dresses[98] caused the editor of the *Unpopular Review* to declare: "At no time and place under Christianity, except the most corrupt periods in France . . . certainly never before in America, has woman's form been so freely displayed in society and on the street."[99]

In addition to following the example of young women in dress and beautification, middle-aged women, especially those from the middle and upper classes, were espousing their permissive manners and morals.[100] Smoking and, to a lesser extent, drinking in public were becoming fashionable for married women of the upper class and were making headway at other class levels.[101] As early as 1910, a prominent clubwoman stated: "It has become a well-established habit for women to drink cocktails. It is thought the smart thing to do."[102] Even before Gertrude Atherton described in the novel *Black Oxen* the phenomenon of the middle-aged women who sought to be attractive to younger men, supposedly typifying the 1920s,[103] it was evident in the play "Years of Discretion." Written by Frederic Hatton and Fanny Locke Hatton, and staged by Belasco, the play was "welcomed cordially both in New York and Chicago" in 1912. It featured a widowed mother forty-eight years of age, who announces, "I intend to look under forty—lots under. I have never attracted men, but I know I can."[104] Again, "I mean to have a wonderful time. To have

98. *Ladies Home Journal*, XXXII (Oct. 1915), 108; *ibid.*, XXXIII (Oct. 1916), 82; *ibid.*, XXXIII (Nov. 1916), 78–79; *ibid.*, XXXIV (Jan. 1917), 53.

99. "The Cult of St. Vitus," *Unpopular Review*, III (Jan.-March 1915), 94.

100. Boston *American*, July 6, 1912. Dix noted "flirtatious" middle-aged women were "aping the airs and graces of the debutante" and "trying to act kittenish" with men.

101. *Ibid.*, Dec. 6, 10, 1912. Anita Stewart, a movie star who wrote "Talks to Girls," though personally opposed to smoking, admitted that "lots of my friends smoke" and "they are nice girls too." *Ibid.*, Dec. 14, 1915. In 1916, the Boston *American* titled a column on a page devoted to women's interests "To Smoke or Not to Smoke." *Ibid.*, April 12, 1916. The *Harvard Lampoon*, LXXI (June 20, 1916), 376, spoofed women smoking: it carried a heading "Roman Society Women Agree to Give Up Smoking" and a commentary below, "Oh, Nero, how times have changed!"

102. Boston *American*, March 7, 1910.

103. Leuchtenburg, *Perils of Prosperity*, 174–75.

104. " 'Years of Discretion'—A Play of Cupid at Fifty," *Current Opinion*, LIV (Feb. 1913), 116.

all sorts and kinds of experience. I intend to love and be loved, to lie and cheat."[105] Dorothy Dix was dismayed over "the interest that women . . . have in what we are pleased to euphoniously term the 'erotic.' " She continued, "I'll bet there are not ten thousand women in the whole United States who couldn't get one hundred in an examination of the life and habits of Evelyn Nesbitt and Harry Thaw. . . ."[106] Married women among the fashionable set held the great parties, at times scandalous ones which made the 1920s seem staid by comparison.[107] They hired the Negro orchestras at Newport and performed and sometimes invented the daring dances.[108] They conscientiously practiced birth control, as did women of other classes.[109] And they initiated divorce proceedings, secure in the knowl-

Perhaps the best insights on the mores and morals of this group are to be found in the writings of the contemporary, realistic novelist, Robert Herrick.[110] Herrick derived his heroines from "the higher income groups, the wealthy, upper middle, and professional classes among which he preferred to move."[111] His heroines resemble literary flappers of the 1920s in their repudiation of childbearing. "It takes a year out of a woman's life, of course, no matter how she is situated," they say, or, "Cows do that."[112] Since their lives were seldom more than a meaningless round of social experiences, relieved principally by romantic literature, many of them either contemplated or consented

105. *Ibid.,* 117.

106. Boston *American,* April 10, 1908. Evelyn Nesbitt, the wife of Harry Thaw, was romantically involved with architect Stanford White, whom Thaw shot to death.

107. *Ibid.,* Aug. 25, Sept. 1, 1912.

108. Most of the dances which became very popular after 1910, such as the Turkey Trot, the Bunny Hug, and the Grizzly Bear, afforded a maximum of motion in a minimum of space. The Chicken Flip was invented by a Boston society woman. *Ibid.,* Nov. 11, 1912. See also "New Reflections on the Dancing Mania," *Current Opinion,* LV (Oct. 1913), 262.

109. Louis I. Dublin, "Birth Control," *Social Hygiene,* VI (Jan. 1920), 6. edge that many of their best friends had done the same thing.

110. Alfred Kazin, "Three Pioneer Realists," *Saturday Review of Literature,* XX (July 8, 1939), 15. Herrick's biographer, Blake Nevius, declares, "It can be argued that Herrick is the most comprehensive and reliable social historian in American fiction to appear in the interregnum between Howells and the writers of the Twenties. . . ." Blake Nevius, *Robert Herrick: The Development of a Novelist* (Berkeley, 1962), Preface.

111. Nevius, *Robert Herrick,* 177.

112. Herrick, *Together,* 91, 392.

to infidelity. Thus Margaret Pole confesses to her friend, Conny Woodyard, " 'I'd like to lie out on the beach and forget children and servants and husbands, and stop wondering what life is. Yes, I'd like a vacation—in the Windward Islands, with somebody who understood.' 'To wit, a man!' added Conny. 'Yes, a man! But only for the trip.' "[113] They came finally to live for love in a manner that is startlingly reminiscent of some of the famous literary women of the Twenties.[114]

Insights regarding the attitudes of married women from the urban lower middle class can be found in the diary of Ruth Vail Randall, who lived in Chicago from 1911 to the date of her suicide, March 6, 1920.[115] A document of urban sociology, the diary transcends mere personal experience and becomes a commentary on group behavior of the times. Mrs. Randall was reared in a family that owned a grocery store, was graduated from high school in Chicago, and was married at twenty to Norman B. Randall, then twenty-one. She worked after marriage in a department store and later for a brief period as a model. She looked to marriage, especially its romance, as the supreme fulfillment of her life and was bitterly disappointed with her husband. She began to turn to other men whom she met at work or places of recreation, and her husband left her. Fearing that her lover would leave her eventually as well, she killed him and herself.

The diary focuses on those conditions which made the revolution in morals a reality. The young couple lived anonymously in a highly mobile neighborhood where their morals were of their own making. Mrs. Randall did not want children; she aborted their only child.[116] She was also averse to the reserved "womanly" role, which her husband insisted that she assume.[117] She complained, "Why cannot a woman do all man does?"[118] She wished that men and women were

113. *Ibid.*, 263, 250–51, 320–24.

114. Herrick describes the temperament of the modern woman as one of "mistress rather than the wife. . . . 'I shall be a person with a soul of my own. To have me man must win me not once, but daily.' " *Ibid.*, 516. The last sentence above nearly duplicates Rosalind's statement to her beau in *This Side of Paradise*, "I have to be won all over again every time you see me." F. Scott Fitzgerald, *This Side of Paradise* (New York, 1920), 194.

115. Chicago *Herald and Examiner*, March 10-17, 1920.

116. *Ibid.*, March 10, 1920.

117. *Ibid.*, March 11, 1920.

118. *Ibid.*

more alike in their social roles.[119] She repudiated involvement in her home, resolved to exploit equally every privilege which her husband assumed, drank, flirted, and lived promiscuously. Telephones and cars made her extramarital liaisons possible. Even before her divorce, she found another companion; flouting convention, she wrote, "He and I have entered a marriage pact according to our own ideas."[120] Throughout her diary she entertained enormous, almost magical, expectations of love. She complained that her lovers no more than her husband provided what she craved—tenderness and companionship. Disillusionment with one of them caused her to cry out, "I am miserable. I have the utmost contempt for myself. But the lake is near and soon it will be warm. Oh, God to rest in your arms. To rest—and to have peace."[121]

That America was experiencing a major upheaval in morals during the Progressive era is nowhere better ascertained than in the comprehensive efforts by civic officials and censorial citizens to control them. Disapproval extended not only to such well-known staples as alcohol, divorce, and prostitution, but also to dancing, woman's dress, cabarets, theaters and movies, and birth control. "Mrs. Warren's Profession" was withdrawn from the New York stage in 1905 after a one night performance, the manager of the theater later being charged with offending public decency.[122] When a grand jury in New York condemned the "turkey trot and kindred dances" as "indecent," the judge who accepted the presentment noted that "Rome's downfall was due to the degenerate nature of its dancers, and I only hope that we will not suffer the same result."[123] Public dancing was henceforth to be licensed. Mayor John Fitzgerald personally assisted the morals campaign in Boston by ordering the removal from a store of an objectionable picture which portrayed a "show-girl" with her legs crossed.[124] Meanwhile, the "X-Ray Skirt" was outlawed in Portland, Oregon, and Los Angeles;[125] and the police chief of Louisville, Kentucky, ordered the arrest of a number of women appearing on the streets with slit skirts.[126] Witnessing to a general fear that the spreading

119. *Ibid.*, March 11, 12, 1920.
120. *Ibid.*, March 13, 14, 1920.
121. *Ibid.*, March 15, 1920.
122. New York *Tribune,* Nov. 1, 1905.
123. New York *Times,* May 28, 1913.
124. *Ibid.*, Dec. 20, 1912.
125. *Ibid.*, Aug. 20, 23, 1913.
126. *Ibid.*, June 29, 1913.

knowledge of contraception might bring on sexual license, the federal and several state governments enacted sumptuary legislation.[127] And in two celebrated incidents, the offenders, Van K. Allison (1916) in Boston and Margaret Sanger (1917) in New York, were prosecuted and sent to jail.[128]

Public officials were apprehensive about the sweeping influence of the movies on the masses, "at once their book, their drama, their art. To some it has become society, school, and even church."[129] They proceeded to set up boards of censorship with powers to review and condemn movies in four states: Pennsylvania (1911), Ohio (1913), Maryland (1916), and Kansas (1917), and in numerous cities beginning with Chicago in 1907.[130] The Pennsylvania board, for example, prohibited pictures which displayed nudity, prolonged passion, women drinking and smoking, and infidelity. It protected Pennsylvanians from such films produced between 1915 and 1918 as "What Every Girl Should Know," "A Factory Magdalene," and "Damaged Goodness."[131]

Such determination proved unavailing, however, even as the regulatory strictures were being applied. According to one critic the "sex drama" using "plain, blunt language" had become "a commonplace" of the theater after 1910 and gave the "tender passion rather the worst for it in recent years."[132] Vice films packed them in every night, especially after the smashing success of "Traffic in Souls," which reportedly grossed $450,000.[133] In Boston the anti-vice campaign itself languished because there was no means of controlling "the kitchenette-apartment section." "In these apartment houses, there are hundreds of women who live as they please and who entertain as they will."[134] Mayor Fitzgerald's "show-girl," evicted from her saucy

127. Carol Flora Brooks, "The Early History of the Anti-Contraceptive Laws in Massachusetts and Connecticut," *American Quarterly,* XVIII (Spring 1966), 3–23; George E. Worthington, "Statutory Restrictions on Birth Control," *Journal of Social Hygiene,* IX (Nov. 1923), 458–65.

128. Boston *American,* July 14, 21, 1916; New York *Times,* Feb. 6, 1917.

129. *Report of the Pennsylvania State Board of Censors,* June 1, 1915 to Dec. 1, 1915 (Harrisburg, 1916), 6.

130. Ellis Paxson Oberholtzer, *The Morals of the Movie* (Philadelphia, 1922), 115–23.

131. *Report of the Pennsylvania State Board of Censors,* 1915, pp. 14–15; *ibid.,* 1916, pp. 24–25; *ibid.,* 1917, pp. 8–9.

132. Boston *American,* Aug. 10, 1913.

133. Ramsaye, *A Million and One Nights,* II, 617.

134. Boston *American,* July 7, 1917.

perch, gained more notoriety when she appeared in a Boston newspaper the following day.[135] Even Anthony Comstock, that indefatigable
guardian of public morals, had probably come to look a bit like
a comic character living beyond his times.[136]

When Mrs. Sanger was arrested for propagating birth control information in 1917, she confidently stated, "I have nothing to fear. . . .
Regardless of the outcome I shall continue my work, supported by
thousands of men and women throughout the country."[137] Her assurance was well founded. Three years earlier her supporters had founded
a National Birth Control League; and in 1919, this organization
opened its first public clinic.[138] But most encouraging for Mrs. Sanger
was the impressive testimony that many Americans were now practicing or interested in birth control.[139] When Paul B. Blanchard, pastor
of the Maverick Congregational Church in East Boston, protested
the arrest of Van K. Allison, he charged, "If the truth were made
public and the laws which prevent the spreading of even oral information about birth control were strictly enforced how very few of the
married society leaders, judges, doctors, ministers, and businessmen
would be outside the prison dock!"[140]

The foregoing demonstrates that a major shift in American manners
and morals occurred in the Progressive era, especially after 1910.
Changes at this time, though developing out of still earlier conditions,
represented such visible departures from the past and were so commonly practiced as to warrant calling them revolutionary. Too often
scholars have emphasized the Twenties as the period of significant
transition and World War I as a major cause of the phenomenon.
Americans of the 1920s, fresh from the innovative wartime atmosphere, undoubtedly quickened and deepened the revolution. Women

135. *Ibid.*, Dec. 20, 1912.

136. Heywood Broun, *Anthony Comstock: Roundsman of the Lord*
(New York, 1927); Mary Alden Hopkins, "Birth Control and Public
Morals: An Interview with Anthony Comstock," *Harper's Weekly*, LX
(May 22, 1915), 489–90.

137. Boston *American,* Jan. 4, 1917.

138. Norman E. Himes, "Birth Control in Historical and Clinical Perspective," *Annals of the American Academy of Political and Social Sciences,*
160 (March 1932), 53.

139. Dublin, "Birth Control," 6.

140. Boston *American,* July 16, 1916. According to International News
Service, "Mrs. Rose Pastor Stokes was literally mobbed by an eager crowd
in Carnegie Hall when she offered, in defiance of the police, to distribute
printed slips bearing a formula for birth control." *Ibid.*, May 6, 1916.

from smaller cities and towns contested what was familiar terrain to an already seasoned cadre of urban women and a formidable group of defectors. Both in their rhetoric and their practices, apparent even before the war, the earlier group had provided the shibboleths for the 1920s; they first asked, "What are Patterns for?" The revolution in manners and morals was, of course, but an integral part of numerous contemporary political and social movements to free the individual by reordering society. Obviously, the Progressive era, more than the 1920s, represents the substantial beginnings of contemporary American civilization.

The revolution in manners and morals, particularly as it affected women, took the twofold form of more permissive sexuality and diminished femininity. Women from the upper classes participated earlier, as is evidenced by their introductory exhibition of fashions, hair styles, dances, cosmetics, smoking, and drinking. Realistic novels concerned with marriage suggest that they entertained ideas of promiscuity and even infidelity before women of the lower classes. Yet the cardinal condition of change was not sophistication but urban living and the freedom it conferred. As technology and economic progress narrowed the gap between the classes, middle-class women and even those below were free to do many of the same things almost at the same time. Above all, the revolution in manners and morals after 1910 demonstrates that sexual freedom and the twentieth-century American city go together.

DIMENSIONS OF PEACEMAKING

ARTHUR S. LINK

Wilson and the Liberal Peace Program

Close behind American intervention in World War I in historical interest has come the matter of peacemaking. It would be hard to judge whether more energy and emotion have been expended in arguments about President Wilson's performance at the Paris peace conference or about the domestic fight over membership in the League of Nations. The following essay by Wilson's leading biographer reconsiders most of the points at issue in assessing Wilson's accomplishments and failures at the conference table. It is also perhaps the most balanced evaluation of the President's attempt to institute his vision of a new international order.

An influential earlier account which emphasized Wilson's mistakes and shortcomings is Thomas A. Bailey, *Woodrow Wilson and the Lost Peace* (New York, 1944). For some strikingly different perspectives on Wilson's intentions at Paris, which stress his counterrevolutionary thrust against Bolshevism and colonial nationalism, see Arno Mayer, *Politics and Diplomacy of Peacemaking* and N. Gordon Levin, *Woodrow Wilson and World Politics*.

The opportunity for which Wilson had waited since 1915 was now almost at hand. No leader in history ever stood on the eve of a fateful undertaking with higher hopes or nobler ambitions; none, it seemed, even approached his task with greater strength, for he had

Reprinted by permission from *Wilson the Diplomatist: A Look at His Major Foreign Policies* (Baltimore, 1957), pp. 109–125. Copyright © 1957 by the Johns Hopkins Press.

wrung explicit Allied approval of a solemn promise to make peace in accord with a program of his own devising.

It is not my purpose here either to write a biography of Wilson during this period or another history of the Paris Peace Conference.[1] Indeed, to tell the story in all its detail would be to obscure my objective in the balance of this lecture. That objective, simply stated, is to determine the degree to which Wilson succeeded or failed in vindicating the liberal peace program. This can best be done by describing the crucial areas of disagreement and by showing what the outcome was when Wilsonian idealism clashed with Allied ambitions.

The overshadowing necessity of the Paris conference was the devising of plans and measures to assure security for the French against future German aggression. Wilson offered safety in the hope of a Reich reformed because democratic, and in a League of Nations that would provide the machinery for preventing any aggression in the future. To the French, whose territory had been twice invaded by the Germans in less than half a century and who were still inferior in manpower and industry to their eastern neighbor, such promises were not enough. Having lived under the shadow of the German colossus, they were determined to destroy it and by so doing to assure a peaceful Europe. Thus Georges Clemenceau, the French Premier, following plans devised by Marshal Foch and approved even before the United States entered the war, proposed to tear the west bank of the Rhine from Germany by the creation of one or more autonomous Rhenish republics under French control.

Arguing that the dismemberment of Germany in the West would outrageously violate the Pre-Armistice Agreement and create a wound on the body of the world community that would fester for generations to come, Wilson opposed this plan with grim determination during long and violent debates with the French spokesmen. The tension

---

1. This might be a good point at which to acknowledge my indebtedness to several secondary works on the Paris Peace Conference. They are Paul Birdsall, *Versailles Twenty Years After* (New York, 1941); Thomas A. Bailey, *Woodrow Wilson and the Lost Peace* (New York, 1944); Louis A. R. Yates, "The United States and French Security, 1917–1921: A Study of the Treaty of Guarantee," unpublished Ph.D. dissertation, University of Southern California, 1950; and Étienne Mantoux, *The Carthaginian Peace, or The Economic Consequences of Mr. Keynes* (New York, 1952). These studies, especially the first two, provide useful and on the whole balanced summaries for the reader who does not have the time or energy to work through the enormous body of source materials on the conference.

reached a climax during late March and early April, 1919, when Clemenceau accused Wilson of being pro-German and the President ordered his ship, the *George Washington,* to prepare to take him back to the United States. Some agreement, obviously, was a compelling necessity; without it the conference would have failed entirely, and the French would have been at liberty to execute their own plans in their own way.

In the showdown it was the French who made the vital concessions, by yielding their demands for the creation of the Rhenish republics and the permanent French occupation of the Rhineland. In return, Wilson and David Lloyd George, the British Prime Minister, who gave the President important support on this issue, agreed to permit a fifteen-year occupation of the Rhineland and signed with Clemenceau treaties promising that the United States and Great Britain would come to the aid of France if she were attacked by Germany. These concessions saved the conference from actual disruption. Coupled with provisions for the permanent demilitarization of the west bank of the Rhine and a strip along the east bank, and for severe limitations upon German land forces, the guarantee treaties afforded such security as the French were determined to achieve.

A second issue, that of reparations and indemnities, evoked perhaps the most protracted debates at the conference and the most lasting bitterness afterward. In cynical disregard of the Pre-Armistice Agreement, which stipulated that Germany should be liable for civilian damages, Clemenceau and Lloyd George demanded that she be made to shoulder the entire costs of the war to the Allied peoples. In the face of an aroused British and French public opinion and heavy pressure by their leaders, Wilson made perhaps his most conspicuous concessions at Paris. First, he agreed that Germany should be forced to bear the costs of disability pensions to Allied veterans and their families, on the ground that these were really civilian damages. Second, he approved the inclusion of Article 231 in the treaty, by which Germany and her allies were forced to accept responsibility for all Allied war losses and damages, although this responsibility was actually limited to civilian damages in Article 232. Third, he agreed that the French should have the right to occupy the Rhineland beyond the stipulated period if the Germans failed to meet their reparations obligations. In addition, the President consented to the immediate Allied seizure of some $5 billion worth of German property; French ownership of the coal mines in the Saar Valley, as compensation for the wanton destruction wrought in France by the retreating German army; and French occupation of the Saar under the supervision of the League of Nations for twenty years.

Actually, the concessions that Wilson made would not have mattered much if he had succeeded in winning the crucial point for which he and his financial advisers fought so hard. It was the proposal that a Reparations Commission be established to fix a schedule of reparations payments to be made for a definite period, the amount to be determined, not upon the basis of Allied hopes, but upon the basis of Germany's capacity to pay. Under the American plan, moreover, the Commission might reduce or cancel reparations payments altogether if they proved to be more than the German economy could sustain.

In the controversy that ensued the British were badly divided, but they finally veered toward the American position. But on April 5, 1919, just at the time when it seemed that the American plan might prevail, Colonel House (speaking for the ailing President) surrendered unconditionally to the French demands, by agreeing that the Reparations Commission should be instructed only to compute the reparations bill and to enforce its complete payment, without any reference to a definite period or to Germany's capacity to pay. It was a disastrous instance of yielding, for it bound the President to the French position and guaranteed that the reparations settlement would embitter international relations until statesmen finally admitted that it had been a fiasco from the beginning.

A third issue, one that threatened to disrupt the conference almost before it could begin, was the question of the disposition of the former German colonies, all of which had been occupied by Allied forces during the war. In the Fourteen Points Wilson had called for an "absolutely impartial adjustment of all colonial claims" with due regard for the interests of the peoples involved. As he explained during preconference discussions in London in December, 1918, what he had in mind was to make the former German colonies the common property of the League and to have them governed by small nations under specific international mandate and supervision. In pressing for this objective, he ran head-on into commitments for annexation that the British government had made to the dominions and to Japan, and into an absolutely stubborn determination on the part of the latter that these promises should be honored.

The issue was fought out during the opening days of the Paris conference, with Wilson alone arrayed against Lloyd George and the spokesmen of the dominions and of Japan. At no time, it is important to note, did the President envisage the return of the disputed colonies to Germany, for he agreed with most experts who accused the Germans of being oppressive and exploitative masters. (This opinion is still held by most specialists in the field of colonial administration.) Wilson, moreover, soon abandoned his plan for mandating the colonies to small nations, on the ground that it was impractical, and accepted the necessity of a division on the basis of occupation. But he refused to yield the chief objective for which he fought, the clear establishment of the principle that the governments to which the former German possessions were awarded should hold those colonies under the specific mandate and supervision of the League for the benefit of the native peoples affected and of the entire world. This was a notable victory, perhaps more notable than Wilson himself realized, because the establishment of the mandate system spelled the eventual doom of colonialism, not merely in the mandates, but throughout the entire world.

Wilson suffered momentary defeat, however, on the closely related issue of Japanese rights in the Shantung Province of China, a matter infinitely more complicated than the disposition of the German colonies because it involved the entire balance of power in the Far East.[2] The Japanese had entered the war in 1914, captured the German naval base at Kiaochow, China, and overrun the entire German concession in the Shantung Province. They had proceeded afterward, from 1915 to 1917, to impose treaties upon the Chinese government recognizing their rights as successors to Germany in the province and to win a similar recognition from the foreign offices in London, Paris, and Petrograd. Legally, therefore, the Japanese claims at the Paris conference were nearly impregnable.

But technical legalities carried little weight with the man who was fighting to help the Chinese people recover a lost province and to avert the danger of Japanese domination of northern China; and with almost incredible effrontery Wilson set out to vindicate the principle of self-determination. He presented the Chinese delegates to the conference, so that they could plead their own case. He appealed

2. In writing this and the following paragraph, I have leaned heavily upon the recent excellent study, Russell H. Fifield, *Woodrow Wilson and the Far East, The Diplomacy of the Shantung Question* (New York, 1952).

to sentiments and principles with unrivaled eloquence, urging the Japanese to make their contribution to a better world by foregoing conquest. Only after it was indelibly clear that the Japanese would sign no treaty that did not recognize their claims did Wilson withdraw his pressure. In agreeing to recognize Japan's right to the former concession, however, the President won verbal promises that full sovereignty in the Shantung Province would be restored to China, a pledge the Japanese later honored.

A fifth issue, the question of Italian claims to former parts of the Austro-Hungarian Empire, provoked the bitterest personal acrimony at the Paris conference. In line with their national traditions, the Italians had bargained astutely with both alliances in 1914 and 1915 and had entered the war against the Central Powers in the latter year under the terms of the Treaty of London, by which the Allies had promised the Italians the Austrian Trentino to the Brenner Pass, the district of Trieste, the Dalmatian coast below the port of Fiume, and other territories.

There would have been no great conflict at Paris over this matter if the Italians had succeeded in keeping their appetites within reasonable bounds. Following the detailed interpretation of the Fourteen Points prepared by Frank Cobb and Walter Lippmann of The Inquiry in October, 1918, Wilson conceded Italy's claim to the Trentino on strategic grounds even before the peace conference opened, although he perhaps later regretted this concession when he realized the degree to which it violated the principle of self-determination. Nor did he object to the Italian claims to Trieste, which were in accord with the Fourteen Points, even though they had been confirmed in the kind of diplomatic bargaining that he detested most.

Conflict between Wilson and the Italian Prime Minister and Foreign Minister, Vittorio Orlando and Sidney Sonnino, arose chiefly because the latter, not satisfied with their more or less legitimate fruits of victory, demanded also the Adriatic port of Fiume, which had been awarded to the South Slavs by the Treaty of London and would be the only good outlet to the sea for the new state of Yugoslavia. By thus overreaching themselves, the Italians alienated their British and French friends and gave Wilson a strategic opportunity that he quickly exploited. In brief, he capitalized upon the weakness of the Italian claim to Fiume to justify a sweeping denial of the Italian right to the Dalmatian coast and, through it, complete control of the Adriatic.

The climax of the grueling battle came on April 23, 1919, when Wilson, sick of making futile pleas to the masters of the old diplomacy, appealed over their heads directly to the Italian people. In a gigantic bluff Orlando and Sonnino left the conference, only to return in early May after it was evident that the President would not yield. There then ensued the most incredible negotiations of the entire conference and a final recognition that the peacemakers could not agree upon the Fiume and Adriatic issues. They were left for settlement by the League of Nations and by direct negotiations between Italy and Yugoslavia.

Four other great issues before the Paris conferees were no less important than the ones we have discussed, but it will serve our purposes here merely to describe the role that Wilson played in helping to find solutions for them.

First, there was the business of redeeming the promise, made by all the belligerents during the war, to establish an independent Poland.[3] The only controversies of any consequence about this matter involved the disposition of the port of Danzig and the German province of Upper Silesia. In both disputes Wilson joined Lloyd George in standing firm against Polish and French demands and in winning the internationalization of Danzig and a plebiscite to determine how Upper Silesia should be partitioned between Germany and Poland.

Second, there was the necessity of deciding the fate of the component remains of the Austro-Hungarian Empire. Wilson's role in this matter has been gravely misunderstood and distorted, especially by certain British critics who have ascribed to him virtually full responsibility for the destruction of the Empire. This is an exaggeration worthy of the good Baron Munchausen. Before the summer of 1918, Wilson had demanded the federalization, not the breaking up, of the realms of the Hapsburgs. Their Empire had already been destroyed from within by centrifugal forces even before Wilson, in the late summer of 1918, specifically amended the Fourteen Points by recognizing the new state of Czechoslovakia and by thus endorsing the idea of breaking up the Austro-Hungarian Empire. By the time that the Paris Peace Conference assembled the new states of Central Europe existed in fact. They would have been created, and their leaders would have demanded the right of self-determination even though Wilson had never uttered that magic word. All that Wilson, or anyone else at

3. See Louis L. Gerson, *Woodrow Wilson and the Rebirth of Poland, 1914–1920* (New Haven, Conn., 1953).

Paris for that matter, could do was to try to draw the least absurd boundary lines possible and to impose arrangements to preserve some degree of economic unity in Central Europe.[4]

Third, there was the even more perplexing necessity of dealing with a chaotic and changing situation in Russia. It is true, as one scholar has recently pointed out, that Wilson's notions about the capacities of the Russian people for effective self-government and self-determination, expressed in Point 6, were romantic.[5] It is also true that he had only a vague understanding of the character of the international communist movement. Yet in spite of it all he arrived intuitively at the right answers, while his Allied conferees, with all their superior knowledge and more "realistic" understanding, arrived at the wrong ones.

In all the inter-Allied discussions about Russia before and during the peace conference, Wilson defended two propositions—first, that the Russian people must be permitted to solve their internal problems without outside intervention, and, second, that communism was a revolutionary answer to egregious wrongs and could be met only by removing its root causes, not by force. As he put it, "In my opinion, trying to stop a revolutionary movement by troops in the field is like using a broom to hold back a great ocean."[6]

Wilson acted throughout in accord with these assumptions.[7] During 1918 he resisted heavy Allied pressure for a general anti-Bolshevik intervention. Finally yielding to what seemed to be military and humane necessities, he sent American troops to Archangel and Vladivostok, but only for specific purposes, not for general political intervention in the Russian Civil War, and only in small numbers and for the briefest time possible, as if to chaperone Allied conduct in

4. As Victor S. Mamatey shows in his excellent study, *The United States and East Central Europe, 1914–1918: A Study in Wilsonian Diplomacy and Propaganda* (Princeton, N.J., 1957).

5. George F. Kennan, *Soviet-American Relations, 1917–1920, Russia Leaves the War,* especially pp. 242–74.

6. Paul Mantoux, *Les Délibérations du Conseil des Quatre* (2 vols., Paris, 1955), I, 55.

7. On this point I have greatly profited by reading Betty Miller Unterberger, *America's Siberian Expedition, 1918–1920* (Durham, N.C., 1956); by my conversations with Professor Chihiro Hosoya of Tokyo, who is presently working upon a large study of the Japanese intervention in Siberia; and by reading parts of the second volume, as yet unpublished, of Professor Kennan's study of Soviet-American relations.

these areas. At the peace conference, moreover, he again resisted all British and French suggestions for intervention in Russia proper and even refused to send American troops to Vienna to help halt what seemed to be an onrushing Bolshevik tide. The British and particularly the French executed their own far-reaching military interventions at this time and later, to be sure, but Wilson was in no way responsible for these fiascos.

Fourth, there was the issue of disarmament, the key, Wilson believed, to peace and security in the future. What the President proposed was that the victors accept virtually the same limitations that they were imposing upon the Germans, by agreeing in the peace treaty itself to abolish conscription, prohibit private manufacture of the implements of war, and maintain armies sufficient only to preserve domestic order and fulfill international obligations. What Wilson encountered was insuperable opposition from the French; what he won, only a vague promise to undertake general disarmament in the future. Perhaps because he made so little progress toward the limitation of land forces, he never seriously proposed naval disarmament at the conference.

We come now to the one issue that took precedence over all the others in Wilson's plans and purposes—the question of the League of Nations, which I mention last because it was so pervasively involved in all the discussions at Paris. There were two divergent concepts of what the League should be and do that cast a revealing light upon the motives and objectives of opposing forces at Paris. One was the French concept of a league of victors, which would be used to guarantee French military domination of the Continent. Embodied in a draft presented at the first meeting of the League of Nations Commission on February 3, 1919, the French plan envisaged the creation of an international army and a general staff with startling supranational powers. The other was Wilson's concept of a league of all nations, the vanquished as well as the victors, in short, a universal alliance for the purpose of creating a concert of power, not really a supranational agency, but one depending upon the leadership of the great powers, the co-operation of sovereign states, and the organized opinion of mankind for its effectiveness.

With strong British support Wilson had his way easily enough in the meetings of the commission that drafted the Covenant, or constitution, of the League. The crucial conflicts came during the discussions of the Council of Ten and the Big Four, when the French, Italians,

Japanese, and even the British at times relentlessly used the threat of refusing to support Wilson's League as a way of exacting concessions on other issues. Time and again Wilson did retreat, but by thus yielding he won the larger goal, a League of Nations constructed almost exactly as he wanted it, the Covenant of which was firmly embedded in all the treaties signed at Paris.

That Covenant was a treaty binding its signatory members in an alliance of nonaggression and friendship and creating the machinery for international co-operation in many fields and for the prevention of war. The heart of the Covenant was embodied in Article 10, which read as follows:

> The Members of the League undertake to respect and preserve as against external aggression the territorial integrity and existing political independence of all Members of the League. In case of any such aggression or in case of any threat or danger of such aggression the Council shall advise upon the means by which this obligation shall be fulfilled.[8]

The structure erected was the League itself, an international parliament with an Assembly in which all members were represented and an executive Council in which the great powers shared a greater responsibility with a minority of smaller states. In addition, there was a judicial branch—a Permanent Court of International Justice—and an administrative arm—a Secretariat and various commissions charged with responsibility for executing the peace treaties and for promoting international co-operation in economic and social fields. It was, Wilson said when he first presented the Covenant to a full session of the conference, "a living thing . . . , a definite guarantee of peace . . . against the things which have just come near bringing the whole structure of civilization into ruin."

Did Wilson fail at Paris? This is a question that has been asked and answered a thousand times by statesmen and scholars since the Versailles Treaty was signed in 1919. It will be asked so long as men remember Woodrow Wilson and the world's first major effort to solve the problem of recurring wars. The answer that one gives depends not only upon the circumstances and mood prevailing at the time it is given, but as well upon the view that one takes of

8. Ray Stannard Baker, *Woodrow Wilson and World Settlement* (3 vols.; Garden City, N.Y., 1922), III, 179.

history and of the potentialities and limitations of human endeavor.
That is to say, it makes a great deal of difference whether one judges
Wilson's work by certain absolute so-called moral standards, or
whether one views what he did remembering the obstacles that he
faced, the pressures under which he labored, the things that were
possible and impossible to achieve at the time, and what would have
happened had he not been present at the conference.

I should perhaps begin my own assessment by saying that the
Versailles Treaty, measured by the standards that Wilson had enunciated from 1916 to 1919, obviously failed to fulfill entirely the liberal
peace program. It was not, as Wilson had demanded in his Peace
without Victory speech and implicitly promised in the Fourteen Points,
a peace among equals. It was, rather, as the Germans contended
then and later, a *diktat* imposed by victors upon a beaten foe. It
shouldered Germany with a reparations liability that was both economically difficult to satisfy and politically a source of future international
conflict.[9] It satisfied the victors' demands for a division of the enemy's
colonies and territories. In several important instances it violated the
principle of self-determination. Finally, it was filled with pin pricks,
like the provision for the trial of the former German Emperor,
that served no purpose except to humiliate the German people. It
does not, therefore, require much argument to prove that Wilson

9. John Maynard Keynes, in his famous *Economic Consequences of
the Peace* (New York, 1920), conclusively proved the utter economic
absurdity of the reparations settlement (the Carthaginian peace) to the
whole postwar generation of scholars in England and America. It is no
longer possible to be quite so dogmatic, for Étienne Mantoux, in *The
Carthaginian Peace, or The Economic Consequences of Mr. Keynes,* has
proved that Keynes was egregiously wrong in his statistical methods and
has demonstrated that German resources were in fact fully adequate to
satisfy the reparations requirements of the Versailles Treaty. This position
is supported by many economists and by Professor Samuel F. Bemis in
his *Diplomatic History of the United States* (New York, 1955 ed.). They
point out that Hitler spent vastly more money on rearmament than the
German nation would have paid in reparations during the 1930's.

These arguments, actually, are unanswerable, but in a larger sense they
are also irrelevant. The question is not whether it was possible for the
Germans to continue reparations payments over a long period, but whether
they were willing to do so; whether the British and French would attempt
to coerce the Germans for a long period if the Germans were not willing
to continue voluntary payments; and whether the monetary returns were
worth all the international ill will that they provoked. To ask the question
this way is, it seems to me, to answer it.

failed to win the settlement that he had demanded and that the Allies had promised in the Pre-Armistice Agreement.

To condemn Wilson because he failed in part is, however, to miss the entire moral of the story of Versailles. That moral is a simple one: The Paris peace settlement reveals more clearly than any other episode of the twentieth century the tension between the ideal and the real in history and the truth of the proposition that failure inheres in all human striving. It does not make much sense merely to list Wilson's failures. We can see their meaning only when we understand *why* he failed as he did.

Wilson failed at Paris not because he did not fight with all his mind and strength for the whole of the liberal peace program. Never before in his career had he fought more tenaciously or pleaded more eloquently. Nor did he fail because, as John Maynard Keynes and Harold Nicolson have portrayed him in their unkind caricatures, he was incompetent, uninformed, and "bamboozled" by men of superior wit and learning.[10] Indeed, after reading the records of the deliberations at Paris one cannot escape the feeling that Wilson was the best informed and on the whole the wisest man among the Big Four.

Wilson failed as he did because his handicaps and the obstacles against which he fought made failure inevitable. In the first place, he had lost most of his strategic advantages by the time that the peace conference opened. German military power, upon which he had relied as a balance against Allied ambitions, was now totally gone. Wilson had no power of coercion over Britain and France, for they were no longer dependent upon American manpower and resources for survival. His only recourse, withdrawal from the conference, would have been utterly fatal to his program. It would have meant inevitably a Carthaginian peace imposed by the French, as the British alone could never have prevented the French from carrying out their plans to destroy Germany. In these circumstances, therefore, compromise was not merely a necessity, but a compelling necessity to avert (from Wilson's point of view) a far worse alternative.

In contrast to the strength of the French were Wilson's other weaknesses. His claim to the right to speak in the name of the American people had been seriously weakened by the election of a Republican Congress in November, 1918, and was denied during the peace confer-

10. Keynes in his *Economic Consequences of the Peace,* cited in the previous footnote, and Nicolson in *Peacemaking 1919, Being Reminiscences of the Paris Peace Conference* (Boston and New York, 1933).

ence itself by Republican leaders like Senator Henry Cabot Lodge. In addition, there was the failure of Colonel House, upon whom Wilson had relied as his strong right arm, to support liberal peace ideals during that period of the conference when House was still the President's spokesman. House was so eager for harmony that he was willing to yield almost any demand and on several crucial occasions seriously undercut and compromised the President.

Another of Wilson's obstacles, namely, the character of his antagonists at Paris, has often been overlooked. Clemenceau, Lloyd George, Orlando, Baron Sonnino, and the Japanese delegates were all tough and resourceful negotiators, masters of the game of diplomacy, quick to seize every advantage that the less experienced American offered.

To overcome such opposition Wilson had at his command the threat of withdrawal, the promise of American support for the right kind of settlement and of leadership in the League of Nations, and the fact that he did speak for liberal groups not only in his own country, but throughout the world as well. These were sources of considerable strength, to be sure, but they were not enough to enable Wilson to impose his own settlement.

In spite of it all Wilson did succeed in winning a settlement that honored more of the Fourteen Points—not to mention the additional thirteen points—than it violated and in large measure vindicated his liberal ideals. There was the restoration of Belgium, the return of Alsace-Lorraine to France, and the creation of an independent Poland with access to the sea. There was the satisfaction of the claims of the Central European and Balkan peoples to self-determination. There was the at least momentary destruction of German military power. Most important, there was the fact that the Paris settlement provided machinery for its own revision through the League of Nations and the hope that the passing of time and American leadership in the League would help to heal the world's wounds and build a future free from fear.

As it turned out, many of Wilson's expectations were fulfilled even though the American people refused to play the part assigned to them. For example, the reparations problem was finally solved in the 1920's in a way not dissimilar from the method that Wilson had proposed. Germany was admitted to the League in 1926, and that organization ceased to be a mere league of victors. Effective naval disarmament was accomplished in 1921 and 1930. Even the great and hitherto elusive goal of land disarmament and the recognition of Germany's right to military equality was being seriously sought by international action in the early 1930's. In brief, the Paris settlement, in spite of its imperfections, did create a new international order that functioned well, relatively speaking. And it failed, not because it was imperfect, but because it was not defended when challenges arose in the 1930's.

Thus I conclude by suggesting that for Woodrow Wilson the Paris Peace Conference was more a time of heroic striving and impressive achievement than of failure. By fighting against odds that would have caused weaker men to surrender, he was able to prevent the Carthaginian kind of peace that we have seen to our regret in our own time; and he was able to create the machinery for the gradual attainment of the kind of settlement that he would have liked to impose at once. The Paris settlement, therefore, was not inevitably a "lost peace." It could have been, rather, the foundation of a viable and secure world order and therefore a lasting memorial to its chief architect, if only the victors had maintained the will to enforce what Wilson signed.

RALPH A. STONE

The Irreconcilables' Alternatives
to the League of Nations

Discussion of the controversy over American membership in the League of Nations has usually centered on the fight between Wilson and his principal adversary, Senator Henry Cabot Lodge. Likewise, most historians who have written on the controversy have shared the assumption that the United States should have joined the League, though several have doubted whether the stakes were so high as either Wilson's supporters or opponents claimed. Until recently, little attention has been paid to the "irreconcilables" of 1919 who, unlike Lodge, absolutely rejected League membership and virtually all overseas political commitments. As in the case of more general treatments of isolationism, the irreconcilables' ideas and motives have usually been dismissed as either ignorant or vindictive forms of obstructionism. Criticism of that view has sprung largely from the work of Ralph A. Stone. In this essay, and later in a book-length study, *The Irreconcilables: The Fight Against the League of Nations* (Lexington, Ky., 1970), Stone has treated them as a diverse set of spokesmen for carefully considered, often humane and idealistic positions toward international affairs.

The fullest account of the League fight, which evenhandedly criticizes Wilson while condemning Lodge and dismissing the irreconcilables, is Thomas A. Bailey, *Woodrow Wilson and the Great Betrayal* (New York, 1945). John A. Garraty, *Henry Cabot Lodge: A Biography* (New York, 1953) is helpful for understanding the role of Wilson's chief antagonist. The fullest treatment of an irreconcilable's foreign policy may be found in Robert J. Maddox, *William E. Borah and American Foreign Policy* (Baton Rouge, La., 1970).

On the night of November 19, 1919, a happy crowd of people, including several Senators and their wives and assorted other guests, gathered

Reprinted by permission from *Mid-America*, XLIX (July 1967), 163–173.

for a victory party at the Washington home of Alice Roosevelt Longworth, daughter of the recently deceased President, Theodore Roosevelt. They had come from the Capitol where, a short time before, the United States Senate had rejected on three separate votes resolutions to approve the Treaty of Versailles and thereby bring the United States into the League of Nations. Four months to the day later, on March 19, 1920, another party was held at Mrs. Longworth's to mark what was to be the final defeat of the Treaty.[1] That afternoon the Senate had failed by a margin of seven votes to give it the necessary two-thirds approval. Of all those who celebrated this result, none had cause to feel more jubilant than a small band of sixteen Senators, sometimes referred to as the bitter-enders or battalion of death, but better known as the irreconcilables, who had fought for the complete rejection of the Treaty, irrespective of any qualifying reservations. They were: William E. Borah of Idaho, Frank B. Brandegee of Connecticut, Albert B. Fall of New Mexico, Bert M. Fernald of Maine, Joseph France of Maryland, Asle J. Gronna of North Dakota, Hiram W. Johnson of California, Philander C. Knox of Pennsylvania, Robert M. La Follette of Wisconsin, Joseph Medill McCormick of Illinois, George H. Moses of New Hampshire, George W. Norris of Nebraska, Miles Poindexter of Washington, James A. Reed of Missouri, Lawrence Y. Sherman of Illinois, and Charles S. Thomas of Colorado.[2]

Despite the national prominence of many of the irreconcilables, surprisingly little of a scholarly nature has been written about them. Biographies of a few of the more outstanding individuals have appeared in recent years and others can be expected soon, but almost nothing is to be found on several less well known bitter-enders.[3] More-

1. Alice Roosevelt Longworth, *Crowded Hours,* New York and London, 1933, 292, 303.

2. There is much confusion about the number and identity of the irreconcilables. Different authors list twelve, thirteen, fourteen, fifteen, sixteen, nineteen, and "a dozen or so." The sixteen named above were the only Senators to vote against the Treaty, to be paired against it, or to have it announced they would have voted against it on each of the four separate resolutions of approval.

3. Only Borah and La Follette have had full biographies. Claudius O. Johnson, *Borah of Idaho,* New York, 1936, and Marian C. McKenna, *Borah,* Ann Arbor, 1961, are good, though neither utilizes related manuscript collections sufficiently. Belle Case La Follette and Fola La Follette, *Robert M. La Follette,* 2 vols., New York, 1953 is packed with information, not all of it critically analyzed. What promises to be a thorough biography

over, biographies do not usually relate their subjects to the group as a whole. Thus, there are still many questions which remain unanswered. For example, did the irreconcilables agree on the Treaty's principal weaknesses, and if not, to what degree were their differences the result of ideology, domestic politics, local pressures, or some other force? Were their criticisms of the League chiefly demagogic, or did they show a realistic grasp of some of the flaws in the concept of collective security? Was their bitter opposition in 1919 consistent with both their earlier and later positions? Also of interest are questions about their parliamentary strategy, their relationship to Henry Cabot Lodge, speaking campaigns outside the Senate, and sources of financial support.

One important question which touches many of the above concerns their alternatives to the League of Nations. Did the bitter-enders offer, along with their wide-ranging attacks on the League, any substitute plans? They spurned as wholly inadequate the reservationists' hope of qualifying the existing Treaty, including the League, so as to make it reasonably acceptable. Were the irreconcilables, then, out-and-out negativists, or, at best, positive defenders of outmoded and largely negative policies, notably isolationism? No single answer will suffice. Some irreconcilables proposed almost nothing except adherence to the isolationist precepts and doctrines that had been formulated in the late 18th and early 19th centuries. Other bitter-enders, however, do not fit this description, and, in fact, offered alternatives of some merit. Divided according to the kinds of alternatives proposed, the irreconcilables fall into three loosely-defined groups.

In the first group were those irreconcilables who were both isolationists and extreme nationalists. These men preached a simple message, one with deep and well-nurtured roots. America, they proclaimed, must be the sole commander of its destiny, proud of its institutions, true to its Founding Fathers, free to act as it chose, uncommitted and unentangled, in a world that respected only naked power. William

---

of Norris, by Richard Lowitt, has reached only the first volume, *George W. Norris, The Making of a Progressive 1861–1912,* Syracuse, 1963. Sewell Thomas, *Silhouettes of Charles S. Thomas, Colorado Governor and United States Senator,* Caldwell, 1959, and Lee Meriwether, *Jim Reed: "Senatorial Immortal,"* Webster Groves, 1948 are superficial. Works on Fall and Poindexter are near publication. Especially needed are biographies of Johnson and Knox.

E. Borah, Hiram Johnson, and James Reed belong to this group. Borah, Johnson, and Reed are probably the best known bitter-enders. They, especially Borah, have received most of the attention and at least by implication have been judged representative of the battalion of death as a whole. Why this is so can be readily explained. These three were the most active irreconcilables: on the floor of Congress, out on the stump, and in their correspondence. They were colorful personalities whose quotable and often sensational remarks garnered headlines. They also had ability, above all in their capacity to obstruct or demolish what they opposed. Finally, these three Senators, but particularly Borah and Johnson, led the forces of Senatorial isolationism for more than two decades; they remained active and in the public eye long after most of the other irreconcilables had departed. Therefore, they have overshadowed the remaining bitter-enders. Yet if one uses different criteria to evaluate them, Borah, Johnson, and Reed were not the most important irreconcilables during the League fight. There were other bitter-enders who gave penetrating analyses of the Treaty, who demonstrated greater parliamentary skill, and most significantly, who offered more reasonable alternatives to the League of Nations. By this last criterion the second and third groups deserve more recognition than the isolationists and nationalists.

The second group of irreconcilables, who will be called the "realists,"[4] agreed with Borah, Johnson, and Reed that nationalism was an instrument of good and that the United States must depend primarily upon military power to advance its interests. But they rejected narrow isolationism in favor of limited cooperation among nations with similar interests. This group includes Brandegee, Fall, Knox, McCormick, Moses, Poindexter, Sherman, and Thomas.[5] By far the most influential was Knox, former Attorney General under Theodore Roosevelt and Secretary of State under William Howard Taft. Re-

4. The term "realists" has been selected mainly because these particular irreconcilables liked to think of themselves as tough-minded yet flexible, and who, prior to the League fight, frequently contrasted their views to those of their senatorial colleagues who were called idealistic sentimentalists. These latter included La Follette, Norris, and Gronna, all of whom voted against going to war in April, 1917, and were bitterly attacked at the time by their future comrades.

5. Bert Fernald probably should be in this group. He said hardly enough to allow a judgment to be made, but his conservatism on domestic issues, his criticisms of the Treaty, and the few positive comments he did make would seem to place him with the "realists."

spected for his legal acumen and with more experience in foreign affairs than his colleagues, he was something of an intellectual spokesman for this group. For this reason and also because he devoted more time than the other "realists" to alternatives, Knox shall be given extended attention.

The Pennsylvania bitter-ender stated his views in the opening months of the debate. His first suggestion was that the peacemakers postpone the creation of a league of nations until they had settled the more immediate problems of reparations and territorial settlements. If the idea of a league had merit, he said, there would be time enough for its careful consideration. He made it clear that he did not, like some Senators, reject the league concept on principle. Nor did he accept George Washington's advice on foreign affairs as a sacred standard. The difficult questions growing out of the war would have to be "decided by the application of present wisdom to present conditions, not by the easy misapplication of old wisdom to entirely new conditions."[6]

He then listed the essential requirements for a successful league of nations: first, that the member nations share a common purpose and similar ideals, and second, that the organization pursue limited objectives. If, he said, "too many and too Utopian proposals and too great abnegation and too difficult obligations are made the *sine qua non* of its preservation," the league would surely fail. To avoid or at least to mitigate the effects of these weaknesses, Knox suggested that the wartime coalition of the allies continue as a league of nations. "The centripetal force of a common danger has created the league we have, the entente alliance. Remove the common danger and the centrifugal forces of national individualism if unrestrained by a firm understanding, will at once come into play." The purposes of such a league would be to examine controversies that threatened war, suppress "with its overwhelming power" any war that broke out, and indicate a solution to the conflict.[7]

In succeeding speeches Knox amplified his views. Declaring that the peace and stability of Europe were of fundamental concern to the United States, he outlined what he called "a new American doctrine." This proposal, which he hoped might stand alongside the Monroe Doctrine, was stated in the following words:

6. *Congressional Record,* 65 Cong., 2 Sess., 11485–88 (Oct. 28, 1918); 65 Cong., 3 Sess., 604–05 (Dec. 18, 1918).
    7. *Ibid.,* 65 Cong., 2 Sess., 11485–88 (Oct. 28, 1918).

If a situation should arise in which any power or combination of powers should, directly or indirectly, menace the freedom and peace of Europe, the United States would regard such [a] situation with grave concern as a menace to its own freedom and peace and would consult with other powers affected with a view to concerted action for the removal of such menace.

To implement this policy, "new free states" should be set up "as a cordon to cut off for the future the 'Mittel Europa' and Near Eastern dream of founding world dominion. . . ." The responsibility for settling minor problems among these new states would devolve primarily upon the European powers. But whenever a major threat to the security of these states posed a danger to general European security, the United States would take action. Such a plan, Knox said, was based on his belief that nations normally did not undertake great obligations unless their vital interests were at stake, and that it was better for the United States to rely, not upon the judgment of a "world league" in making crucial commitments, but upon its own judgment in conjunction with that of other nations whose interests paralleled its own, in this case America's allies during the war. A practicable league rested upon the "principle of the creation of community of interest, of self-interest in peace and welfare. . . ." "If we perfect our diplomacy," he concluded, "with due practical regard to" and "the gradual extension of . . . this common-sense principle, we shall enable it . . . to render great service to the world at large."[8]

While Knox was the most articulate "realist" among the irreconcilables, there were others who offered similar alternatives. Brandegee, Fall, McCormick, Moses, Poindexter, Sherman, and Thomas all favored some kind of an understanding between the United States and her wartime allies. They differed only on the form this understanding

8. *Ibid.*, 65 Cong., 3 Sess., 603–06 (Dec. 18, 1918). For Knox's later speeches see *ibid.*, 66 Cong., 3 Sess., 4687–94 (Mar. 1, 1919); 66 Cong., 1 Sess., 894 (June 17, 1919), 4493–4501 (Aug. 29, 1919). Knox offered other alternatives in the course of the debates. He proposed, for example, compulsory arbitration; outlawry of aggressive war; and making the United States a "consulting member" of the League, "with the probability that as time goes on . . . we would become a full member. . . ." However, these were random proposals; his primary alternative was the "new American doctrine." See, in addition to the above, Salmon Levinson to William E. Borah, Dec. 8, 1921, and Levinson to Medill McCormick, Jan. 24, 1922, Salmon O. Levinson Papers, University of Chicago Library; *Cong. Record*, 66 Cong., 2 Sess., 540, 544 (Dec. 13, 1919).

should take. Poindexter wanted a loose entente based "upon nothing more than common sense and good will."[9] Brandegee, Fall, and Sherman preferred an agreement more along the lines Knox had suggested.[10] McCormick and Moses expressed approval of a modified Treaty of Guarantee expressly designed to protect France.[11] Thomas argued for a permanent military alliance of the English-speaking peoples.[12]

The proposals of the "realists" emanated to some degree from a pessimistic philosophy of man. Man was, according to their way of thinking, a selfish, vain, cruel, stupid, and power-hungry animal; and man did not change, or if he did, he changed only imperceptibly. What was true of man was even more so of nations. Motives of self-interest governed; morality was given only lip service. The struggle for power inevitably produced conflicts, violence, and war. These philosophical assumptions were stated most precisely in the words of Thomas:

9. *Cong. Record,* 65 Cong., 3 Sess., 1803 (January 21, 1919); Poindexter to W. H. Cowles, January 28, 1919, Miles Poindexter Papers, University of Virginia Library, Charlottesville; *New York Tribune,* Nov. 13, 1918; *New York Sun,* Mar. 6, 1919. Poindexter announced later in the debates that he would support Knox's "doctrine" if it were not made a part of the League. *Cong. Record,* 66 Cong., 1 Sess., 8435 (Nov. 13, 1919).

10. See *Cong. Record.* 66 Cong., 1 Sess., 7009 (Oct. 16, 1919) and 9777 (Nov. 19, 1919) for Brandegee's remarks; *ibid.,* 2062 (June 30, 1919) for statement by Fall; *ibid.,* 65 Cong., 3 Sess., 4866 (Mar. 3, 1919), Lawrence Sherman to Ruth F. Bonsall, Jan. 6, 1919, and Sherman to C. W. Baldridge, Jan. 6, 1919, Lawrence Sherman Papers, in possession of his daughter, Mrs. Marion W. Graham, Daytona Beach, Florida, for Sherman's position.

11. McCormick to Wiliam Jennings Bryan, Nov. 22, 1919, William Jennings Bryan Papers, Manuscript Division, Library of Congress; McCormick to Arthur W. Page, Aug. 12, 1921, Medill McCormick Papers in possession of his daughter, Mrs. Garvin E. Tankersley, Washington, D.C. See Louis A. R. Yates, *The United States and French Security, 1917–1921,* New York, 1957, 120 and fn. 140 for the views of Moses; and *New York Tribune,* Mar. 23, 1919. Fall also announced that he would accept, with certain limitations, the Guarantee Treaty; Yates, *The United States and French Security,* 128.

12. Thomas thought that an alliance might grow into a league of nations; but "in the nature of things a league must be a growth. It can only find its rudiments in conventions." *Cong. Record,* 65 Cong., 3 Sess., 997–98 (Jan. 3, 1919); 66 Cong., 1 Sess., 3320 (July 29, 1919), 7502 (Oct. 25, 1919). An address to the New York State Bar Association on Jan. 17, 1920, contains a clear statement of his views, Charles Thomas Papers, State Historical Society of Colorado, Denver.

Morality is a static element in human affairs, which neither grows nor diminishes. The observance of its essentials may be more active in one age or country than in another, but its quality is essentially unchangeable. . . .

If it be true . . . that man advances and his social condition improves with his extending grasp and domination of material things, and that his happiness and comfort are the outgrowth of the same forces which breed strife and conflict, then it must be true that their peaceful adjustment can not depend with safety upon the possible concentration of static elements upon them. For man is a fighting animal, and life even in the most orderly communities is a continuing contest. We speak of our ambitions, our difficulties, our accomplishments, and our affections in terms of conflict. We practice self-restraint with indifferent success and transfer our battles wherever possible from the field to the forum. This does not change the nature of man, but only his methods of waging wars. Morality is an invaluable ally of peace and of war when its precepts are duly observed by all. But if depended upon as a controlling influence in international affairs, it is apt, like a poorly tempered sword, to break in the hands at the moment of its greatest need.[13]

The conclusion was inescapable: any association of heterogeneous nations that placed much reliance on moral force was doomed to fail. The only solution to evil in the world, and a limited solution at best, was military power and friendly ties with nations whose good will counted for something.

This pessimistic "realism" was flatly rejected by the third group

13. *Cong. Record,* 65 Cong., 3 Sess., 997–98 (Jan. 3, 1919). To be sure, this pessimistic outlook was not limited to the "realists." Borah, Johnson, and Reed took a similar view. However, they drew different conclusions than the "realists" as to what could and should be done about man's perversities. All three, for example, rejected the Treaty of Guarantee; and Knox's "new American doctrine" provoked such a hostile reaction from Borah and Johnson that Knox agreed to drop the "doctrine" from a general peace resolution rather than risk a floor fight that might have harmed the anti-League cause. For their objections to the Treaty of Guarantee see Borah to the *New York World,* May 8, 1919, William E. Borah Papers, Manuscript Division, Library of Congress; Hiram Johnson to Albert J. Beveridge, Nov. 24, 1919, Albert J. Beveridge Papers, Manuscript Division, Library of Congress; and Yates, *The United States and French Security,* 130.

of irreconcilables, to be called the "idealists," as they often were so referred to at the time. These bitter-enders were philosophical optimists who, in contrast to the "realists," believed strongly in the effectiveness of non-military force as a means to almost unlimited ends. Robert La Follette and George Norris were the best known "idealists," but the most articulate was Joseph France, a relatively obscure Senator from Maryland.[14]

France's approach diverged sharply from that of Knox and the "realists." Knox spoke of man's depravity, his failures, ultimately his wars; France condemned this attitude as barren of hope. "I do not subscribe to any of the doctrines of materialism," he once remarked. "I do not regard the universe as a fortunate or unfortunate but wholly fortuitous aggregation of forces. . . . Beneath all the vast ebb and flow of human events, a divine purposiveness moves resistlessly on to the achievement of great and ethical ends."[15] The "realists" thought primarily in terms of relations between the United States and Europe, and emphasized the preservation of the status quo; the "idealists" addressed themselves to relations between the United States and the world at large, and insisted that progressive change was the key to peace and to ends even greater than peace. "Peace in itself is no purpose," France declared.[16] Simply to maintain the status quo was self-defeating because there were underlying problems that eventually would upset it. The problems he had in mind were worldwide—in Latin America and Africa as well as in Europe—and they demanded the concerted attention of every nation in the world. The United States, as the most progressive nation, had an opportunity and a duty to lead in the search for answers.

As a first step, France said, the United States should call a meeting of the nations in the Western Hemisphere to discuss "plans for the closer cooperation of these Governments in promoting justice, progress, and friendship. . . ." After this meeting the President should invite all of the world's nations to attend a conference in Washington for the purpose of creating a league of nations or, as France sometimes called it, a world federation. The Maryland irreconcilable envisaged a league that would be universal in membership and subject to popular

14. Asle Gronna belongs with France, La Follette, and Norris. A close personal friend of the latter two, Gronna also agreed with them on most domestic and foreign policies.

15. *Cong. Record*, 65 Cong., 1 Sess., 2049 (May 10, 1917).

16. *Ibid.*, 65 Cong., 3 Sess., 5002 (Mar. 4, 1919).

control. It would have only advisory powers, but its purposes would be varied and dynamic: to formulate international law; to reduce commercial rivalries; to devise methods for raising the living standards of "backward" countries, specifically by reclaiming waste land, wisely utilizing natural resources, and educating people to assume their rightful place in the world community; to consider the problems of population and attempt to strike a balance between congestion and sparsity; to "localize hostilities between States by cooperative policing of the high seas . . . "; to provide international credits for Russia, Germany, Austria, China, and other countries to purchase needed agricultural materials so that they might resume production.[17]

France was especially interested in seeing the United States adopt a positive policy toward Africa and Russia. It should, at a minimum, assume primary responsibility for administering the formerly German colonies in Africa:

> The time may come when the maintenance of an open door in Africa may be most important, when our right to make our voice heard in African affairs may result in maintaining the peace of the world, and . . . it would be a grave and perhaps a fatal mistake for us . . . to lose forever our power to exercise that right. . . .

Then, in cooperation with Great Britain, Belgium, and other powers with interests in Africa, the United States should create "a permanent, progressive, and upbuilding policy for the development of all of the people and resources" of that continent.[18] It was no less imperative, France continued, that friendly relations be established with Russia. A first step would be to extend congratulations for her Revolution and to express a desire to assist in establishing institutions of her own choosing. On a more practical level American troops should immediately be withdrawn from Russia, and negotiations should begin "concerning any explanations or reparations" that might be due be-

17. *Ibid.*, 1383 (Jan. 14, 1919); 66 Cong., 2 Sess., 3161 (Feb. 20, 1920).

18. *Ibid.*, 66 Cong., 1 Sess., 8140 (Nov. 8, 1919), 8633 (Nov. 17, 1919). One historian states that France "had given more serious consideration to the mandates than had any other senator." "Rarely have the halls of the Senate resounded with such an eloquent plea in behalf of the African nations." Rayford Logan, *The Senate and the Versailles Mandate System*, Washington, 1945, 37–8.

cause of the Allied invasion. In addition, the embargo should be raised on exports, and credits should be made easily available. Only by taking such measures could the foundations be laid for a lasting peace.[19]

France's proposals were not unlike those suggested by La Follette and Norris. Both of these midwestern bitter-enders were sympathetic to a league of nations that was committeed to the speedy reduction of armaments.[20] Norris wanted a league to go, further and provide for the end of secret diplomacy, abolish the right of conquest, and create an international court of arbitration. That such a league might encroach on American sovereignty did not trouble him. He was prepared to relinquish American sovereignty and even abandon the Monroe Doctrine in return for a league embodying his suggestions. Absolute freedom of action, he maintained, was impossible in any civilized society and the attempt to practice it meant anarchy. Even entangling alliances could not be avoided:

> The world is much smaller than it used to be. The invention of steam, the telegraph, telephone, flying machine, and electrical appliances, have brought the nations of the earth much nearer together. Whether we wish it or not, we are next door neighbors to every nation on earth. If it were possible for us to keep out of European alliances, it would of course, be desirable. But we are only now emerging from an European war, that demonstrates that, try as we may, we cannot keep out of world entanglements.

Disarmament, self-determination, and progressive change were the important objectives, and a truly democratic league dedicated to those objectives could perform a noble service in the cause of peace and

19. *Cong. Record,* 66 Cong., 2 Sess., 3554 (Feb. 27, 1920). Borah and Johnson held a similar view toward Russia and they are sometimes cited as the champions of a more liberal policy. Neither, however, went as far as France. France visited Russia in 1921, had several interviews with Lenin, married a widow of a prominent member of the government, and returned to the United States only to be defeated for re-election in 1922. Royal W. France, *My Native Grounds,* New York, 1957, 23–7; interview with Royal France, the Senator's brother.

20. Ellen Torelle, *The Political Philosophy of Robert M. La Follette,* Madison, Wis., 1920, 417; Belle Case La Follette and Fola La Follette, *Robert M. La Follette,* New York, 1953, II, 993; *La Follette's Magazine* (Madison, Wis., 1909–1929), X (Dec. 1918), 1; XI (Sept. 1919), 134.

justice.[21] Hence, Norris and the "idealists" wanted to encourage its formation. Therein they diverged from the other two groups: from the isolationists who feared that a league would undermine American sovereignty, and from the "realists" who regarded the idea as hopelessly utopian.

In their diverse alternatives to collective security the irreconcilables revealed themselves as more than just a united little band of nay-saying isolationists. They were united, but mainly in their conviction that the Treaty of Versailles must be rejected, not in their reasons for rejecting it, for a similar split of the group is evident in their opposition to the Treaty, and much less in their alternatives to its central provision, the League of Nations. They were nay-sayers, some from long habit and on almost every issue; but on this occasion, it should be noted, the parliamentary situation encouraged negativism. The irreconcilables' immediate and strategically necessary task, as they saw it, was to attack what to them were the Treaty's shortcomings. The Treaty first had to be defeated; alternatives could be discussed later. To suggest substitutes prematurely might be interpreted, as it sometimes was, as a weakening of their resistance. That in turn could affect the actions of Henry Cabot Lodge, Republican majority leader and chairman of the Foreign Relations Committee. Lodge, who saw his role, or one part of it, as that of an honest broker between the irreconcilables on one side of his party and the pro-Treaty mild reservationists on the other, might be forced closer to the mild reservationists in order to maintain his position in the center. If that should lead to an overall weakening of the Republican reservations, enough Democrats might be persuaded to support the Treaty with the reservations despite President Wilson's advice to the contrary. The President himself might even agree to accept reservations in this form. Additionally, there was the possibility that alternatives by the irreconcilables would split the group even further and thereby lessen their cooperation on tactical moves.

Nevertheless, the irreconcilables did offer alternatives. Consistency and well-worked-out details were often lacking, partly because of the parliamentary conditions, but also because of their own intellectual limitations and confusion. In the form presented, the alternatives of

21. See an article by Norris written for the *Lincoln State Journal* (Nebraska), Mar. 30, 1919, copy in the George W. Norris Papers, Manuscript Division, Library of Congress; and *Cong. Record,* 65 Cong., 3 Sess., 77 (Dec. 4, 1918).

the "realists" and "idealists" may not have been as viable as Wilson's concept of collective security, but neither were they valueless, and they surely bear closer scrutiny than those of Borah, Johnson, and Reed. At the very least, the irreconcilables must be viewed as an ideologically diverse group. To categorize the irreconcilables as isolationists is perhaps possible. Isolationism was a broad tradition encompassing a variety of emotional and intellectual commitments. On the other hand, it could be argued that the bitter-enders were more divided among themselves than they were separated from many of their fellow Senators, including some Republicans who voted for the Treaty with reservations and some Democrats who followed Wilson's advice and rejected the Treaty with reservations. The important thing is to examine their ideas, and, as has long been recognized in the case of the Lodge Republicans and Wilsonian Democrats, votes did not fully reflect ideas. The same was true of the battalion of death.

EDWIN A. WEINSTEIN

Woodrow Wilson's Neurological Illness

As in few other events in the twentieth century, the pattern of American participation in World War I was determined by a single man. Woodrow Wilson held entirely in his hands both the decision to enter the war and the choice of accepting or rejecting limitations on membership in the League of Nations in 1919. Much of the historical controversy surrounding the United States' part in the war has thus concerned Wilson's thought and singular personality. Medical, psychological, and psychoanalytic analyses have proliferated in an attempt to explain his actions, especially his obdurate role in the League fight. Of all such studies, by far the best is this essay, written by a distinguished medical specialist who draws upon extensive research and practice in an effort to interpret the President's physiological condition and its influence on his behavior.

The two main psychoanalytic treatments of Wilson are Alexander and Juliette George, *Woodrow Wilson and Colonel House: A Personality Study* (New York, 1956), and Sigmund Freud and William C. Bullitt, *Thomas Woodrow Wilson: Twenty-Eighth President of the United States—A Psychological Study* (Boston, 1967). For an evaluation of Wilson's performance in 1919 which uses medical evidence, see Perry Laukhuff, "The Price of Woodrow Wilson's Illness," *Virginia Quarterly Review,* XXXII (Autumn 1956), 598–610.

Woodrow Wilson had a long history of cerebral vascular disease, beginning when he was a professor at Princeton and culminating in September 1919, when he had a massive stroke which paralyzed the left side of his body and affected his vision and sensation on that side. His illness was also associated with alterations in behavior and personality, and there is a relationship between these changes and the events of Woodrow Wilson's later professional and political careers.

Reprinted by permission from the *Journal of American History,* LVII (September 1970), 324–351.

This study is limited by the paucity of medical records, by the state of medical knowledge in his time, and by the circumstances connected with the unique office of President of the United States. Following his major stroke, President Wilson was not hospitalized; case records were not kept (or they may have been kept and subsequently destroyed); no technical procedures to define the exact location and extent of the brain lesion were carried out; and no tests to evaluate mental function were made. The medical data are restricted further by the nature of the relationship of the President's physicians to their patient, and some of the observations of other persons on the scene are biased for personal and political reasons. There is also the methodological problem of clinical versus historical evidence. The report of one observer may be credited more than that from a more qualified source if the event fits into some clinical syndrome or meets with medical expectations.

The demonstration on neurological grounds of impaired brain function does not necessarily mean that such impairment will contribute in a major way to political inefficiency. In a political system with checks and correctives an executive may respond to reduced capacity by accepting more help and delegating more responsibility. The behavioral sequelae of brain damage, also, may appear predominantly in the area of "private" activity rather than in the political sphere. Moreover, grossly irrational political behavior may occur in the presence of normal brain function. The changes in behavior associated with brain damage take a number of forms. They may involve not only a deficit in intellectual performance but also alterations in social, emotional, and "moral" behavior, which may exist relatively independently of defects in memory and thinking ability. The form is determined by a number of factors. The first is the type, location, extent, and rapidity of development of the brain lesion. The second is the premorbid personality, particularly as it influences the patient's attitude toward his disability and the way he adapts to and compensates for it. The third is the social milieu in which the person functions and the way others in the environment respond to and reinforce his behavior.

In the consideration that one is dealing with a complex interaction of many factors, three tentative criteria for the acceptance of impaired brain function as an etiological or causal agent in political behavior may be set up. First, the appearance of clinical evidence of brain damage should coincide with behavioral change. Second, the behavioral change should involve some impairment in performance. Third, it should be possible to classify actions in the political field into behavioral syndromes known to be associated with certain types of brain damage.

Woodrow Wilson's medical history may be divided conveniently into three stages. The first period, during which his ailments were largely psychosomatic, consisting of a nervous stomach and tension headaches, goes up to 1896 when the first definite manifestations of cerebral vascular disease occurred. The second phase extends to the fall of 1919 when he had his massive stroke resulting in the left hemiplegia (paralysis of the left face, arm, and leg). The third takes up the remainder of his presidential term when much of his ineffective political behavior can be explained on the basis of the changes in symbolic organization that occur after certain lesions of the right cerebral hemisphere.

A great deal has been written about Woodrow Wilson's personality from both the descriptive and psychodynamic points of view, and this account does not attempt to give a rounded picture. Rather, it provides a baseline along which later behavioral changes can be evaluated. A formulation of personality that has been useful in previous studies of the effects of brain damage concerns the behaviors and forms of language with which the person has habitually adapted to stress.[1] The approach involves the way a person organizes his environment and relates to people so that new experiences can be symbolically represented and fitted into coherent patterns. These patterns of relatedness in the social environment include those based on family and gender roles; on religious, political, and social class orientation; on attitudes toward work and accomplishment, the physical self, health, and illness; and on general styles of language and communication. These values are a guide to an individual's perception of reality and furnish the context in which feelings, motives, and goals take on form and meaning. They also provide a means whereby dissonant information can be screened out, disbelieved, reclassified, or otherwise altered so that it fits into what are felt as stable, predictable systems.

The importance of Woodrow Wilson's close relationship with his family, especially his father, has been emphasized by him and his biographers. He grew up enjoying the complete loyalty, interest, devotion, and admiration of his parents, sisters, and younger brother.

1. Edwin A. Weinstein and Robert L. Kahn, *Denial of Illness: Symbolic and Physiological Aspects* (Springfield, Ill., 1955).

His mother was wholly approving and uncritical, and on the occasions when his father criticized or reproached him, he did so in the context of Christian love, duty, and morality. For example, when Joseph Wilson scolded his son for cutting classes at law school, he wrote that he did so only because love made him tell the truth.[2] The family relationships were characterized by the absence of any overt expressions of anger, resentment, envy, or other negative feelings. Woodrow Wilson not only was a dutiful son but also took responsibility for and supported many relatives in his home. Each of his wives adored him, and his children found him enchanting. The strong identification with his family was linked with a certain reticence with outsiders until they had shown what he felt was their complete loyalty and devotion. It also led to his treating close friends—John Grier Hibben and Colonel Edward M. House—as family members and to the intense sorrow that resulted after the break with them.

Woodrow Wilson's concepts of masculine and feminine roles were also shaped by his family and regional background. His parents appeared quite opposite in personality. His father was handsome, forceful, talkative, outgoing, and a leader in the community. His mother, quiet and retiring, confined her interests to her family. He made a sharp dichotomy in his expectations of the behavior of men and women. Toward women he had a chivalrous and patronizing attitude, a view that doubtless contributed to his difficulties at Bryn Mawr where he encountered such "strong-minded women" as Carey Thomas and Lucy Salmon. Throughout his life, he cherished the companionship of loving and devoted women, a need that may have led to his early remarriage. He saw intellectual power, leadership, and logical thinking as masculine qualities, and with men he tended to be competitive and challenging, relishing the opportunity to "match minds."

He and his father had similar attitudes toward work and accomplishment. Their correspondence emphasizes application, success, and self-improvement. In his letters, Joseph Wilson constantly exhorted, encouraged, evaluated, and criticized his son and himself. Each man was firmly convinced that any goal could be reached provided one had enough faith and self-discipline. Achievement and failure, alike, were incentives for further effort. Thus, when Woodrow Wilson was a senior at Princeton, his father wrote, "That you are yourself dissatis-

2. Joseph R. Wilson to Woodrow Wilson, May 6, 1880, Arthur S. Link and others, eds., *The Papers of Woodrow Wilson* (7 vols., Princeton, 1966–1969), I, 654.

fied with your performance I am glad to know. For dissatisfaction with present achievement implies further progress. And *I* do not pronounce what you have written, perfect. It might be considerably improved—and you *will* improve upon it."[3] While praising his son for some accomplishment, Joseph Wilson might point out how things could have been done even more efficiently and might warn him not to let success go to his head. The father motivated his son to aspire to perfection and gave him confidence in his capabilities, but, at times, he inculcated the feeling that, even at the peak of success, Woodrow Wilson had not fully realized his capacity. Even in the moments of his greatest triumphs, Woodrow Wilson was made cognizant of tasks which lay ahead.

An extremely methodical and efficient worker, he functioned deliberately and systematically without wasted time or motion. He dictated letters without hesitations, repetitions, or later corrections. He did not, as a rule, work long hours at Wesleyan or Princeton, and, prior to 1896, he seemed to have a good deal of time for conversation, quiet walks, bicycle rides, and tennis.[4] For him, orderly work habits were a sign of an orderly mind. He told Irwin "Ike" Hoover, the White House usher, that "if a man knows his job, he does not have to work hard."[5] Prior to the outbreak of the war, Woodrow Wilson completed his work as President in three or four hours a day. He had a remarkable ability to grasp and formulate the essentials of a problem with which he had had little or no previous experience. In preparing many of his speeches he would set down the main points and then fill in the illustrations and details, usually in extemporaneous fashion.

Woodrow Wilson's motivations to work and his confidence in his ability were a part of his religious belief. In the Calvinistic ethic of the Wilsons, God used men for His purposes; and in carrying them out, one could strive for goals and face crises with supreme confidence. This orientation sometimes led to overconfidence and rigidity, and to greater concern for success and victory than for the nature of the achievement itself. It also tended to make Woodrow Wilson feel anxious and guilty when not achieving. Work also served to

3. Joseph R. Wilson to Woodrow Wilson, Feb. 25, 1879, *ibid.*, I, 459.

4. Interview of Ray Stannard Baker with Stockton Axson, Ray Stannard Baker Papers (Manuscript Division, Library of Congress).

5. Irwin Hood Hoover, *Forty-Two Years in the White House* (New York, 1934), 267.

overcome feelings of loneliness, depression, and grief. He worked to get over the "blues" when he was separated from Ellen L. Axson in his Johns Hopkins years, and after the death of his mother in 1888, he worked to deaden the pain of the loss.[6]

An important facet of Woodrow Wilson's character was his conviction that one had the ability to control one's actions, feelings, and thoughts. This belief is expressed in his enormous powers of concentration, in his habitual self-discipline, and in his idea that one could, by force of will, put certain thoughts out of one's mind and make one's self feel or think in certain ways. While a professor at Princeton, he told a colleague, Bliss Perry, that when he could not think of a word that he wanted, he did not light up his pipe and walk across the room but would force himself to sit with his fingers on the typewriter keys and make the right word come to him.[7] The quality is also seen in his mastery, prior to his brain illness, of his temper and impatience.

The separation of the controlling and observing self from the experiencing self is illustrated in his habit of self-scrutiny, expressed in his methodical and detailed recording of his thoughts and feelings and his habit of giving a reason for them. In his earlier years, particularly, he was apt to include in his letters a statement of his motive for writing. At Johns Hopkins he began a letter to his fiancée, "I feel justified in writing on this particular day because . . ."[8] He deplored his self-consciousness, comparing it unfavorably to smallpox.[9] The dichotomy is indicated, also, in his statement of how, in a crisis, he felt guided by some intelligent power outside of himself,[10] and is vividly described when, shortly after his inauguration as President, he wrote: "The old kink in me is still there. Everything is persistently *impersonal*. I am administering a great office,—no doubt the greatest in the world,—but I do not seem to be identified with it; it is not me, and I am not it. I am only a commissioner, in charge of its apparatus, living in its offices, and taking upon myself its functions.

6. Ray Stannard Baker, *Woodrow Wilson: Life and Letters* (8 vols., Garden City, 1927–1939), I, 294–95.

7. John A. Garraty, *Woodrow Wilson: A Great Life in Brief* (New York, 1956), 22.

8. Woodrow Wilson to Ellen L. Axson, Oct. 14, 1883, Link and others, eds., *Papers of Woodrow Wilson*, II, 473.

9. Baker, *Woodrow Wilson*, IV, 179.

10. *Ibid.*, I, 70.

This impersonality of my life is a very odd thing, and perhaps robs it of intensity, as it certainly does of pride and self-consciousness (and, maybe, of enjoyment) but at least prevents me from becoming a fool, and thinking myself *It!*"[11]

Woodrow Wilson had a rather ascetic attitude toward the material self. He felt that the body was the servant of the mind and totally disliked pomp and show. He never took more food on his plate than he could consume and, although neat in dress, did not pay attention to the style of his clothes until after he had entered the White House. He seemed indifferent to physical danger and showed no fear of assassination. He demonstrated his belief that the principle transcended the physical aspect of a situation when, wearing a high hat and a cutaway coat and mounted on a horse, he reviewed a regiment of the New Jersey National Guard.[12]

All of these features of Woodrow Wilson's personality entered into his attitudes toward health and illness. His mother was frequently ill and was extremely apprehensive for the health and safety of her family. Her letters to him at college regularly expressed concern, and if he had not written for several days, she was apt to inquire if he had fallen ill. One letter reads: "I shall not be quite satisfied till I hear that you are *quite* rid of your cold. Please tell me particularly how it affects you now—and how it sickened you so seriously at first. Now dont [sic] forget to tell me all this, dear, please. . . ."[13] She worried greatly that he might have to go to a doctor, possibly a not too irrational fear at the time. She avoided upsetting her son with news of her own ailments, about which he would learn later from his father. Her worries were in some degree a projection of her own fears for her health and a means of controlling and feeling close to her son. One senses in Woodrow Wilson's dutiful reporting of his symptoms the fulfilling of a filial obligation.

Joseph Wilson's concern for his son's health was expressed in the context of religious principles and moral exhortation. To feel well and be in good spirits depended on carrying out the laws of right

11. *Ibid.,* IV, 38–39.
12. Cary T. Grayson, *Woodrow Wilson: An Intimate Memoir* (New York, 1959), 44–45; Hoover, *Forty-Two Years in the White House,* 234; Edith Bolling Wilson, *My Memoir* (Indianapolis, 1938), 107.
13. Janet W. Wilson to Woodrow Wilson, March 7, 1877, Link and others, eds., *Papers of Woodrow Wilson,* I, 251–52.

living and having a good conscience before God. The maintenance of one's health was part of one's responsibility to God, and illness was seen as a kind of sin or enemy force to be overcome by the power of will and moral rectitude. Joseph Wilson was himself subject to spells of depression, and, noting the tendency in his son, advised him to throw himself into his daily studies and trust in God.[14] When Woodrow Wilson confessed that he was depressed about the study of the law, his father replied that he could think of no reason for the blues to come to him except that he might fight and conquer them.[15]

While Woodrow Wilson could use his symptoms as a way of gaining sympathy and affection, as shown in his letters to Ellen L. Axson during their courtship, his numerous ailments never interfered with what he considered his duty; and his response to threatened incapacity was to work harder. Prior to 1896, he rarely went to a doctor; and the few consultations recorded were mainly casual encounters and correspondence with medical friends and relatives. From Johns Hopkins in November 1883, he wrote that he had caught a cold and felt thickheaded, but "I am so seldom unwell that it fills me with impatience to be deprived of the full use and command of myself by sickness—which may be proof that discipline is needed; . . . "[16] In apparently incongruous fashion, after complaining to Ellen L. Axson about headaches brought on by too much work and loneliness, he assured her that there was nothing wrong with him. Here, again, is the idea that the physical manifestations of illness are something apart from the responsible self.

The way in which complaints of illness and refusal to admit incapacity can be combined is illustrated in the circumstances of Woodrow Wilson's withdrawal from the University of Virginia Law School. Soon after he entered in the fall of 1879, his letters to his parents became filled with complaints of feelings of depression, dyspepsia, and a cold. Despite these reports of his suffering, he refused to accept the advice of his parents that he withdraw; and eventually left only when his father insisted that it was his duty not to endanger his life and his mother begged him not to sacrifice his health to stubborn pride.[17] He departed suddenly without the usual amenities of leave-

14. *Ibid.,* I, 596–97.
15. *Ibid.*
16. Woodrow Wilson to Ellen L. Axson, Nov. 27, 1883, *ibid.,* II, 551.
17. *Ibid.,* I, 702–03.

taking, suggesting that he had some feelings of guilt. On his return home, his recovery was instantaneous.[18]

Woodrow Wilson's language was an important mode of shaping his social environment and adapting to stress. Someone said that he was born halfway between the Bible and the dictionary, and he was fond of telling how his own clear, precise speech was the result of his father's insistence that he be able to say exactly what he meant. Speaking, especially in public addresses, was a stimulating experience for him. He could establish an emotional bond with and sway his audiences by his use of figures of speech. He had the ability to represent complex political, economic, and social issues in homely illustrations and could make a moral issue of some mundane event. He depended on verbal content for his impact and did not use vocal effects or much gesture. William Bayard Hale, a one-time associate and, later, severe critic, made a valuable content analysis of Woodrow Wilson's linguistic style. Hale cites his predilection for adjectives and tropes and his repetition of favorite words like "counsel" and process." He pokes fun at the affectations and romantic rhetoric of Woodrow Wilson's *George Washington*. Writing in 1919, when knowledge of the functions of symbols was limited, he claimed that Woodrow Wilson's fondness for images and figures of speech was the sign of an inferior mind and a substitute for rational thought.[19] Actually, Woodrow Wilson used metaphorical speech because through it he could relate to people by reason of the way such language enlivens one's sense of reality and evokes a feeling of consensual experience. As Woodrow Wilson once told his fiancée, his speeches gave him a sense of power in dealing with men collectively that he did not feel with them individually.[20] Henry W. Bragdon, a biographer of Woodrow Wilson's Princeton years, tells how during the stress of the Quadrangle Plan, Woodrow Wilson at a meeting with three close faculty friends in his study rose to address them.[21]

The language of Woodrow Wilson's early biographical essays reinforced his sense of identity and served as an antidote to depression. He wrote his articles on William Gladstone and John Bright in March and April of 1880 when he was discontented with the study of law

18. *Ibid.*, II, 9.

19. William Bayard Hale, *The Story of a Style* (New York, 1920).

20. Woodrow Wilson to Ellen L. Axson, Dec. 18, 1884, Link and others, eds., *Papers of Woodrow Wilson*, II, 553.

21. Henry Wilkinson Bragdon, *Woodrow Wilson: The Academic Years* (Cambridge, 1967), 319.

at the University of Virginia, feeling depressed and discouraged, and complaining of bad health. In the ornate figures of speech in which he admired the minds of these great men and in his praise of Bright for maintaining an "undeviating purpose and a will that knows no discouragement and no defeat," he was raising his own spirits.[22]

Woodrow Wilson wrote *George Washington* in 1895–1896 when he was under a great financial strain and heavy pressures of work and time. Probably, his flowery style with its archaisms was a playful indulgence and a means of relaxation. He loved to play with language. As a child he was fascinated by symbols—by names, titles, ranks, and orders. His fondness for reciting poetry, limericks, and nonsense rhymes and doing parodies and comic imitations for his family is well known. The security-making aspects of these activities is emphasized by his repetition of certain passages of which he never tired. He had a large stock of jokes and anecdotes and liked puns. Some people, who had known him at Princeton, felt that he used these to cover up his self-consciousness.[23] Certainly, he used humor to create rapport, disarm opponents, and dominate situations. He was apt to joke about his medical ailments, saying that he had worn out his pen hand, and referring to his digestive troubles as "disturbances in the equatorial regions" and "turmoil in Central America."[24]

While most of Woodrow Wilson's biographers have stated that he had delicate health as a child, there is no firsthand evidence of any ailment in his early years. He complained of a cold during his freshman year at Davidson but completed the term before withdrawing from the college. At Princeton, he had occasional headaches, feelings of dizziness and dullness, gastro-intestinal disturbances, and colds. These symptoms were not frequent and did not cause him to miss classes, and their severity may have been exaggerated by biographers in view of his later record of illness. Dr. Hiram Woods, a Princeton classmate, did not recall that Woodrow Wilson had ever been ill in college. At the University of Virginia Law School, his dyspepsia and headaches were clearly psychosomatic manifestations of anxiety and depression brought on by conflicts over the study of the law, his failure to meet his own and his parents' expectations, and his

22. Woodrow Wilson, "John Bright," Link and others, eds., *Papers of Woodrow Wilson,* I, 608–21.

23. Interview of Henry W. Bragdon with Professor and Mrs. Westcott, Professor and Mrs. Osgood, and Mrs. Scott Agar, July 13, 1940, Woodrow Wilson Collection (Princeton University Library).

24. Grayson, *Woodrow Wilson,* 2.

inability or reluctance to express opposition more openly. These symptoms returned during his unhappy practice of law in Atlanta where they were ascribed to "biliousness." By this time his father had diagnosed their cause and advised him to conquer his real enemy, his *"mental* liver."[25]

Woodrow Wilson entered Johns Hopkins for graduate study in the fall of 1883. There he complained of headaches, occasionally at first but more frequently in the spring of 1884. In February 1884, he saw his friend, Dr. Woods, who assured him they were harmless. Woodrow Wilson attributed his headaches to overwork, to uncertainty over his plans, and to his longing for Ellen L. Axson. At Bryn Mawr, his headaches continued along with bowel disturbances. His illnesses at Bryn Mawr could have been related to general unhappiness, to the stress of writing *The State,* and to the preparation of lectures for numerous courses. Disgusted with his "treacherous digestive organs," he went to a physician who *"laughed"* at him and prescribed some pills, but Woodrow Wilson did not take them and was soon relieved in "mind and bowel."[26] His move to Wesleyan in 1888 was accompanied by a marked improvement in health, which he maintained during his early Princeton years.

Woodrow Wilson's gastrointestinal disturbances recurred in severe fashion in the winter of 1895–1896 when he was teaching post-graduate courses at Johns Hopkins. It was a period when he was under heavy pressure of work and finances. He treated his symptoms by siphoning out the contents of his stomach with a pump that had been recommended by Dr. Francis Delafield of New York. Also, on the advice of his friend, Dr. Charles Mitchell of Baltimore, he planned a vacation trip to England for the summer. The first clinical evidence of structural damage to his nervous system came in late May 1896, probably while he was spending a weekend in Princeton. He suddenly developed weakness and pain in his right arm and numbness in the fingers of his right hand. Over the summer, his condition improved; and in July he wrote from England that his only disability was slight numbness of the ends of his first and second fingers.[27] However, his

25. Joseph Wilson to Woodrow Wilson, Feb. 13, 1883, Link and others, eds., *Papers of Woodrow Wilson,* II, 303–04.

26. Woodrow Wilson to Ellen Axson Wilson, May 26, 1886, *ibid.,* V, 260.

27. Woodrow Wilson to Ellen Axson Wilson, July 3, 1896, Woodrow Wilson Collection.

symptoms persisted after his return to Princeton and it was not until
March 1897, that he was able to write consistently with his right
hand. Subsequent attacks of weakness and paresthesia (abnormal
sensation) in the right upper extremity, necessitating the use of a
special, large penholder and a rubber signature stamp, were to recur
intermittently in transient fashion throughout his career at Princeton.

His response to the events of 1896 was typical of the way he
reacted to incapacity. According to Ray Stannard Baker, Woodrow
Wilson expressed neither worry nor complaint and was so reticent
about letting some of his friends know that they felt aggrieved because
of his seeming neglect of them.[28] To some friends, he wrote apologizing
for not using his right hand. His family, in contrast, was alarmed;
Joseph Wilson exclaimed: "I am afraid Woodrow is going to die."[29]
There is no record that Woodrow Wilson consulted a doctor prior
to his return from England. In characteristic fashion, he learned to
write extremely well with his left hand and, later, to hit a golf ball
left-handed. In his letters to his wife from abroad, he complained
more of his clumsy *left* hand[30] and his hemorrhoids,[31] as if these
were his major concerns. (He habitually complained more about his
relatively minor psychosomatic ills than he did about serious organic
symptoms, which he tended to deny.) The condition was diagnosed
as "neuritis," and he himself called it "writer's cramp."

The nature of his ailment becomes clear in the light of the cata-
strophic events of 1906. On May 28, he awoke completely blind
in his left eye. He was taken by his close friend Hibben to Philadelphia
to consult the famous ophthalmologist, Dr. George de Schweinitz.
De Schweinitz found that the blindness had been caused by the burst-
ing of a blood vessel in the eye and that this was a manifestation
of a more general disease of the arteries, probably high blood pressure,
and told Woodrow Wilson that he must give up active work. In
a letter to her cousins, Ellen Axson Wilson describes the condition
as "incurable" and due to "premature old age," and notes that it
is the same disease that killed his father. Woodrow Wilson was also
seen by an internist, Dr. Alfred Stengel, who found a moderate degree

28. Baker, *Woodrow Wilson,* II, 31.
29. Memo of conversations of Baker and Stockton Axson, Feb. 8, 10,
11, 1923, Ray Stannard Baker Papers.
30. Woodrow Wilson to Ellen Axson Wilson, June 9, 1896, Woodrow
Wilson Collection.
31. Woodrow Wilson to Ellen Axson Wilson, June 17, 1896. *ibid.*

of arterial tension that did not suggest a progressive course, and he felt confident that a rest of three months would restore the patient.[32]

The sequence of episodes of paresthesia in one hand and blindness in the opposite eye is characteristic of occlusive disease of the internal carotid artery, the major supplier of blood to the brain. This vessel gives off a branch, the ophthalmic artery, whose continuation, the central retinal artery, goes to the homolateral retina, and continues on to supply the cerebral hemisphere. Interference with circulation to the hemisphere gives impairment of motion and sensation on the opposite, contralateral side of the body. Thus, the combination of symptoms indicates that there was blocking of the left internal carotid artery. There is no medical evidence for the diagnosis of neuritis because the findings point so clearly to involvement of the brain rather than the peripheral nerves.

The exact way in which occlusive and stenotic disease—a narrowing of the internal carotid artery—produces symptoms is not clearly understood, but it is likely that the paresthesias in the right hand and blindness in the left eye result when clots from the larger vessel block the smaller branches. The clinical course is variable, but tends to be episodic with frequent remissions. The age of onset is between thirty and sixty. The overall duration may be very long with periods of up to twenty-five years reportedly elapsing from initial manifestations to final incapacity. Transient, brief episodes lasting from thirty minutes to several hours, especially involving the hand, are common. These either abate spontaneously or terminate in an enduring hemiplegia (paralysis of a side of the body).[33] The attacks of blindness do not occur at the same time as the other neurological disturbances, and, in contrast to the transitory nature of the paresthesias and weakness, the blindness is enduring. Some of Woodrow Wilson's vision returned, but he had impaired sight in his left eye for the rest of his life.[34] He had another attack involving his right hand in 1908, but no further episodes of paresthesia occurred during his terms as governor and President.[35]

Wilson probably was seen in 1906 by the neurologist Dr. Francis

32. Ellen Axson Wilson to Florence Hoyt, June 27, 1906, Baker, *Woodrow Wilson*, II, 202.

33. P. Bradshaw and E. Casey, "Outcome of Medically Treated Strokes Associated with Stenosis or Occlusion of the Internal Carotid Artery," *British Medical Journal*, 1 (Jan. 1967), 201–05.

34. Grayson, *Woodrow Wilson*, 81.

35. *Ibid.*, 28.

X. Dercum of Philadelphia, who also attended him after his massive stroke of 1919. Dercum's files were destroyed under the terms of his will, but de Schweinitz continued to examine Wilson at approximately yearly intervals. His records have also been discarded, but Dr. Edward S. Gifford, Jr., of Philadelphia, who took over the practice from de Schweinitz's associate, observed: "Woodrow Wilson suffered from a very high blood pressure and his fundi (retinas) showed hypertensive vascular changes with advanced atherosclerosis (thickening of vessel walls), angiospasticity (spasm of retinal vessels), retinal hemorrhages and exudates. These observations were made while Wilson was President."[36]

Eleanor Wilson vividly recalled her father's return from the examination by Dr. de Schweinitz. While the family was engulfed in panic and despair, he was outwardly calm and even gay.[37] Dr. Cary T. Grayson, Woodrow Wilson's physician during his presidency, later told Baker that Woodrow Wilson was extremely despondent. Whatever his feelings, Woodrow Wilson continued in his routine duties as president of Princeton. His letters during his three-month vacation abroad were optimistic despite the minimal improvement in vision. "I am puzzled what to report about myself," he wrote his sister, "I have never felt as if there were anything the matter with me, you know, except for my eye and I can only guess I am improving from the unmistakable increase in energy that comes to me from week to week." He consulted an ophthalmologist, Dr. George A. Berry, and an internist, Dr. F. D. Boyd, in Edinburgh. He cites their opinion that he is fit for work and that a man of his temperament should not stay away from work for too long.[38] It is likely that the Scottish physicians' knowledge of Woodrow Wilson's temperament came from Woodrow Wilson himself. (Boyd was ten years younger than Woodrow Wilson and Berry his approximate age.)

According to Stockton Axson, a subtle change took place in Wilson after 1896. He relaxed less and appeared more intense and all business. He became more impatient of theoretical discussion and more demanding of facts. He no longer would take long bicycle rides on which he would sit by the roadside and chat. It is not likely that the relatively

36. Edward S. Gifford, M.D. to author, Sept. 25, 1967.
37. Eleanor Wilson McAdoo, *The Woodrow Wilsons* (New York, 1937), 93.
38. Woodrow Wilson to Annie Wilson Howe, Aug. 2, 1906; Woodrow Wilson to Ellen Axson Wilson, Sept. 2, 1960, Woodrow Wilson Collection.

slight degree of brain damage was directly involved in these changes in behavior. One does not know whether Wilson suspected that he had sustained a stroke, but he must have experienced a great deal of anxiety over an ailment which, unlike his previous ones, did not yield to rest and relaxation of tension, and which recurred in unpredictable fashion.

From 1906, the behavioral changes were more marked. He became irritable and impulsive, more openly aggressive and less tolerant of criticism and opposition. In the Quadrangle Plan and graduate school controversies he was inconsistent in his statements and actions. This behavior is commonly associated with cerebral vascular disease and in the early stages may be the only clinical manifestation. However, the symptoms are not specific for brain damage and may occur in other situations of stress unassociated with structural brain pathology. While the coincidence with clear evidence of brain damage makes it likely that the latter was a causal factor, it does not, in itself, explain the behavior. Another person similarly afflicted might have responded in a different way. Other factors were his personality and the responses of others to the way he adapted to the stress of his disability.

With the dismal prognosis that he received in 1906, he must have felt that he did not have long to live and that his mental faculties might deteriorate as his father's had. In characteristic fashion, he sought his salvation in work. In April 1907, he said he had originally thought that the Quadrangle Plan would take twenty years, but that now it seemed immediately obtainable.[39] He methodically reorganized his life in the interests of conserving his strength. He obtained a full-time secretary, played golf faithfully, and went on regular vacations to Bermuda. He took naps and learned to fall asleep at will. He reduced his personal contacts and tended to meet members of the Princeton community only on official business. This lack of informal communication proved a serious handicap as, prior to presenting his plan for the abolition of the eating clubs in June 1907, he had mentioned the idea only to three of his intimate friends on the faculty and had ignored the alumni.[40]

The content of the language in which Woodrow Wilson put forth his proposals can be interpreted from the standpoint of his adaptation to stress. He could have made a good case if he had fought the issue of the eating clubs on the basis of social snobbery. Yet, over

39. Baker, *Woodrow Wilson,* II, 226–27.
40. Bragdon, *Woodrow Wilson,* 319.

and over again he asserted that the aim was not social but intellectual and academic. He reiterated that he stood for the attainment of the full intellectual life of the University.[41] Here he may have been symbolically representing and compensating for what he felt was a danger to his own intellectual capacity and morale. One notes his emphasis on "restoration," on "revitalization," and on the "life of the mind." In July 1907, he wrote, "the fight is on, and I regard it, not as a fight for development, but as a fight for the restoration of Princeton. My heart is in it more than it has been in anything else because it is a scheme for salvation."[42] In his December 1906 supplementary report to the Princeton trustees he charged that the club system had disintegrated undergraduate morale. These remarks, however, were interpreted by his adversaries not as self-referential representations but as distortions of fact.

On the whole, Woodrow Wilson made a good clinical recovery which, in retrospect, is not surprising in view of the episodic nature of his illness. At the time, however, his improvement ran counter to the medical knowledge, as evidenced by the later prediction of Dr. S. Weir Mitchell, the eminent neurologist, that Woodrow Wilson would not live through his presidential term of office. The President's recovery also, in a person of his beliefs, may have given him the conviction that God had preserved him and destined him for some great purpose. When he entered the White House in 1913, Woodrow Wilson looked extremely well.[43] Grayson stated that "careful examination and all the medical tests revealed that there was no organic disease,"[44] a statement of doubtful validity in view of de Schweinitz's report on the condition of Woodrow Wilson's eye grounds.

In the spring of 1915, Woodrow Wilson experienced several days of severe, blinding headaches; and he saw de Schweinitz in August of that year. The headaches persisted intermittently,[45] and he continued to consult de Schweinitz semi-annually.[46] Over this period he had frequent "colds," the nature of which is not stated. From about early

41. Arthur S. Link, *Wilson: The Road to the White House* (Princeton, 1947), 51.
42. Woodrow Wilson to Cleveland Dodge, July 1, 1907, Woodrow Wilson Collection.
43. Baker, *Woodrow Wilson,* IV, 13.
44. Grayson, *Woodrow Wilson,* 81.
45. Wilson, *My Memoir,* 116.
46. Cary T. Grayson to Harry A. Garfield, Oct. 1, 1919, Ray Stannard Baker Papers.

1916, he began to show signs of increased tension in the form of irritability and intolerance of opposition.[47] Edmund W. Starling, the Secret Service agent assigned to protect the President, says that Woodrow Wilson first showed signs of strain in December 1917, with outbursts of anger in relatively trivial situations.[48] In view of the great stress to which the President was subject during the war, it is impossible to judge to what degree impaired vascular supply to the brain was a factor in his behavior.

The relationship of Wilson to his physician, Grayson, is of great significance. Grayson was a young navy doctor, who had served in the White House in the William Howard Taft administration. Woodrow Wilson took a liking to him when he did a prompt first aid job on Woodrow Wilson's sister when she fell at a White House reception. Grayson was highly personable and the President was probably wary of doctors in their professional roles after the virtual death sentence passed on him in 1906. He needed a doctor with whom he could have a warm relationship, who was thoroughly devoted to him and whom he could treat as a member of his family. Grayson carried out these roles admirably, much as House did in the political sphere. Grayson gave the President emotional support and supervised his routine of diet and regular exercise.

Grayson's close relationship with the Wilson family, however, created difficulties in his functioning as a physician because his emotional identification contributed to his overlooking or denying the seriousness of illnesses. During the progressively downhill course of Ellen Axson Wilson's fatal sickness (she died in 1914 of tuberculosis of the kidneys), the President and Grayson continued to give out optimistic forecasts. When Stockton Axson saw his sister at the William G. McAdoo wedding, at which Grayson was best man, Stockton Axson was shocked to see how feeble she had become. When he expressed his apprehension, he was reassured by Woodrow Wilson that she was getting well and that Grayson had expressed full expectation of her recovery.[49] Shortly before the end, the facts were given to the President by a friend and former family physician, Dr. E. P. Davis.

47. James Kerney, *The Political Education of Woodrow Wilson* (New York, 1926), 348.

48. Thomas Sugrue and Edmund W. Starling, *Starling of the White House: The Story of the man whose Secret Service detail guarded five presidents from Woodrow Wilson to Franklin D. Roosevelt . . .* (New York, 1946), 47.

49. Interview of Baker and Stockton Axson, Ray Stannard Baker Papers.

It is generally agreed that Woodrow Wilson's first great political mistake was the issuing of an appeal to the people, in October 1918, to show their confidence in his leadership by electing a Democratic Congress. The action itself was, of course, not indicative of any impairment of brain function, but what was disturbing was the language, which Seward W. Livermore describes as "splenetic in temper and petulant in tone."[50] Even Edith Wilson called it undignified.[51] Although the President changed the wording, he insisted on issuing the statement, which contained bitter references to the Republicans, such as the charge that "the return of a Republican majority to either House of Congress would be interpreted on the other side of the water as a repudiation of my leadership." In a similar incident, Richard Hooker, the editor of the Springfield *Republican,* a paper friendly to the administration, urged Wilson to select Taft and another Republican on the peace delegation. Hooker states, "his reply, while personally gracious in the extreme . . . disturbed me at the time by the severity of its condemnation of Taft and made me feel that Wilson's judgment owing to increasing irritation was not as good as it had been."[52] According to Arthur S. Link, the deciding factor in the Democratic defeat of 1918 was not Woodrow Wilson's offense to the supporters of a bipartisan foreign policy, but the resentment of midwestern wheat farmers over a price ceiling while southern cotton was uncontrolled.[53] The President, however, blamed the defeat on the insufficient loyalty to him of Democratic congressmen. As if to compensate further for any feeling of not maintaining his leadership, he told the American experts traveling with him to Paris that the French and British leaders did not represent their people.[54]

On April 3, 1919, at the Paris Peace Conference, Woodrow Wilson was taken sick suddenly with high fever, cough, vomiting, diarrhea, and insomnia. Because of the suddenness and the gastro-intestinal symptoms, Grayson first suspected that the President had been poisoned and then made a diagnosis of influenza.[55] Despite his condition,

50. Seward W. Livermore, *Politics Is Adjourned: Woodrow Wilson and the War Congress, 1916–1918* (Middletown, 1966), 220.

51. Baker, *Woodrow Wilson,* VIII, 510.

52. Memo of Richard Hooker, Ray Stannard Baker Papers.

53. Arthur S. Link, *Woodrow Wilson: A Brief Biography* (Cleveland, 1963), 139.

54. Ray Stannard Baker, *Woodrow Wilson and World Settlement* (3 vols., Garden City, 1923), I, 10.

55. Grayson, *Woodrow Wilson,* 85.

Woodrow Wilson, in characteristic fashion, insisted on working; and business was conducted from his bedside for several days. According to William C. Bullitt, the President, on April 4, had bloody urine and twitching of the left leg and the left side of his face.[56] Ike Hoover states that the President developed markedly irrational behavior. While still in bed, he issued an order forbidding members of the American delegation to use automobiles for recreation, in exact contrary fashion to his previous solicitous suggestions that they take as much diversion motoring as possible. After getting back on his feet, Woodrow Wilson expressed the idea that all the French servants were spies, who spoke perfect English and overheard everything that was said. According to Ike Hoover's account, Woodrow Wilson also claimed that he was personally responsible for the furniture in the palace and became disturbed because some of it had been removed.[57]

These reports pose problems of clinical diagnosis and in the evaluation of the evidence. Bullitt was not present in Woodrow Wilson's bedroom, and his book contains so many inaccuracies and so much anti-Wilson prejudice that he hardly qualifies as a competent witness. However, during the preceding month, the President's left facial muscles had been observed by others as twitching involuntarily,[58] and, in the fall of 1919, he did go on to a full-fledged paralysis of his left side. The President did have an enlarged prostate gland, and urinary obstruction was a serious complication after the September 1919 stroke. The veracity of Ike Hoover's account has been disputed by Thomas A. Bailey,[59] who calls him "not-too-reliable" because Ike Hoover knew nothing of Woodrow Wilson's pre-conference ill health. Yet, Wilson would hardly complain in front of the White House domestic staff. Moreover, Ike Hoover admired Woodrow Wilson's intellect and his considerate attitude toward the staff, and can be considered an impartial witness.

The best reason for accepting Ike Hoover's account of the President's irrational behavior is that the symbolic themes of his delusions and preoccupations were those which Woodrow Wilson had habitually used to express his thoughts and feelings and to adapt to stress.

56. Sigmund Freud and William C. Bullitt, *Thomas Woodrow Wilson, Twenty-eighth President of the United States: A Psychological Study* (Boston, 1967), 246.
57. Hoover, *Forty-Two Years in the White House*, 98–99.
58. Harold Nicolson, *Peacemaking, 1919* (New York, 1965), 196.
59. Thomas A. Bailey, *Woodrow Wilson and the Great Betrayal* (Chicago, 1963), 98.

Automobiles were a favorite figure of speech. (Woodrow Wilson, incidentally, was the first President to ride to his inaugural in an automobile.) In 1906, he had predicted ominously that the automobile would spread socialism in the United States because it gave people the picture of the arrogance of great wealth.[60] In his speeches, Woodrow Wilson liked to use the metaphor to express his ideas about the abuses of trusts, saying that he objected not to automobiles but to people taking joy rides in them.[61] Along with golf, motoring was his favorite relaxation and recreation. In the White House, motoring was a daily activity with each trip numbered and no deviation permitted from a set route.[62] To emphasize his convictions about special privileges before the law, he had insisted that no member of his family or staff exceed the speed limit.[63] The theme was to recur in disturbed behavior when, after his stroke, he was permitted to take automobile rides. When his car was passed by another vehicle, the President would demand that the offending motorists be arrested and tried for speeding.[64] If one considers Woodrow Wilson's habitual passion for motoring and his previous generosity with the staff, his strange action in forbidding the use of cars suggests that he was projecting some sense of guilt and was symbolically punishing himself.

The delusion that all the French servants were spies who spoke perfect English is a highly condensed symbolic representation of his problems with the French, which were acute at the time. In a delusion, one represents his problems in symbols that explain and impart a particularly vivid feeling to the experience by reason of the way the language is an expression of personal identity. "Perfect English" was a favorite idiom and a mainstay of his identity system. The idea that everything he said was overheard by the French suggests that he was symbolizing his defeat by Georges Clemenceau on the Saar and other matters of French security.

In view of Woodrow Wilson's history and his subsequent massive stroke six months later, the most likely cause of his illness in Paris was a cerebral vascular occlusion (blood clot in the brain). A less feasible diagnosis is a virus inflammation of the brain, associated

60. Interview of Bragdon with Professor Jacob N. Beam, Sept. 14, 1942, Woodrow Wilson Collection.
61. Link, *Wilson: The Road to the White House,* 179.
62. Hoover, *Forty-Two Years in the White House,* 61.
63. Grayson, *Woodrow Wilson,* 47–48.
64. Sugrue and Starling, *Starling of the White House,* 157.

with influenza. The episode is an example of what Dr. Walter Alvarez has called "little strokes," as differentiated from "big strokes" associated with gross paralyses and aphasia (loss of speech).[65]

There is also some scattered evidence of other neurological sequelae. Bernard Baruch describes the President coming in to ask Grayson to look at his eye while Baruch and the doctor were conversing. After joining them for a time, the President left and Grayson told Baruch, "He didn't have anything the matter with his eye. He just wanted to come up and be with us."[66] Knowing Grayson's attitude, the remark may have been made to remove any suspicion of Baruch's that the President was ailing. Edith Benham, Edith Bolling Wilson's social secretary, states that in Paris the President avoided walking.[67] This would be a marked change, as walking had long been a favorite diversion. That some motor weakness or incoordination may have been present is suggested by Starling's recollection of how on shipboard returning to America the President stumbled repeatedly over an iron ring set in the deck.[68]

Various observers comment on the change in the President after the April episode. Starling says that he tired more easily and never did regain his old grasp. Herbert Hoover states that prior to the acute illness, Woodrow Wilson was incisive, quick to grasp essentials, unhesitating in his conclusions, and willing to listen to advice. Afterward, he groped for ideas and his mind constantly strove for precedents and previous decisions even in minor matters.[69] In later years, David Lloyd George told Harold Nicolson that he thought Woodrow Wilson had sustained some sort of a stroke and that after April 1 he had fallen increasingly under the influence of Clemenceau.[70] There was a striking change in the President's sleep and work habits. Although feeling tired, he slept poorly in contrast to his usual ability to put himself to sleep regardless of the stress. According to Grayson, Woodrow Wilson deliberately neglected his health by working all

65. Walter C. Alvarez, *Little Strokes* (Philadelphia, 1966).

66. Bernard M. Baruch, *Baruch, the Public Years* (New York, 1960), 127–28.

67. Edith Benham Helm, *The Captains and the Kings* (New York, 1954), 92.

68. Sugrue and Starling, *Starling of the White House*, 145.

69. Herbert Hoover, *The Memoirs of Herbert Hoover: Years of Adventure 1874–1920* (New York, 1951), 468.

70. Harold Nicolson, *Diaries and Letters, 1930–39* (New York, 1966), 123.

hours of the day and night, and even on Sunday.[71] His tour of the western states in September was taken against the advice of his physician.

The episode of April 2 to 5 suggests that he sustained a lesion in the right cerebral hemisphere extending to include deeper structures in the limbic-reticular system. With the history of lesions of the left side of the brain, indicated by the attacks of right-sided paresthesia and left monocular blindness from 1896 to 1908, he now had evidence of bilateral damage, a condition affecting emotional and social behavior more severely than a unilateral lesion. With such involvement, there occur changes in the patient's perception and classification of his environment, so that his designation and recall of issues, events, and people tend to become *metaphorical* representations of his own problems and feelings. This appears in selective fashion so that one may forget and falsify events connected with one's personal problems without showing an overall deficit in memory or thinking. One may recall an incident accurately in one context but not in another where it is being used as the vehicle for the representation of some aspect of illness or incapacity. These patterns of language occur in some degree in any situation of stress, but they are more marked and persistent with structural brain damage. Also, the person becomes less aware of the self-referential aspects.

The President's use of ostensibly referential language to represent aspects of his illness symbolically can be seen in the record of the meeting of the American delegation on June 3. General Tasker Howard Bliss stated his opposition to a French military occupation of Germany. In answer, the President proposed that the matter be taken up by a small group who would meet to exchange views without the usual roundabout expressions of international intercourse, "to learn each others' minds, read minds. . . ."[72] In this statement he may have been resolving concern about his own mind. At the same session, he dismissed the fears of the British and some of his American colleagues that the terms of the treaty in respect to Germany's eastern frontier, reparations, period of occupation, and admission to the League were so harsh that the Germans would not sign the treaty. The President said: "It makes me a little tired for people to come and say now that they are afraid the Germans won't sign, and their fear is based on things that they insisted upon at the time of the

71. Grayson, *Woodrow Wilson,* 83.
72. Baker, *Woodrow Wilson and World Settlement,* III, 493.

writing of the treaty; that makes me very sick. And that is the thing that happened. These people that over-rode our judgment and wrote things into the treaty that are now the stumbling blocks, are falling over themselves to remove these stumbling blocks. . . ."[73] He then specifically cited the British: "They are all unanimous . . . in their funk. Now that makes me very tired. They ought to have been rational to begin with and then they would not have needed to have funked at the end. . . ."[74] One might wonder less at the vehemence of this tirade when it is considered that he may have been referring also to his sickness, fatigue, and stumbling gait.

The President's most direct symbolic representation of his illness came up in a discussion of reparations. Thomas W. Lamont had said that the difficulties would be cleared up if the President, Lloyd George, and Clemenceau would instruct their technical experts to arrive at a definite sum in twenty-four hours. The President replied: "We instructed them once to find a definite sum. And then we got Klotz on the brain."[75] (Louis L. Klotz was the French minister of finance.)

The choice of metaphor in which the patient represents his problems depends on the nature of the problems and the concepts in which he has habitually classified his environment and related to people. For Woodrow Wilson, the significant concepts were those of God, Christian morality and duty, democracy and the people. These were the categories to which experiences were assimilated and given meaning and unity. Under the conditions of altered brain function, he continued to use the same organizing principles and the same "problem solving" language. However, the symbols were now more highly condensed, and the categories contained many more diverse and otherwise unconnected referents. With increasing impairment of brain function, the meaning of events depended less on the actual situation in which they occurred and more on the way they fitted into Wilson's personal identity system. Whereas formerly Woodrow Wilson had used language to shape his environment and control the behavior of others, now his own behavior was to come increasingly under the control of his language.

Much of the controversy over the treaty had to do with changes in the language. Most Democrats saw the alterations in wording that

73. *Ibid.*, 503.
74. *Ibid.*
75. *Ibid.*, 480.

moderate reservations would have required as inconsequential if the treaty could only be ratified, particularly when it was evident that it would not pass the Senate in its original form. For Woodrow Wilson, however, the words had a different order of significance because they were such highly condensed symbols of intense personal experience. This preoccupation with language contributed to the unfavorable result of his meeting with the Senate Foreign Relations Committee in August 1919. The President was asked whether the United States would be obligated to go to war to punish an aggressor should a commercial boycott fail. He replied that while there was no legal obligation, there was a moral one. He agreed that each country would determine for itself what was aggression, but he rejected the suggestion that it be explicitly stated that Congress use its own judgment, insisting that a moral obligation was superior to a legal one and in itself carried the force of truth and righteousness. He maintained that if the United States lived up to its moral obligation, then its judgment would of necessity be right. While a person might escape legal technicalities, he could not escape his own conscience.

This kind of language produced the Republican charge that the President had been evasive, although the Democrats considered his performance eloquent and high-minded. Woodrow Wilson was probably using the word "moral" in an idiosyncratic, personalized context. He had asked for a declaration of war only after a period of great reluctance and had sought justification for the war on moral grounds. His insistence on the specific language appears to have been his defense against feelings of guilt and inadequacy, especially after the compromises that he had been forced to make at Paris. When he said that moral obligations were superior to legal ones and that one could not escape one's conscience, he may well have meant his own conscience and the feeling that, while he was legally justified in declaring war, he had not absolved himself of the moral guilt.

At this meeting the President also denied having had knowledge of the secret treaties prior to going to Europe. These were the arrangements to divide up the territory of the defeated Central Powers that the Allies had made among themselves, and they proved to be the greatest obstacle in the way of the President's aim of a just peace. Despite his denial, the treaties were known to him, and the provision in the Fourteen Points about open covenants was deliberately designed to offset the effect of Soviet revelations about the treaties after the Bolshevik Revolution. For a long time the President had probably wished to deny their existence and consequently acted as though they did not exist. However, it was only under the conditions of altered brain function that he could deny them in the form of a selective amnesia. This explanation is more plausible than the charge that the President was deliberately lying or had become grossly incompetent. Bailey points out that during the questioning the President freely and accurately gave intimate details of subjects that were no less important.[76] In his monograph, Alvarez comments that after a "little stroke" a patient may remember quickly and easily a hundred thousand scientific facts and the meaning of thousands of words in languages not his own, but may forget the name of an old friend whom he wants to introduce to someone.[77] Possibly the same type of amnesia had occurred at the Princeton trustees' meeting of January 13, 1910, when Woodrow Wilson denied that he had read Dean Andrew F. West's graduate school brochure, which he had not only read but also for which he had written a laudatory preface.

On the ill-fated western tour in September 1919, the President had definite signs of cardiac decompensation and brain involvement. He experienced nocturnal episodes of coughing which forced him to sleep in a sitting position, and he complained of severe headaches and double vision. In his last speech at Pueblo on September 25, he stumbled when getting onto the platform, and, uncharacteristically, allowed Starling to assist him. His voice was weak, he mumbled, and there were long pauses as if he were having difficulty in following a train of thought.[78] In the early morning of the next day, September 26, Joseph Tumulty, the President's secretary, found him dressed and sitting in a chair. His whole left side was paralyzed, and he had difficulty in articulating. He pleaded with Tumulty not to cut the trip short as the President's friends and Senator Lodge would say that he was a quitter, and the treaty would be lost. He went on to tell Tumulty that he would be all right if the trip could be postponed for twenty-four hours.[79] By the time the party reached Washington, some power in the left limbs had returned, and the

76. Thomas A. Bailey, *Woodrow Wilson and the Lost Peace* (Chicago, 1963), 148.

77. Alvarez, *Little Strokes*, 33.

78. David Lawrence, *The True Story of Woodrow Wilson* (New York, 1924), 279; Sugrue and Starling, *Starling of the White House*, 152.

79. Joseph P. Tumulty, *Woodrow Wilson as I Know Him* (Garden City, 1921), 446–48.

President was able to walk from the train. He felt better over the next few days, but Grayson was alarmed enough to make appointments for de Schweinitz and Dercum to see the President.[80] On the evening of October 1, he appeared cheerful and played some billiards,[81] but early the next morning Edith Bolling Wilson found him unable to use his left arm and complaining of loss of feeling in it. When she returned from calling Grayson, she found him unconscious on the floor.[82] The hemiplegia proved to be permanent. On November 17, he was able to sit up in a specially braced wheel chair, for the first time; but Woodrow Wilson never recovered any power in his left arm and was able to walk only a short distance with support. Weakness of the left face and jaw persisted. In addition, he probably had sensory loss on his left side and absent vision in the left visual field of both eyes. Superimposed on the visual loss sustained in 1906, the probable hemianopia must have caused almost complete blindness in the left eye and made it extremely difficult for the President to read. He was not aphasic, but after speaking for a time his voice would become weak and indistinct. The illness was complicated by a threat of uremia from a urinary obstruction, which became acute on October 17, but which relieved itself spontaneously.

Following his stroke, the outstanding feature of the President's behavior was his denial of his incapacity. Denial of illness, or anosognosia, literally lack of knowledge of disease, is a common sequel of the type of brain injury received by Wilson. In this condition, the patient denies or appears unaware of such deficits as paralysis or blindness. While recognizing a limb as paralyzed, he may regard it as not a part of his body, attributing its ownership to another person, or referring to it as an inanimate object, often in humorous fashion. Patients commonly talk of their incapacities in the "third person," as if they were occurring in someone else, as in saying that another person is weak or incompetent. When denial is well established, patients are bland and serene or mildly paranoid, as in cases where the patient attributes his paralysis to a faulty injection or mistreatment by the doctors and nurses. Improvement in brain function is often accompanied by weakening of the denial with outbursts of irritability and the appearance of depression. To casual observers, anosognosic patients may appear quite normal and even bright and witty. When

80. Grayson to Garfield, Oct. 1, 1919, Ray Stannard Baker Papers.
81. Grayson, *Woodrow Wilson*, 100.
82. Wilson, *My Memoir*, 287.

not on the subject of their disabilities, they are quite rational; and tests of intelligence may show no deficit. The syndrome of anosognosia, given the necessary conditions of brain dysfunction, is most marked in persons, who, like Woodrow Wilson, have habitually perceived the physical manifestations and consequences of illness in the context of principles and values, and as separate from the real self, who are highly work and efficiency oriented, and who have been accustomed to the overcoming of physical indispositions by force of will and character.[83]

The President did not deny that his left side was paralyzed, but neither he nor Edith Bolling Wilson was aware, or would admit, that the paralysis was a symptom of brain damage. He referred to himself as "lame" and refused to accept the fact that he could not carry on his office. Three days after his stroke, he attempted to dictate to his stenographer, but was dissuaded by his wife on the grounds that it was Sunday.[84] On October 7, he dictated a diplomatic note and communicated his displeasure that a cabinet meeting had been held in his absence.[85] For the President to admit that the meeting was held properly would have meant the admission that he was too ill to attend. Immediately after recovering from his near-fatal urinary obstruction he began to work, sending letters and signing bills. During November he received a few visitors, but he carried on only in a very limited way. Messages were screened by Edith Bolling Wilson and Grayson, and the President was seen for only occasional, brief periods by Tumulty, cabinet members, and Democratic leaders. Usually, Edith Bolling Wilson received them in her sitting room and repeated to them what the President had told her should be done about a particular problem. Memoranda were either not acknowledged or were answered in a short note, in Edith Bolling Wilson's handwriting, quoting the President. Cabinet members did what they could on their own or waited on the President. A factor in Woodrow Wilson's isolation is that he may have felt ashamed of his incapacity. Visitors noted, for example, that he would cover himself in such a way as to conceal

83. Edwin A. Weinstein and Robert L. Kahn, "Personality Factors in Denial of Illness," *American Medical Association Archives of Neurology and Psychiatry,* 69 (March 1953), 355–67.

84. Alden Hatch, *Edith Bolling Wilson: First Lady Extraordinary* (New York, 1961), 223.

85. E. David Cronon, ed., *The Cabinet Diaries of Josephus Daniels 1913–1921* (Lincoln, 1963), 445.

the paralyzed side. He did not resign his office, and he was to seek a third nomination.[86]

In January 1920, the President drafted a remarkable proposal suggesting that his Republican opponents, whom he listed by name, resign and seek reelection on the issue of the League. If a majority were returned, then he, with his vice-president, would resign after appointing a Republican as secretary of state, who, according to the order of succession, would assume the presidency. To assume that Republicans would resign was, of course, unrealistic, and the President was persuaded to pigeonhole his proposals. Yet, in his denial system the gesture was highly meaningful. He was coping with the issue of resignation by representing it in the "third person plural," by talking about the resignation of other people. Also, he was indicating that he might resign not because he was disabled but because he was carrying out the will of the people.

The attitudes of other persons toward the illness were determined by their relationships to the President in personal, professional, and political contexts. Edith Bolling Wilson indignantly rejected the idea that her husband was disabled or had sustained brain damage, regarding these facts as scurrilous rumors.[87] She states that Dercum advised that the President remain in office because he would lose his greatest incentive to get well should he resign and quotes Dercum as pointing out that Louis Pasteur had recovered from the same condition and had gone on to do some of his most brilliant work.

Grayson similarly expressed a great deal of denial of the seriousness of the President's condition. When he met with the cabinet on October 6, he refused to tell the members anything beyond that Woodrow Wilson was suffering from "a nervous breakdown, indigestion and a depleted condition," adding the warning that any excitement might kill him.[88] Later, Grayson told Secretary of the Navy Josephus Daniels that he did not want the truth disclosed[89] and it was not until February 10, 1920, that any reference to Woodrow Wilson's hemiplegia appeared in the press. At that time, Dr. Hugh Young, the urologist

86. Kurt Wimer, "Woodrow Wilson and a Third Term Nomination," *Pennsylvania History*, XXIX (April 1962), 193–211.

87. Wilson, *My Memoir*, 298.

88. David F. Houston, *Eight Years with Wilson's Cabinet, 1913–1920* (2 vols., Garden City, 1926), II, 38.

89. Josephus Daniels, *The Wilson Era: Years of War and After 1917–1923* (Chapel Hill, 1946), 512.

who had been called in when the President developed his urinary obstruction, said that there had been some impairment of function in the left limbs but that now the President was organically sound and that only the inclement weather prevented him from leaving the White House. Young maintained that the vigor and lucidity of the President's mental processes had not been affected in the slightest degree.[90]

Grayson was in conflict over his professional, personal, and family roles. When Stockton Axson asked him if the President had had a stroke, the doctor replied that he did not know.[91] Possibly Grayson was mindful of Ellen Axson Wilson's request to him, on her deathbed, that he "take good care of my husband."[92] Grayson also could not bring himself to tell the President that he could not adequately perform the duties of his office, and his behavior, like that of Edith Bolling Wilson, strongly reinforced Wilson's denial. When, on March 25, Woodrow Wilson brought up the third term issue with Grayson, the doctor stated that "for medical reasons, I preferred not to volunteer any advice. I did not want to tell him that it would be impossible for him to take part in such a campaign, as I was fearful that it might have a depressing effect upon him."[93] In a conversation of April 13, he asked his doctor's advice about resignation in view of the time it would take for him to recover his health and strength. Grayson replied by assuring the President how well he was keeping in touch with and conducting the affairs of the government. He then persuaded the President to call his first cabinet meeting, which was held the next day.[94] In June, however, evidently without Woodrow Wilson's knowledge, Grayson asked Senator Carter Glass of Virginia to convince the President not to seek a third term.[95]

In recalling the cabinet meeting of April 14, Secretary of Agriculture David F. Houston commented on his surprise at hearing his and the others' names announced as they entered,[96] a procedure evidently necessitated by the President's poor vision. Woodrow Wilson appeared

90. Baltimore *Sun,* Feb. 10, 1920.

91. Interview of Baker and Stockton Axson, Sept. 2, 1931, Ray Stannard Baker Papers.

92. Interview of Baker and Grayson, Feb. 18-19, 1926, *ibid.*

93. Grayson, *Woodrow Wilson,* 117.

94. *Ibid.,* 112.

95. Rixey Smith and Norman Beasley, *Carter Glass: A Biography* (New York, 1939), 205.

96. Houston, *Eight Years with Wilson's Cabinet,* II, 69–70.

bright and cheerful and began the session by telling a joke about the Chicago aldermen who got their heads together to form a solid surface. Then there was a silence as the President did not follow up the initiative. When the critical railroad situation was brought up, he seemed to have difficulty at first in fixing his mind on the topic. Grayson looked in several times as if to warn against tiring the President, and at the end of an hour Edith Bolling Wilson suggested that the members leave.

According to Stockton Axson, the President alternated between states of abject depression and periods of a week or so when he would be in good spirits and would dictate. He had uncontrolled outbursts of emotion and temper, often without apparent reason, directed even at his wife and Grayson.[97] This behavior suggests some improvement in brain function because it meant that his denial was not being maintained as completely. It coincided with an increase in initiative expressed in the abrupt dismissal of Secretary of State Robert Lansing in February 1920 and the issuance of optimistic reports of his condition to the press as a part of the campaign for renomination.[98] Lansing's dismissal can be interpreted as a symbolic gesture of presidential authority, which Woodrow Wilson accused Lansing of usurping.

While the President was incapable of sustained work, he could, at times, appear to be bright and witty, as in his famous encounter with Senator Albert B. Fall of New Mexico who, with Senator Gilbert M. Hitchcock of Nebraska, had been delegated by the Senate Foreign Relations Committee ostensibly to discuss the Mexican situation but actually to report on the clarity of the President's mind. When Fall unctuously observed: "Well, Mr. President, we have all been praying for you," the President responded with, "Which way, Senator?"[99] Much of his humor symbolized his physical disabilities—his inability to walk and to make speeches. He called his cane his "third leg" and recited the following limerick:

There was a young girl from Missouri,
Who took her case to the jury.
She said, "Car Ninety-three

97. Stockton Axson to Baker, Ray Stannard Baker Papers.
98. Wimer, "Woodrow Wilson and a Third Term Nomination," 205.
99. Wilson, *My Memoir,* 298–99.

Ran over my knee,"
But the jury said "We're from Missouri."[100]

One of his favorite stories was about a Scotsman, who let his wife fall out of an airplane to win a wager dependent on his not speaking. His sardonic references to the League and jokes about its death in cabinet meetings[101] seem to be defenses against feelings of failure and despair.

To some degree, his anosognosia shielded him from the impact of political misfortune. When Houston tried to prepare him for the shock of Warren G. Harding's almost certain victory, Houston was assured that the people would not elect Harding.[102] When Stockton Axson brought up the subject, the President smiled indulgently and said, "You pessimist! You don't know the American people. They always rise to a moral occasion. Harding will be deluged." Stockton Axson stated, "Up to the last day I could make no impression on him. The day after the election I was so nervous about him that I called up the White House early and was told he was all right. As soon as I knew I could see him, I went over. He was as serene as in the moments of his own preceding victories (and the matter can't be stated stronger than that). His first words, after greetings, were (and I remember them verbatim), 'I have not lost faith in the American people. They have merely been temporarily deceived. They will realize their error in a little while.' "[103] With great insight, Stockton Axson wondered if Wilson's attitude might not be a symptom of his illness.

This account of Woodrow Wilson's neurological illnesses may help to explain some of his political actions and should be of value to students of his personality. While it is quite true that the character traits formed in his childhood were important determinants of his political career, attempts to interpret his defeats as predestined or as stemming inevitably from insatiable ambition or unconscious self-destructive drives are unwarranted oversimplifications. If one has all the variables, then there is some value in an interpretation of political events based on the tenets of a particular psychological theory, as in Alexander and Juliette George's application of Harold Lasswell's

100. Kerney, *The Political Education of Woodrow Wilson,* 481–82.
101. Cronon, ed., *Cabinet Diaries of Josephus Daniels,* 520.
102. *Ibid.*
103. Stockton Axson to Baker, Ray Stannard Baker Papers.

hypothesis that a drive to power is a compensation for self-esteem damaged in childhood.[104] However, neither the Georges' study nor the more recent one by Sigmund Freud and Bullitt take into account the factor of brain damage. If one were to judge Woodrow Wilson's potentialities for political success on the basis of his personality make-up, the major emphasis should be his behavior prior to 1906.

104. Alexander L. George and Juliette L. George, *Woodrow Wilson and Colonel House: A Personality Study* (New York, 1964), 195–96.

E. H. CARR

Conditions of Peace

In the study of history, unlike other fields of knowledge, the
latest interpretation is not always the best one. This essay, the
earliest of the selections in this book, was written in 1942,
while World War II raged and its outcome, much less the shape
of a future peace, still lay shrouded in doubt. Yet for both
breadth of perspective and depth of perception about what
World War I meant to the international system and more generally in the course of human affairs, no one has matched the
insight of the English historian E. H. Carr.

The civilised world on which the war of 1914 broke so suddenly
was on the whole a prosperous and orderly world. It was a world
of contented and reasoned optimism—a world which, looking back
on the past hundred years with a pardonable self-satisfaction, believed
in progress as a normal condition of civilised human existence. The
war was regarded not as a symptom that mankind had got on to
the wrong path (for that seemed almost inconceivable), but as a
shocking and meaningless digression. "We were sure . . . in 1914,"
says Lord Halifax, "that once we had dealt with the matter in hand
the world would return to old ways, which, in the main, we thought
to be good ways."[1] Some grains of optimism could even be extracted
from the awful experience. In the closing stages of the war the belief
became current that the result of an Allied victory would be to create
a still better world than had been known before, a world safe for
democracy and fit for heroes to live in, a world in which a new
international order would assure universal justice and perpetual peace.
There was felt to be nothing revolutionary about this conception.
A return to the old ways, which were also good ways, naturally
meant a resumption of the orderly march of human progress. "There
is no doubt," wrote General Smuts in 1918 in a much-quoted passage,
"that mankind is once more on the move. . . . The tents have been

Reprinted by permission from E. H. Carr, *Conditions of Peace* (London,
1942), pp. ix–xxiv. Copyright © Macmillan, London and Basingstoke.
  1. Viscount Halifax, *Speeches on Foreign Policy, 1934–1939*, p. 360.

struck, and the great caravan of humanity is once more on the march."[2]

This vision of a resumption of the age-long march of mankind towards a better world did not last. It faded through the long months of the Peace Conference, and perished in the first post-war economic crisis of 1920. In laying aside their arms, the war-weary peoples of the victorious countries seemed to have abandoned their exalted ambitions for the future. Still obsessed with the idea of a return to the good old ways, they thought of it no longer as the return to an interrupted path of effort and progress, but as the return to a static condition of automatic and effortless prosperity. No longer expecting or demanding a key to paradise, they sank into a mood of comfortable resignation. Mr. Lloyd George, the restless innovator, was replaced by Mr. Baldwin smoking the pipe of peace and security. Woodrow Wilson, the prophet of the new order, was succeeded by Harding and Coolidge, the dispensers of "normalcy." Security and normalcy became the twin pillars of the temple. Both were interpreted in terms of the halcyon age before 1914. For twenty years, this unadventurous and backward-looking view was the characteristic attitude of the three Great Powers who were mainly responsible for the Versailles settlement.[3]

Far different was the psychological reaction of the so-called "dissatisfied" Powers. These included Germany, the only defeated Great Power; Soviet Russia, who was conducting a revolution against the whole political, social and economic system which the peace settlement was designed to perpetuate; Italy, driven into the rebel camp by disappointment with her share in the proceeds of victory; and Japan, whose successes in the past fifty years have imparted a strain of caution and conservatism to her policy, but whose jealousy of British and American influence in the Pacific range her on the side of the dissatisfied Powers. None of these countries was disposed to look back on the past with complacency. The satisfied Powers continued to draw their inspiration from the conditions of the period which had witnessed their rise to power and their triumph, and too often failed to realise that those conditions had passed away. The dissatisfied Powers were in the position of revolutionaries renouncing and challenging the past

2. J. C. Smuts, *The League of Nations: A Practical Suggestion*, p. 18.

3. This statement requires qualification for the United States after 1933: the point will be discussed later.

in the name of new ideologies. The psychological background of the twenty years between the two wars may be observed in the respective reactions of the satisfied and dissatisfied Powers to military, political and economic problems.

The backward-looking view of the satisfied Powers is particularly well illustrated in the attitude of their military chiefs. Soldiers and sailors alike clung eagerly to the glorious traditions of nineteenth-century warfare. After the victorious struggle of 1914–18, security could best be assured by putting back the clock, or at any rate by seeing that it did not move on any further. The programme of the British and American General Staffs at the Peace Conference of 1919 contained two main desiderata: to abolish the submarine and to deprive Germany of military aviation. If only these two major innovations of the war could be somehow shuffled out of existence, we could return to the familiar and comfortable dispositions of nineteenth-century strategy. At the Disarmament Conference, Great Britain once more proposed the abolition of twentieth-century weapons: the submarine, the large tank, gas and bombing from the air. So reluctant were successive British Governments to recognise the potentialities of the air arm that Great Britain ranked at one time as the seventh air Power of the world. The Royal Air Force, being the youngest, was also the Cinderella of the services.[4] It was considered important that the British navy should be three times as strong as is the German. But in the air no more than equality with Germany was aimed at, and this was far from being achieved. "The sea gives us time," Campbell-Bannerman had exclaimed in 1871 arguing against an expansion of the army.[5] The same factor was felt to be valid more than sixty years later. If Britannia ruled the waves, then British supremacy was surely as secure in the twentieth century as in the nineteenth: British mentality was slow to adapt itself to any other view.

French strategy was still more retrograde. The two famous French memoranda on security submitted to the Peace Conference of 1919—the "Foch memorandum" of January 10 and the "Tardieu

4. "The importance of this professional departmentalism in determining the actual allocation of our resources is greater than anyone who is not closely acquainted with the Government machine can well recognise. If we ask why, in the first allocation of the additional resources, the Air Ministry did not get more, the true answer is that it is the youngest of the fighting services" (A. Salter, *Security: Can We Retrieve It?* p. 183).

5. J. A. Spender, *The Life of the Right Hon. Sir Henry Campbell-Bannerman*, i, p. 40.

memorandum" of February 26—discussed military transport exclusively in terms of railways; and neither of them so much as mentioned air power. The one important French strategical conception of the inter-war period was the Maginot Line—an attempt to immobilise warfare and to freeze the *status quo*. Throughout this period, the French and British General Staffs appear to have assumed without question that immobile trench warfare would be the main form of land fighting in any future war—for no better reason than that this had been true of the last war. "Everything is being done," complained a prescient French critic in 1928, "as though the Versailles Treaty, which has compelled Germany to modernise her military ideas, permits us to go back to the military routine of 1914—and then fall asleep."[6] It is perhaps unfair to pass a similar stricture on the military policy of the smaller satisfied Powers, since their conservative outlook was dictated by lack of resources as well as by lack of imagination. Holland and Belgium failed to recognise that an army deprived of the assistance of air forces and mechanised units of appreciable strength is a negligible factor in modern warfare. Polish strategy assigned an important rôle to cavalry; and Switzerland based her plan to defence on a militia mounted on bicycles and renowned for its personal courage and for the accuracy of its marksmanship with the rifle.

While therefore the strategy of the satisfied Powers was dominated by an amalgam of nineteenth-century preconceptions and of the lessons of the war of 1914–18, the initiative passed to the rival group. The aeroplane was a French, the tank a British, invention. Yet in the period between the two wars, it was the German army which elaborated and perfected the tactics of aerial and mechanised warfare, while the British and French military mind was unable to clear itself of the precepts and habits of a bygone age. The parachutist landing behind enemy lines was a Russian device, studied and perfected by Germany and ignored by the satisfied Powers. It is difficult to exaggerate advantage ultimately derived by Germany from the destruction of her armaments and of her whole military machine in 1919–a circumstance which obliged her not only to modernise her material but to think out again from the start every problem of equipment and organisation, while Britain and France remained embedded in the legacy of the past.[7] When war began, the enterprising nature

6. Quoted from *L'Œuvre* by M. Werner, *The Military Strength of the Powers*, p. 210.

7. It has been observed that German industry enjoyed an exactly similar

of German tactics completely bewildered the British and French General Staffs. The German army, explained *The Times,* "is prepared to take risks of a character which, rightly or wrongly, has been condemned by French and British military doctrine."[8] "The truth is," said the French Prime Minister a few days later, "that our classic conception of the conduct of war has come up against a new conception."[9] The significant fact about the first year of war was not so much that the Germans took the offensive throughout, but that every novelty in strategy or tactics, every new military invention of any importance, appeared on the German side.[10] Technically speaking, revolutionary conceptions of warfare were matched against pure conservatism.

The politicians of the satisfied Powers, no less than the soldiers and the sailors, had their eyes fixed on the past. "Our apparent inability to innovate or do any really original thinking," wrote an independent observer of British political life in 1934, "is the most exasperating feature of modern politics."[11] The democracy for which the world had been made safe in 1918 was understood to be the particular form of liberal democracy which had grown up in the special conditions of the nineteenth century. Conceived in these terms, it became one of those things which, being taken for granted, cease to be a living force. Democracy relied on the prestige of a glorious tradition and seemed to have nothing but its past achievements to offer as a contribution to the problems of the new world. It became the prerogative of the well-to-do and the privileged who could regard

---

advantage over British in the latter part of the nineteenth century: "The country being . . . not committed to antiquated sites and routes for its industrial plant, the men who exercised the discretion were free to choose with a single eye to the mechanical expediency of locations for the pursuit of industry. Having no obsolescent equipment and no out-of-date trade connexions to cloud the issue, they were also free to take over the processes of the new industry at their best and highest efficiency, rather than content themselves with compromises between the best equipment known and what used to be the best a few years or a few decades ago" (T. Veblen, *Imperial Germany,* pp. 187–8).

8. *The Times* (leading article), May 14, 1940.

9. Statement to French Senate of May 21, reported in *The Times,* May 2, 1940.

10. The *Deutsche Allgemeine Zeitung* of August 24, 1940, tauntingly remarked that the one initiative taken by Great Britain in the first year of the war had been to declare it.

11. E. Percy, *Government in Transition,* p. 99.

past and present with a substantial measure of satisfaction. In 1939 democratic governments survived in most of the ten or twelve countries of the world possessing the highest income per head of population—and hardly anywhere else. Prior to 1933, no attempt had been made to reinterpret democracy to meet the conditions of the post-war world; and in democratic countries few people recognised that it could not continue to function exactly as it had functioned before 1914. After 1933, opinion in the United States began to move, in face of considerable opposition,[12] towards a radically new conception of democracy. But this movement had scarcely spread to Europe before the outbreak of war in 1939. In politics as in strategy, it was difficult to imagine that anything had happened to put an end for ever to the glorious and easy-going days of the nineteenth century.

Politically, too, therefore the initiative was left to the dissatisfied Powers. The first to take it was Soviet Russia. From 1921 onwards her example was followed by country after country which combined rebellion against the Versailles settlement with rejection of democracy, sometimes paying lip-service to democracy, as the Russians had done, by purporting to set up a new and more perfect form of it. The attraction of Bolshevism, Fascism and National Socialism lay not in their obscure, elastic and sometimes incoherent doctrines, but in the fact that they professedly had something new to offer and did not invite their followers to worship a political ideal enshrined in the past. Like the new strategy, the new political order had the merit of not having been tried before. A revolutionary frame of mind confronted an attitude of political complacency and nostalgia for the past.

In international affairs, the same confrontation appeared in a more overt and more dramatic form. Here there was a direct clash of interest between conservative Powers satisfied with the *status quo* and revolutionary Powers seeking to overthrow it. The League of Nations, more than any other institution, was overtaken by the reaction from the brief interlude of optimism of 1918–19 to the static complacency of the 'twenties. Created in a mood of burning faith in human progress, of which it was to be the principal instrument, it was quickly

12. The backward-looking view was still firmly entrenched even in the United States. In 1937 a well-known American publicist prepared an "agenda of liberalism" which recommended a return to the point where "latter-day" liberals had gone off the rails somewhere about 1870 in order to complete "the unfinished mission of liberalism" (W. Lippmann, *The Good Society*, p. 225 and *passim*).

perverted into a tool of the satisfied Powers, who had been careful even at the Peace Conference to emasculate the only radical article in the Covenant. Every attempt to "strengthen" the Covenant meant another bulwark to uphold the *status quo.* The Geneva Protocol was the political counterpart of the Maginot Line. To make the Geneva trenches impregnable and wait for the enemy to attack was the summit of political wisdom. Like all privileged groups, the satisfied Powers insisted on the supreme importance of peace, and capitalised the fear of war in the same way in which conservatives at home capitalise the fear of revolution. "No special circumstances, no individual aspirations, however justifiable," said Briand to the Assembly in the palmiest days of the League, "can be allowed to transcend the interests of peace. Peace must prevail, must come before all. If any act of justice were proposed which would disturb world peace and renew the terrible disaster of yesterday, I should be the first to call on those promoting it to stop, to abandon it in the supreme interests of peace."[13] Let injustice persist rather than that the sacred rights of the existing order should be infringed. "The first purpose of the League," declared one of its English champions, "is the defence of its members—self-preservation which is the first law of life of any organization."[14] The obsession of "security" hung like a millstone about the neck of the League and excluded every breath of life and freshness from its body. Politically, Geneva became the home of pure conservatism. "Govern and change nothing" had been Metternich's motto. The League changed nothing and failed only to govern.

Every movement for international change came therefore from the dissatisfied Powers, and was at once confronted by the vested interests of the *status quo.* It is true that some of the desired changes were destructive in character. But the absence of any proposals for constructive change, or indeed of any recognition of the need for change at all, from any other quarter left the field open to the challengers. The fund of prestige inherited by the League of Nations from its radical and idealistic origins was soon exhausted. The political offensive, like the strategic offensive, passed exclusively to the dissatisfied Powers.

In the economic field complacency was less easy to justify and a policy of inaction more difficult to maintain. Politically, the bank-

13. League of Nations, *Ninth Assembly,* p. 83.
14. N. Angell in *The Future of the League of Nations* (Royal Institute of International Affairs, 1936), p. 17.

ruptcy of the *status quo* was not fully revealed or recognised before the middle and later 'thirties. Strategically, the unmitigated conservatism of the satisfied Powers was exploded only by the military disasters of 1940. Economically, the break came far sooner. The first economic crisis of 1920 had created widespread disquiet, which was aggravated by the controversies over reparations and the Ruhr occupation. In the heyday of military predominance and political quiescence, the demon of economic insecurity was already raising is head. Even in 1924, amid the enthusiasm inspired by the Geneva Protocol, a French Delegate to the Assembly of the League sounded a warning note:

> If we are ever to rest secure in the edifice of peace, the great and grave problems of the distribution of raw materials, of markets, of emigration and immigration, will one day have to be taken in hand by the financial and economic organisations of the League and by its Assemblies. If they are left unsolved—let us make no mistake—they will cause internal disruption which will bring down in ruins the fabric we have reared.[15]

To dig oneself in might suffice as a guiding principle for soldiers or politicians. It was lamentably defective as an economic panacea. Economically, conservatism was not enough; for there was not even the semblance of a satisfactory *status quo* to conserve. The problem was urgent and inescapable. What remedy could be applied?

The answer given to this question was the completest expression of the backward-looking attitude of the satisfied Powers. Belief in progress was dead. If the *status quo* did not secure economic prosperity, if some change was unavoidable, then change could be conceived only in the form of a step backwards. If conservatism was not enough, the alternative was reaction. Economic man was no longer marching forward by new and untried paths towards hitherto unscaled heights. The aim was now to retrieve a false move, to undo what had been done, to erase from the fair page everything written on it since 1914. A return to the past meant a return to "normal" prosperity. "Lancashire is perfectly sanguine of success," wrote an observer in 1924, "once normal conditions have been restored."[16] "Business men," remarks another commentator, "wistfully awaited a return to 'normal,'

---

15. League of Nations, *Fifth Assembly*, p. 219.
16. A. Siegfried, *Post-War Britain*, p. 110.

and convinced themselves that 'normal' meant the world of 1913.'"[17]
In this fatal atmosphere even steps which were at the time hailed
as landmarks of progress turned out on a longer view to be pure
reaction. Thus the Dawes Plan, which seemed a highly enlightened
way of disposing of reparations, was in essence a reactionary attempt
to set up again the humpty-dumpty of nineteenth-century private international capitalism with its centre in New York instead of in London.
When American financiers in 1929 found the burden too heavy, the
world no longer had any shelter from the sweeping storm of economic
revolution.

Yet nostalgia for the past still remained the dominant obsession.
It is curious to reflect how many of the economic slogans of the
period between the two wars began with the prefix *re*. We were
successively concerned with reconstruction, retrenchment, reparations,
repayment of war debts, revaluation of currencies, restoration of the
gold standard, recovery and removal of trade barriers. Even inflation
could be made respectable by calling it "reflation." In the 'thirties
a leading British expert on international economic relations wrote
two books of which the first was called *Recovery* and the second
Security: Can We Retrieve It?[18] The collective wisdom of the economic
world as expressed by the experts of the two international economic
conferences of 1927 and 1933 taught that practically every trend
of economic policy which had developed since 1914 was wrong and
ought to be arrested or reversed.

It will not be pretended that those responsible for the economic
policy of the satisfied Powers always listened to the pleas of their
economic advisers for a return to nineteenth-century principles. Down
to 1931, lip-service did indeed continue to be paid by the governments
of almost all these countries to economic orthodoxy, though there
were many derogations from it in practice. From 1931 onwards even
the lip-service grew faint and perfunctory, and governments were
driven before the economic hurricane into new and unprecedented
courses. But the point is that this action was taken haphazard, under
compulsion of circumstances, in defiance of accepted economic theory,
yet without any understanding why that theory had broken down

17. W. K. Hancock, *Survey of British Commonwealth Affairs*, ii, Pt. 1,
p. 199.
18. The "expert" is Sir Arthur Salter. The comment is intended not
as a criticism of the books, but as an expression of admiration for titles
so exactly calculated to appeal to the mood of the contemporary reader.

and what was being substituted for it. The statesmen who sponsored these new policies were on the defensive. The new course was represented as a temporary and distasteful necessity. It was adopted only to meet "unfair" competition. Appearances notwithstanding, it would expand, not limit, the volume of international trade. It was designed to pave the way for an eventual return to orthodoxy. These absurd and mutually contradictory explanations had only one significance. The statesmen who sponsored the policies neither understood nor believed in them. They had lost the initiative, and were being driven, hesitant, bewildered and apologetic, by forces too powerful for them to control.

In these conditions economic inventiveness, like military inventiveness, was honoured and practised only among the dissatisfied Powers. The innovations which, for good or evil, transformed the face of the economic world in the inter-war period were developed and exploited by the revolutionary Powers who challenged the existing order. "Planned economy"—the regulation and organisation of national economic life by the state for the needs of the community as a whole—may be said to have made its first appearance in all the principal belligerent countries (though predominantly in Germany, where the term originated) in the war of 1914–18. But whereas Great Britain, the United States and France made haste at the end of the war to cast off state control in the vain hope of returning to the *laissez-faire* principles of the pre-war period, Soviet Russia, soon to be followed by Fascist Italy and Nazi Germany, found in "planned economy" the new twentieth-century concept which was to replace nineteenth-century liberalism; and having gained the initiative, these countries at length compelled the conservative Powers to follow slowly and reluctantly in their train. State control of foreign trade and its use as a political weapon, invented by Soviet Russia, were perfected by Nazi Germany; and in 1938–39 Great Britain, under extreme German pressure, had begun to take some faltering steps in the same direction. The techniques of a managed currency and of foreign exchange control were elaborately studied by the dissatisfied Powers while these things were still regarded in Great Britain and the United States with contemptuous horror. Necessity was, of course, the mother of invention. But those on whom the necessity first descended scored an immense advantage through the rapid development of the spirit of enterprise and innovation. The fact that Soviet Russia and Nazi Germany had virtually eliminated unemployment was slightingly dismissed with the retort that this had been achieved only by methods, and at the cost of sacrifices, which the satisfied countries would never tolerate. The answer was clearly inadequate, so long as the satisfied Powers could find no answer of their own to a problem whose acuteness could not be denied. If a considerable part of the younger generation in many European countries came to believe that either Soviet Russia or Nazi Germany held the key to the future, this was because both these countries propounded new economic systems based on new principles and therefore opening up a prospect of hope, whereas the political and intellectual leaders of the satisfied countries appeared to offer no solution of the economic problem but the return to a past whose bankruptcy had been sufficiently demonstrated. Nothing did more to discredit the satisfied Powers than the way in which they allowed the effective initiative, in the critical field of economic theory and practice, to pass to the rival group. Only the United States began, after 1933, to move hesitatingly, and with much lip-service to antiquated ideals, in the direction of a new economic, as well as a new political, orientation.

If in the light of this outline, military, political and economic, we now review the whole psychological background of the past twenty years, we shall see that the attitude of the satisfied Powers was stultified by two defects of outlook common to almost all privileged and possessing groups. In the first place, the privileged group tends to idealise the period in which it has risen to the height of its power, and to see its highest good in the maintenance of those conditions. Secondly, the privileged group is preoccupied with the question of its own security rather than with the need for reform or even for progress. "Nothing is more certain," observed J. S. Mill eighty years ago, "than that improvement in human affairs is wholly the work of the uncontented characters."[19] In the satisfied countries, privileged groups have for a long time past been too powerful, and "uncontented characters" not sufficiently numerous or influential. The widespread diffusion of privilege in the English-speaking countries has been the foundation of the stability of their political institutions. But in revolutionary times the number of the privileged may present a positive danger by hindering the prompt recognition of new and vital needs.

The first moral for the victors in the present war is then not to look backwards in search of principles to guide the post-war settlement. This precept should be less difficult to follow than it was in

19. J. S. Mill, *Considerations on Representative Government,* ch. iii.

1919; for we are no longer blinded, as we were then, by the "old ways" of the pre-war world which we thought of as good ways. The most encouraging feature of the present situation is the prevalence, especially among the younger generation, of a deep-seated conviction that the world of the past decade has been a bad and mad world, and that almost everything in it needs to be uprooted and replanted. A revolutionary current is in the air. Nevertheless, there are many disquieting features, one of them being the very high average age of those who hold the key positions in the public life of Great Britain. Most men of sixty and over are more susceptible to impressions of the past than to future needs. The younger generation will hardly achieve its goal if it continues to rely, as exclusively as it appears to rely at present, on the leadership of veterans. France and Great Britain suffered military disaster in 1940 largely because they had prepared to fight the last war over again. Will it be said hereafter that we failed in peace-making because we had prepared only for the last peace?

The second moral, equally important and perhaps more easily forgotten, is the fatal consequence of undue preoccupation with security. This preoccupation is a constant pitfall of privileged groups. "The prosperous middle classes who ruled the nineteenth century," observes a distinguished scientist, "placed an excessive value on placidity of existence. . . . The middle-class pessimism over the future of the world comes from a confusion between civilisation and security. In the immediate future there will be less security than in the immediate past, less stability. . . . On the whole, the great ages have been unstable ages."[20] The quest for security inevitably becomes an instrument of reaction. "The clash of progress and security," which Professor Fisher has discussed in a stimulating book under that title, has a significance far beyond the specifically economic application which he has given to it. Everyone who followed the history of the League of Nations knows the stifling effect exercised at Geneva by the word "security" on any progressive movement. It is both shocking and alarming to learn from an American business man, a President of the International Chamber of Commerce, that "the thing that gives us most satisfaction in life is security."[21] If this is indeed true, our civilisation is doomed to perish.

20. Sir Alfred Whitehead, quoted in B. L. Richmond, *The Pattern of Freedom*, p. 68.
21. *International Conciliation*, No. 362 (September 1940), p. 328.

It cannot be too often repeated—for it is still not widely under-stood—that neither security nor peace can properly be made the object of policy. "Personal security is like happiness," writes Professor Fisher, "in that it is likely to elude a direct search. In a progressive economy, stability and personal security are to be found only as a by-product of the search for something else."[22] International peace is another such by-product.[23] It cannot be achieved by the signing of pacts or covenants "outlawing" war any more than revolutions are prevented by making them illegal. A generation which makes peace and security its aim is doomed to frustration. The only stability attainable in human affairs is the stability of the spinning-top or the bicycle. If the victors in the present war are able to create the conditions for an orderly and progressive development of human society, peace and security will be added unto them. But they will have to learn the paradoxical lesson that the condition of security is continuous advance. The political, social and economic problems of the post-war world must be approached with the desire not to stabilise, but to revolutionise.

A further warning is necessary. We have seen how rapidly the idealistic urge generated at the end of the last war faded away into indolence and complacency. The perfectly natural phenomenon of war-weariness, coupled with the desire of the individual to return to "normal" life, completely eclipsed the vague inclination to play an effective part in the building of a new world. "The demand for 'demobilisation' in every sphere was so strong that even the victorious governments were carried along by the tide, and the statesmen at Paris had hardly begun to grapple with their task before they found their omnipotence ebbing away."[24] There is grave danger that war-weariness may play the same rôle at the end of the present war with still more disastrous results. "The true measure of nations," remarked Mr. Churchill in February 1919, "is what they can do when they are tired."[25] But much will depend on the existence of

22. A. G. B. Fisher, *The Clash of Progress and Security,* p. 106.

23. The thesis that peace is not, and never can be, a direct object of policy, is developed at greater length in E. H. Carr, *The Twenty Years' Crisis,* pp. 68–9. As Dorothy Sayers has wittily remarked, "we wooed peace as a valetudinarian woos health, by brooding over it until we became really ill" (*The Spectator,* November 24, 1939, p. 736).

24. A. J. Toynbee, *The World After the Peace Conference,* p. 2.

25. Speech at the English-Speaking Union, February 23, 1919, quoted in R. Sencourt, *Winston Churchill,* p. 169.

a government ready to give a clear and decisive lead; and this lead will not be forthcoming unless policy has been considered and plans carefully formulated in advance. This is one of several cogent answers to those who argue that reconstruction is an affair of the post-war period, and that it is premature or superfluous to examine such problems so long as hostilities continue.

A NOTE TO THE EDITOR

John Milton Cooper, Jr., was born in Washington, D.C., and studied at Princeton University and Columbia University, where he received a Ph.D. and was a Woodrow Wilson Fellow. His articles have appeared in various scholarly journals, and he has written *The Vanity of Power: American Isolationism and the First World War, 1914–1917*. Mr. Cooper is now Associate Professor of History at the University of Wisconsin.